W9-CNK-498

Explorations in
CORE MATH

for Common Core GPS
Coordinate Algebra

© Houghton Mifflin Harcourt Publishing Company

HOUGHTON MIFFLIN HARCOURT

Copyright © by Houghton Mifflin Harcourt Publishing Company

All rights reserved. No part of this work may be reproduced or transmitted in any form or by any means, electronic or mechanical, including photocopying or recording, or by any information storage and retrieval system, without the prior written permission of the copyright owner unless such copying is expressly permitted by federal copyright law. Requests for permission to make copies of any part of the work should be addressed to Houghton Mifflin Harcourt Publishing Company, Attn: Contracts, Copyrights, and Licensing, 9400 Southpark Center Loop, Orlando, Florida 32819-8647.

Common Core State Standards © Copyright 2010. National Governors Association Center for Best Practices and Council of Chief State School Officers. All rights reserved.

This product is not sponsored or endorsed by the Common Core State Standards Initiative of the National Governors Association Center for Best Practices and the Council of Chief State School Officers.

Cover photo credit: ©Hisham Ibrahim/Getty Images

Printed in the U.S.A.

8 9 10 0928 23 22 21 20 19 18 17 16 15 14

4500483813   C D E F G H I

If you have received these materials as examination copies free of charge, Houghton Mifflin Harcourt Publishing Company retains title to the materials and they may not be resold. Resale of examination copies is strictly prohibited.

Possession of this publication in print format does not entitle users to convert this publication, or any portion of it, into electronic format.

Contents

GPS
COMMON
CORE

© Houghton Mifflin Harcourt Publishing Company

© Houghton Mifflin Harcourt Publishing Company

© Houghton Mifflin Harcourt Publishing Company

Module 11 Graphs and Equations of Linear Functions

Module 12 Exponential Functions

Module 13 Comparing and Modeling with Functions

© Houghton Mifflin Harcourt Publishing Company

© Houghton Mifflin Harcourt Publishing Company

© Houghton Mifflin Harcourt Publishing Company

© Houghton Mifflin Harcourt Publishing Company

Correlation of *Explorations in Core Math* to the Common Core GPS for Coordinate Algebra

Standards	Lessons
Number and Quantity: Quantities*	
Reason quantitatively and use units to solve problems	
MCC9-12.N.Q.1 Use units as a way to understand problems and to guide the solution of multi-step problems; choose and interpret units consistently in formulas; choose and interpret the scale and the origin in graphs and data displays.*	Lessons 2-1, 2-2, 8-2, 10-1, 18-1
MCC9-12.N.Q.2 Define appropriate quantities for the purpose of descriptive modeling.*	Lessons 15-1, 15-2, 18-1
MCC9-12.N.Q.3 Choose a level of accuracy appropriate to limitations on measurement when reporting quantities.*	Lesson 2-3
Algebra: Seeing Structure in Expressions	
Interpret the structure of expressions	
MCC9-12.A.SSE.1 Interpret expressions that represent a quantity in terms of its context.*	Lessons 1-1, 2-1, 11-2, 11-3, 11-4, 12-1, 12-2
MCC9-12.A.SSE.1a a. Interpret parts of an expression, such as terms, factors, and coefficients.*	Lessons 1-1, 2-1, 11-2, 11-3, 11-4, 12-1, 12-2
MCC9-12.A.SSE.1b b. Interpret complicated expressions by viewing one or more of their parts as a single entity. For example, interpret $P(1 + r)^n$ as the product of P and a factor not depending on P.*	Lessons 12-1, 12-2
Algebra: Creating Equations*	
Create equations that describe numbers or relationships	
MCC9-12.A.CED.1 Create equations and inequalities in one variable and use them to solve problems. Include equations arising from linear and quadratic functions, and simple rational and exponential functions.*	Lessons 1-2, 1-3, 2-2, 3-1, 3-2, 4-1, 4-2, 4-3, 5-1, 5-2
MCC9-12.A.CED.2 Create equations in two or more variables to represent relationships between quantities; graph equations on coordinate axes with labels and scales.*	Lessons 8-3, 9-1, 11-1, 11-2, 11-4, 12-2, 13-1, 18-1
MCC9-12.A.CED.3 Represent constraints by equations or inequalities, and by systems of equations and/or inequalities, and interpret solutions as viable or non-viable options in a modeling context. *For example, represent inequalities describing nutritional and cost constraints on combinations of different foods.**	Lessons 6-1, 6-2, 7-1, 7-3, 8-3, 11-2, 18-1
MCC9-12.A.CED.4 Rearrange formulas to highlight a quantity of interest, using the same reasoning as in solving equations. *For example, rearrange Ohm's law V = IR to highlight resistance R.**	Lesson 3-3

(+) Advanced   * = Also a Modeling Standard

© Houghton Mifflin Harcourt Publishing Company

Standards	Lessons
Algebra: Reasoning with Equations and Inequalities	
Understand solving equations as a process of reasoning and explain the reasoning	
MCC9-12.A.REI.1 Explain each step in solving a simple equation as following from the equality of numbers asserted at the previous step, starting from the assumption that the original equation has a solution. Construct a viable argument to justify a solution method.	Lessons 1-2, 1-3, 3-1, 3-2
Solve equations and inequalities in one variable	
MCC9-12.A.REI.3 Solve linear equations and inequalities in one variable, including equations with coefficients represented by letters.	Lessons 1-2, 1-3, 1-9, 3-1, 3-2, 3-3, 4-2, 4-3, 5-1, 5-2, 5-3
Solve systems of equations	
MCC9-12.A.REI.5 Prove that, given a system of two equations in two variables, replacing one equation by the sum of that equation and a multiple of the other produces a system with the same solutions.	Lesson 6-3
MCC9-12.A.REI.6 Solve systems of linear equations exactly and approximately (e.g., with graphs), focusing on pairs of linear equations in two variables.	Lessons 6-1, 6-2, 6-3, 7-1, 7-2
Represent and solve equations and inequalities graphically	
MCC9-12.A.REI.10 Understand that the graph of an equation in two variables is the set of all its solutions plotted in the coordinate plane, often forming a curve (which could be a line).	Lessons 9-1, 10-2, 12-2
MCC9-12.A.REI.11 Explain why the x-coordinates of the points where the graphs of the equations $y = f(x)$ and $y = g(x)$ intersect are the solutions of the equation $f(x) = g(x)$; find the solutions approximately, e.g., using technology to graph the functions, make tables of values, or find successive approximations. Include cases where $f(x)$ and/or $g(x)$ are linear, polynomial, rational, absolute value, exponential, and logarithmic functions.*	Lessons 11-2, 13-1
MCC9-12.A.REI.12 Graph the solutions to a linear inequality in two variables as a half-plane (excluding the boundary in the case of a strict inequality), and graph the solution set to a system of linear inequalities in two variables as the intersection of the corresponding half-planes.	Lessons 7-2, 7-3
Functions: Interpreting Functions	
Understand the concept of a function and use function notation	
MCC9-12.F.IF.1 Understand that a function from one set (called the domain) to another set (called the range) assigns to each element of the domain exactly one element of the range. If f is a function and x is an element of its domain, then $f(x)$ denotes the output of f corresponding to the input x. The graph of f is the graph of the equation $y = f(x)$.	Lessons 8-2, 10-1, 12-3
MCC9-12.F.IF.2 Use function notation, evaluate functions for inputs in their domains, and interpret statements that use function notation in terms of a context.	Lessons 8-2, 8-3, 9-1, 9-3, 10-1, 11-1, 11-4, 12-2
MCC9-12.F.IF.3 Recognize that sequences are functions, sometimes defined recursively, whose domain is a subset of the integers. *For example, the Fibonacci sequence is defined recursively by $f(0) = f(1) = 1$, $f(n + 1) = f(n) + f(n - 1)$ for $n \geq 1$ (n is greater than or equal to 1).*	Lessons 9-3, 10-1

(+) Advanced   * = Also a Modeling Standard

© Houghton Mifflin Harcourt Publishing Company

Standards	Lessons
Interpret functions that arise in applications in terms of the context	
MCC9-12.F.IF.4 For a function that models a relationship between two quantities, interpret key features of graphs and tables in terms of the quantities, and sketch graphs showing key features given a verbal description of the relationship. Key features include: intercepts; intervals where the function is increasing, decreasing, positive, or negative; relative maximums and minimums; symmetries; end behavior; and periodicity.*	**Lessons 8-1, 9-1, 10-3, 11-1, 11-2, 11-4, 12-2, 13-2**
MCC9-12.F.IF.5 Relate the domain of a function to its graph and, where applicable, to the quantitative relationship it describes. *For example, if the function h(n) gives the number of person-hours it takes to assemble n engines in a factory, then the positive integers would be an appropriate domain for the function.**	**Lessons 8-2, 9-1, 10-1, 12-3**
MCC9-12.F.IF.6 Calculate and interpret the average rate of change of a function (presented symbolically or as a table) over a specified interval. Estimate the rate of change from a graph.*	**Lessons 10-3, 10-4**
Analyze functions using different representations	
MCC9-12.F.IF.7 Graph functions expressed symbolically and show key features of the graph, by hand in simple cases and using technology for more complicated cases.*	**Lessons 9-1, 10-1, 11-1, 11-2, 11-4, 12-2, 12-3**
MCC9-12.F.IF.7a a. Graph linear ,,, functions and show intercepts, maxima, and minima.*	**Lessons 9-1, 10-1, 11-1, 11-2, 11-4**
MCC9-12.F.IF.7e e. Graph exponential ... functions, showing intercepts and end behavior, ...*	**Lessons 12-2, 12-3**
MCC9-12.F.IF.9 Compare properties of two functions each represented in a different way (algebraically, graphically, numerically in tables, or by verbal descriptions). *For example, given a graph of one quadratic function and an algebraic expression for another, say which has the larger maximum.*	**Lessons 10-1, 13-2**

(+) Advanced   * = Also a Modeling Standard

© Houghton Mifflin Harcourt Publishing Company

Standards	Lessons
Functions: Building Functions	
Build a function that models a relationship between two quantities	
MCC9-12.F.BF.1 Write a function that describes a relationship between two quantities.*	**Lessons 8-3, 9-1, 11-1, 12-1**
MCC9-12.F.BF.1a a. Determine an explicit expression, a recursive process, or steps for calculation from a context.	**Lessons 8-3, 9-1, 9-3, 11-1, 12-1**
MCC9-12.F.BF.1b b. Combine standard function types using arithmetic operations. *For example, build a function that models the temperature of a cooling body by adding a constant function to a decaying exponential, and relate these functions to the model.*	**Lessons 8-3, 9-1, 11-1, 12-1**
MCC9-12.F.BF.2 Write arithmetic and geometric sequences both recursively and with an explicit formula, use them to model situations, and translate between the two forms.*	**Lessons 9-3, 12-1**
Build new functions from existing functions	
MCC9-12.F.BF.3 Identify the effect on the graph of replacing $f(x)$ by $f(x) + k$, $k\,f(x)$, $f(kx)$, and $f(x + k)$ for specific values of k (both positive and negative); find the value of k given the graphs. Experiment with cases and illustrate an explanation of the effects on the graph using technology. *Include recognizing even and odd functions from their graphs and algebraic expressions for them.*	**Lessons 11-1, 11-4 12-2**

(+) Advanced   * = Also a Modeling Standard

© Houghton Mifflin Harcourt Publishing Company

Standards	Lessons
Functions: Linear, quadratic, and Exponential Models*	
Construct and compare linear, quadratic, and exponential models and solve problems	
MCC9-12.F.LE.1 Distinguish between situations that can be modeled with linear functions and with exponential functions.*	Lessons 12-3, 13-3
MCC9-12.F.LE.1a a. Prove that linear functions grow by equal differences over equal intervals, and that exponential functions grow by equal factors over equal intervals.*	Lessons 12-3, 13-3
MCC9-12.F.LE.1b b. Recognize situations in which one quantity changes at a constant rate per unit interval relative to another.*	Lessons 12-3, 13-3
MCC9-12.F.LE.1c c. Recognize situations in which a quantity grows or decays by a constant percent rate per unit interval relative to another.*	Lessons 12-3, 13-3
MCC9-12.F.LE.2 Construct linear and exponential functions, including arithmetic and geometric sequences, given a graph, a description of a relationship, or two input-output pairs (include reading these from a table).*	Lessons 8-3, 9-3, 11-2, 11-3, 12-1, 12-2, 12-3, 13-1
MCC9-12.F.LE.3 Observe using graphs and tables that a quantity increasing exponentially eventually exceeds a quantity increasing linearly, quadratically, or (more generally) as a polynomial function.*	Lesson 13-2
Interpret expressions for functions in terms of the situation they model	
MCC9-12.F.LE.5 Interpret the parameters in a linear or exponential function in terms of a context.*	Lessons 8-3, 15-2, 11-4, 12-3, 13-1

(+) Advanced * = Also a Modeling Standard

© Houghton Mifflin Harcourt Publishing Company

Standards	Lessons
Geometry: Congruence	
Experiment with transformations in the plane	
MCC9-12.G.CO.1 Know precise definitions of angle, circle, perpendicular line, parallel line, and line segment, based on the undefined notions of point, line, distance along a line, and distance around a circular arc.	Lessons 16-1, 16-2, 16-3, 16-4, 18-1, 18-2
MCC9-12.G.CO.2 Represent transformations in the plane using, e.g., transparencies and geometry software; describe transformations as functions that take points in the plane as inputs and give other points as outputs. Compare transformations that preserve distance and angle to those that do not (e.g., translation versus horizontal stretch).	Lessons 16-1, 16-2, 16-3, 16-4
MCC9-12.G.CO.3 Given a rectangle, parallelogram, trapezoid, or regular polygon, describe the rotations and reflections that carry it onto itself.	Lesson 17-2
MCC9-12.G.CO.4 Develop definitions of rotations, reflections, and translations in terms of angles, circles, perpendicular lines, parallel lines, and line segments.	Lessons 16-2, 16-3, 16-4
MCC9-12.G.CO.5 Given a geometric figure and a rotation, reflection, or translation, draw the transformed figure using, e.g., graph paper, tracing paper, or geometry software. Specify a sequence of transformations that will carry a given figure onto another.	Lessons 16-1, 16-2, 16-3, 16-4, 17-1, 17-3

(+) Advanced   * = Also a Modeling Standard

© Houghton Mifflin Harcourt Publishing Company

Standards	Lessons
Geometry: Expressing Geometric Properties with Equations	
Use coordinates to prove simple geometric theorems algebraically	
MCC9-12.G.GPE.4 Use coordinates to prove simple geometric theorems algebraically. For example, prove or disprove that a figure defined by four given points in the coordinate plane is a rectangle; prove or disprove that the point $(1, \sqrt{3})$ lies on the circle centered at the origin and containing the point $(0, 2)$.	Lessons 18-1, 18-2
MCC9-12.G.GPE.5 Prove the slope criteria for parallel and perpendicular lines and use them to solve geometric problems (e.g., find the equation of a line parallel or perpendicular to a given line that passes through a given point).	Lesson 18-1
MCC9-12.G.GPE.6 Find the point on a directed line segment between two given points that partitions the segment in a given ratio.	Lesson 18-2
MCC9-12.G.GPE.7 Use coordinates to compute perimeters of polygons and areas of triangles and rectangles, e.g., using the distance formula.*	Lesson 18-2
Statistics and Probability: Interpreting Categorical and Quantitative Data*	
Summarize, represent, and interpret data on a single count or measurable variable	
MCC9-12.S.ID.1 Represent data with plots on the real number line (dot plots, histograms, and box plots).*	Lessons 14-1, 14-2, 14-4
MCC9-12.S.ID.2 Use statistics appropriate to the shape of the data distribution to compare center (median, mean) and spread (interquartile range, standard deviation) of two or more different data sets.*	Lessons 14-2, 14-4
MCC9-12.S.ID.3 Interpret differences in shape, center, and spread in the context of the data sets, accounting for possible effects of extreme data points (outliers).*	Lesson 14-4

(+) Advanced   * = Also a Modeling Standard

© Houghton Mifflin Harcourt Publishing Company

Standards	Lessons
Summarize, represent, and interpret data on two categorical and quantitative variables	
MCC9-12.S.ID.5 Summarize categorical data for two categories in two-way frequency tables. Interpret relative frequencies in the context of the data (including joint, marginal, and conditional relative frequencies). Recognize possible associations and trends in the data.*	Lesson 14-3
MCC9-12.S.ID.6 Represent data on two quantitative variables on a scatter plot, and describe how the variables are related.*	Lesson 13-1, 15-1, 15-2
MCC9-12.S.ID.6a a. Fit a function to the data; use functions fitted to data to solve problems in the context of the data. Use given functions or choose a function suggested by the context. Emphasize linear and exponential models.*	Lessons 13-1, 15-1, 15-2
MCC9-12.S.ID.6b b. Informally assess the fit of a function by plotting and analyzing residuals.*	Lessons 13-1, 15-1, 15-2
MCC9-12.S.ID.6c c. Fit a linear function for a scatter plot that suggests a linear association.*	Lessons 15-1, 15-2
Interpret linear models	
MCC9-12.S.ID.7 Interpret the slope (rate of change) and the intercept (constant term) of a linear model in the context of the data.*	Lessons 15-1, 15-2
MCC9-12.S.ID.8 Compute (using technology) and interpret the correlation coefficient of a linear fit.*	Lesson 15-1
MCC9-12.S.ID.9 Distinguish between correlation and causation.*	Lesson 15-1

(+) Advanced   * = Also a Modeling Standard

© Houghton Mifflin Harcourt Publishing Company

Learning the Standards for Mathematical Practice

The Common Core Georgia Performance Standards include eight Standards for Mathematical Practice. Here's how *Explorations in Core Math* helps you learn those standards as you master the Standards for Mathematical Content.

1 Make sense of problems and persevere in solving them.

In *Explorations in Core Math*, you will work through Explores and Examples that present a solution pathway for you to follow. You will be asked questions along the way so that you gain an understanding of the solution process, and then you will apply what you've learned in the Practice for the lesson.

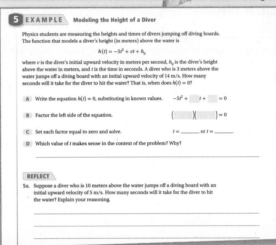

5 EXAMPLE Modeling the Height of a Diver

Physics students are measuring the heights and times of divers jumping off diving boards. The function that models a diver's height (in meters) above the water is

$$h(t) = -5t^2 + vt + h_0$$

where v is the diver's initial upward velocity in meters per second, h_0 is the diver's height above the water in meters, and t is the time in seconds. A diver who is 3 meters above the water jumps off a diving board with an initial upward velocity of 14 m/s. How many seconds will it take for the diver to hit the water? That is, when does $h(t) = 0$?

A Write the equation $h(t) = 0$, substituting in known values. $-5t^2 + \boxed{}\, t + \boxed{} = 0$

B Factor the left side of the equation. $(\boxed{})(\boxed{}) = 0$

C Set each factor equal to zero and solve. $t = \underline{\hspace{1cm}}$ or $t = \underline{\hspace{1cm}}$

D Which value of t makes sense in the context of the problem? Why?

_____

REFLECT

5a. Suppose a diver who is 10 meters above the water jumps off a diving board with an initial upward velocity of 5 m/s. How many seconds will it take for the diver to hit the water? Explain your reasoning.

_____
_____
_____

2 Reason abstractly and quantitatively.

When you solve a real-world problem in *Explorations in Core Math*, you will learn to represent the situation symbolically by translating the problem into a mathematical expression or equation. You will use these mathematical models to solve the problem and then state your answer in terms of the problem context. You will reflect on the solution process in order to check your answer for reasonableness and to draw conclusions.

2 EXAMPLE Writing and Solving Inequalities

Kristin can afford to spend at most $50 for a birthday dinner at a restaurant, including a 15% tip. Describe some costs that are within her budget.

A Which inequality symbol can be used to represent "at most"? _____

B Complete the verbal model for the situation.

Cost before tip (dollars)		15%		Cost before tip (dollars)		Budget limit (dollars)

C Write and simplify an inequality for the model. _____

REFLECT

2a. Can Kristin spend $40 on the meal before the tip? Explain.

_____
_____

2b. What whole dollar amount is the most Kristin can spend before the tip? Explain.

_____
_____

© Houghton Mifflin Harcourt Publishing Company

③ Construct viable arguments and critique the reasoning of others.

Throughout *Explorations in Core Math*, you will be asked to make conjectures, construct a mathematical argument, explain your reasoning, and justify your conclusions. Reflect questions offer opportunities for cooperative learning and class discussion. You will have additional opportunities to critique reasoning in Error Analysis problems.

REFLECT

1a. Why should the parts of the domain of a piecewise function $f(x)$ have no common x-values?

REFLECT

2a. Describe how the graph of $f(x) = ab^x$ compares with the graph of $f(x) = b^x$ for a given value of b when $a > 1$ and when $0 < a < 1$.

23. **Error Analysis** A student says that the graph of $g(x) = |x + 3| - 1$ is the graph of the parent function, $f(x) = |x|$, translated 3 units to the right and 1 unit down. Explain what is incorrect about this statement.

④ Model with mathematics.

Explorations in Core Math presents problems in a variety of contexts such as science, business, and everyday life. You will use mathematical models such as expressions, equations, tables, and graphs to represent the information in the problem and to solve the problem. Then you will interpret your results in context.

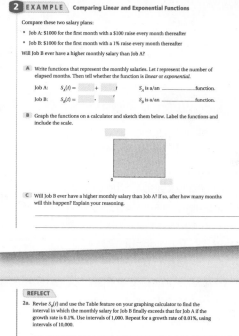

2 EXAMPLE Comparing Linear and Exponential Functions

Compare these two salary plans:

* Job A: $1000 for the first month with a $100 raise every month thereafter
* Job B: $1000 for the first month with a 1% raise every month thereafter

Will Job B ever have a higher monthly salary than Job A?

A Write functions that represent the monthly salaries. Let t represent the number of elapsed months. Then tell whether the function is *linear* or *exponential*.

Job A: $S_A(t) = \boxed{} + \boxed{}\,t$ S_A is a/an _____ function.

Job B: $S_B(t) = \boxed{} \cdot \boxed{}^t$ S_B is a/an _____ function.

B Graph the functions on a calculator and sketch them below. Label the functions and include the scale.

C Will Job B ever have a higher monthly salary than Job A? If so, after how many months will this happen? Explain your reasoning.

REFLECT

2a. Revise $S_B(t)$ and use the Table feature on your graphing calculator to find the interval in which the monthly salary for Job B finally exceeds that for Job A if the growth rate is 0.1%. Use intervals of 1,000. Repeat for a growth rate of 0.01%, using intervals of 10,000.

2b. Why does a quantity increasing exponentially eventually exceed a quantity increasing linearly?

© Houghton Mifflin Harcourt Publishing Company

Getty Images/Image Source

⑤ Use appropriate tools strategically.

You will use a variety of tools in *Explorations in Core Math,* including manipulatives, paper and pencil, and technology. You might use manipulatives to develop concepts, paper and pencil to practice skills, and technology (such as graphing calculators, spreadsheets, or geometry software) to investigate more complicated mathematical ideas.

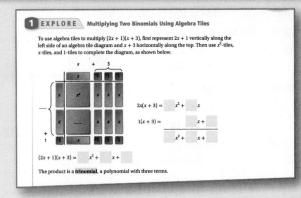

1 EXPLORE Multiplying Two Binomials Using Algebra Tiles

To use algebra tiles to multiply $(2x + 1)(x + 3)$, first represent $2x + 1$ vertically along the left side of an algebra tile diagram and $x + 3$ horizontally along the top. Then use x^2-tiles, x-tiles, and 1-tiles to complete the diagram, as shown below.

$2x(x + 3) =$ ☐ $x^2 +$ ☐ x

$1(x + 3) =$ ☐ $x +$ ☐

☐ $x^2 +$ ☐ $x +$ ☐

$(2x + 1)(x + 3) =$ ☐ $x^2 +$ ☐ $x +$ ☐

The product is a **trinomial**, a polynomial with three terms.

3 EXPLORE Changing the Value of b in $f(x) = b^x$

A Graph the functions $Y_1 = 1.2^x$ and $Y_2 = 1.5^x$ on a graphing calculator. Use a viewing window from −5 to 5 for x and from −2 to 5 for y, with a scale of 1 for both. Sketch the curves.

B Use the TBLSET and TABLE features to make a table of values starting at −2 with an increment of 1. Then complete the table below.

x	Y_1	Y_2
−2	0.694	
−1		0.667
0		
1	1.2	1.5
2		

C Which graph rises more quickly as x increases to the right of 0? Which graph falls, or approaches 0, more quickly as x decreases to the left of 0?

D Identify the y-intercepts of the graphs of Y_1 and Y_2.

⑥ Attend to precision.

Precision refers not only to the correctness of arithmetic calculations, algebraic manipulations, and geometric reasoning but also to the proper use of mathematical language, symbols, and units to communicate mathematical ideas. Throughout *Explorations in Core Math* you will demonstrate your skills in these areas when you are asked to calculate, describe, show, explain, prove, and predict.

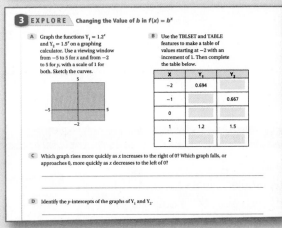

REFLECT

1a. Identify the property being illustrated.

* $2x + 7x = (2 + 7)x$, which equals $9x$
* $(x + 1) + 9 = x + (1 + 9)$, which equals $x + 10$
* $5 + x + 3 = x + 5 + 3$, which equals $x + 8$

1b. *Like terms* contain the same variables raised to the same power. In part a, how was the Distributive Property used to combine like terms?

1c. Constant terms are also considered like terms. In part a, how were properties used to combine constant terms?

3c. If you write only the units for the expression $100 + 12.5t$, you get $mi + \frac{mi}{h} \cdot h$ where "mi" is the abbreviation for miles and "h" is the abbreviation for hours. Explain what the following *unit analysis* shows:

$$mi + \frac{mi}{\not{h}} \cdot \not{h} = mi + mi = mi$$

© Houghton Mifflin Harcourt Publishing Company

⑦ Look for and make use of structure.

In *Explorations in Core Math*, you will look for patterns or regularity in mathematical structures such as expressions, equations, geometric figures, and graphs. Becoming familiar with underlying structures will help you build your understanding of more complicated mathematical ideas.

This method of using the distributive property to multiply two binomials is referred to as the FOIL method. The letters of the word FOIL stand for **F**irst, **O**uter, **I**nner, and **L**ast and will help you remember how to use the distributive property to multiply binomials.

You apply the FOIL method by multiplying each of the four pairs of terms described below and then simplifying the resulting polynomial.

- **First** refers to the first terms of each binomial.
- **Outer** refers to the two terms on the outside of the expression.
- **Inner** refers to the two terms on the inside of the expression.
- **Last** refers to the last terms of each binomial.

Now multiply $(7x - 1)(3x - 5)$ using FOIL. Again, think of $7x - 1$ as $7x + (-1)$ and $3x - 5$ as $3x + (-5)$. This results in a positive constant term of 5 because $(-1)(-5) = 5$.

$$(7x - 1)(3x - 5) = 21x^2 - 35x - 3x + 5$$

$$(7x - 1)(3x - 5) = 21x^2 - 38x + 5$$

Notice that the trinomials are written with variable terms in descending order of exponents and with the constant term last. This is a standard form for writing polynomials: Starting with the variable term with the greatest exponent, write the other variable terms in descending order of their exponents, and put the constant term last.

⑧ Look for and express regularity in repeated reasoning.

In *Explorations in Core Math,* you will have the opportunity to explore and reflect on mathematical processes in order to come up with general methods for performing calculations and solving problems.

1 EXPLORE Deriving the Quadratic Formula

Solve the general form of the quadratic equation, $ax^2 + bx + c = 0$, by completing the square to find the values of x in terms of a, b, and c.

A Subtract c from both sides of the equation.

$$ax^2 + bx = \boxed{}$$

B Multiply both sides of the equation by $4a$ to make the coefficient of x^2 a perfect square.

$$4a^2x^2 + \boxed{}\, x = -4ac$$

C Add b^2 to both sides of the equation to complete the square. Then write the trinomial as the square of a binomial.

$$4a^2x^2 + 4abx + b^2 = -4ac + \boxed{}$$

$$\left(\boxed{}\right)^2 = b^2 - 4ac$$

D Apply the definition of a square root and solve for x.

$$\boxed{} = \pm\sqrt{\boxed{}}$$

$$2ax = -\boxed{} \pm \sqrt{\boxed{}}$$

$$x = \underline{}$$

The formula $x = \frac{-b \pm \sqrt{b^2 - 4ac}}{2a}$ is called the **quadratic formula**.
For any quadratic equation written in standard form, $ax^2 + bx + c = 0$,
the quadratic formula gives the solutions of the equation.

© Houghton Mifflin Harcourt Publishing Company

PhotoDisc/Getty Images

Relationships Between Quantities

© Houghton Mifflin Harcourt Publishing Company

Unpacking the Standards

Understanding the standards and the vocabulary terms in the standards will help you know exactly what you are expected to learn in this unit.

UNIT 1

 GPS COMMON CORE MCC9-12.A.SSE.1

Interpret expressions that represent a quantity in terms of its context.

Key Vocabulary
expression *(expresión)* A mathematical phrase that contains operations, numbers, and/or variables.

What It Means For You

Variables in formulas and other math expressions are used to represent specific quantities.

EXAMPLE

$A = \frac{1}{2}bh$

A = area of the triangle

b = length of the base

h = height

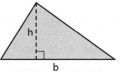

 GPS COMMON CORE MCC9-12.A.CED.1

Create equations … in one variable and use them to solve problems.

Key Vocabulary
equation *(ecuación)* A mathematical statement that two expressions are equivalent.
variable *(variable)* A symbol used to represent a quantity that can change.

What It Means For You

You can write an equation to represent a real-world problem and then use algebra to solve the equation and find the answer.

EXAMPLE
Michael is saving money to buy a trumpet. The trumpet costs $670. He has $350 saved, and each week he adds $20 to his savings. How long will it take him to save enough money to buy the trumpet?

Let w represent the number of weeks.

cost of trumpet	=	current savings	+	additional savings
670	=	350	+	20w
320	=	20w		
16	=	w		

It will take Michael 16 weeks to save enough money.

© Houghton Mifflin Harcourt Publishing Company; Photo credit: © Tetra Images / Tetra Images / Corbis

© Houghton Mifflin Harcourt Publishing Company

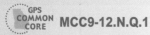 **MCC9-12.N.Q.1**

Use units as a way to understand problems and to guide the solution of multi-step problems; …

Key Vocabulary

unit analysis/dimensional analysis *(análisis dimensional)*
A process that uses rates to convert measurements from one unit to another.

What It Means For You

Keeping track of units in problem solving will help you identify a solution method and interpret the results.

EXAMPLE
Li's car gets 40 miles per gallon of gas. At this rate, she can go 620 miles on a full tank. She has driven 245 miles on the current tank. How many gallons of gas g are left in the tank?

$$\underbrace{620 \text{ mi}}_{\text{Distance}} = \underbrace{245 \text{ mi}}_{\text{Distance}} + \underbrace{\frac{40 \text{ mi}}{1 \text{ gal}} \cdot g \text{ gal}}_{\text{Distance}}$$

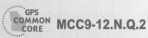 **MCC9-12.N.Q.2**

Define appropriate quantities for the purpose of descriptive modeling.

What It Means For You

Defining quantities carefully helps guide your problem solving when you model a situation.

EXAMPLE
To find all sets of 3 consecutive even integers with sums from 60 to 70, let x be any integer. Then $2x$ is an even integer, and $2x + 2$ and $2x + 4$ are the next consecutive even integers.

$$60 \leq 2x + (2x + 2) + (2x + 4) \leq 70$$

$$60 \leq 6x + 6 \leq 70$$

$$54 \leq \quad 6x \quad \leq 64$$

$$9 \leq \quad x \quad \leq 10\tfrac{2}{3}$$

Because x can be 9 or 10, the first even integer is $2(9) = 18$ or $2(10) = 20$. The sets are 18, 20, 22, or 20, 22, 24.

UNIT 1

Key Vocabulary

coefficient *(coeficiente)* A number that is multiplied by a variable.

constant *(constante)* A value that does not change.

corresponding angles *(ángulos correspondientes)* Angles in the same relative position in polygons with an equal number of angles.

corresponding sides of polygons *(lados correspondientes de los polígonos)* Sides in the same relative position in polygons with an equal number of sides.

equation *(ecuación)* A mathematical statement that two expressions are equivalent.

evaluate *(evaluar)* To find the value of an algebraic expression by substituting a number for each variable and simplifying by using the order of operations.

expression *(expresión)* A mathematical phrase that contains operations, numbers, and/or variables.

linear equation in one variable *(ecuación lineal en una variable)* An equation that can be written in the form $ax = b$ where a and b are constants and $a \neq 0$.

order of operations *(orden de las operaciones)* A process for evaluating expressions:
First, perform operations in parentheses or other grouping symbols.
Second, simplify powers and roots.
Third, perform all multiplication and division from left to right.
Fourth, perform all addition and subtraction from left to right.

precision *(precisión)* The level of detail of a measurement, determined by the unit of measure.

similar *(semejantes)* Two figures are similar if they have the same shape but not necessarily the same size.

solution of an equation in one variable *(solución de una ecuación en una variable)* A value or values that make the equation true.

term of an expression *(término de una expresión)* The parts of the expression that are added or subtracted.

unit analysis/dimensional analysis *(análisis dimensional)* A process that uses rates to convert measurements from one unit to another

variable *(variable)* A symbol used to represent a quantity that can change.

Variables and Expressions
Going Deeper

Essential question: *How do you interpret, evaluate and write algebraic expressions that model real-world situations?*

MCC9–12.A.SSE.1a

1 ENGAGE Interpreting Expressions

Video Tutor

An **expression** is a mathematical phrase that contains operations, numbers, and/or variables. A **numerical expression** contains only numbers and operations, while an **algebraic expression** contains at least one variable.

A **term** is a part of an expression that is added. The **coefficient** of a term is the numerical factor of the term. A numerical term in an algebraic expression is referred to as a *constant term*.

Algebraic Expression	Terms	Coefficients
$2x^2 - 16x + 32$	$2x^2$, $-16x$, constant term 32	2 is the coefficient of $2x$. -16 is the coefficient of $-16x$.

Recall that the **order of operations** is a rule for simplifying a numerical expression:

1. **P**arentheses (simplify inside parentheses) $1 - 6 \cdot (7 - 4) + 5^2 = 1 - 6 \cdot \mathbf{3} + 5^2$

2. **E**xponents (simplify powers) $= 1 - 6 \cdot 3 + \mathbf{25}$

3. **M**ultiplication and **D**ivision (from left to right) $= 1 - \mathbf{18} + 25$

4. **A**ddition and **S**ubtraction (from left to right) $= \mathbf{8}$

REFLECT

1a. Write the expression $3m - 4n - 8$ as a sum. How does this help you identify the terms of the expression? Identify the terms.

_____

_____

1b. Explain and illustrate the difference between a term and a coefficient.

_____

_____

1c. What is the coefficient of x in the expression $x - 2$? Explain your reasoning.

_____

1d. What is the value of $1 - 18 + 25$ if you subtract then add? If you add then subtract? Why is the order of operations necessary?

_____

© Houghton Mifflin Harcourt Publishing Company

To **evaluate** an algebraic expression, substitute the value(s) of the variable(s) into the expression and simplify using the order of operations.

MCC9–12.A.SSE.1b

2 EXAMPLE   **Evaluating Algebraic Expressions**

Evaluate the algebraic expression $x(4x - 10)^3$ for $x = 2$.

A   Substitute 2 for x in the expression. $\boxed{} \cdot \left(4 \cdot \boxed{} - 10\right)^3$

B   Simplify the expression according to the order of operations.

- Multiply within parentheses.   _____

- Subtract within parentheses.   _____

- Simplify powers.   _____

- Multiply.   _____

REFLECT

2a. Explain why x and $4x - 10$ are factors of the expression $x(4x - 10)^3$ rather than terms of the expression. What are the terms of the factor $4x - 10$?

_____

_____

2b. Evaluate $5a + 3b$ and $(5 + a)(3 + b)$ for $a = 2$ and $b = 4$. How is the order of the steps different for the two expressions?

_____

_____

2c. In what order would you perform the operations to correctly evaluate the expression $2 + (3 - 4) \cdot 9$? What is the result?

_____

2d. Show how to move the parentheses in the expression $2 + (3 - 4) \cdot 9$ so that the value of the expression is 9.

_____

© Houghton Mifflin Harcourt Publishing Company

The table shows some words associated with the four arithmetic operations.
They can help you translate verbal phrases into algebraic expressions.

Operation	Words	Examples
addition	plus, the sum of, added to, more than, increased by, how many altogether	• the sum of a number and 3 • a number increased by 3 $n + 3$
subtraction	minus, less, less than, the difference of, subtracted from, reduced by, how many more, how many less	• the difference of a number and 3 • 3 less than a number $n - 3$
multiplication	times, multiply, the product of, twice, double, triple, percent of	• the product of 0.4 and a number • 40% of a number $0.4n$
division	divide, divided by, divide into, the quotient of, half of, one-third of, the ratio of	• the quotient of a number and 3 • one-third of a number $n \div 3$, or $\frac{n}{3}$

REFLECT

The verbal phrase "the quotient of 3 more than a number and 5" can be modeled
as follows:

$$\boxed{\text{Quantity 1}} \div \boxed{\text{Quantity 2}}$$

3a. What words in the phrase represent Quantity 1? Translate these words into
an algebraic expression using n for the variable.

_____

3b. Write an algebraic expression to represent the overall phrase. Explain why you
have to use some sort of grouping symbol.

_____

3c. Show two ways to rewrite the verbal phrase so that it could be represented by the
algebraic expression $5 \div (n + 3)$.

_____

_____

© Houghton Mifflin Harcourt Publishing Company

You can create a verbal model to help you translate a verbal expression into an algebraic expression.

MCC9–12.A.SSE.1

4 EXAMPLE Modeling with Algebraic Expressions

Write an algebraic expression to model the following phrase: the price of a meal plus a 15% tip for the meal.

A Complete the verbal model.

| Price of meal (dollars) | | 15% | | Price of meal (dollars) |

B Choose a variable for the unknown quantity. Include units.

Let _____ represent the _____.

C Write an algebraic expression for the situation. Simplify, if possible.

_____

REFLECT

4a. A 15% tip represents the ratio 15 cents to 100 cents. Why does this make 15% a *unit-less* factor?

_____

_____

4b. What units are associated with the total cost? Explain.

_____

_____

4c. What could the expression $\frac{p + 0.15p}{2}$ represent, including units?

_____

_____

_____

4d. What if the tip is 20% instead of 15%? How can you represent the total cost with a simplified algebraic expression? Identify the units for the expression.

_____

4e. What if the tip is 20% instead of 15% and 3 people are sharing the cost evenly? How can you represent the amount that each person pays with a simplified algebraic expression? Identify the units for the expression.

_____

© Houghton Mifflin Harcourt Publishing Company

Identify the terms of each expression and the coefficient of each term.

1. $7x + 8y$

2. $a - b$

3. $3m^2 - 6n$

_____

_____

_____

Evaluate each expression for $a = 2$, $b = 3$, and $c = -6$.

4. $7a - 5b + 4$

5. $b^2(c + 4)$

6. $8 - 2ab$

_____

_____

_____

7. $a^2 + b^2 - c^2$

8. $(a - c)(c + 5)$

9. $12 - 2(a - b)^2$

_____

_____

_____

10. $a + (b - c)^2$

11. $(a + b) - ab$

12. $5a^2 + bc^2$

_____

_____

_____

13. Alex purchased a 6-hour calling card. He has used t minutes of access time. Write an algebraic expression to represent how many minutes he has remaining and identify the units for the expression.

_____

14. A store is having a sale on used video games. Each game costs $12. Write an algebraic expression to represent the cost of buying v video games. Identify the units for the expression.

_____

15. Sara is driving home from college for the weekend. The average speed of her car for the trip is 45 miles per hour. Write a verbal model and algebraic expression to represent the distance Sara's car travels in h hours. Identify the units for the expression.

_____

16. It costs $20 per hour to bowl and $3 for shoe rental. Write a verbal model and an algebraic expression to represent the cost for n hours and identify the units for the expression.

_____

17. Jared earns 0.25 vacation days for every week that he works in a calendar year. He also gets 10 paid company holidays per year. Write a verbal model and an algebraic expression to represent the amount of time he gets off from work in a year after working for w weeks and identify the units for the expression.

_____

_____

© Houghton Mifflin Harcourt Publishing Company

18. Sam collects baseball cards. He currently has 112 cards in his collection. He plans to buy 5 new cards every month. Write a verbal model and algebraic expression to represent the total number of cards Sam has after m months. Identify the units for the expression.

_____

_____

19. There are 575 fireworks to be shot off in a fireworks display. Every minute 12 new fireworks are shot off for the display. Write a verbal model and algebraic expression to represent the number of fireworks left to be shot off after t minutes. Identify the units for the expression.

_____

_____

20. Lindsay gets paid a base salary of $400 per week plus a 0.15 commission on each sale she makes. Write a verbal model and algebraic expression to represent Lindsay's total salary for the week if she makes d dollars worth of sales during the week. Identify the units for the expression.

_____

_____

© Houghton Mifflin Harcourt Publishing Company

Additional Practice

Give two ways to write each algebraic expression in words.

1. $15 - b$

2. $\dfrac{x}{16}$

_____

_____

_____

_____

3. $x + 9$

4. $(2)(t)$

_____

_____

_____

_____

5. $z - 7$

6. $4y$

_____

_____

_____

_____

7. Sophie's math class has 6 fewer boys than girls, and there are g girls. Write an expression for the number of boys.

_____

8. A computer printer can print 10 pages per minute. Write an expression for the number of pages the printer can print in m minutes.

_____

Evaluate each expression for $r = 8$, $s = 2$, and $t = 5$.

9. st

10. $r \div s$

11. $s + t$

_____

_____

_____

12. $r - t$

13. $r \cdot s$

14. $t - s$

_____

_____

_____

15. Paula always withdraws 20 dollars more than she needs from the bank.

   a. Write an expression for the amount of money Paula withdraws if she needs d dollars.

_____

   b. Find the amount of money Paula withdraws if she needs 20, 60, and 75 dollars.

_____

© Houghton Mifflin Harcourt Publishing Company

Problem Solving

Write the correct answer.

1. For her book club, Sharon reads for 45 minutes each day. Write an expression for the number of hours she reads in *d* days.

   _____

2. The minimum wage in 2003 was $5.15. This was *w* more than the minimum wage in 1996. Write an expression for the minimum wage in 1996.

   _____

3. According to the 2000 census, the number of people per square mile in Florida was about 216 more than the number of people per square mile in Texas. Write an expression for the number of people per square mile in Florida if there were *t* people per square mile in Texas.

   _____

4. The cost of a party is $550. The price per person depends on how many people attend the party. Write an expression for the price per person if *p* people attend the party. Then find the price per person if 25, 50, and 55 people attend the party.

   _____

   _____

Use the table below to answer questions 5–6, which shows the years five states entered the Union. Select the best answer.

5. North Carolina entered the Union *x* years after Pennsylvania. Which expression shows the year North Carolina entered the Union?

   A 1845 + *x*   C 1787 + *x*

   B 1845 − *x*   D 1787 − *x*

6. The expression *f* − 26 represents the year Alabama entered the Union, where *f* is the year Florida entered. In which year did Alabama enter the Union?

   F 1819   H 1837

   G 1826   J 1871

7. The number of states that entered the Union in 1889 was half the number of states *s* that entered in 1788. Which expression shows the number of states that entered the Union in 1889?

   A 2*s*   C *s* + 2

   B *s* ÷ 2   D 2 − *s*

State	Year Entered into Union
Florida	1845
Indiana	1816
Pennsylvania	1787
Texas	1845
West Virginia	1863

© Houghton Mifflin Harcourt Publishing Company

Solving Equations by Adding or Subtracting
Going Deeper

Essential question: *What are some different methods for solving linear equations?*

The solution of an equation can be given as an equation of the form $x = a$ where a is a solution, as in $x = 6$, or listed in set notation, as $\{6\}$.

MCC9–12.A.REI.3

1 EXPLORE Solving Equations Using Different Methods

Find the solution set for the linear equation.

A Use guess and check to find the solution set of the equation $x - 5 = 4$.

Guess $x = 10$.　　$10 - 5 = $ ____　　$5 > 4$, so 10 is too great.

Guess $x = 8$.　　$8 - 5 = $ ____　　$3 < 4$, so 8 is too little.

Guess $x = 9$.　　$9 - 5 = $ ____　　$4 = 4$, so 9 is correct.

The solution set is $\{$ ____ $\}$.

B Use a table to find the solution set of the equation $y + 7 = 10$.

y	1	2	3	4
$y + 7$	$1 + 7$	$2 + 7$	$3 + 7$	$4 + 7$
Sum				

The solution set is $\{$ ____ $\}$.

C Work backward to find the solution set of the equation $z - 2 = 8$.

Start with the number being subtracted, _____.

Working backward, add _____ since it is the inverse of subtracting _____.

You get $z - 2 + 2 = 8 + 2 = $ _____ or $z = 10$. The solution set is $\{$_____$\}$.

REFLECT

1a. Could you solve each of the three equations above by all three methods? Explain.

_____

_____

_____

© Houghton Mifflin Harcourt Publishing Company

Two equations are **equivalent equations** if they have the same solution set. The two equations below are equivalent because they have the same solution set, {6}.

$$x + 3 = 9 \qquad x - 3 = 3$$
$$\mathbf{6} + 3 = 9 \qquad \mathbf{6} - 3 = 3$$

To solve an equation algebraically, you perform a series of inverse operations to isolate the variable on one side. When these inverse operations are completed, the other side of the equation is the solution. The Addition and Subtraction Properties of Equality can be used to justify the steps taken to solve an equation. These properties, as well as other useful properties, are listed below.

Addition Property of Equality	If $a = b$, then $a + c = b + c$.
Subtraction Property of Equality	If $a = b$, then $a - b = b - c$.
Inverse Property of Addition	$a + (-a) = -a + a = 0$
Identity Property of Addition	$a + 0 = 0 + a = a$
Associative Property of Addition	$(a + b) + c = a + (b + c)$

MCC9–12.A.REI.1

2 EXAMPLE   **Adding or Subtracting to Find the Solution Set**

Add or subtract to find the solution set.

A $x + 5 = 13$

$x + 5 - \boxed{} = 13 - \boxed{}$ _____ Property of Equality

$x + \boxed{} = 13 - \boxed{}$ _____ Property of Addition

$x = 13 - \boxed{}$ _____ Property of Addition

$x = \boxed{}$ Simplify.

The solution set is {   }.

B $y - 11 = 2$

$y - 11 + \boxed{} = 2 + \boxed{}$ _____ Property of Equality

$y + \boxed{} = 2 + \boxed{}$ _____ Property of Addition

$y = 2 + \boxed{}$ _____ Property of Addition

$y = \boxed{}$ Simplify.

The solution set is {   }.

REFLECT

2a. Which property of equality would you use to solve $x - 47 = 100$? Explain.

_____

_____

© Houghton Mifflin Harcourt Publishing Company

3 EXAMPLE   Using the Associative Property

Use properties to find the solution set of $(x + 5) + 4 = 16$.

$(x + 5) + 4 = 16$	Original equation
$x + (5 +) = 16$	Associative Property
$x + = 16$	Simplify.
$x + 9 - 9 = 16 - $	_____ Property of Equality
$x + = 16 - 9$	Inverse Property of Addition
$ = 16 - $	_____ Property of Addition
$x = $	Simplify.

The solution set is {   }.

REFLECT

3a. Solve $(x + 5) + 4 = 16$ by first subtracting 4 and then subtracting 5. Show your work and justify each step.

_____

_____

_____

_____

_____

_____

_____

_____

_____

_____

3b. Does performing the steps in a different order affect the solution of the equation? Compare the steps in the example with the steps for the question above. How do the two methods differ? Explain.

_____

_____

_____

_____

© Houghton Mifflin Harcourt Publishing Company

Find the solution set for each equation. State the property you used.

1. $m - 7 = 13$

2. $r + 12 = 21$

_____

_____

3. $17 + p = 22$

4. $7 = q + 4$

_____

_____

5. $81 = 8 + z$

6. $42 = b - 21$

_____

_____

Solve using the Associative Property first. Justify your steps.

7. $(y + 8) - 3 = 16$

_____

_____

_____

_____

_____

_____

Solve using the Properties of Equality first. Justify your steps.

8. $(m - 3) + 5 = 12$

_____

_____

_____

_____

_____

_____

_____

© Houghton Mifflin Harcourt Publishing Company

Additional Practice

Solve each equation. Check your answers.

1. $g - 7 = 15$

2. $t + 4 = 6$

3. $13 = m - 7$

_____   _____   _____

4. $x + 3.4 = 9.1$

5. $n - \dfrac{3}{8} = \dfrac{1}{8}$

6. $p - \dfrac{1}{3} = \dfrac{2}{3}$

_____   _____   _____

7. $-6 + k = 32$

8. $7 = w + 9.3$

9. $8 = r + 12$

_____   _____   _____

10. $y - 57 = -40$

11. $-5.1 + b = -7.1$

12. $a + 15 = 15$

_____   _____   _____

13. Marietta was given a raise of $0.75 an hour, which brought her hourly wage to $12.25. Write and solve an equation to determine Marietta's hourly wage before her raise. Show that your answer is reasonable.

_____

_____

14. Brad grew $4\dfrac{1}{4}$ inches this year and is now $56\dfrac{7}{8}$ inches tall. Write and solve an equation to find Brad's height at the start of the year. Show that your answer is reasonable.

_____

_____

15. Heather finished a race in 58.4 seconds, which was 2.6 seconds less than her practice time. Write and solve an equation to find Heather's practice time. Show that your answer is reasonable.

_____

_____

16. The radius of Earth is 6378.1 km, which is 2981.1 km longer than the radius of Mars. Write and solve an equation to determine the radius of Mars. Show that your answer is reasonable.

_____

_____

© Houghton Mifflin Harcourt Publishing Company

Problem Solving

Write the correct answer.

1. Michelle withdrew $120 from her bank account. She now has $3345 in her account. Write and solve an equation to find how much money m was in her account before she made the withdrawal.

   _____

   _____

2. Max lost 23 pounds while on a diet. He now weighs 184 pounds. Write and solve an equation to find his initial weight w.

   _____

   _____

3. Earth takes 365 days to orbit the Sun. Mars takes 687 days. Write and solve an equation to find how many more days d Mars takes than Earth to orbit the Sun.

   _____

   _____

4. In 1990, 53.4% of commuters took public transportation in New York City, which was 19.9% greater than the percentage in San Francisco. Write and solve an equation to find what percentage of commuters p took public transportation in San Francisco.

   _____

   _____

Use the circle graph below to answer questions 5–7. Select the best answer. The circle graph shows the colors for SUVs as percents of the total number of SUVs manufactured in 2000 in North America.

5. The percent of silver SUVs increased by 7.9% between 1998 and 2000. If x% of SUVs were silver in 1998, which equation represents this relationship?

   A $x + 7.9 = 14.1$ C $7.9x = 14.1$

   B $x - 7.9 = 14.1$ D $7.9 - x = 14.1$

6. Solve the equation from problem 5. What is the value of x?

   F 1.8   H 7.1

   G 6.2   J 22

7. The sum of the percents of dark red SUVs and white SUVs was 26.3%. What was the percent of dark red SUVs?

   A 2.3%   C 12.2%

   B 3.2%   D 18%

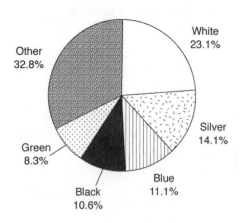

Percent of SUVs by Color

White 23.1%
Other 32.8%
Silver 14.1%
Green 8.3%
Blue 11.1%
Black 10.6%

© Houghton Mifflin Harcourt Publishing Company

Video Tutor

Solving Equations by Multiplying or Dividing
Going Deeper

Essential question: *How can you use properties to justify solutions to equations that involve multiplication and division?*

You have solved addition and subtraction equations by performing a series of inverse operations that isolate the variable on one side of the equation. Multiplication and division equations can be solved in a similar way. The Multiplication and Division Properties of Equality, as well as the other properties below, can be used to justify the steps taken to solve a multiplication or division equation.

Multiplication Property of Equality	If $a = b$, then $ac = bc$.
Division Property of Equality	If $a = b$, and $c \neq 0$, then $\frac{a}{c} = \frac{b}{c}$.
Inverse Property of Multiplication	If $a \neq 0$, then $a\left(\frac{1}{a}\right) = \left(\frac{1}{a}\right)a = 1$.
Identity Property of Multiplication	$a \cdot 1 = 1 \cdot a = a$
Associative Property of Multiplication	$a(bc) = (ab)c$

MCC9–12.A.REI.1

1 EXAMPLE Multiplying or Dividing to Find the Solution Set

Find the solution set.

$$\frac{5y}{3} = 20$$

$$\boxed{}\left(\frac{5y}{3}\right) = \boxed{}(20) \qquad \underline{\hspace{3cm}}\text{Property of Equality}$$

$$\frac{\boxed{}}{3}(5y) = \boxed{}(20) \qquad \text{Associative Property of Multiplication}$$

$$\boxed{}(5y) = \boxed{}(20) \qquad \underline{\hspace{3cm}}\text{Property of Multiplication}$$

$$(5y) = \boxed{}(20) \qquad \underline{\hspace{3cm}}\text{Property of Addition}$$

$$5y = \boxed{} \qquad \text{Simplify.}$$

$$\frac{5y}{\boxed{}} = \frac{60}{\boxed{}} \qquad \underline{\hspace{3cm}}\text{Property of Equality}$$

$$y = \boxed{} \qquad \text{Simplify.}$$

The solution set is { $\boxed{}$ }.

© Houghton Mifflin Harcourt Publishing Company

1a. Solve $\frac{5y}{3} = 20$ using only the Multiplication Property of Equality. Show your work and justify each step.

_____

_____

_____

_____

_____

_____

_____

1b. Which method of solving $\frac{5y}{3} = 20$ is more efficient? Explain.

_____

_____

PRACTICE

Find the solution set for each equation. State the property you used.

1. $\frac{4}{5}b = 16$ **2.** $7w = 105$

_____   _____

3. Solve $\frac{3}{4}\left(\frac{2}{3}m\right) = 24$. Use the Properties of Equality first. Justify each step.

_____

_____

_____

_____

_____

_____

_____

_____

_____

© Houghton Mifflin Harcourt Publishing Company

Additional Practice

Solve each equation. Check your answers.

1. $\frac{d}{8} = 6$

2. $-5 = \frac{n}{2}$

3. $2p = 54$

_____

4. $\frac{-t}{2} = 12$

5. $-40 = -4x$

6. $\frac{2r}{3} = 16$

_____

7. $-49 = 7y$

8. $-15 = -\frac{3n}{5}$

9. $9m = 6$

_____

10. $\frac{v}{-3} = -6$

11. $2.8 = \frac{b}{4}$

12. $\frac{3r}{4} = \frac{1}{8}$

_____

Answer each of the following.

13. The perimeter of a regular pentagon is 41.5 cm. Write and solve an equation to determine the length of each side of the pentagon.

14. In June 2005, Peter mailed a package from his local post office in Fayetteville, North Carolina to a friend in Radford, Virginia for $2.07. The first-class rate at the time was $0.23 per ounce. Write and solve an equation to determine the weight of the package.

15. Lola spends one-third of her allowance on movies. She spends $8 per week at the movies. Write and solve an equation to determine Lola's weekly allowance.

© Houghton Mifflin Harcourt Publishing Company

Problem Solving

Write the correct answer.

1. John threw a surprise birthday party for his friend. Food, drinks, and a DJ cost $480 for a group of 32 people. Write and solve an equation to find the cost c per person.

   _____

   _____

2. One serving of soybeans contains 10 grams of protein, which is 4 times the amount in one serving of kale. Write and solve an equation to find the amount of protein x in one serving of kale.

   _____

   _____

3. Maria earned $10.50 per hour working at an ice cream shop. She earned $147 each week before taxes. Write and solve an equation to find the number of hours h she worked each week.

   _____

   _____

4. Ben is saving $\frac{1}{5}$ of his weekly pay to buy a car. Write and solve an equation to find what weekly pay w results in savings of $61.50.

   _____

   _____

Use the table below to answer questions 5–7. Select the best answer.
The table shows the maximum speed in miles per hour for various animals.

5. The speed of a snail is how many times that of a cat?

   A $\frac{1}{1000}$ C 100

   B $\frac{1}{100}$ D 1000

Animal	mi/h
Falcon	200
Zebra	40
Cat (domestic)	30
Black Mamba Snake	20
Snail	0.03

6. A cheetah's maximum speed of 70 mi/h is x times faster than a black mamba snake's maximum speed. Which equation shows this relationship?

   F $20 + x = 70$ H $70 = \frac{20}{x}$

   G $20 = 70x$ J $70 = 20x$

7. Use your equation in problem 6 to find how many times faster a cheetah is than a black mamba snake if they are both traveling at their maximum speed.

   A 0.3 times   C 10 times

   B 3.5 times   D 50 times

© Houghton Mifflin Harcourt Publishing Company

Rates, Ratios, and Proportions
Extension: Dimensional Analysis

Essential question: *How can you use units to help solve real-world problems?*

Unit Analysis When evaluating expressions that represent real-world situations, you should pay attention to the units of measurement attached to the parts of the expression. For instance, if p people go to a restaurant and agree to split the $50 cost of the meal equally, then the units in the numerator of the expression $\frac{50}{p}$ are *dollars*, the units in the denominator are *people*, and the units for the value of the expression are *dollars per person*.

Video Tutor

MCC9–12.A.SSE.1

1 EXAMPLE **Evaluating Real-World Expressions**

A Sheila is participating in a multi-day bike trip. On the first day, she rode 100 miles in 8 hours. Use the expression $\frac{d}{t}$ where d is the distance traveled and t is the travel time to find her average rate of travel. Include units when evaluating the expression.

$$\frac{d}{t} = \frac{}{} = $$

B If Sheila continues riding at her average rate for the first day, then the expression $100 + 12.5t$ gives the total distance that she has traveled after riding for t hours on the second day. Evaluate this expression when $t = 7$, and include units.

$$100 + 12.5t = 100\,\underline{} + 12.5\,\underline{} \cdot \underline{}$$

$$= \underline{}$$

REFLECT

1a. What are the terms in the expression $100 + 12.5t$? What does each term represent in the context of Sheila's bike trip?

_____

_____

1b. What is the coefficient of the term $12.5t$? What does it represent in the context of Sheila's bike trip?

_____

_____

© Houghton Mifflin Harcourt Publishing Company

1c. If you write only the units for the expression $100 + 12.5t$, you get

$mi + \frac{mi}{h} \cdot h$ where "mi" is the abbreviation for miles and "h" is the abbreviation for hours. Explain what the following *unit analysis* shows:

$$mi + \frac{mi}{\cancel{h}} \cdot \cancel{h} = mi + mi = mi$$

_____

_____

1d. How can you modify the expression $100 + 12.5t$ so that the units are feet when the expression is evaluated?

_____

MCC9–12.N.Q.1

2 EXAMPLE **Using Unit Analysis to Guide Modeling**

Lizzie has volunteered 20 hours at her town library. From now on, she plans to volunteer 5 hours per week at the library. Write an algebraic expression to represent the total number of hours she will volunteer.

A Use unit analysis to help you get the correct units for the expression.

$$\boxed{hours} + \frac{\boxed{hours}}{\boxed{\cancel{week}}} \cdot \boxed{} = \boxed{hours}$$

B Write a verbal model.

_____

C Choose a variable for the unknown quantity.

Let _____ represent the _____.

D Write an algebraic expression to represent the situation.

_____

REFLECT

2a. Explain why you chose the units you chose in Part A.

_____

_____

_____

_____

© Houghton Mifflin Harcourt Publishing Company

2b. How many hours will Lizzie have volunteered at the library by the end of 10 weeks?

_____

2c. Lizzie has also volunteered 10 hours at an animal shelter and she plans to volunteer there for 3 hours a week beginning in 1 week. Rewrite the algebraic expression you wrote in Part D above based on this new information. (Assume that the number of weeks is at least 1.) Simplify, if possible.

_____

2d. How many hours will Lizzie have volunteered at the library and the animal shelter combined by the end of 20 weeks?

_____

PRACTICE

1. Henry drives in town at a rate of 25 miles per hour. It takes him 15 minutes to go to the library from his house. The algebraic expression rt represents distance traveled, where r is the average rate (in miles per hour) and t is the travel time (in hours).

  a. Can you multiply 25 and 15 to find the distance Henry traveled to the library? Explain.

  _____

  b. Show how to find the distance from Henry's house to the library. Include units in your calculation.

  _____

2. Sarah works 4 hours her first week of a part-time job and earns $60. Her total pay after the second week can be represented by the expression $60 + \frac{p}{t} \cdot s$ where p represents her pay for t hours of work and s represents the hours she works in the second week.

  a. What are the units of the fraction?

  _____

  b. Rewrite the expression substituting the given values for p and t. What are the units of each term of your new expression? Explain.

  _____

  c. Evaluate your expression for $s = 5$. Include units.

  _____

© Houghton Mifflin Harcourt Publishing Company

3. To convert dog years to human years, you count 10.5 dog years per human year for the first two human years and then 4 dog years per human year for each human year thereafter.

    a. Show how to use unit analysis to get the correct units when you convert dog years to human years.

    _____

    b. Write and simplify an algebraic expression for converting dog years to human years when the number of human years is 2 or more. Define what the variable represents.

    _____

4. Tracie buys tickets to a concert for herself and two friends. There is an 8% tax on the cost of the tickets and an additional $10 booking fee. Write an algebraic expression to represent the cost per person. Simplify the expression, if possible. Define what the variable represents and identify the units for the expression.

_____

_____

5. Write two different algebraic expressions that could represent the phrase "a number plus 2 times the number." Then rewrite the phrase so that only one of the algebraic expressions could be correct.

_____

_____

© Houghton Mifflin Harcourt Publishing Company

Additional Practice

1. Julia drove 135 miles in 4.5 hours. Find her average rate in miles per hour.   _____

Find the average rate.

2. Four pounds of apples cost $1.96.

3. Sal washed 5 cars in 50 minutes.

_____   _____

4. A giraffe can run 32 miles per hour. What is this speed in feet per second? Round your answer to the nearest tenth.   _____

Use unit analysis to write an algebraic expression to represent the situation.

5. Billie and Toni are driving from Chicago to Phoenix. The first day they drove 420 miles. They want to drive at 65 miles per hour for the rest of their trip.

   a. Write an algebraic expression to represent the situation.   _____

   b. If they drive 8 hours a day for the next two days, how far have they traveled by the end of the third day?   _____

6. Frank ordered playoff tickets for himself and three friends. There is a $7 service fee per ticket and an additional shipping cost of $12 for the entire ticket order.

   a. Write an algebraic expression to represent the situation.   _____

   b. Write an algebraic expression to represent the ticket cost per person.   _____

7. Sam is building a model of an antique car. The scale of his model to the actual car is 1:10. His model is $18\frac{1}{2}$ inches long.

How long is the actual car in feet? Round your answer to the nearest tenth of a foot.   _____

8. The scale on a map of Virginia shows that 1 centimeter represents 30 miles. The actual distance from Richmond, VA to Washington, DC is 110 miles. On the map, how many centimeters are between the two cities? Round your answer to the nearest tenth.   _____

© Houghton Mifflin Harcourt Publishing Company

Problem Solving

Write the correct answer.

1. A donut shop bakes 4 dozen donuts every 18 minutes. Find the average rate to the nearest hundredth.

   _____

2. Sally volunteers at the youth center 14 hours per week. If Sally volunteers 4 days a week, what is her average rate in hours per day?

   _____

3. The birth rate in Namibia is 35 babies to every 1000 people. In 2001, the country had a population of about 1,800,000 people. How many babies were there?

   _____

4. A boat travels 160 miles in 5 hours. What is its speed in miles per minute to the nearest hundredth?

   _____

The Hendersons are driving cross country from Boston to Los Angeles. The first day they drove 300 miles. They plan to drive at an average speed of 60 miles per hour for the rest of the trip so that the trip will be completed in less than one week.

5. Write an algebraic expression to represent the length of the total trip.

   A $300t + 60$ C $60t + 300$

   B $300 - 60t$ D $60t - 300$

6. What are the units in the expression from Problem 5?

   F hours   H days

   G miles   J weeks

7. If the Hendersons drive for 9 hours per day, how many miles will they travel in a day?

   A 300 miles   C 60 miles

   B $9t$ miles   D 540 miles

8. The distance from Boston to Los Angeles is approximately 3000 miles. How many days should the Henderson's trip take if they drive 9 hours per day after the first day?

   F 4 days

   G 5 days

   H 6 days

   J 7 days

© Houghton Mifflin Harcourt Publishing Company

Applications of Proportions
Connection: Dimensional analysis

Essential question: *How can you use units to write and solve proportions?*

MCC9–12.N.Q.1

1 ENGAGE Writing Valid Proportions

Video Tutor

Similar figures are figures that have the same shape, but not necessarily the same size. **Corresponding sides** of two similar figures are in the same relative position in the figures. Two figures are similar if and only if the lengths of the corresponding sides are proportional.

$\triangle ABC$ is similar to $\triangle DEF$. This can be written as $\triangle ABC \sim \triangle DEF$, with the corresponding vertices written in the same order.
It is not correct to write $\triangle ABC \sim \triangle FED$.

Side $\overline{AC}$ corresponds to side $\overline{DF}$.
Side $\overline{AB}$ corresponds to side $\overline{DE}$.
Side $\overline{BC}$ corresponds to side $\overline{EF}$.

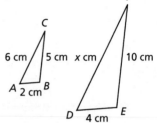

In similar figures, the lengths of corresponding sides are proportional. To correctly set up a proportion, the corresponding side lengths must be in the same position in both ratios.

Correct: $\frac{AC}{DF} = \frac{AB}{DE}$

(corresponding sides; same position)

Incorrect: $\frac{AC}{DF} = \frac{DE}{AB}$

(second ratio reversed)

Incorrect: $\frac{AC}{DF} = \frac{AB}{EF}$

(non-corresponding sides)

Also, in a valid proportion the units must be the same for all entries.

Incorrect: $\frac{3 \text{ cm}}{8 \text{ m}} = \frac{9 \text{ cm}}{x}$

Correct: $\frac{3 \text{ cm}}{800 \text{ cm}} = \frac{9 \text{ cm}}{x}$

REFLECT

1a. What change was made to make $\frac{3 \text{ cm}}{8 \text{ m}} = \frac{9 \text{ cm}}{x}$ into a valid proportion? Why and how was this change made?

_____

_____

_____

1b. Two figures are similar. One is measured in inches and the other is measured in feet. How could you write a valid proportion for these figures?

_____

_____

1c. Is it possible to write the proportion $\frac{6 \text{ m}}{x} = \frac{2 \text{ m}}{4 \text{ m}}$ in another way? If so, rewrite the proportion and then explain how you know that the new proportion is valid.

_____

_____

© Houghton Mifflin Harcourt Publishing Company

2 EXAMPLE   Solving Real-World Proportions

A flagpole casts a shadow that is 12 feet long. At the same time, a 6-foot-tall man casts a shadow that is 2 feet long. Write and solve a proportion to find the height of the flagpole.

The man and the flagpole are both perpendicular to the ground, so they form right angles with the ground. The sun shines at the same angle on both, so similar triangles are formed.

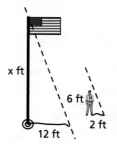

A Write a proportion.

$$\frac{\text{man's height}}{\text{pole's height}} = \frac{\text{man's shadow}}{\text{pole's shadow}} \qquad \frac{6}{x} = \frac{2}{12}$$

B Solve using cross products.

$$\frac{6}{x} = \frac{2}{12}$$

$6 \times 12 =$ _____

_____

_____

_____

REFLECT

2a. Write and solve a different proportion to find the height of the flagpole.

_____

_____

_____

_____

_____

2b. Explain why your new proportion and solution are valid.

_____

_____

_____

© Houghton Mifflin Harcourt Publishing Company

3 EXAMPLE   Using Dimensional Analysis

A can of tuna has a shape similar to the shape of a large holding tank. The can of tuna has a diameter of 3 inches and a height of 2 inches. The holding tank has a diameter of 6 yards. What is the height of the holding tank?

You can change the units by using dimensional analysis. In order to avoid using fractions or decimals, change yards to inches.

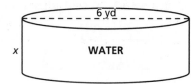

A Use dimensional analysis.

$$6 \text{ yd} \times \frac{\boxed{} \text{ ft}}{1 \text{ yd}} \times \frac{\boxed{}}{1 \text{ ft}} = \boxed{} \times \boxed{} \times \boxed{} = \boxed{}$$

B Write and solve a proportion.

$$\frac{2 \text{ in.}}{3 \text{ in.}} = \underline{\hspace{6cm}}$$

_____

_____

_____

_____

The holding tank is _____ tall.

REFLECT

3a. Use dimensional analysis to write the height in feet and in yards.

_____

_____

3b. What other proportions could be used to find the height of the holding tank? Explain why these proportions could be used.

_____

_____

_____

© Houghton Mifflin Harcourt Publishing Company

Solve each problem using a proportion.

1. △*ABC* ~ △*DEF*. What is the length of $\overline{DF}$?

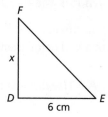
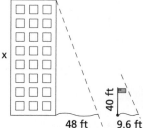

_____

_____

_____

_____

_____

_____

2. A building casts a shadow 48 feet long. At the same time, a 40-foot tall flagpole casts a shadow 9.6 feet long. What is the height of the building?

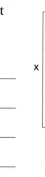

_____

_____

_____

_____

_____

_____

3. Rectangle *ABCD* is similar to rectangle *WXYZ*. Rectangle *ABCD* has a length of 8 inches and a height of 5 inches. Rectangle *WXYZ* has a height of 3 feet. What is the length of rectangle *WXYZ* in inches?

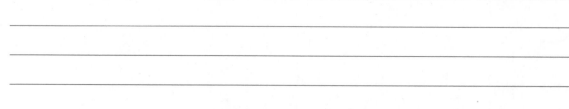

© Houghton Mifflin Harcourt Publishing Company

Additional Practice

Find the value of *x* in each diagram.

1. △ABC ~ △DEF

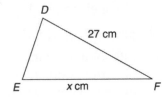

2. FGHJK ~ MNPQR

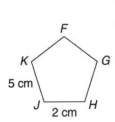
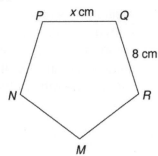

_____   _____

3. A utility worker is 5.5 feet tall and is casting a shadow 4 feet long. At the same time, a nearby utility pole casts a shadow 20 feet long. Write and solve a proportion to find the height of the utility pole.   _____

4. A cylinder has a radius of 3 cm and a length of 10 cm. Every dimension of the cylinder is multiplied by 3 to form a new cylinder. How is the ratio of the volumes related to the ratio of corresponding dimensions?

_____

5. A rectangle has an area of 48 in^2. Every dimension of the rectangle is multiplied by a scale factor, and the new rectangle has an area of 12 in^2.
What was the scale factor?   _____

© Houghton Mifflin Harcourt Publishing Company

Problem Solving

Write the correct answer.

1. A 4 by 5 inch photo is enlarged by multiplying every dimension by 2 to form a similar 8 by 10 inch photo. What is the ratio of the perimeter of the smaller rectangle to that of the larger? What is the ratio of the two areas?

_____

_____

2. Pamela wants to buy a suitcase whose dimensions are $1\frac{1}{2}$ times those of her $28 \times 16 \times 8$ inch suitcase. How is the ratio of the volumes related to the ratio of corresponding dimensions? What is the ratio of the volumes?

_____

_____

_____

_____

3. The Taylors plan to expand their 80 square foot garage by tripling the dimensions. What will be the area of the new garage?

_____

4. A tent has a volume of 26.25 in^3. Every dimension is multiplied by a scale factor so that the new tent has a volume of 1680 in^3. What was the scale factor?

_____

Complete the table below and use it to answer questions 5–8. Select the best answer. Assume the shadow lengths were measured at the same time of day.

5. The flagpole casts an 8 foot shadow, as shown in the table. At the same time, the oak tree casts a 12 foot shadow. How tall is the oak tree?

   A 4.8 ft   C 30 ft

   B 24 ft   D 32 ft

Object	Length of Shadow (ft)	Height (ft)
Flagpole	8	20
Oak tree	12	
Goal post	18	
Telephone pole		17.5
Fence		6.5

6. How tall is the goal post?

   F 7.2 ft   H 38 ft

   G 30 ft   J 45 ft

7. What is the length of the telephone pole's shadow?

   A 5.5 ft   C 25.5 ft

   B 7 ft   D 43.8 ft

8. What is the length of the fence's shadow?

   F 1.5 ft   H 16.25 ft

   G 2.6 ft   J 21.5 ft

© Houghton Mifflin Harcourt Publishing Company

Precision and Accuracy
Extension: Significant Digits

Essential question: *How do you use significant digits to report the results of calculations based on measurements?*

Precision is the level of detail an instrument can measure. For example, a ruler marked in millimeters is more precise than a ruler that is marked only in centimeters.

You can use precision to compare measurements. For example, a measurement of 25 inches is more precise than a measurement of 2 feet because an inch is a smaller unit than a foot. Similarly, 9.2 kg is more precise than 9 kg because a tenth of a kilogram is a smaller unit than a kilogram.

In the following activity, you will investigate how precision affects calculated measurements, such as area.

MCC9–12.N.Q.3

1 EXPLORE   Making Measurements to Calculate an Area

A   Work with a partner. One of you should measure the width of a book cover to the nearest centimeter. Record the width below.

Width of book cover: _____

The other person should measure the length of the book cover to the nearest tenth of a centimeter. Record the length below.

Length of book cover: _____

B   Determine the minimum and maximum possible values for the actual width and length of the book cover.

Example: When you measure an object to the nearest centimeter and get a measurement of 3 cm, the actual measurement is between 2.5 cm and 3.5 cm.

When measuring to the nearest centimeter, lengths in this range are rounded to 3 cm.

Minimum width: _____   Maximum width: _____

Minimum length: _____   Maximum length: _____

C   Use the minimum width and minimum length to calculate the minimum possible area of the book cover. Then use the maximum width and maximum length to calculate the maximum possible area of the book cover.

Minimum area: _____   Maximum area: _____

© Houghton Mifflin Harcourt Publishing Company

1a. How does the precision of the linear measurements (width and length) affect the calculated measurement (area)?

_____

_____

In the preceding Explore, you may have discovered that there was a wide range of possible values for the actual area of the book cover. This raises the question of how a calculated measurement, like an area, should be reported. Significant digits offer one way to resolve this dilemma.

Significant digits are the digits in a measurement that carry meaning contributing to the precision of the measurement. The table gives rules for determining the number of significant digits in a measurement.

Rules for Determining Significant Digits			
Rule	Example	Significant Digits (Bold)	Number of Significant Digits
All nonzero digits	37.85	**37.85**	4
Zeros after the last nonzero digit and to the right of the decimal point	0.0070	0.00**70**	2
Zeros between significant digits	6500.0	**6500.0**	5

Note that zeros at the end of a whole number are usually not considered to be significant digits. For example, 4550 ft has 3 significant digits.

MCC9–12.N.Q.3

2 EXAMPLE Determining the Number of Significant Digits

Determine the number of significant digits in each measurement.

A 840.09 m **B** 36,000 mi **C** 0.010 kg

A The digits 8, 4, and 9 are significant digits because _____.

The zeros are significant digits because _____.

So, 840.09 m has _____ significant digits.

B The digits 3 and 6 are significant digits because _____.

The zeros are not significant because _____.

So, 36,000 mi has _____ significant digits.

© Houghton Mifflin Harcourt Publishing Company

C The digit 1 is a significant digit because _____.

The zero after the 1 is a significant digit because _____

_____

So, 0.010 kg has _____ significant digits.

REFLECT

2a. A student claimed that 0.045 m and 0.0045 m have the same number of significant digits. Do you agree or disagree? Why?

_____

_____

When you perform operations on measurements, use these rules for determining the number of significant digits you should report.

Rules for Significant Digits in Calculations	
Operations	**Rule**
Addition Subtraction	Round the sum or difference to the same place as the last significant digit of the least precise measurement.
Multiplication Division	The product or quotient must have the same number of significant digits as the measurement with the fewest significant digits.

MCC9–12.N.Q.3

3 EXAMPLE   **Calculating with Significant Digits**

A student measures the width of a book cover to the nearest centimeter and finds that the width is 16 cm. Another student measures the length of the cover to the nearest tenth of a centimeter and finds that the length is 23.6 cm. Use the correct number of significant digits to write the perimeter and area of the cover.

A Find the perimeter: 16 cm + 23.6 cm + 16 cm + 23.6 cm = 79.2 cm

The least precise measurement is 16 cm. Its last significant digit is in the units place. Round the sum to the nearest whole number.

So, the perimeter is _____.

B Find the area: 16 cm × 23.6 cm = 377.6 cm^2

The measurement with the fewest significant digits is 16 cm. It has 2 significant digits. Round the product to 2 significant digits.

So, the area is _____.

© Houghton Mifflin Harcourt Publishing Company

3a. Suppose the first student had measured the book cover to the nearest tenth of a centimeter and found that the width was 16.0 cm. Does this change how you would you report the perimeter and area? Explain.

_____

_____

PRACTICE

Choose the more precise measurement in each pair.

1. 18 cm; 177 mm

2. 3 yd; 10 ft

3. 40.23 kg; 40.3 kg

_____   _____   _____

4. One student measures the length of a rectangular wall to the nearest meter and finds that the length is 5 m. Another student measures the height of the wall to the nearest tenth of a meter and finds that the height is 3.2 m. What are the minimum and maximum possible values for the area of the wall?

_____

Determine the number of significant digits in each measurement.

5. 12,080 ft

6. 0.8 mL

7. 1.0065 km

_____   _____   _____

8. You measure a rectangular window to the nearest tenth of a centimeter and find that the length is 81.4 cm. A friend measures the width to the nearest centimeter and finds that the width is 38 cm. Use the correct number of significant digits to write the perimeter and area of the window.

_____

9. Error Analysis A student measured the length and width of a square rug to the nearest hundreth of a meter. He found that the length and width were 1.30 m. The student was asked to report the area using the correct number of significant digits and he wrote the area as 1.7 m^2. Explain the student's error.

_____

10. Measure the length and width of the rectangle to the nearest tenth of a centimeter. Then use the correct number of significant digits to write the perimeter and area of the rectangle.

_____

© Houghton Mifflin Harcourt Publishing Company

Additional Practice

Choose the more precise measurement in each pair.

1. 2.78 L; 2782 mL

2. 6 ft; 72.3 in.

3. 2 c; 15 oz

_____ _____ _____

4. 52 mm; 5.24 cm

5. 3 lb; 47 oz

6. 5.2 km; 5233 m

_____ _____ _____

Determine the number of significant digits.

7. 4700

8. 16.005

9. 301,000

_____ _____ _____

10. 0.1760

11. 7.0080

12. 0.000705

_____ _____ _____

Use the following information for 13 and 14.

Marcel is measuring the volume of a liquid for chemistry class. He uses a beaker, a measuring cup, and a test tube. The teacher measures the liquid with a graduated cylinder, which gives the most accurate reading of 26.279 milliliters (mL). Marcel's measurements are shown below.

Measuring Device	Measurement (mL)
Beaker	26.3
Measuring Cup	25
Test Tube	26.21

13. Which device used by Marcel recorded the most precise measurement?

_____

14. Which device used by Marcel recorded the most accurate measurement?

_____

© Houghton Mifflin Harcourt Publishing Company

Problem Solving

Write the correct answer.

1. Rolondo is measuring the length of his lawn. Using a board that is 10 feet long, he measures his lawn to be 70 feet long. He then uses his foot, which is 12 inches long, to measure his lawn to be 864 inches. Which is the more precise measurement? Which is the more precise tool?

_____

2. A bolt used to assemble a car must have a length of 37.5 mm or 3.75 cm. Which is the more precise measurement?

_____

3. A bin contains 15 steel balls of various diameters. Give the number of significant digits in each measurement.

Ball	1	2	3	4	5
Diameter (in.)	1.062	1.100	0.072	0.802	2.010
Ball	6	7	8	9	10
Diameter (in.)	1.401	0.690	0.090	1.008	0.066
Ball	11	12	13	14	15
Diameter (in.)	0.810	2.100	0.068	0.590	0.009

_____

_____

_____

_____

Select the best answer.

4. Ann is measuring the capacity of a 16-oz water bottle. She first uses a measuring cup and finds that the water bottle holds 16.2 oz of water. She then uses a graduated cylinder and finds that the water bottle holds 16.18 oz of water. Which is the more precise measurement? Which is the more precise tool?

   A 16.2 oz; measuring cup

   B 16.2 oz; graduated cylinder

   C 16.18 oz; measuring cup

   D 16.18 oz; graduated cylinder

5. Ina added 32.155 milliliters (mL) of HCL to 64 mL of H_2O. How much solution does Ina have to the nearest milliliter?

   F 95 mL   H 97 mL

   G 96 mL   J 98 mL

6. Jesse mixed 8.24 oz of paprika with 12.23 oz of pepper. How much of the spice combination does Jesse have to the nearest tenth of an ounce?

   A 20.0 oz   C 20.5 oz

   B 20.4 oz   D 21.0 oz

7. An aquarium must be heated to 30.040°C. How many significant digits are there in this measurement?

   F two

   G three

   H four

   J five

© Houghton Mifflin Harcourt Publishing Company

Performance Tasks

GPS
COMMON
CORE

MCC9-12.A.CED.1
MCC9-12.N.Q.1
MCC9-12.N.Q.3

1. Mike scored 17 points in the first half of the basketball game, and he scored p points in the second half of the game.

    a. Write an expression to determine the number of points he scored in all.

    b. Then, find the number of points he scored in all if he scored 12 points in the second half of the game.

2. A certain breakfast cereal has 9.0 g of protein in a 120-g serving. How many grams of protein are in a 200-oz serving? (1 oz ≈ 28.3 g)

3. A company sells furniture for home assembly. Their largest bookcase has shelves that should be 105 cm, with a tolerance of 0.8 cm (105 cm ± 0.8 cm). A set of six shelves had lengths of 105.3 cm, 105.2 cm, 105.0 cm, 104.1 cm, 105.1 cm, and 105.9 cm.

    a. Find the minimum and maximum allowable shelf length.

    b. Which, if any, of the shelves are not within the specified tolerance?

© Houghton Mifflin Harcourt Publishing Company

4. Ayn went to the hospital for a broken leg. Upon admission, she paid a co-payment of $150 to the hospital. Later she received a hospital bill for $714, the amount her insurance did not cover. Ayn's insurance policy covers 80% of her total hospital expenses minus the co-pay.

    a. Write an equation that represents the amount of money Ayn pays the hospital if x is the total amount charged by the hospital. What was the total amount charged by the hospital?

    b. Write an equation that represents the amount of money Ayn's insurance paid the hospital. Use the total charges from part **a** to find the amount the insurance paid. Does this make sense? Explain.

    c. Ayn's policy is called an 80/20 policy because the insurance pays 80% and she pays 20%. Choose a policy with percentages that would be more favorable to Ayn, and use it to calculate how much she would have to pay for this visit under your plan, including the $150 co-payment. Show your work.

© Houghton Mifflin Harcourt Publishing Company

Name _____ Class _____ Date _____

SELECTED RESPONSE

1. Evaluate $x^2 + 3x - 18$ for $x = 3$.

A. -6

B. 0

C. 6

D. 9

2. Simplify $4n + 2(3n - 5) - 8 + n$.

F. $8n - 13$

G. $9n - 8$

H. $10n - 2$

J. $11n - 18$

3. It costs $75 per hour plus a $65 service fee to have a home theater system set up for you. Let t represent the number of hours. Which expression represents the total cost?

A. $75t + 65$

B. $65t + 75$

C. $140t$

D. $75t$

4. Elizabeth and her friend purchase identical team shirts to wear to a football game. There is a 7% sales tax. If c represents the cost of the two shirts without tax, which algebraic expression represents the tax for one shirt?

F. $\frac{c}{2}$

G. $\frac{0.07c}{2}$

H. $\frac{1.07c}{2}$

J. $1.07c$

5. Which property of equality can be used to justify this step?

$$\begin{array}{rcr} 15 - 10x = & & 6x \\ + 10x & & + 10x \\ \hline 15 & = & 16x \end{array}$$

A. Substitution Property of Equality

B. Summation Property of Equality

C. Addition Property of Equality

D. Subtraction Property of Equality

6. Give two ways to write the algebraic expression $m \div 20$ in words.

F. the quotient of m and 20, m divided by 20

G. m subtracted from 20, m less than 20

H. the quotient of 20 and m, 20 divided by m

J. the product of m and 20, m times 20

7. The range of a set of scores is 28, and the lowest score is 31. Write and solve an equation to find the highest score. (*Hint*: In a data set, the range is the difference between the highest and the lowest values.)

A. $h + 31 = 28$
The highest score is -3.

B. $h - 31 = 2 \cdot 28$
The highest score is 87.

C. $h + 28 = 31$
The highest score is 3.

D. $h - 31 = 28$
The highest score is 59.

8. Solve the proportion $\frac{5}{6} = \frac{x}{36}$.

F. $x = 0.02$ **H.** $x = 31$

G. $x = 43.2$ **J.** $x = 30$

9. Write the possible range of the measurement to the nearest hundredth. $60 \text{ lb} \pm 0.6 \text{ lb}$

A. 59.7 lb—60.3 lb   **C.** 59.99 lb—60.01 lb

B. 59 lb—61 lb   **D.** 59.4 lb—60.6 lb

© Houghton Mifflin Harcourt Publishing Company

10. What solution(s) does the equation represented by the graph have in common with the equation $y = 1$?

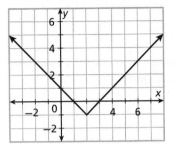

F. $x = 2$

G. $x = 1$ and $x = 3$

H. $x = 0$ and $x = 4$

J. No solutions

11. A student measures the length of a rectangular poster to the nearest centimeter and finds that the length is 75 cm. Another student measures the poster's width to the nearest tenth of a centimeter and finds that the width is 50.3 cm. How should the students report the area of the poster using the correct number of significant digits?

A. 3700 cm^2 **C.** 3772.5 cm^2

B. 3770 cm^2 **D.** 3800 cm^2

CONSTRUCTED RESPONSE

12. Student enrollment in a county's schools during a 16-year period is modeled by the equation $n = -0.3|t - 8| + 11$ where n is the number of students (in thousands) at time t (in number of years since 1990).

a. What was the enrollment in 1990? Show how you found your answer.

_____

_____

b. In what year(s) was the enrollment closest to 10,000? Explain how to find the answer.

_____

_____

_____

_____

13. Find the value of x in the diagram.

$\triangle ABC \sim \triangle DEF$

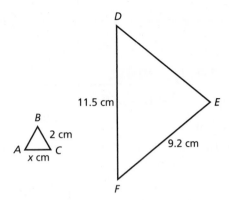

_____

14. A weight that measures *exactly* 5.000 ounces is placed on three different balance scales. Scale 1 shows a weight of 4.99 ounces, scale 2 shows a weight of 5.04 ounces, and scale 3 shows a weight of 5.047 ounces.

a. Which scale is the most precise? Explain your answer.

_____

_____

_____

b. Which is the most accurate? Explain your answer.

_____

_____

_____

_____

© Houghton Mifflin Harcourt Publishing Company

Reasoning with Equations and Inequalities

© Houghton Mifflin Harcourt Publishing Company

Unpacking the Standards

Understanding the standards and the vocabulary terms in the standards will help you know exactly what you are expected to learn in this unit.

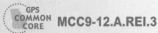 **MCC9-12.A.REI.3**

Solve linear ... inequalities in one variable, ...

Key Vocabulary
linear equation in one variable *(desigualdad lineal en una variable)* An inequality that can be written in one of the following forms: $ax < b$, $ax > b$, $ax \leq b$, $ax \geq b$, or $ax \neq b$, where a and b are constants and $a \neq 0$.

What It Means For You

Solving inequalities lets you answer questions where a range of solutions is possible.

EXAMPLE
The final exam counts as two grades in calculating Cleo's course grade. Solve the inequality for t to find what grades on the final exam will give Cleo a course grade of "A."

$705 + 2t \geq 895$ *Cleo has 705 points and needs at least 895.*

$2t \geq 190$ *Subtract 705 from both sides.*

$t \geq 95$ *Divide both sides by 2.*

Cleo needs to earn a 95 or above on the final exam.

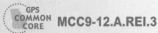 **MCC9-12.A.REI.6**

Solve systems of linear equations exactly and approximately (e.g., with graphs), focusing on pairs of linear equations in two variables.

Key Vocabulary
system of linear equations *(sistema de ecuaciones lineales)* A system of equations in which all of the equations are linear.

What It Means For You

You can solve systems of equations to find out when two relationships involving the same variables are true at the same time.

EXAMPLE
The cost of bowling at bowling alley **A** or **B** is a function of the number of games g.

$$\text{Cost } \mathbf{A} = 2.5g + 2$$
$$\text{Cost } \mathbf{B} = 2g + 4$$

When are the costs the same?

$$\text{Cost } \mathbf{A} = \text{Cost } \mathbf{B}$$
$$2.5g + 2 = 2g + 4$$

The cost is $12 at both bowling alleys when g is 4.

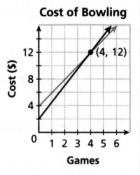

Cost of Bowling

© Houghton Mifflin Harcourt Publishing Company; Photo credit: © Adams Picture Library/t/a apl/Alamy

© Houghton Mifflin Harcourt Publishing Company

MCC9-12.A.REI.12

Graph the solutions to a linear inequality in two variables as a half-plane (excluding the boundary in the case of a strict inequality), and graph the solution set to a system of linear inequalities in two variables as the intersection of the corresponding half-planes.

Key Vocabulary

half-plane *(semiplano)* The part of the coordinate plane on one side of a line, which may include the line.

solution of a linear inequality in two variables *(solución de una desigualdad lineal en dos variables)* An ordered pair or ordered pairs that make the inequality true.

system of linear inequalities *(sistema de desigualdades lineales)* A system of inequalities in which all of the inequalities are linear.

What It Means For You

Systems of linear inequalities model many real-life situations where you want to know when one or more conditions are met, but where there are many possible solutions.

EXAMPLE   **Linear Inequality**

$y > \frac{2}{3}x - 1$

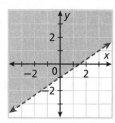

EXAMPLE   **System of Two Linear Inequalities**

$$\begin{cases} y > \frac{2}{3}x - 1 \\ y \leq -2x - 2 \end{cases}$$

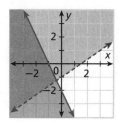

EXAMPLE   **System of Three Linear Inequalities**

Tracy works at least 5 hours per week as a cashier: $c \geq 5$

Tracy works at least 10 hours per week at a library: $p \geq 10$

Tracy works at most 24 hours per week: $c + p \leq 24$

How can Tracy divide her time between the two jobs?

Sample Solutions	
Cashier (hours)	Page (hours)
5	10
5	16
8	12
8	16
10	12
12	12

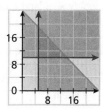

UNIT 2

Key Vocabulary

absolute value *(valor absoluto)* The absolute value of x is the distance from zero to x on a number line, denoted $|x|$.

$$|x| = \begin{cases} x \text{ if } x \geq 0 \\ -x \text{ if } x < 0 \end{cases}$$

compound inequality *(desigualdad compuesta)* Two inequalities that are combined into one statement by the word *and* or *or*.

consistent system *(sistema consistente)* A system of equations or inequalities that has at least one solution.

dependent system *(sistema dependiente)* A system of equations that has infinitely many solutions.

empty set *(conjunto vacío)* A set with no elements.

formula *(fórmula)* A literal equation that states a rule for a relationship among quantities.

inequality *(desigualdad)* A statement that compares two expressions by using one of the following signs: $<, >, \leq, \geq$, or $\neq$.

intersection *(intersección de conjuntos)* The intersection of two sets is the set of all elements that are common to both sets, denoted by $\cap$.

inconsistent system *(sistema inconsistente)* A system of equations or inequalities that has no solution.

independent system *(sistema independiente)* A system of equations that has exactly one solution.

linear inequality in one variable *(desigualdad lineal en una variable)* An inequality that can be written in one of the following forms: $ax < b, ax > b, ax \leq b, ax \geq b$, or $ax \neq b$, where a and b are constants and $a \neq 0$.

literal equation *(ecuación literal)* An equation that contains two or more variables.

linear inequality in two variables *(desigualdad lineal en dos variables)* An inequality that can be written in one of the following forms: $Ax + By < C, Ax + By > C, Ax + By \leq C, Ax + By \geq C$, or $Ax + By \neq C$, where A, B, and C are constants and A and B are not both 0.

solution of an inequality in one variable *(solución de una desigualdad en una variable)* A value or values that make the inequality true.

system of linear equations *(sistema de ecuaciones lineales)* A system of equations in which all of the equations are linear.

system of linear inequalities *(sistema de desigualdades lineales)* A system of inequalities in which all of the inequalities are linear.

union *(unión)* The union of two sets is the set of all elements that are in either set, denoted by $\cup$.

Solving Two-Step and Multi-Step Equations
Going Deeper

Essential question: *How can you justify solutions to multi-step equations?*

The Properties of Equality, as well as the Commutative Properties, can be used to solve multi-step equations.

Addition Property of Equality	If $a = b$, then $a + c = b + c$.
Subtraction Property of Equality	If $a = b$, then $a - c = b - c$.
Multiplication Property of Equality	If $a = b$, then $ac = bc$.
Division Property of Equality	If $a = b$ and $c \neq 0$, then $\frac{a}{c} = \frac{b}{c}$.
Commutative Property of Addition	$a + b = b + a$
Commutative Property of Multiplication	$ab = ba$

MCC9–12.A.REI.1

1 EXAMPLE Solving Multi-Step Equations

Find the solution. Justify each step.

$x + 3 + 3x = 7 + 4$

$(x + 3x) + \boxed{} = 7 + 4$ Commutative Property of Addition

$\boxed{} = \boxed{}$ Combine like terms.

$4x + 3 - 3 = \boxed{} - \boxed{}$ Subtraction Property of Equality

$\boxed{} = \boxed{}$ Inverse Property of Addition; Simplify.

 $\dfrac{4x}{4} = \underline{}$ Division Property of Equality

$x = \boxed{}$ Simplify.

REFLECT

1a. In the equation $4x - 8 + x = 18 - 7$, would you use the Addition Property of Equality to add 7 to each side? Why or why not?

_____

You may need to use the Distributive Property to solve an equation.

Distributive Property	If a, b, and c are real numbers, then $a(b + c) = ab + ac$.

© Houghton Mifflin Harcourt Publishing Company

2 EXAMPLE   Using the Distributive Property

Find the solution. Justify each step.

$$2(x - 6) = -18$$

$$2x - 12 = -18 \qquad \underline{\hspace{6cm}}$$

$$2x - 12 + 12 = \boxed{} \qquad \underline{\hspace{6cm}}$$

$$\boxed{} = \boxed{} \qquad \text{Inverse Property of Addition; Simplify.}$$

$$\frac{2x}{2} = \frac{-6}{2} \qquad \underline{\hspace{6cm}}$$

$$\boxed{} = \boxed{} \qquad \text{Simplify.}$$

REFLECT

2a. Could you have solved $2(x - 6) = -18$ by dividing first? If so, how? When does it make sense to do this and when does it not?

_____

_____

_____

_____

_____

PRACTICE

1. Solve $4(5x + 3) = 92$. Justify each step.

_____

_____

_____

_____

_____

Without solving, explain which properties you would use to solve these equations. List the properties in order of use.

2. $\frac{x}{3} + 5 = 11$

_____

_____

_____

3. $4(x + 6) = 30$

_____

_____

_____

© Houghton Mifflin Harcourt Publishing Company

Additional Practice

Solve each equation. Check your answers.

1. $-4x + 7 = 11$

2. $17 = 5y - 3$

3. $-4 = 2p + 10$

_____   _____   _____

4. $3m + 4 = 1$

5. $12.5 = 2g - 3.5$

6. $-13 = -h - 7$

_____   _____   _____

7. $-6 = \dfrac{y}{5} + 4$

8. $\dfrac{7}{9} = 2n + \dfrac{1}{9}$

9. $-\dfrac{4}{5}t + \dfrac{2}{5} = \dfrac{2}{3}$

_____   _____   _____

10. $-(x - 10) = 7$

11. $-2(b + 5) = -6$

12. $8 = 4(q - 2) + 4$

_____   _____   _____

13. If $3x - 8 = -2$, find the value of $x - 6$.   _____

14. If $-2(3y + 5) = -4$, find the value of $5y$.   _____

Answer each of the following.

15. The two angles shown
form a right angle.
Write and solve an
equation to find the
value of x.

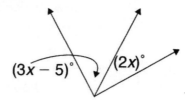

$(3x - 5)°$ $(2x)°$

_____

16. For her cellular phone service, Vera pays $32 a
month, plus $0.75 for each minute over the
allowed minutes in her plan. Vera received a bill
for $47 last month. For how many minutes did
she use her phone beyond the allowed minutes?   _____

© Houghton Mifflin Harcourt Publishing Company

Problem Solving

Write the correct answer.

1. Stephen belongs to a movie club in which he pays an annual fee of $39.95 and then rents DVDs for $0.99 each. In one year, Stephen spent $55.79. Write and solve an equation to find how many DVDs d he rented.

   _____

   _____

2. In 2003, the population of Zimbabwe was about 12.6 million, which was 1 million more than 4 times the population in 1950. Write and solve an equation to find the population p of Zimbabwe in 1950.

   _____

   _____

3. Maggie's brother is three years younger than twice her age. The sum of their ages is 24. How old is Maggie?

   _____

4. Kate is saving to take an SAT prep course that costs $350. So far, she has saved $180, and she adds $17 to her savings each week. How many more weeks must she save to be able to afford the course?

   _____

Use the graph below to answer questions 5–7. Select the best answer. The graph shows the population density (number of people per square mile) of various states given in the 2000 census.

5. One seventeenth of Rhode Island's population density minus 17 equals the population density of Colorado. What is Rhode Island's population density?

   A 425   C 714

   B 697   D 1003

6. One more than sixteen times the population density of New Mexico equals the population density of Texas. To the nearest whole number, what is New Mexico's population density?

   F 5   H 13

   G 8   J 63

7. Three times the population density of Missouri minus 26 equals the population density of California. What is Missouri's population density?

   A 64   C 98

   B 81   D 729

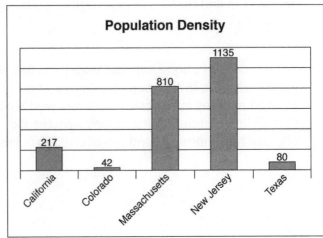

Population Density

California 217, Colorado 42, Massachusetts 810, New Jersey 1135, Texas 80

© Houghton Mifflin Harcourt Publishing Company

3-2

Solving Equations with Variables on Both Sides
Going Deeper

Video Tutor

Essential question: *How can you use properties to justify solutions to equations that have variables on both sides?*

You can use the Properties of Equality and the Distributive Property to justify the steps to solutions of equations that have variables on both sides.

MCC9–12.A.REI.1

1 EXAMPLE **Solving with Variables on Both Sides**

Justify the steps in solving $3x + 2 = -x + 10$ by using the properties of equality.

$3x + 2 = -x + 10$ Original equation

$3x + 2 + x = -x + 10 + x$ _____

$\boxed{} = \boxed{}$ Simplify.

$4x + 2 - 2 = 10 - 2$ _____

$4x = \boxed{}$ Simplify.

$\dfrac{4x}{\boxed{}} = \dfrac{8}{\boxed{}}$ _____

$x = \boxed{}$ Simplify.

The solution set is $\{\ \boxed{}\ \}$.

REFLECT

1a. In the first step, suppose that you subtracted $3x$ from both sides. How would the rest of the steps change? Would the solution set be different?

_____

_____

_____

_____

1b. What is the solution set of $x = x$? Why?

_____

_____

1c. What statement do you get if you try to solve the equation $x + 2 = x$? Is this statement true or false? What does this mean in terms of the solution set?

_____

_____

© Houghton Mifflin Harcourt Publishing Company

2 E X A M P L E Solving a Multi-Step Linear Equation

Justify the steps in solving $\frac{3x}{2} + 7x - 7 = 3(2x + 1)$ by using the properties of equality and other properties.

$\frac{3x}{2} + 7x - 7 = 3(2x + 1)$	Original equation
$\frac{3x}{2} + 7x - 7 = 6x + 3$	_____
$2 \cdot \left(\frac{3x}{2} + 7x - 7\right) = 2 \cdot (6x + 3)$	_____
$3x + 14x - 14 = 12x + 6$	_____
$(3 + 14)x - 14 = 12x + 6$	_____
$17x - 14 = 12x + 6$	Simplify.
$17x - 14 - 12x = 12x + 6 - 12x$	_____
$5x - 14 = 6$	Simplify.
$5x - 14 + 14 = 6 + 14$	_____
$5x = 20$	Simplify.
$\frac{5x}{5} = \frac{20}{5}$	_____
$x = 4$	

The solution set is { ⬚ }.

REFLECT

2a. In the example, could the steps have been performed in a different order? Explain.

_____

_____

_____

2b. Would performing the steps in a different order affect the solution to the equation? Why or why not?

_____

_____

© Houghton Mifflin Harcourt Publishing Company

Find the solution set for the equation. Use the properties of equality and other properties to justify your solution.

1. $2x - 3 = 9 - x$

_____

_____

_____

_____

_____

_____

_____

2. $4x - 7 = x + 5$

_____

_____

_____

_____

_____

_____

_____

3. $25 + 10(12 - x) = 5(2x - 7)$

_____

_____

_____

_____

_____

_____

_____

_____

_____

© Houghton Mifflin Harcourt Publishing Company

4. $\frac{1}{2}(6x + 4) = x + 2(x + 1)$

_____

_____

_____

_____

_____

_____

_____

5. Find the set of values of x such that $5x - 9 = 6$. Justify your solution by using the properties of equality.

_____

_____

_____

_____

_____

_____

_____

6. Find the set of values of x such that $-12x + 7 = 4x - 9$. Justify your solution by using the properties of equality.

_____

_____

_____

_____

_____

_____

_____

_____

_____

© Houghton Mifflin Harcourt Publishing Company

Additional Practice

Solve each equation. Check your answers.

1. $3d + 8 = 2d - 17$

2. $2n - 7 = 5n - 10$

3. $p - 15 = 13 - 6p$

_____   _____   _____

4. $-t + 5 = t - 19$

5. $15x - 10 = -9x + 2$

6. $1.8r + 9 = -5.7r - 6$

_____   _____   _____

7. $2y + 3 = 3(y + 7)$

8. $4n + 6 - 2n = 2(n + 3)$

9. $6m - 8 = 2 + 9m - 1$

_____   _____   _____

10. $-v + 5 + 6v = 1 + 5v + 3$

11. $2(3b - 4) = 8b - 11$

12. $5(r - 1) = 2(r - 4) - 6$

_____   _____   _____

Answer each of the following.

13. Janine has job offers at two companies. One company offers a starting salary of $28,000 with a raise of $3000 each year. The other company offers a starting salary of $36,000 with a raise of $2000 each year.

    a. After how many years would Janine's salary be the same with both companies? _____

    b. What would that salary be? _____

14. Xian and his cousin both collect stamps. Xian has 56 stamps, and his cousin has 80 stamps. Both have recently joined different stamp-collecting clubs. Xian's club will send him 12 new stamps per month, and his cousin's club will send him 8 new stamps per month.

    a. After how many months will Xian and his cousin have the same number of stamps? _____

    b. How many stamps will that be? _____

© Houghton Mifflin Harcourt Publishing Company

Problem Solving

Write the correct answer.

1. Claire purchased just enough fencing to border either a rectangular or triangular garden, as shown, whose perimeters are the same.

   How many feet of fencing did she buy?

   _____

2. Celia and Ryan are starting a nutrition program. Celia currently consumes 1200 calories a day and will increase that number by 100 calories each day. Ryan currently consumes 3230 calories a day and will decrease that number by 190 each day. They will continue this pattern until they are both consuming the same number of calories per day. In how many days will that be?

   _____

3. A moving company charges $800 plus $16 per hour. Another moving company charges $720 plus $21 per hour. How long is a job that costs the same no matter which company is used?

   _____

4. Aaron needs to take out a loan to purchase a motorcycle. At one bank, he would pay $2500 initially and $150 each month for the loan. At another bank, he would pay $3000 initially and $125 each month. After how many months will the two loan payments be the same?

   _____

Use the table below to answer questions 5–7. Select the best answer.
The table shows the membership fees of three different gyms.

5. After how many months will the fees for Workout Now and Community Gym be the same?

   A 2.5   C 25

   B 15   D 30

6. Sal joined Workout Now for the number of months found in problem 5. How much did he pay?

   F $695   H $1325

   G $875   J $1550

7. After how many months will the fees for Workout Now and Ultra Sports Club be the same?

   A 7   C 12

   B 10   D 15

Gym	Fees
Workout Now	$200 plus $45 per month
Community Gym	$50 plus $55 per month
Ultra Sports Club	$20 plus $60 per month

© Houghton Mifflin Harcourt Publishing Company

Solving for a Variable
Going Deeper

Essential question: *How do you solve literal equations and rewrite formulas?*

A **literal equation** is an equation in which the coefficients and constants have been replaced by letters. In the following Explore, you will see how a literal equation can be used to represent specific equations having the same form.

Video Tutor

MCC9–12.A.REI.3

1 EXPLORE **Understanding Literal Equations**

A For each equation given below, solve the equation by writing two equivalent equations: one where the *x*-term is isolated and then one where *x* is isolated.

$$3x + 1 = 7 \qquad\qquad -2x + 5 = 11 \qquad\qquad 4x + 3 = -1$$

_____ _____ _____

_____ _____ _____

B Identify the two properties of equality that you used in part A. List them in the order that you used them.

_____

C Each equation in part A has the general form $ax + b = c$ where $a \neq 0$. Solve this literal equation for *x* using the properties of equality that you identified in part B.

$ax + b = c$ Write the literal equation.

$ax = \boxed{} - \boxed{}$ Subtract *b* from both sides.

$x = \dfrac{\boxed{} - \boxed{}}{\boxed{}}$ Divide both sides by *a*.

D Show that the solution of the literal equation gives the same solution of $3x + 1 = 7$ as you found in part A. Recognize that when $a = 3$, $b = 1$, and $c = 7$, the literal equation $ax + b = c$ gives the specific equation $3x + 1 = 7$.

$x = \dfrac{\boxed{} - \boxed{}}{\boxed{}}$ Write the literal equation's solution.

$x = \dfrac{\boxed{} - \boxed{}}{\boxed{}}$ Substitute 3 for *a*, 1 for *b*, and 7 for *c*.

$x = \boxed{}$ Simplify.

REFLECT

1a. Why must the restriction $a \neq 0$ be placed on the literal equation $ax + b = c$?

_____

© Houghton Mifflin Harcourt Publishing Company

1b. Choose one of the other specific equations from part A. Show that the solution of the literal equation gives the solution of the specific equation.

_____

_____

When you solve a literal equation, you use properties of equality and other properties to isolate the variable. The result is not a number, but rather an expression involving the letters that represent the coefficients and constants.

MCC9–12.A.REI.3

2 E X A M P L E   Solving a Literal Equation and Evaluating Its Solution

Solve the literal equation $a(x + b) = c$ where $a \neq 0$. Then use the literal equation's solution to obtain the solution of the specific equation $2(x + 7) = -6$.

A Solve $a(x + b) = c$ for x. Use the properties of equality to justify your solution steps.

$a(x + b) = c$ Original equation

$x + b = \dfrac{\square}{\square}$ _____ Property of Equality

$x = \dfrac{\square}{\square} - \square$ _____ Property of Equality

B Obtain the solution of $2(x + 7) = -6$ from the literal equation's solution by letting $a = 2$, $b = 7$, and $c = -6$.

$x = \dfrac{\square}{\square} - \square$ Write the literal equation's solution.

$x = \dfrac{\square}{\square} - \square$ Substitute 2 for a, 7 for b, and -6 for c.

$x = \square$ Simplify.

REFLECT

2a. When solving $a(x + b) = c$, why do you divide by a before you subtract b?

_____

_____

_____

2b. Write an equation that has the form $a(x + b) = c$. Find the solution of your equation using the literal equation's solution.

_____

© Houghton Mifflin Harcourt Publishing Company

2c. Another way to solve $a(x + b) = c$ is to start by using the Distributive Property. Show and justify the solution steps using this method.

_____

_____

_____

_____

2d. When you start solving $a(x + b) = c$ by dividing by a, you get $x = \frac{c}{a} - b$. When you start solving $a(x + b) = c$ by distributing a, you get $x = \frac{c - ab}{a}$. Use the fact that you can rewrite $\frac{c - ab}{a}$ as the difference of two fractions to show that the two solutions are equivalent.

_____

MCC9–12.A.CED.4

3 EXAMPLE Solving a Formula for a Variable

Solve the formula for the given variable. Justify each step in your solution.

A The formula $V = lwh$ gives the volume of a rectangular prism with length l, width w, and height h. Solve the formula for h to find the height of a rectangular prism with a given volume, length, and width.

$V = lwh$ Original equation

$\dfrac{V}{\boxed{}} = \dfrac{lwh}{\boxed{}}$ _____

$h = \dfrac{\boxed{}}{\boxed{}}$ Simplify.

B The formula $E = \frac{1}{2}kx^2$ gives the potential energy E of a spring with spring constant k that has been stretched by length x. Solve the formula for k to find the constant of a spring with a given potential energy and stretch.

$E = \frac{1}{2}kx^2$ Original equation

$\boxed{} \cdot E = \boxed{} \cdot \frac{1}{2}kx^2$ _____

$2E = kx^2$ _____

$\dfrac{2E}{\boxed{}} = \dfrac{kx^2}{\boxed{}}$ _____

$k = \dfrac{\boxed{}}{\boxed{}}$ Simplify.

© Houghton Mifflin Harcourt Publishing Company

REFLECT

3a. The formula $T = p + sp$ gives the total cost of an item with price p and sales tax s, expressed as a decimal. Describe a situation in which you would want to solve the formula for s.

_____

3b. What is true about the restrictions on the value of a variable in a formula that might not be true of other literal equations?

_____

_____

4 **EXAMPLE**   **Writing and Rearranging a Formula**

The flower garden at the right is made up of a square and an isosceles triangle. Write a formula for the perimeter P in terms of x, and then solve for x to find a formula for the side length of the square in terms of P.

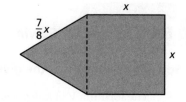

A Write a formula for the perimeter of each shape. Use only the sides of the square and the triangle that form the outer edges of the figure.

Perimeter of square = _____

Perimeter of triangle = _____

B Combine the formulas. $P = $ ▢

C Solve the formula for x.

$P = $ ▢   Write the combined formula.

$P = x\left(\boxed{} + \boxed{} \right)$ Distributive Property

$P = x\left(\dfrac{\boxed{}}{\boxed{}} \right)$ Find the sum. Write the result as an improper fraction.

$P\left(\dfrac{\boxed{}}{\boxed{}} \right) = x\left(\dfrac{\boxed{}}{\boxed{}} \right)\left(\dfrac{\boxed{}}{\boxed{}} \right)$ Multiplication Property of Equality

$\dfrac{\boxed{}}{\boxed{}} = x$ Simplify.

© Houghton Mifflin Harcourt Publishing Company

4a. What are the restrictions on the values of P and x? Explain.

_____

4b. How could you write a formula for the area of the square in terms of P?

_____

_____

PRACTICE

1. Show and justify the steps for solving $x + a = b$. Then use the literal equation's solution to obtain the solution of $x + 2 = -4$.

_____

_____

_____

2. Show and justify the steps for solving $ax = b$ where $a \neq 0$. Then use the literal equation's solution to obtain the solution of $3x = -15$.

_____

_____

_____

3. Show and justify the steps for solving $ax = bx + c$ where $a \neq b$. Then use the literal equation's solution to obtain the solution of $2x = x + 7$.

_____

_____

_____

_____

_____

_____

© Houghton Mifflin Harcourt Publishing Company

Solve each formula for the indicated variable.

4. Formula for the surface area of a rectangular prism: $SA = 2(lw + hw + hl)$, for w

_____

_____

_____

_____

_____

_____

5. Formula for the area of a trapezoid: $A = \frac{1}{2}(a + b)h$, for b

_____

_____

_____

_____

_____

_____

6. An electrician sent Bonnie an invoice in the amount of a dollars for 6 hours of work that was done on Saturday. The electrician charges a weekend fee f in addition to an hourly rate r. Bonnie knows what the weekend fee is. Write a formula Bonnie can use to find r, the rate the electrician charges per hour.

_____

_____

_____

_____

7. The swimming pool below is made up of a square and two semicircles. Write a formula for the perimeter P in terms of x, and then solve for x to find a formula for the side length of the square in terms of P.

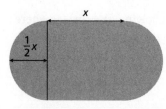

_____

_____

_____

_____

_____

© Houghton Mifflin Harcourt Publishing Company

Additional Practice

Answer each of the following.

1. The formula $C = 2\pi r$ relates the radius r of a circle to its circumference C. Solve the formula for r.

2. The formula $y = mx + b$ is called the slope-intercept form of a line. Solve this formula for m.

_____

_____

Solve for the indicated variable.

3. $4c = d$ for c

4. $n - 6m = 8$ for n

5. $2p + 5r = q$ for p

_____

6. $-10 = xy + z$ for x

7. $\dfrac{a}{b} = c$ for b

8. $\dfrac{h-4}{j} = k$ for j

_____

Answer each of the following.

9. The formula $c = 5p + 215$ relates c, the total cost in dollars of hosting a birthday party at a skating rink, to p, the number of people attending.

   a. Solve the formula $c = 5p + 215$ for p.   _____

   b. If Allie's parents are willing to spend $300 for a party, how many people can attend?   _____

10. The formula for the area of a triangle is $A = \dfrac{1}{2}bh$, where b represents the length of the base and h represents the height.

    a. Solve the formula $A = \dfrac{1}{2}bh$ for b.   _____

    b. If a triangle has an area of 192 mm², and the height measures 12 mm, what is the measure of the base?   _____

© Houghton Mifflin Harcourt Publishing Company

Problem Solving

Use the table below, which shows some track and field gold medal winners, to answer questions 1–4. Round all answers to the nearest tenth.

1. Solve the formula $d = rt$ for r.

   _____

2. Find Johnson's average speed in meters per second.

   _____

3. Find Garcia's average speed in meters per second.

   _____

4. The world record of 19.32 seconds in the 200-meter race was set by Michael Johnson in 1996. Find the difference between Johnson's average speed and Kenteris' average speed.

2000 Summer Olympics		
Gold Medal Winner	Race	Time (s)
M. Greene, USA	100 m	9.87
K. Kenteris, Greece	200 m	20.09
M. Johnson, USA	400 m	43.84
A. Garcia, Cuba	110 m hurdles	13.00

_____

Select the best answer.

5. The cost to mail a letter in the United States in 2008 was $0.41 for the first ounce and $0.26 for each additional ounce. Solve $C = 0.41 + 0.26(z - 1)$ for z.

   A $z = \dfrac{C - 0.41}{0.26}$

   B $z = \dfrac{C - 0.41}{0.26} + 1$

   C $z = \dfrac{C + 0.15}{0.26}$

   D $z = C - 0.67$

7. Degrees Celsius and degrees Fahrenheit are related by the equation $C = \dfrac{5}{9}(F - 32)$. Solve for F.

   A $F = 9C + 27$ C $F = \dfrac{5}{9}C + 32$

   B $F = \dfrac{9}{5}C$ D $F = \dfrac{9}{5}C + 32$

6. The formula $V = \dfrac{Bh}{3}$ shows how to find the volume of a pyramid. Solve for B.

   F $B = \dfrac{3V}{h}$ H $B = 3Vh$

   G $B = 3V - h$ J $B = 3V + h$

8. The cost of operating an electrical device is given by the formula $C = \dfrac{Wtc}{1000}$ where W is the power in watts, t is the time in hours, and c is the cost in cents per kilowatt-hour. Solve for W.

   F $W = 1000C - tc$

   G $W = \dfrac{Ctc}{1000}$

   H $W = 1000C + tc$

   J $W = \dfrac{1000C}{tc}$

© Houghton Mifflin Harcourt Publishing Company

Graphing and Writing Inequalities
Going Deeper

Video Tutor

Essential question: *How can you represent relationships using inequalities?*

An **inequality** is a statement that compares two expressions that are not strictly equal by using one of the following inequality signs.

Symbol	Meaning
<	is less than
≤	is less than or equal to
>	is greater than
≥	is greater than or equal to
≠	is not equal to

A **solution of an inequality** is any value of the variable that makes the inequality true. You can find solutions by making a table.

MCC9–12.A.CED.1

1 EXAMPLE   Writing and Solving Inequalities

Kristin can afford to spend at most $50 for a birthday dinner at a restaurant, including a 15% tip. Describe some costs that are within her budget.

A   Which inequality symbol can be used to represent "at most"? _____

B   Complete the verbal model for the situation.

Cost before tip (dollars)		15%		Cost before tip (dollars)		Budget limit (dollars)

C   Write and simplify an inequality for the model. _____

© Houghton Mifflin Harcourt Publishing Company

D Complete the table to find some costs that are within Kristin's budget.

Cost	Substitute	Compare	Solution?
$47	$1.15(47) \leq 50$	$54.05 \leq 50$ ✗	No
$45	$1.15(45) \leq 50$		
$43			
$41			

REFLECT

1a. Can Kristin spend $40 on the meal before the tip? Explain.

_____

_____

1b. What whole dollar amount is the most Kristin can spend before the tip? Explain.

_____

_____

1c. The *solution set* of an equation or inequality consists of all values that make the statement true. Describe the whole dollar amounts that are in the solution set for this situation.

_____

1d. Suppose Kristin also has to pay a 6% meal tax. Write an inequality to represent the new situation. Then identify two solutions.

_____

PRACTICE

Tell whether each value of the variable is a solution of the inequality $4p < 64$. Show your reasoning.

1. $p = 40$

_____

2. $p = 45$

_____

3. $p = 5$

_____

4. $p = 22$

_____

© Houghton Mifflin Harcourt Publishing Company

Tell whether each value of the variable is a solution of the inequality $7p \geq 105$. Show your reasoning.

5. $p = 6$

_____

6. $p = 21$

_____

7. $p = 4$

_____

8. $p = 15$

_____

Tell whether the value is a solution of the inequality. Explain.

9. $x = 36; 3x < 100$

_____

10. $m = 12; 5m + 4 > 50$

_____

11. $b = 5; 60 - 10b \leq 20$

_____

12. $y = -4; 7y + 6 < -20$

_____

13. $n = -4; 18 - 2n \geq 26$

_____

14. $d = -6; 27 + 8d > -14$

_____

15. Brent is ordering books for a reading group. Each book costs $11.95. If he orders at least $200 worth of books, he will get free shipping.

a. Complete the verbal model for the situation.

Price per book		Number of books		Amount for free shipping

b. Choose a variable for the unknown quantity. Include units.

Let _____ represent the _____.

c. Write an inequality from the verbal model.

_____

d. Complete the table to find some numbers of books Brent can order and receive free shipping.

Books	Substitute	Compare	Solution?
15	$11.95(15) \geq 200$	$179.25 \geq 200$ ✗	No
16			
17			
18			

© Houghton Mifflin Harcourt Publishing Company

16. Farzana has a prepaid cell phone that costs $1 per day plus $.10 per minute she uses. She has a daily budget of $5 for phone costs.

   a. Write an inequality to represent the situation.

   _____

   _____

   _____

   b. What is the maximum number of minutes Farzana can use and still stay within her daily budget? Show your reasoning.

   _____

   _____

   _____

   c. Describe the solution set of the inequality.

   _____

   _____

   _____

© Houghton Mifflin Harcourt Publishing Company

Additional Practice

Tell whether the value is a solution of the inequality.

1. $m = 8$; $2m \geq 6$ _____

2. $t = 5$; $t + 3 < 8$ _____

3. $x = 2$; $1 < x - 5$ _____

4. $c = -28$; $-10 \geq \frac{1}{2}c$ _____

5. $n = 6$; $2n + 9 \geq 31$ _____

6. $d = -4$; $5d + 8 > -12$ _____

7. $h = -11$; $3h + 20 \leq -13$ _____

8. $y = 0$; $4y - 11 < 17$ _____

Define a variable and write an inequality for each situation.

9. Josephine sleeps more than 7 hours each night.

    _____

10. In 1955, the minimum wage in the U.S. was $0.75 per hour.

    _____

11. Sam can spend no more than $75 on school supplies. He has to spend
    $12 on paper and pencils. What is the maximum amount Sam can spend
    on a graphing calculator?

    _____

12. Sally and Tim need more than 24 bags of grass seed to reseed their lawn.
    The seed they want to buy is sold in cartons that contain 4 bags each.
    What is the minimum number of cartons of grass seed they need to buy?

    _____

© Houghton Mifflin Harcourt Publishing Company

Problem Solving

Write the correct answer.

1. A citizen must be at least 35 years old in order to run for the Presidency of the United States. Define a variable and write an inequality for this situation.

   _____

   _____

2. A certain elevator can hold no more than 2500 pounds. Define a variable and write an inequality for this situation.

   _____

   _____

3. Approximately 30% of the land on Earth is forested, but this percent is decreasing due to construction. Write an inequality for this situation.

   _____

   _____

4. Khalil weighed 125 pounds before he started to gain weight to play football. Write an inequality for this situation.

   _____

   _____

The Sanchez family is visiting an amusement park. When they enter the park, they receive a brochure which lists several requirements and restrictions. Select the best answer.

5. You must be at least 50 inches tall to ride The Wild Tornado roller coaster. Which of the following inequalities fits this situation?

   A $h \leq 50$ C $h \geq 50$

   B $h < 50$ D $h > 50$

6. Children less than 12 years old must be accompanied by an adult inside The Haunted House. Which of the following inequalities shows the ages of children who require an adult inside the house?

   F $y \leq 12$ H $y \geq 12$

   G $y < 12$ J $y > 12$

7. Totland is an area of the amusement park set aside for children who are 6 years old or younger. Which of the following inequalities represents the ages of children who are allowed in Totland?

   A $a \leq 6$ C $a \geq 6$

   B $a < 6$ D $a > 6$

8. The Bumpy Cars will not be turned on if there are 5 or more empty cars. Which of the following inequalities shows the possible numbers of empty cars if the ride is going to start?

   F $c \leq 5$ H $c \geq 5$

   G $c < 5$ J $c > 5$

© Houghton Mifflin Harcourt Publishing Company

Solving Inequalities by Adding or Subtracting
Going Deeper

Essential question: *How can you use properties to justify solutions to inequalities that involve addition and subtraction?*

Video Tutor

MCC9–12.A.REI.3

1 ENGAGE   Properties of Inequality

You have solved addition and subtraction equations by performing inverse operations that isolate the variable on one side. The value on the other side is the solution. Inequalities involving addition and subtraction can be solved similarly using the following inequality properties. These properties are also true for $\geq$ and $\leq$.

Addition Property of Inequality	If $a > b$, then $a + c > b + c$.
	If $a < b$, then $a + c < b + c$.
Subtraction Property of Inequality	If $a > b$, then $a - c > b - c$.
	If $a < b$, then $a - c < b - c$.

REFLECT

1a. How do the Addition and Subtraction Properties of Inequality compare to the Addition and Subtraction Properties of Equality?

_____

_____

_____

_____

Most linear inequalities have infinitely many solutions. When using set notation, it is not possible to list all the solutions in braces. The solution $x \leq 1$ in set notation is $\{x \mid x \leq 1\}$. Read this as "the set of all x such that x is less than or equal to 1."

$$\{ x \mid x \leq 1 \}$$

the set of ⟶ all x — such that — x is less than or equal to 1

A number line graph can be used to represent the solution set of a linear inequality.

- To represent $<$ or $>$, mark the endpoint with an empty circle.

- To represent $\leq$ or $\geq$, mark the endpoint with a solid circle.

- Shade the part of the line that contains the solution set.

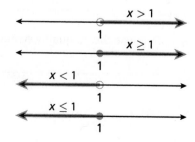

© Houghton Mifflin Harcourt Publishing Company

2 EXAMPLE Adding to Find the Solution Set

Solve. Write the solution using set notation. Graph your solution.

A $x - 3 < 2$

$x - 3 + \boxed{} < 2 + \boxed{}$ _____ Property of Inequality;

add _____ to both sides.

$x < \boxed{}$ Simplify.

Write the solution set using set notation.

_____

Graph the solution set on a number line.

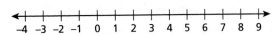

B $x - 5 \geq -3$

$x - 5 + \boxed{} \geq -3 + \boxed{}$ _____ Property of Inequality;

add _____ to both sides.

$x \geq \boxed{}$ Simplify.

Write the solution set using set notation.

_____

Graph the solution set on a number line.

REFLECT

2a. Is 5 in the solution set of the inequality in Part A? Explain.

_____

_____

2b. Suppose the inequality symbol in Part A had been >. Describe the solution set.

_____

2c. Suppose the inequality symbol in Part B had been ≤. Describe the solution set.

_____

© Houghton Mifflin Harcourt Publishing Company

3 EXAMPLE Subtracting to Find the Solution Set

Solve. Write the solution using set notation. Graph your solution.

A $x + 4 > 3$

$x + 4 - \boxed{} > 3 - \boxed{}$ _____ Property of Inequality

$x > \boxed{}$ Simplify.

Write the solution set using set notation.

_____

Graph the solution set on a number line.

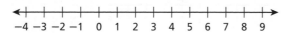

−4 −3 −2 −1　0　1　2　3　4　5　6　7　8　9

B $x + 2 \leq -1$

$x + 2 - \boxed{} \leq -1 - \boxed{}$ _____ Property of Inequality

$x \leq \boxed{}$ Simplify.

Write the solution set using set notation.

_____

Graph the solution set on a number line.

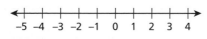

−5 −4 −3 −2 −1　0　1　2　3　4

REFLECT

3a. Is −3 in the solution set of the inequality in Part B? Explain.

_____

_____

3b. Suppose the inequality symbol in Part A had been ≥. Describe the solution set.

_____

3c. Suppose the inequality symbol in Part B had been <. Describe the solution set.

_____

© Houghton Mifflin Harcourt Publishing Company

Solve. Justify your steps. Write the solution in set notation. Graph your solution.

1. $x + 1 \leq -2$

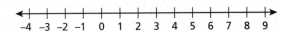

_____

_____

_____

2. $x - 2 > 1$

_____

_____

_____

3. $x + 6 < 6$

_____

_____

_____

4. $x + 3 < 2$

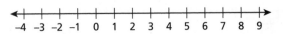

_____

_____

_____

5. $x - 4 \geq -4$

_____

_____

_____

© Houghton Mifflin Harcourt Publishing Company

Additional Practice

Solve each inequality and graph the solutions.

1. $b + 8 > 15$

2. $t - 5 \geq -2$

3. $-4 + x \geq 1$

4. $g + 8 < 2$

5. $-9 \geq m - 9$

6. $15 > d + 19$

Answer each question.

7. Jessica makes overtime pay when she works more than 40 hours in a week. So far this week she has worked 29 hours. She will continue to work h hours this week. Write, solve, and graph an inequality to show the values of h that will allow Jessica to earn overtime pay.

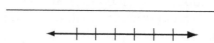

8. Henry's MP3 player has 512MB of memory. He has already downloaded 287MB and will continue to download m more megabytes. Write and solve an inequality that shows how many more megabytes he can download.

9. Eleanor needs to read at least 97 pages of a book for homework. She has read 34 pages already. Write and solve an inequality that shows how many more pages p she must read.

© Houghton Mifflin Harcourt Publishing Company

Problem Solving

Write the correct answer.

1. Sumiko is allowed to watch no more than 10 hours of television each week. She has watched 4 hours of television already. Write and solve an inequality to show how many more hours of television Sumiko can watch.

   _____

2. A satellite will be released into an orbit of more than 400 miles above the Earth. The rocket carrying it is currently 255 miles above Earth. Write and solve an inequality to show how much higher the rocket must climb before it releases the satellite.

   _____

3. Wayne's homework is to solve at least 20 questions from his textbook. So far, he has completed 9 of them. Write, solve, and graph an inequality to show how many more problems Wayne must complete.

   _____

4. Felix wants to get at least one hour of exercise each day. Today, he has run for 40 minutes. Write, solve, and graph an inequality that shows how much longer Felix needs to exercise to reach his goal.

   _____

The high school has been raising money for charity and the class that raises the most will be awarded a party at the end of the year. The table below shows how much money each class has raised so far. Use this information to answer questions 5–7.

5. The school has a goal of raising at least $3000. Which inequality shows how much more money m they need to raise to reach their goal?

   A $m \geq 215$

   B $m < 215$

   C $m \leq 215$

   D $m > 2785$

Class	Amount Raised ($)
Seniors	870
Juniors	650
Sophomores	675
First-Years	590

6. The juniors would like to raise more money than the seniors. The seniors have completed their fundraising for the year. Which expression shows how much more money j the juniors must raise to overtake the seniors?

   F $j \leq 220$

   G $j < 220$

   H $j \geq 220$

   J $j > 220$

7. A local business has agreed to donate no more than half as much as the senior class raises. Which inequality shows how much money b the business will contribute?

   A $\frac{1}{2}(870) \leq b$

   B $870 \leq \frac{1}{2}b$

   C $\frac{1}{2}(870) \geq b$

   D $870 \geq \frac{1}{2}b$

© Houghton Mifflin Harcourt Publishing Company

Solving Inequalities by Multiplying or Dividing
Going Deeper

Essential question: *How can you use properties to justify solutions to inequalities that involve multiplication and division?*

MCC9–12.A.REI.3

1 EXPLORE   Multiplying or Dividing by a Negative Number

The following two inequalities are true.

$$4 < 5 \qquad\qquad\qquad 15 > 12$$

What happens to the inequalities if you multiply both sides of the first inequality by 4 and divide both sides of the second inequality by 3?

$$4 < 5 \qquad\qquad\qquad 15 > 12$$

_____   _____

_____   _____

Both statements are still true: 16 is less than 20, and 5 is greater than 4.

Now, multiply the first inequality by −4 and divide the second inequality by −3. Do not change the inequality symbol when you do these multiplications.

$$4 < 5 \qquad\qquad\qquad 15 > 12$$

_____   _____

_____   _____

Is −16 less than −20? No, −16 is closer to 0 than −20 is, so it is greater than −20. Is −5 greater than −4? No, −5 is farther from 0 than −4, so it is less than −4.

Repeat the multiplication by −4 and the division by −3, but this time reverse the inequality symbol when you do.

$$4 < 5 \qquad\qquad\qquad 15 > 12$$

_____   _____

_____   _____

Do you get a true statement in each case? _____

REFLECT

1a. When solving inequalities, if you multiply by a negative number, you must

_____

1b. When solving inequalities, if you divide by a negative number, you must

_____

© Houghton Mifflin Harcourt Publishing Company

You can use the following inequality properties to solve inequalities involving multiplication and division. These properties are also true for $\geq$ and $\leq$.

Multiplication Property of Inequality	If $a > b$ and $c > 0$, then $ac > bc$. If $a < b$ and $c > 0$, then $ac < bc$. If $a > b$ and $c < 0$, then $ac < bc$. If $a < b$ and $c < 0$, then $ac > bc$.
Division Property of Inequality	If $a > b$ and $c > 0$, then $\frac{a}{c} > \frac{b}{c}$. If $a < b$ and $c > 0$, then $\frac{a}{c} < \frac{b}{c}$. If $a > b$ and $c < 0$, then $\frac{a}{c} < \frac{b}{c}$. If $a < b$ and $c < 0$, then $\frac{a}{c} > \frac{b}{c}$.

MCC9–12.A.REI.3

2 EXAMPLE **Multiplying to Find the Solution Set**

Solve. Write the solution using set notation. Graph your solution.

A $\quad \dfrac{x}{2} > 3$

$\boxed{} \left(\dfrac{x}{2}\right) > \boxed{} (3)$ _____ Property of Inequality

$x > \boxed{}$ \qquad\qquad Simplify.

Solution set: _____

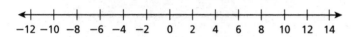

B $\quad \dfrac{x}{-4} \leq -2$

$\boxed{} \left(\dfrac{x}{-4}\right) \geq \boxed{} (-2)$ _____ Property of Inequality;

_____ $\leq$ symbol.

$x \geq \boxed{}$ \qquad\qquad Simplify.

Solution set: _____

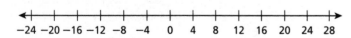

REFLECT

2a. Suppose the inequality symbol in Part A had been $\geq$. Describe the solution set.

_____

2b. Suppose the inequality symbol in Part B had been $<$. Describe the solution set.

_____

© Houghton Mifflin Harcourt Publishing Company

3 **EXAMPLE** Dividing to Find the Solution Set

Solve. Write the solution using set notation. Graph your solution.

A $3x \geq -9$

$\dfrac{3x}{\boxed{}} \geq \dfrac{-9}{\boxed{}}$ _____ Property of Inequality

$x \geq \boxed{}$ Simplify.

Solution set: _____

$-4\ -3\ -2\ -1\ \ \ 0\ \ \ 1\ \ \ 2\ \ \ 3\ \ \ 4\ \ \ 5\ \ \ 6\ \ \ 7\ \ \ 8\ \ \ 9$

B $-5x < 20$

$\dfrac{-5x}{\boxed{}} > \dfrac{20}{\boxed{}}$ _____ Property of Inequality;

_____ < symbol.

$x > \boxed{}$ Simplify.

Solution set: _____

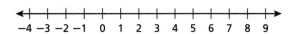

$-4\ -3\ -2\ -1\ \ \ 0\ \ \ 1\ \ \ 2\ \ \ 3\ \ \ 4\ \ \ 5\ \ \ 6\ \ \ 7\ \ \ 8\ \ \ 9$

REFLECT

3a. There is a negative number in both Parts A and B. Why is the inequality symbol only reversed in Part B?

_____

_____

_____

3b. Suppose the inequality symbol in Part A had been >. Describe the solution set.

_____

3c. Suppose the inequality symbol in Part B had been ≤. Describe the solution set.

_____

© Houghton Mifflin Harcourt Publishing Company

PRACTICE

Solve. Justify your steps. Write each solution using set notation. Graph your solution.

1. $4x < 32$

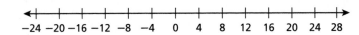

_____

_____

_____

2. $\frac{x}{5} > -3$

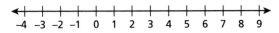

_____

_____

_____

3. $\frac{x}{-4} \leq -4$

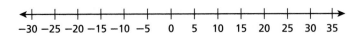

_____

_____

_____

4. $-2x \geq -6$

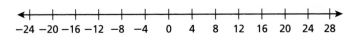

_____

_____

_____

5. $\frac{x}{-6} < 3$

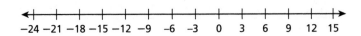

_____

_____

_____

© Houghton Mifflin Harcourt Publishing Company

Additional Practice

Solve each inequality and graph the solutions.

1. $4a > 32$

2. $-7y < 21$

3. $1.5n \le -18$

4. $-\frac{3}{8}c \ge 9$

5. $\frac{y}{5} > 4$

6. $2s \le -3$

7. $-\frac{1}{3}b < -6$

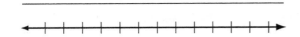

8. $\frac{z}{-8} \ge -0.25$

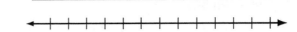

Write and solve an inequality for each problem.

9. Phil has a strip of wood trim that is 16 feet long. He needs 5-foot pieces to trim some windows. What are the possible numbers of pieces he can cut?

10. A teacher buys a 128-ounce bottle of juice and serves it in 5-ounce cups. What are the possible numbers of cups she can fill?

11. At an online bookstore, Kendra bought 4 copies of the same book for the members of her book club. She got free shipping because her total was at least $50. What was the minimum price of each book?

© Houghton Mifflin Harcourt Publishing Company

Write and solve an inequality for each situation.

1. Karin has $3 to spend in the arcade. The game she likes costs 50¢ per play. What are the possible numbers of times that she can play?

_____

_____

2. Tyrone has $21 and wants to buy juice drinks for his soccer team. There are 15 players on his team. How much can each drink cost so that Tyrone can buy one drink for each person?

_____

_____

3. A swimming pool is 7 feet deep and is being filled at the rate of 2.5 feet per hour. How long can the pool be left unattended without the water overflowing?

_____

_____

4. Megan is making quilts that require 11 feet of cloth each. She has 50 feet of cloth. What are the possible numbers of quilts that she can make?

_____

_____

Alyssa, Reggie, and Cassie are meeting some friends at the movies and have stopped at the refreshment stand. The table below shows some of the items for sale and their prices. Use this information to answer questions 5–7.

5. Alyssa has $7 and would like to buy fruit snacks for as many of her friends as possible. Which inequality below can be solved to find the number of fruit snacks f she can buy?

   A $2f \le 7$ C $7f \le 2$

   B $2f < 7$ D $7f < 2$

Menu Item	Price($)
Popcorn	3.50
Drink	3.00
Hot Dog	2.50
Nachos	2.50
Fruit Snack	2.00

6. Reggie brought $13 and is going to buy popcorn for the group. Which answer below shows the possible numbers of popcorns p Reggie can buy for his friends?

   F 0, 1, or 2   H 0, 1, 2, 3, or 4

   G 0, 1, 2, or 3   J 0, 1, 2, 3, 4, or 5

7. The movie theater donates 12% of its sales to charity. From Cassie's purchases, the theater will donate at least $2.15. Which inequality below shows the amount of money m that Cassie spent at the refreshment stand?

   A $m \ge 17.92$ C $m \ge 25.80$

   B $m \le 17.92$ D $m \le 25.80$

© Houghton Mifflin Harcourt Publishing Company

Solving Two-Step and Multi-Step Inequalities
Going Deeper

Essential question: *How can you use properties to justify solutions to multi-step inequalities?*

You can use the properties of inequality you learned in the previous lessons, as well as other properties, to justify your solutions to multi-step inequalities.

Video Tutor

MCC9–12.A.RE1.3

1 E X A M P L E   **Solving Inequalities With More Than One Step**

Find the solution set. Justify each step and graph the solution set.

$$4x - 3 + x + 8 > 20$$

$$4x + \boxed{} - \boxed{} + 8 > 20 \qquad \underline{\hspace{3cm}} \text{ Property of Addition}$$

$$\boxed{} + \boxed{} > 20 \qquad \text{Combine like terms.}$$

$$5x + 5 - \boxed{} > 20 - \boxed{} \qquad \underline{\hspace{3cm}} \text{ Property of Inequality}$$

$$\boxed{} > \boxed{} \qquad \text{Simplify.}$$

$$\frac{5x}{\boxed{}} > \frac{15}{\boxed{}} \qquad \underline{\hspace{3cm}} \text{ Property of Inequality}$$

$$x > \boxed{} \qquad \text{Simplify.}$$

Solution set: _____

−4 −3 −2 −1 0 1 2 3 4 5 6 7 8 9

REFLECT

1a. How would the solution set change if the inequality symbol in the above inequality were ≥ rather than >?

_____

1b. How would the above solution process be different if the first term were −4x?

_____

_____

You may need to use the Distributive Property before you can solve an inequality.

Distributive Property	If *a*, *b*, and *c* are real numbers, then $a(b + c) = ab + ac$.

© Houghton Mifflin Harcourt Publishing Company

2 EXAMPLE   Using the Distributive Property

Find the solution set. Justify each step and graph the solution set.

$$-2(3x - 8) < 10$$

     ▢ + ▢ < 10 _____ Property

$-6x + 16 -$ ▢ $< 10 -$ ▢   _____ Property of Inequality

     ▢ $<$ ▢   Simplify.

$$\frac{6x}{▢} < \frac{-6}{▢}$$ _____ Property of Inequality

     x ▢ ▢   _____ the inequality symbol; simplify.

Solution set: _____

REFLECT

2a. Why was the inequality symbol not reversed when you multiplied by -2 using the Distributive Property?

_____

_____

PRACTICE

Find the solution set. Justify each step and graph the solution set.

1. $12 - 3x \le 6$

_____

_____

_____

_____

Solution set: _____

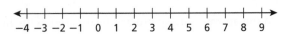

2. $2(x + 4) < 14$

_____

_____

_____

_____

_____

Solution set: _____

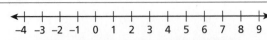

© Houghton Mifflin Harcourt Publishing Company

Additional Practice

Solve each inequality and graph the solutions.

1. $-3a + 10 < -11$

_____

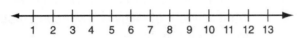

2. $4x - 12 \geq 20$

_____

3. $\dfrac{2k - 3}{-5} > 7$

_____

4. $-\dfrac{1}{5}z + \dfrac{2}{3} \leq 2$

_____

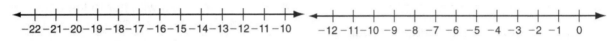

5. $6(n - 8) \geq -18$

_____

6. $10 - 2(3x + 4) < 11$

_____

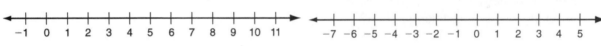

7. $7 + 2c - 4^2 \leq -9$

_____

8. $15p + 3(p - 1) > 3(2^3)$

_____

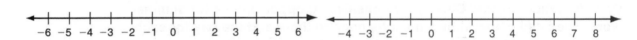

Write and solve an inequality for each problem.

9. A full-year membership to a gym costs $325 upfront with no monthly charge. A monthly membership costs $100 upfront and $30 per month. For what numbers of months is it less expensive to have a monthly membership?

_____

10. The sum of the lengths of any two sides of a triangle must be greater than the length of the third side. What are the possible values of x for this triangle?

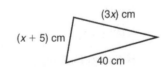
(3x) cm
(x + 5) cm
40 cm

_____

© Houghton Mifflin Harcourt Publishing Company

Problem Solving

Write and solve an inequality for each situation.

1. Jillene is playing in a basketball tournament and scored 24 points in her first game. If she averages over 20 points for both games, she will receive a trophy. How many points can Jillene score in the second game and receive a trophy?

   _____

   _____

2. Marcus has accepted a job selling cell phones. He will be paid $1500 plus 15% of his sales each month. He needs to earn at least $2430 to pay his bills. For what amount of sales will Marcus be able to pay his bills?

   _____

   _____

3. A 15-foot-tall cedar tree is growing at a rate of 2 feet per year beneath power lines that are 58 feet above the ground. The power company will have to prune or remove the tree before it reaches the lines. How many years can the power company wait before taking action?

   _____

   _____

4. Binh brought $23 with her to the county fair. She purchased a $5 T-shirt and now wants to buy some locally grown plants for $2.50 each. What are the numbers of plants that she can purchase with her remaining money?

   _____

   _____

Benedict, Ricardo, and Charlie are considering opportunities for summer work. The table below shows the jobs open to them and the pay for each. Use this information to answer questions 5–7.

5. Benedict has saved $91 from last year and would like to baby-sit to earn enough to buy a mountain bike. A good quality bike costs at least $300. What numbers of hours h can Benedict baby-sit to reach his goal?

   A $h \geq 14$ C $h \geq 38$

   B $h \geq 23$ D $h \geq 71$

Job	Pay
Mowing Lawns	$15 per lawn
Baby-Sitting	$5.50 per hour
Tutoring	$9 per session

6. Ricardo has agreed to tutor for the school. He owes his older brother $59 and would like to end the summer with at least $400 in savings. How many sessions s can Ricardo tutor to meet his goal?

   F $s \geq 31$ H $s \geq 51$

   G $s \geq 38$ J $s \geq 83$

7. Charlie has agreed to mow his neighbor's lawn each week and will also baby-sit some hours. If he makes $100 or more each week, his parents will charge him rent. How many hours h should Charlie agree to baby-sit each week to avoid paying rent?

   A $h \leq 15$ C $h \leq 21$

   B $h \geq 15$ D $h \geq 21$

© Houghton Mifflin Harcourt Publishing Company

Solving Inequalities with Variables on Both Sides

Going Deeper

Essential question: *How can you use properties to justify solutions of inequalities with variables on both sides?*

You can use the Properties of Inequality and the Distributive Property to justify the steps in a solution when solving inequalities that have variables on both sides.

MCC9–12.A.REI.3

1 EXAMPLE Using Properties to Justify Solutions

Find the solution set. Justify each step and graph your solution.

$3(2x - 3) \leq x + 1$

$6x - 9 \leq x + 1$ _____ Property

$6x \boxed{} - 9 \leq x \boxed{} + 1$ _____

$\boxed{} \leq \boxed{}$ Simplify.

$5x - 9 + 9 \leq \boxed{}$ _____

$\boxed{} \leq \boxed{}$ Simplify.

$\boxed{} \leq \boxed{}$ _____

$\boxed{} \leq \boxed{}$ Simplify.

Solution set: _____

-4 -3 -2 -1 0 1 2 3 4 5 6 7 8 9

REFLECT

1a. Why is the Distributive Property applied first in the solution?

_____

_____

1b. Could the properties have been applied in a different order than shown above? If so, would this make finding the solution easier or more difficult? Explain.

_____

_____

_____

1c. How would the solution change if the simplified coefficient of *x* were negative?

_____

_____

© Houghton Mifflin Harcourt Publishing Company

Find the solution set. Justify each step and graph your solution.

1. $21x + 28 < 10 - 3x$

_____

_____

_____

_____

_____

_____

Solution set: _____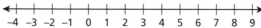

2. $-\frac{1}{3}(x + 2) \geq 7x + 3$

_____

_____

_____

_____

_____

_____

_____

_____

Solution set: _____

3. $2(4 - 3x) \leq 4x - 2$

_____

_____

_____

_____

_____

_____

_____

Solution set: _____

© Houghton Mifflin Harcourt Publishing Company

Additional Practice

Solve each inequality and graph the solutions.

1. $2x + 30 \geq 7x$

2. $2k + 6 < 5k - 3$

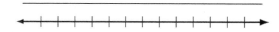

3. $3b - 2 \leq 2b + 1$

4. $2(3n + 7) > 5n$

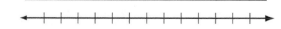

5. $5s - 9 < 2(s - 6)$

6. $-3(3x + 5) \geq -5(2x - 2)$

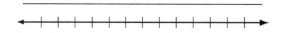

7. $1.4z + 2.2 > 2.6z - 0.2$

8. $\frac{7}{8}p - \frac{1}{4} \leq \frac{1}{2}p$

Solve each inequality.

9. $v + 1 > v - 6$

10. $3(x + 4) \leq 3x$

11. $-2(8 - 3x) \geq 6x + 2$

Write and solve an inequality for each problem.

12. Ian wants to promote his band on the Internet. Site A offers website hosting for $4.95 per month with a $49.95 startup fee. Site B offers website hosting for $9.95 per month with no startup fee. For how many months would Ian need to keep the website for Site B to be less expensive than Site A?

13. For what values of x is the area of the rectangle greater than the perimeter?

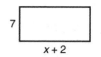

© Houghton Mifflin Harcourt Publishing Company

Problem Solving

Write and solve an inequality for each situation.

1. Rosa has decided to sell pet rocks at an art fair for $5 each. She has paid $50 to rent a table at the fair and it costs her $2 to package each rock with a set of instructions. For what numbers of sales will Rosa make a profit?

_____

_____

2. Jamie has a job paying $25,000 and expects to receive a $1000 raise each year. Wei has a job paying $19,000 a year and expects a $1500 raise each year. For what span of time is Jamie making more money than Wei?

_____

_____

3. Sophia types 75 words per minute and is just starting to write a term paper. Patton already has 510 words written and types at a speed of 60 words per minute. For what numbers of minutes will Sophia have more words typed than Patton?

_____

_____

4. Keith is racing his little sister Pattie and has given her a 15 foot head start. She runs 5 ft/sec and he is chasing at 8 ft/sec. For how long can Pattie stay ahead of Keith?

_____

_____

The table below shows the population of four cities in 2004 and the amount of population change from 2003. Use this table to answer questions 5–6.

5. If the trends in this table continue, after how many years y will the population of Manchester, NH, be more than the population of Vallejo, CA? Round your answer to the nearest tenth of a year.

   A $y > 0.2$ C $y > 34.6$

   B $y > 6.4$ D $y > 78.6$

6. If the trends in this table continue, for how long x will the population of Carrollton, TX be less than the population of Lakewood, CO? Round your answer to the nearest tenth of a year.

   F $x < 11.7$ H $x < 20.1$

   G $x < 14.6$ J $x < 28.3$

City	Population (2004)	Population Change (from 2003)
Lakewood, CO	141,301	−830
Vallejo, CA	118,349	−1155
Carrollton, TX	117,823	+1170
Manchester, NH	109,310	+261

© Houghton Mifflin Harcourt Publishing Company

Solving Compound Inequalities
Extension: Solving Special Compound Inequalities

Essential question: *How can you solve special compound inequalities?*

Compound inequalities are two inequalities joined by AND (∩) or OR (∪).

To solve a compound inequality:

1. Solve each inequality independently.

2. Graph the solutions above the same number line.

3. Decide which parts of the graphs represent the solution. If AND is used, it's the common points. If OR is used, it's all points. Then graph the solution on the number line.

Video Tutor

MCC9–12.A.REI.3

1 EXAMPLE Solving Compound Inequalities

Solve. Write the solution in set notation. Graph the solution.

A $2x < 8$ AND $3x + 2 > -4$
   $x < 4$ $3x > -6$
                   $x > -2$

Solution set: $\left\{x \mid x < \boxed{}\right\} \cap \left\{x \mid x < \boxed{}\right\}$ or $\left\{x \mid \boxed{} < x < \boxed{}\right\}$

B $3x + 2 \geq -1$ OR $4 - x \geq 2$
   $3x \geq -3$ $-x \geq -2$
   $x \geq -1$ $x \leq 2$

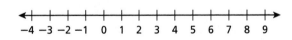

Solution set: $\left\{x \mid x \geq \boxed{}\right\} \cup \left\{x \mid x \leq \boxed{}\right\}$ or the set of all _____ numbers

C $2x - 3 > 3$ AND $x + 4 \leq 1$
   $2x > 6$ $x \leq -3$
   $x > 3$

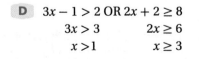

Solution set: $\left\{x \mid x > \boxed{}\right\} \cap \left\{x \mid x \leq \boxed{}\right\}$ or the _____ set or $\boxed{}$

D $3x - 1 > 2$ OR $2x + 2 \geq 8$
   $3x > 3$ $2x \geq 6$
   $x > 1$ $x \geq 3$

Solution set: $\left\{x \mid x > \boxed{}\right\} \cup \left\{x \mid x \geq \boxed{}\right\}$ or $\left\{x \mid x > \boxed{}\right\}$

© Houghton Mifflin Harcourt Publishing Company

1a. In Part C, why is the solution set the empty set?

_____

_____

1b. In Part D, why is the solution set $\{x \mid x > 1\}$?

_____

_____

PRACTICE

Solve. Write the solution in set notation. Graph the solution.

1. $4x + 2 > 14$ AND $x + 6 \le 4$

_____

_____

Solution set: _____

_____

2. $-3x < 3$ OR $2x + 3 \ge 11$

_____

_____

Solution set: _____

_____

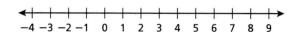

3. $2 + x < 1$ OR $-5x + 1 < 16$

_____

_____

Solution set: _____

_____

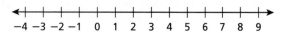

4. $4x - 3 > -7$ AND $3x - 2 \ge 7$

_____

_____

Solution set: _____

_____

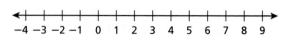

© Houghton Mifflin Harcourt Publishing Company

Additional Practice

Write the compound inequality shown by each graph.

1.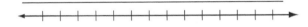

_____

2.

_____

3.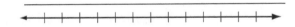

_____

4.

_____

Solve each compound inequality and graph the solutions.

5. $-15 < x - 8 < -4$

_____

6. $12 \leq 4n < 28$

_____

7. $-2 \leq 3b + 7 \leq 13$

_____
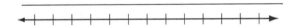

8. $x - 3 < -3$ OR $x - 3 \geq 3$

_____
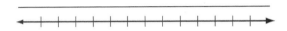

9. $5k \leq -20$ OR $2k \geq 8$

_____

10. $2s + 3 \leq 7$ OR $3s + 5 > 26$

_____

Write a compound inequality for each problem. Graph the solutions.

11. The human ear can distinguish sounds between 20 Hz and 20,000 Hz, inclusive.

_____

12. For a man to box as a welterweight, he must weigh more than 140 lbs, but at most 147 lbs.

_____

© Houghton Mifflin Harcourt Publishing Company

Problem Solving

Write and solve an inequality for each situation.

1. The Mexican Tetra is a tropical fish that requires a water temperature between 68 and 77 degrees Fahrenheit, inclusive. An aquarium is heated 8 degrees so that a Tetra can live in it. What temperatures could the water have been before the heating?

_____

_____

2. Nerissa's car can travel between 380 and 410 miles on a full tank of gas. She filled her gas tank and drove 45 miles. How many more miles can she drive without running out of gas?

_____

3. A local company is hiring trainees with less than 1 year of experience and managers with 5 or more years of experience. Graph the solutions.

_____

_____

4. Marty's allowance is doubled and is now between $10 and $15, inclusive. What amounts could his allowance have been before the increase? Graph the solutions.

_____

_____

The elliptical orbits of planets bring them closer to and farther from the Sun at different times. The closest (perihelion) and furthest (aphelion) points are given for three planets below. Use this data to answer questions 5–7.

5. Which inequality represents the distances d from the sun to Neptune?

   A $d \le 4444.5$

   B $d \le 4545.7$

   C $4444.5 \le d \le 4545.7$

   D $d = 4444.5$ OR $d \ge 4545.7$

Planet	Perihelion (in 10^6 km)	Aphelion (in 10^6 km)
Uranus	2741.3	3003.6
Neptune	4444.5	4545.7
Pluto	4435.0	7304.3

6. A NASA probe is traveling between Uranus and Neptune. It is currently between their orbits. Which inequality shows the possible distance p from the probe to the Sun?

   F $1542.1 < p < 1703.2$

   G $2741.3 < p < 4545.7$

   H $3003.6 < p < 4444.5$

   J $7185.8 < p < 7549.3$

7. At what distances o do the orbits of Neptune and Pluto overlap?

   A $4435.0 \le o \le 4444.5$

   B $4435.0 \le o \le 4545.7$

   C $4444.5 \le o \le 7304.3$

   D $4545.7 \le o \le 7304.3$

© Houghton Mifflin Harcourt Publishing Company

Solving Systems by Graphing
Going Deeper

Essential question: *How do you approximate the solution of a system of linear equations by graphing?*

A **system of linear equations** consists of two or more linear equations that have the same variables. A **solution of a system of linear equations** with two variables is an ordered pair that satisfies both equations in the system. The values of the variables in the ordered pair make each equation in the system true.

Systems of linear equations can be solved by graphing and by using algebra. In this lesson you will learn to solve linear systems by graphing the equations of the system and analyzing how those graphs are related.

Video Tutor

MCC9–12.A.REI.6

1 EXAMPLE Solving a Linear System by Graphing

Solve the system of equations below by graphing. Check your answer.

$$\begin{cases} -x + y = 3 \\ 2x + y = 6 \end{cases}$$

A Graph each equation.

Step 1: Find the intercepts for $-x + y = 3$, plus a third point for a check. Graph the line.

x-intercept: _____   *y*-intercept: _____

Check: The *y*-value for $x = 2$ is $y =$ _____.

Is that point (x, y) on the line? _____

Step 2: Find the intercepts for $2x + y = 6$ and graph the line.

x-intercept: _____   *y*-intercept: _____

Check: The *y*-value for $x = 2$ is $y =$ _____.

Is that point (x, y) on the line? _____

B Find the point of intersection.

The two lines appear to intersect at _____.

How is the point of intersection related to the solution of the linear system?

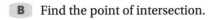

_____

_____

© Houghton Mifflin Harcourt Publishing Company

C Check if the ordered pair is a solution.

The solution of the system appears to be _____.

To check, substitute the ordered pair (x, y) into each equation.

$-x + y = 3$		
$-$ ▢ $+$ ▢		3
▢		$3\ \checkmark$

$2x + y = 6$		
$2\big(\ ▢\ \big) +$ ▢		6
▢ $+$ ▢		6
▢		$6\ \checkmark$

The ordered pair _____ makes both equations _____.

So, _____ is a solution of the system.

REFLECT

1a. How is the graph of each equation related to the solutions of the equation?

_____

_____

1b. Explain why the solution of a linear system with two equations is represented by the point where the graphs of the two equations intersect.

_____

_____

1c. Describe the graphs of $x = 4$ and $y = 2$. Explain how to solve the linear system by graphing.

$$\begin{cases} x = 4 \\ y = 2 \end{cases}$$

What would the graph look like? What is the solution of the linear system? Can systems of this type be solved by examining the equations without graphing them?

_____

_____

_____

_____

_____

_____

© Houghton Mifflin Harcourt Publishing Company

2 EXAMPLE   **Estimating a Solution by Graphing**

Estimate the solution for the linear system by graphing.

$$\begin{cases} x + 2y = 2 \\ 2x - 3y = 12 \end{cases}$$

A   Graph each equation by finding intercepts.

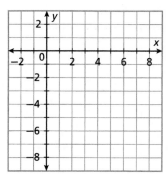

$x + 2y = 2$ $2x - 3y = 12$

x-intercept: _____   *x*-intercept: _____

y-intercept: _____   *y*-intercept: _____

B   Find the point of intersection.

The two lines appear to intersect at _____ .

C   Check if the ordered pair is an approximate solution.

$x + 2y$	$= 2$
▢ $+ 2\left(\right)$	2
▢ $+$ ▢	2
▢	2 ✓

$2x - 3y$	$= 12$
$2\left(\right) - 3\left(\right)$	12
▢ $-$ ▢	12
▢	12 ✓

Does the approximate solution make both equations true? If not, explain why not and whether the approximate solution is acceptable.

_____

_____

_____

REFLECT

2a. How could you adjust the graph to make your estimate more accurate?

_____

_____

2b. Can an approximate solution make both equations true? Explain.

_____

© Houghton Mifflin Harcourt Publishing Company

PRACTICE

Solve each system by graphing. Check your answer.

1. $\begin{cases} x - y = -2 \\ 2x + y = 8 \end{cases}$

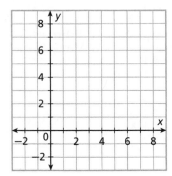

Solution: _____

2. $\begin{cases} x - y = -5 \\ 2x + 4y = -4 \end{cases}$

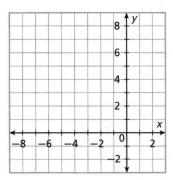

Solution: _____

Estimate the solution for the linear system by graphing. Check your answer.

3. $\begin{cases} x + y = 5 \\ x - 3y = 3 \end{cases}$

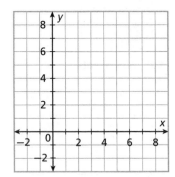

Approximate solution: _____

4. $\begin{cases} 3x = 8 \\ 2x - 2y = -3 \end{cases}$

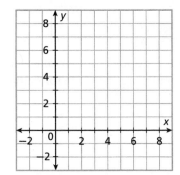

Approximate solution: _____

5. $\begin{cases} 3x - 2y = 12 \\ 2x - 6y = 9 \end{cases}$

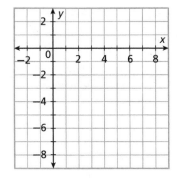

Approximate solution: _____

6. $\begin{cases} x + 2y = -6 \\ 2x + y = -4 \end{cases}$

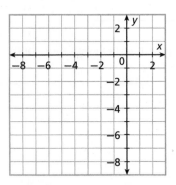

Approximate solution: _____

© Houghton Mifflin Harcourt Publishing Company

Additional Practice

Tell whether the ordered pair is a solution of the given system.

1. $(3, 1)$; $\begin{cases} x + 3y = 6 \\ 4x - 5y = 7 \end{cases}$ _____

2. $(6, -2)$; $\begin{cases} 3x - 2y = 14 \\ 5x - y = 32 \end{cases}$ _____

$x + 3y = 6$ _____ $4x - 5y = 7$ _____

$3x - 2y = 14$ _____ $5x - y = 32$ _____

Solve each system by graphing. Check your answer.

3. $\begin{cases} y = x + 4 \\ y = -2x + 1 \end{cases}$ Solution : _____

4. $\begin{cases} y = x + 6 \\ y = -3x + 6 \end{cases}$ Solution : _____

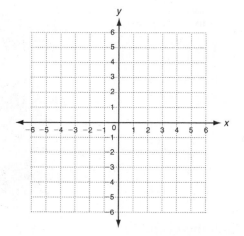

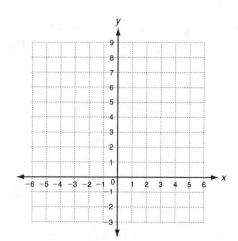

5. Maryann and Carlos are each saving for new scooters. So far, Maryann has $9 saved, and can earn $6 per hour babysitting. Carlos has $3 saved, and can earn $9 per hour working at his family's restaurant. After how many hours of work will Maryann and Carlos have saved the same amount? What will that amount be?

four hours 4 =27 dollars

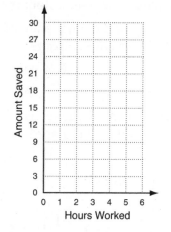

© Houghton Mifflin Harcourt Publishing Company

Problem Solving

Write the correct answer.

1. Mr. Malone is putting money in two savings accounts. Account A started with $200 and Account B started with $300. Mr. Malone deposits $15 in Account A and $10 in Account B each month. In how many months will the accounts have the same balance? What will that balance be?

_____

2. Tom currently has 5 comic books in his collection and has subscribed to receive 5 new comic books each month. His uncle has 145 comic books, but sends 5 to each of his 3 nieces each month. In how many months will they have the same number of comic books? How many books will that be?

_____

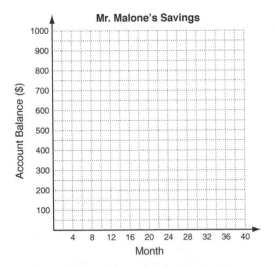

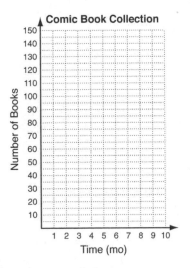

The graph below compares the heights of two trees. Use the graph to answer questions 3–6. Select the best answer.

3. How many years after planting will the trees be the same height?

   A 1 years   C 4 years

   B 2 years   D 6 years

4. Which system of equations is represented by the graph?

   F $\begin{cases} y = x + 2 \\ y = 0.5x + 2 \end{cases}$ H $\begin{cases} y = 2x + 4 \\ y = x + 4 \end{cases}$

   G $\begin{cases} y = x + 2 \\ y = 0.5x + 4 \end{cases}$ J $\begin{cases} y = 4x - 2 \\ y = 2x + 2 \end{cases}$

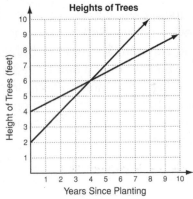

5. How fast does the tree that started at 2 feet tall grow?

   A 0.5 ft/yr   C 1.5 ft/yr

   B 1 ft/yr   D 2 ft/yr

6. How fast does the tree that started at 4 feet tall grow?

   F 0.5 ft/yr   H 1.5 ft/yr

   G 1 ft/yr   J 2 ft/yr

© Houghton Mifflin Harcourt Publishing Company

Solving Systems by Substitution
Going Deeper

Essential question: *How do you use substitution to solve a system of linear equations?*

The **substitution method** is used to solve systems of linear equations by solving an equation for one variable and then substituting the resulting expression for that variable into the other equation. The steps for this method are as follows:

1. Solve one of the equations for one of its variables.

2. Substitute the expression from step 1 into the other equation and solve for the other variable.

3. Substitute the value from step 2 into either original equation and solve to find the value of the variable in step 1.

MCC9–12.A.REI.6

1 E X A M P L E   Solving a Linear System by Substitution

Solve the system of linear equations by substitution. Check your answer.

$$\begin{cases} -3x + y = 1 \\ 4x + y = 8 \end{cases}$$

A   Solve an equation for one variable.

$-3x + y = 1$ Select one of the equations.

$y = \boxed{}$ Solve for the variable y. Isolate y on one side.

B   Substitute the expression for y in the other equation and solve.

$4x + \left(\boxed{} \right) = 8$ Substitute the expression for the variable y.

$\boxed{} + 1 = 8$ Combine like terms.

$\boxed{} = 7$ Subtract _____ from each side.

$x = \boxed{}$ Divide each side by _____.

C   Substitute the value of x you found into one of the equations and solve for the other variable, y.

$-3\left(\boxed{} \right) + y = 1$ Substitute the value of x into the first equation.

$\boxed{} + y = 1$ Simplify.

$y = \boxed{}$ Add _____ to each side.

So, _____ is the solution of the system.

© Houghton Mifflin Harcourt Publishing Company

Video Tutor

D Check the solution by graphing.

$$-3x + y = 1 \qquad\qquad 4x + y = 8$$

x-intercept: _____   **x-intercept:** _____

y-intercept: _____   **y-intercept:** _____

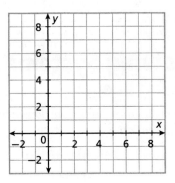

The point of intersection is _____.

REFLECT

1a. Is it more efficient to solve $-3x + y = 1$ for x? Why or why not?

_____

1b. Is there another way to solve the system?

_____

1c. What is another way to check your solution?

_____

PRACTICE

Solve each system by substitution. Check your answer.

1. $\begin{cases} x + y = 3 \\ 2x + 4y = 8 \end{cases}$

Solution: _____

2. $\begin{cases} x + 2y = 7 \\ 4x + 3y = 3 \end{cases}$

Solution: _____

3. $\begin{cases} -4x + y = 3 \\ 5x - 2y = -9 \end{cases}$

Solution: _____

4. $\begin{cases} 8x - 7y = -2 \\ -2x - 3y = 10 \end{cases}$

Solution: _____

5. $\begin{cases} 2x + 7y = 2 \\ 4x + 2y = -2 \end{cases}$

Solution: _____

6. $\begin{cases} 2x - y = 7 \\ 2x + 7y = 31 \end{cases}$

Solution: _____

Tell whether it is more efficient to solve for *x* and then substitute for *x* or to solve for *y* and then substitute for *y*. Explain your reasoning. Then solve the system.

7. $\begin{cases} 6x - 3y = 15 \\ x + 3y = -8 \end{cases}$

_____

_____

Solution: _____

© Houghton Mifflin Harcourt Publishing Company

Additional Practice

Solve each system by substitution. Check your answer.

1. $\begin{cases} y=x-2 \\ y=4x+1 \end{cases}$

2. $\begin{cases} y=x-4 \\ y=-x+2 \end{cases}$

3. $\begin{cases} y=3x+1 \\ y=5x-3 \end{cases}$

_____ _____ _____

4. $\begin{cases} 2x-y=6 \\ x+y=-3 \end{cases}$

5. $\begin{cases} 2x+y=8 \\ y=x-7 \end{cases}$

6. $\begin{cases} 2x+3y=0 \\ x+2y=-1 \end{cases}$

_____ _____ _____

7. $\begin{cases} 3x-2y=7 \\ x+3y=-5 \end{cases}$

8. $\begin{cases} -2x+y=0 \\ 5x+3y=-11 \end{cases}$

9. $\begin{cases} \frac{1}{2}x+\frac{1}{3}y=5 \\ \frac{1}{4}x+y=10 \end{cases}$

_____ _____ _____

Write a system of equations to represent the situation. Then, solve the system by substitution.

10. The length of a rectangle is 3 more than its width. The perimeter of the rectangle is 58 cm. What are the rectangle's dimensions?

_____

11. Carla and Benicio work in a men's clothing store. They earn commission from each suit and each pair of shoes they sell. For selling 3 suits and one pair of shoes, Carla has earned $47 in commission. For selling 7 suits and 2 pairs of shoes, Benicio has earned $107 in commission. How much do the salespeople earn for the sale of a suit? for the sale of a pair of shoes?

_____

© Houghton Mifflin Harcourt Publishing Company

Problem Solving

Write the correct answer.

1. Maribel has $1.25 in her pocket. The money is in quarters and dimes. There are a total of 8 coins. How many quarters and dimes does Maribel have in her pocket?

_____

_____

2. Fabulously Fit offers memberships for $35 per month plus a $50 enrollment fee. The Fitness Studio offers memberships for $40 per month plus a $35 enrollment fee. In how many months will the fitness clubs cost the same? What will the cost be?

_____

_____

3. Vong grilled 21 burgers at a block party. He grilled the same number of pounds of turkey burgers as hamburgers. Each turkey burger weighed $\frac{1}{4}$ pound and each hamburger weighed $\frac{1}{3}$ pound. How many of each did Vong grill?

_____

_____

4. Kate bought 3 used CDs and 1 used DVD at the bookstore. Her friend Joel bought 2 used CDs and 2 used DVDs at the same store. If Kate spent $20 and Joel spent $22, determine the cost of a used CD and a used DVD.

_____

_____

Use the chart below to answer questions 5–8. Select the best answer.
The chart compares the quotes that the Masons received from four different flooring contractors to tear out and replace a floor.

5. Which expression shows the total cost if the work is done by Dad's Floors?

   A $8 + 150x$ C $150(8x)$

   B $150 + 8x$ D $158x$

6. How many square feet would the Masons need to have installed to make the total cost of V.I.P. Inc. the same as the total cost of Floorshop?

   F 10 sq ft   H 100 sq ft

   G 200 sq ft   J 350 sq ft

7. When the total costs of V.I.P. Inc. and Floorshop are the same, what is the total cost?

   A $1125.00   C $1950.00

   B $1900.00   D $3187.50

Contractor	Cost to tear out old floor	Cost of new floor per square foot
Smith & Son	$250	$8.00
V.I.P. Inc.	$350	$7.75
Dad's Floors	$150	$8.00
Floorshop	$300	$8.25

8. How many square feet would the Masons need to have installed to make the total cost of Smith & Son the same as the total cost of V.I.P. Inc.?

   F 80 sq ft   H 400 sq ft

   G 100 sq ft   J 1000 sq ft

© Houghton Mifflin Harcourt Publishing Company

Solving Systems by Elimination
Going Deeper

Essential question: *How do you solve a system of linear equations by adding or subtracting?*

The **elimination method** is another method used to solve a system of linear equations. In this method, one variable is *eliminated* by adding or subtracting the two equations of the system to obtain a single equation in one variable. The steps for this method are as follows:

1. Add or subtract the equations to eliminate one variable.

2. Solve the resulting equation for the other variable.

3. Substitute the value into either original equation to find the value of the eliminated variable.

Video Tutor

MCC9–12.A.REI.6

1 EXAMPLE Solving a Linear System by Adding

Solve the system of equations by adding. Check your answer.

$$\begin{cases} 4x - 2y = 12 \\ x + 2y = 8 \end{cases}$$

A Add the equations.

$4x - 2y = 12$ Write the equations so that like terms are aligned.

$\underline{+ \; x + 2y = 8}$ Notice that the terms _____ and _____ are opposites.

$5x + 0 = 20$ Add to eliminate the variable _____.

$5x = 20$ Simplify and solve for x.

$\frac{5x}{5} = \frac{20}{5}$ Divide both sides by 5.

$x = \boxed{}$ Simplify.

B Substitute the solution into one of the equations and solve for y.

$x + 2y = 8$ Use the second equation.

$\left(\boxed{}\right) + 2y = 8$ Substitute _____ for the variable _____.

$2y = \boxed{}$ Subtract _____ from each side.

$y = \boxed{}$ Divide each side by _____.

C Write the solution as an ordered pair: _____

© Houghton Mifflin Harcourt Publishing Company

D Check the solution by graphing.

$4x - 2y = 12$ $x + 2y = 8$

x-intercept: _____   *x*-intercept: _____

y-intercept: _____   *y*-intercept: _____

The point of intersection is _____.

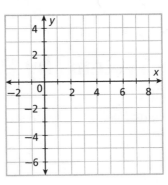

REFLECT

1a. Can this linear system be solved by subtracting one of the original equations from the other? Why or why not?

_____

_____

1b. What is another way to check your solution?

_____

MCC9–12.A.REI.6

2   E X A M P L E   Solving a Linear System by Subtracting

Solve the system of equations by subtracting. Check your answer.

$$\begin{cases} 2x + 6y = 6 \\ 2x - y = -8 \end{cases}$$

A Subtract the equations.

$2x + 6y = 6$ Write the equations so that like terms are aligned.

$\underline{-\,(2x - y = -8)}$ Notice that both equations contain the term _____.

$0 + 7y = 14$ Subtract to eliminate the variable _____.

$7y = 14$ Simplify and solve for *y*.

$\frac{7y}{7} = \frac{14}{7}$ Divide both sides by 7.

$y = \boxed{}$ Simplify.

B Substitute the solution into one of the equations and solve for *x*.

$2x - y = -8$ Use the second equation.

$2x - \left(\boxed{}\right) = -8$ Substitute _____ for the variable _____.

$2x = \boxed{}$ Add _____ to each side.

$x = \boxed{}$ Divide each side by _____.

C Write the solution as an ordered pair: _____

© Houghton Mifflin Harcourt Publishing Company

D Check the solution by graphing.

$2x + 6y = 6$ $2x - y = -8$

x-intercept: _____   *x*-intercept: _____

y-intercept: _____   *y*-intercept: _____

The point of intersection is _____.

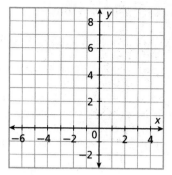

2a. What would happen if you added the original equations instead of subtracting?

_____

_____

2b. Instead of subtracting $2x - y = -8$ from $2x + 6y = 6$, what equation can you add to get the same result? Explain.

_____

_____

2c. How can you decide whether to add or subtract to eliminate a variable in a linear system? Explain your reasoning.

_____

_____

_____

In some linear systems, neither variable can be eliminated by adding or subtracting the equations directly. In systems like these, you need to multiply one or both of the equations by a constant so that adding or subtracting the equations will eliminate one variable. The steps for this method are as follows:

1. Decide which variable to eliminate.

2. Multiply one or both equations by a constant so that adding or subtracting will eliminate that variable.

3. Solve the system using the elimination method.

© Houghton Mifflin Harcourt Publishing Company

3 EXPLORE   Understanding Linear Systems and Multiplication

A Use the equations in the linear system below to write a third equation.

$$\begin{cases} 2x - y = 1 \\ x + y = 2 \end{cases}$$

$x + y = 2$	Write the second equation in the system.
$2(x + y = 2)$	Multiply each term in the equation by 2.
$2x + 2y = 4$	Simplify.
$+ \quad 2x - y = 1$	Write the first equation in the system.
$\boxed{} \, x + \boxed{} \, y = \boxed{}$	Add the equations to write a third equation.

B Graph and label each equation in the original linear system.

The solution of the system is _____.

C Graph and label the third equation.

How is the graph of the third equation related to the graphs of the two equations in the original system?

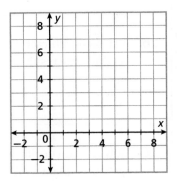

_____

_____

Is the solution of the original system also a solution of the system formed by the equation $2x - y = 1$ and the third equation? Explain.

_____

REFLECT

3a. Examine your results from the Explore. Does it appear that a new linear system composed of one of the equations from the original system and a new equation created by adding a multiple of one original equation to the other equation will have the same solution as the original system? Explain.

_____

_____

_____

© Houghton Mifflin Harcourt Publishing Company

3b. If the two equations in the original system are represented by $Ax + By = C$ and $Dx + Ey = F$, where A, B, C, D, E, and F are constants, then the third equation you wrote can be represented by doing the following:

Multiply the second equation by a nonzero constant k to get $kDx + kEy = kF$.

Then add this equation to the first equation to get the third equation.

$$
\begin{array}{rl}
Ax + & By = C \\
+\quad kDx + & kEy = \quad kF \\
\hline
(A + kD)x + (B + kE)y = & C + kF
\end{array}
$$

Complete the proof below to show that if (x_1, y_1) is a solution of the original system, then it is also a solution of the new system below.

$$\begin{cases} Ax + By = C \\ (A + kD)x + (B + kE)y = C + kF \end{cases}$$

$Ax_1 + By_1 = C$	(x_1, y_1) is a solution of $Ax + By = C$.
$Dx_1 + Ey_1 = F$	(x_1, y_1) is a solution of $Dx + Ey = F$.
$\boxed{}(Dx_1 + Ey_1) = kF$	Multiplication Property of _____
$kDx_1 + kEy_1 = kF$	_____ Property
$C + kDx_1 + kEy_1 = \boxed{} + kF$	_____ Property of Equality
$Ax_1 + \boxed{} + kDx_1 + kEy_1 = C + kF$	Substitute $Ax_1 + By_1$ for C on the left side.
$Ax_1 + kDx_1 + \boxed{} + kEy_1 = C + kF$	_____ Property of Addition
$(Ax_1 + kDx_1) + (By_1 + kEy_1) = C + kF$	Associative Property of Addition
$(A + kD)x_1 + (\boxed{} + kE)y_1 = C + kF$	Distributive Property

Since $(A + kD)x_1 + (B + kE)y_1 = C + kF$, (x_1, y_1) is a solution of the new system.

MCC9–12.A.REI.6

4 EXAMPLE Solving a Linear System by Multiplying One Equation

Solve the system of equations by multiplying.

$$\begin{cases} 3x + 8y = 7 \\ 2x - 2y = -10 \end{cases}$$

A Explain how to multiply one of the equations by a number so that the coefficients for one of the variables are opposites.

_____

_____

© Houghton Mifflin Harcourt Publishing Company

B Multiply the second equation by the constant you found in part A and add this new equation to the first equation.

$\boxed{}\,(2x - 2y = -10)$ Multiply each term in the second equation by _____ to get opposite coefficients for the y-terms.

$$8x - 8y = -40$$ Simplify.
$$\underline{+\ 3x + 8y = 7}$$ Add the first equation to the new equation.

$$11x + 0y = -33$$ Add to eliminate the variable _____.

$$11x = -33$$ Simplify and solve for x.

$$\frac{11x}{11} = \frac{-33}{11}$$ Divide both sides by 11.

$$x = \boxed{}$$ Simplify.

C Substitute the solution into one of the equations and solve.

$$3x + 8y = 7$$ Use the first equation.

$$3\left(\boxed{}\right) + 8y = 7$$ Substitute _____ for the variable _____.

$$\boxed{} + 8y = 7$$ Simplify.

$$8y = \boxed{}$$ Add _____ to each side.

$$y = \boxed{}$$ Divide each side by _____.

D Write the solution as an ordered pair: _____

REFLECT

4a. How can you solve this linear system by subtracting? Which is more efficient, adding or subtracting? Explain your reasoning.

_____

_____

4b. Can this linear system be solved by adding or subtracting without multiplying? Why or why not?

_____

4c. What would you need to multiply the second equation by to eliminate x by adding? Why might you choose to eliminate y instead of x?

_____

_____

© Houghton Mifflin Harcourt Publishing Company

5 EXAMPLE — Solving a Linear System by Multiplying Both Equations

Solve the system of equations by multiplying.

$$\begin{cases} -3x + 9y = -3 \\ 4x - 13y = 5 \end{cases}$$

A Explain how to multiply both of the equations by different integers so that the coefficients for one of the variables are opposites.

_____

_____

B Multiply both of the equations and add.

▢ $(-3x + 9y = -3)$	Multiply the first equation by _____.
▢ $(4x - 13y = 5)$	Multiply the second equation by _____.

$$\begin{aligned} -12x + 36y &= -12 \\ +\quad 12x - 39y &= 15 \end{aligned}$$

Simplify the multiple of the first equation.
Simplify the multiple of the second equation.

$-3y = 3$ Add to eliminate the variable _____.

$\frac{-3y}{-3} = \frac{3}{-3}$ Divide both sides by -3.

$y =$ ▢   Simplify.

C Substitute the solution into one of the equations and solve.

$4x - 13y = 5$ Use the second equation.

$4x - 13($ ▢ $) = 5$ Substitute _____ for the variable _____.

$4x - ($ ▢ $) = 5$ Simplify.

$4x =$ ▢   Add _____ to each side.

$\frac{4x}{4} = \frac{-8}{4}$ Divide each side by _____.

$x =$ ▢   Simplify.

D Write the solution as an ordered pair: _____

© Houghton Mifflin Harcourt Publishing Company

5a. What numbers would you need to multiply both equations by to eliminate y? Why might you choose to eliminate x instead?

_____

_____

_____

_____

5b. Describe how to find the numbers by which you would multiply both equations to eliminate a variable.

_____

_____

_____

_____

_____

5c. If both equations must be multiplied in order to eliminate a variable, how can you decide which variable will be easier to eliminate?

_____

_____

_____

PRACTICE

Solve each system by adding or subtracting. Check your answer.

1. $\begin{cases} -5x + y = -3 \\ 5x - 3y = -1 \end{cases}$

Solution: _____

2. $\begin{cases} 2x + y = -6 \\ -5x + y = 8 \end{cases}$

Solution: _____

3. $\begin{cases} 2x - 3y = -2 \\ 2x + y = 14 \end{cases}$

Solution: _____

4. $\begin{cases} 6x - 3y = 15 \\ 4x + 3y = -5 \end{cases}$

Solution: _____

© Houghton Mifflin Harcourt Publishing Company

5. Error Analysis Which solution is incorrect? Explain the error.

A

$$\begin{cases} x + y = -4 \\ 2x + y = -3 \end{cases} \qquad \begin{array}{r} x + y = -4 \\ -(2x + y = -3) \\ \hline -x = -7 \\ x = 7 \end{array}$$

$7 + y = -4$

$\quad y = -11$

Solution is $(7, -11)$.

B

$$\begin{cases} x + y = -4 \\ 2x + y = -3 \end{cases} \qquad \begin{array}{r} x + y = -4 \\ -(2x + y = -3) \\ \hline -x = -1 \\ x = 1 \end{array}$$

$1 + y = -4$

$\quad y = -5$

Solution is $(1, -5)$.

_____

_____

6. Is it possible to solve the system in the first Example by using substitution? If so, explain how. Which method is easier to use? Why?

_____

_____

_____

_____

_____

Solve each system by multiplying. Check your answer.

7. $\begin{cases} -2x + 2y = 2 \\ 5x - 6y = -9 \end{cases}$

Solution: _____

8. $\begin{cases} 3x + 3y = 12 \\ -6x - 11y = -14 \end{cases}$

Solution: _____

9. $\begin{cases} 4x + 3y = 11 \\ 2x - 2y = -12 \end{cases}$

Solution: _____

10. $\begin{cases} 6x + 3y = -24 \\ 7x - 5y = 6 \end{cases}$

Solution: _____

11. $\begin{cases} 3x + 8y = 17 \\ -2x + 9y = 3 \end{cases}$

Solution: _____

12. $\begin{cases} 11x + 6y = -20 \\ 15x + 9y = -33 \end{cases}$

Solution: _____

13. $\begin{cases} 12x - 6y = 12 \\ 8x - 16y = -16 \end{cases}$

Solution: _____

14. $\begin{cases} 5x + 9y = -3 \\ -4x - 7y = 3 \end{cases}$

Solution: _____

© Houghton Mifflin Harcourt Publishing Company

15. Error Analysis A linear system has two equations, $Ax + By = C$ and $Dx + Ey = F$. A student multiplies the x- and y-coefficients in the second equation by a constant k to get $kDx + kEy = F$. The student then adds the result to $Ax + By = C$ to write a new equation.

a. What is the new equation that the student wrote?

_____

b. If the ordered pair (x_1, y_1) is a solution of the original system, will it also be a solution of $Ax + By = C$ and the new equation? Why or why not?

_____

_____

_____

© Houghton Mifflin Harcourt Publishing Company

Additional Practice

Follow the steps to solve each system by elimination.

1. $\begin{cases} 2x - 3y = 14 \\ 2x + y = -10 \end{cases}$

Subtract the second equation:

$2x - 3y = 14$
$- (2x + y = -10)$
_____

_____

Solve the resulting equation:

$y = $ _____
Use your answer to find the value of x:

$x = $ _____
Solution: (____, ____)

2. $\begin{cases} 3x + y = 17 \\ 4x + 2y = 20 \end{cases}$

Multiply the first equation by –2. Then, add the equations:

___ $x - $ ___ $y = $ ____
$+ 4x + 2y = 20$
_____

_____

Solve the resulting equation:

$x = $ _____
Use your answer to find the value of y:

$y = $ _____
Solution: (____, ____)

Solve each system by elimination. Check your answer.

3. $\begin{cases} x + 3y = -7 \\ -x + 2y = -8 \end{cases}$

4. $\begin{cases} 3x + y = -26 \\ 2x - y = -19 \end{cases}$

5. $\begin{cases} x + 3y = -14 \\ 2x - 4y = 32 \end{cases}$

6. $\begin{cases} 4x - y = -5 \\ -2x + 3y = 10 \end{cases}$

7. $\begin{cases} y - 3x = 11 \\ 2y - x = 2 \end{cases}$

8. $\begin{cases} -10x + y = 0 \\ 5x + 3y = -7 \end{cases}$

Solve.

9. Brianna's family spent $134 on 2 adult tickets and 3 youth tickets at an amusement park. Max's family spent $146 on 3 adult tickets and 2 youth tickets. What is the price of a youth ticket? _____

10. Carl bought 19 apples of 2 different varieties to make a pie. The total cost of the apples was $5.10. Granny Smith apples cost $0.25 each and Gala apples cost $0.30 each. How many of each type of apple did Carl buy? _____

© Houghton Mifflin Harcourt Publishing Company

Problem Solving

Write the correct answer.

1. Mr. Nguyen bought a package of 3 chicken legs and a package of 7 chicken wings. Ms. Dawes bought a package of 3 chicken legs and a package of 6 chicken wings. Mr. Nguyen bought 45 ounces of chicken. Ms. Dawes bought 42 ounces of chicken. How much did each chicken leg and each chicken wing weigh?

_____

_____

3. The Lees spent $31 on movie tickets for 2 adults and 3 children. The Macias spent $26 on movie tickets for 2 adults and 2 children. What are the prices for adult and child movie tickets?

_____

_____

2. Jayce bought 2 bath towels and returned 3 hand towels. His sister Jayna bought 3 bath towels and 3 hand towels. Jayce's bill was $5. Jayna's bill was $45. What are the prices of a bath towel and a hand towel?

_____

_____

4. Last month Stephanie spent $57 on 4 allergy shots and 1 office visit. This month she spent $9 after 1 office visit and a refund for 2 allergy shots from her insurance company. How much does an office visit cost? an allergy shot?

_____

_____

Use the chart below to answer questions 5–6. Select the best answer.
The chart shows the price per pound for dried fruit.

Dried Fruit Price List			
Pineapple	Apple	Mango	Papaya
$7.50/lb	$7.00/lb	$8.00/lb	$7.25/lb

5. A customer bought 5 pounds of mango and papaya for $37.75. How many pounds of each fruit did the customer buy?

   A 2 lbs mango and 3 lbs papaya

   B 3 lbs mango and 2 lbs papaya

   C 1 lb mango and 4 lbs papaya

   D 4 lbs mango and 1 lb papaya

6. A store employee made two gift baskets of dried fruit, each costing $100. The first basket had 12 pounds of fruit x and 2 pounds of fruit y. The second basket had 4 pounds of fruit x and 9 pounds of fruit y. Which two fruits did the employee use in the baskets?

   F pineapple and apple

   G apple and mango

   H mango and papaya

   J papaya and pineapple

© Houghton Mifflin Harcourt Publishing Company

Solving Special Systems
Going Deeper

Essential question: *How do you solve systems with no or infinitely many solutions?*

Video Tutor

MCC9–12.A.REI.6

1 EXAMPLE Solving Special Systems by Graphing

Use the graph to solve each system of linear equations.

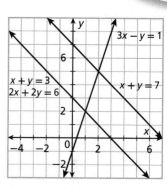

A $\begin{cases} x + y = 7 \\ 2x + 2y = 6 \end{cases}$

Is there a point of intersection? Explain.

_____

_____

Does this linear system have a solution? Use the graph to explain.

_____

_____

B $\begin{cases} 2x + 2y = 6 \\ x + y = 3 \end{cases}$

Is there a point of intersection? Explain.

_____

Does this linear system have a solution? Use the graph to explain.

_____

_____

REFLECT

1a. Use the graph to identify two lines that represent a linear system with exactly one solution. What are the equations of the lines? Explain your reasoning.

_____

1b. If each equation in a system of two linear equations is represented by a different line when graphed, what is the greatest number of solutions the system can have? Explain your reasoning.

_____

_____

© Houghton Mifflin Harcourt Publishing Company

1c. Identify the three possible numbers of solutions for a system of linear equations. Explain when each type of solution occurs.

_____

_____

MCC9–12.A.REI.6

2 EXAMPLE   **Solving Special Systems Algebraically**

A   Solve the system of linear equations by substitution.

$$\begin{cases} x - y = -2 \\ -x + y = 4 \end{cases}$$

Step 1 Solve $x - y = -2$ for x: $x = $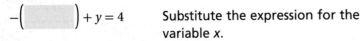

Step 2 Substitute the resulting expression into the other equation and solve.

$-\left(\right) + y = 4$ Substitute the expression for the variable x.

$ = 4$ Simplify.

Step 3 Interpret the solution. Graph the equations to provide more information.

What does the graph tell you about the solution?

_____

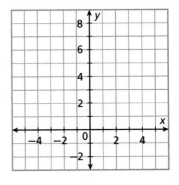

How is this solution represented algebraically when the system is solved using substitution?

_____

B   Solve the system of linear equations by elimination.

$$\begin{cases} 2x + y = -2 \\ 4x + 2y = -4 \end{cases}$$

Step 1 Multiply the first equation by -2.

$-2(2x + y = -2) \rightarrow -4x + (-2y) = 4$

Step 2 Add the new equation from Step 1 to the original second equation.

$$
\begin{array}{r}
-4x + (-2y) = 4 \\
+ \quad 4x + 2y = -4 \\
\hline
0x + 0y = 0 \\
0 = 0
\end{array}
$$

© Houghton Mifflin Harcourt Publishing Company

Step 3 Interpret the solution. Graph the equations to provide more information.

What does the graph tell you about the solution?

_____

_____

How is this solution represented algebraically when the linear system is solved using substitution?

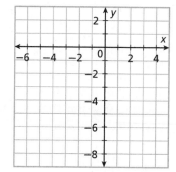

_____

_____

_____

REFLECT

2a. If x represents a variable and a and b represent constants such that $a \neq b$, interpret what each result means when solving a system of linear equations by substitution.

$x = a$ _____

$a = b$ _____

$a = a$ _____

2b. In part B of Example 2, why is it more efficient to solve and substitute for y than to solve and substitute for x?

_____

_____

2c. Give two possible solutions of the system in part B of Example 2. How are all the solutions of this system related to one another?

_____

PRACTICE

Solve each system by graphing. Check your answer.

1. $\begin{cases} x + 2y = -8 \\ -2x - 4y = 4 \end{cases}$

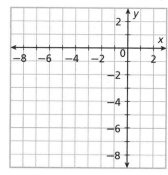

Solution: _____

2. $\begin{cases} 2x - y = -6 \\ 4x - 2y = -12 \end{cases}$

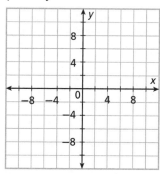

Solution: _____

© Houghton Mifflin Harcourt Publishing Company

Solve each system by substitution. Check your answer.

3. $\begin{cases} 2x - 2y = 5 \\ 4x - 4y = 9 \end{cases}$

   Solution: _____

4. $\begin{cases} x - 2y = -4 \\ 4y = 2x + 8 \end{cases}$

   Solution: _____

Tell whether it is more efficient to solve for *x* and then substitute for *x* or to solve for *y* and then substitute for *y*. Explain your reasoning. Then solve the system.

5. $\begin{cases} \frac{x}{2} + y = 6 \\ \frac{x}{4} + \frac{y}{2} = 3 \end{cases}$

   _____

   _____

   Solution: _____

Solve each system by adding or subtracting. Check your answer.

6. $\begin{cases} -4x + y = -3 \\ 4x - y = -2 \end{cases}$

   Solution: _____

7. $\begin{cases} x - 6y = 7 \\ -x + 6y = -7 \end{cases}$

   Solution: _____

8. If a linear system has no solution, what happens when you try to solve the system by adding or subtracting?

   _____

   _____

9. If a linear system has infinitely many solutions, what happens when you try to solve the system by adding or subtracting?

   _____

   _____

Solve each system by multiplying. Check your answer.

10. $\begin{cases} 2x + 3y = -6 \\ 10x + 15y = -30 \end{cases}$

    Solution: _____

11. $\begin{cases} 3x - 4y = -1 \\ -6x + 8y = 3 \end{cases}$

    Solution: _____

© Houghton Mifflin Harcourt Publishing Company

Additional Practice

Solve each system of linear equations.

1. $\begin{cases} y = 2x - 3 \\ y - 2x = -3 \end{cases}$

2. $\begin{cases} 3x + y = 4 \\ -3x = y - 7 \end{cases}$

Infinite

3. $\begin{cases} y = -4x + 1 \\ 4x = -y - 6 \end{cases}$

4. $\begin{cases} y - x + 3 = 0 \\ x = y + 3 \end{cases}$

Classify each system. Give the number of solutions.

5. $\begin{cases} y = 3(x - 1) \\ -y + 3x = 3 \end{cases}$

6. $\begin{cases} y - 2x = 5 \\ x = y - 3 \end{cases}$

7. Sabina and Lou are reading the same book. Sabina reads 12 pages a day. She had read 36 pages when Lou started the book, and Lou reads at a pace of 15 pages per day. If their reading rates continue, will Sabina and Lou ever be reading the same page on the same day? Explain.

8. Brandon started jogging at 4 miles per hour. After he jogged 1 mile, his friend Anton started jogging along the same path at a pace of 4 miles per hour. If they continue to jog at the same rate, will Anton ever catch up with Brandon? Explain.

© Houghton Mifflin Harcourt Publishing Company

Problem Solving

Write the correct answer.

1. Tyra and Charmian are training for a bike race. Tyra has logged 256 miles so far and rides 48 miles per week. Charmian has logged 125 miles so far and rides 48 miles per week. If these rates continue, will Tyra's distance ever equal Charmian's distance? Explain.

_____

_____

2. Metroplexpress and Local Express are courier companies. Metroplexpress charges $15 to pick up a package and $0.50 per mile. Local Express charges $10 to pick up a package and $0.55 per mile. Classify this system and find its solution, if any.

_____

_____

3. The Singhs start savings accounts for their twin boys. The accounts earn 5% annual interest. The initial deposit in each account is $200. Classify this system and find its solution, if any.

_____

_____

4. Frank earns $8 per hour. Madison earns $7.50 per hour. Frank started working after Madison had already earned $300. If these rates continue, will Frank's earnings ever equal Madison's earnings? If so, when?

_____

_____

Select the best answer.

5. A studio apartment at The Oaks costs $400 per month plus a $350 deposit. A studio apartment at Crossroads costs $400 per month plus a $300 deposit. How many solutions does this system have?

   A no solutions

   B 1 solution

   C 2 solutions

   D an infinite number of solutions

6. Jane and Gary are both landscape designers. Jane charges $75 for a consultation plus $25 per hour. Gary charges $50 for a consultation plus $30 per hour. For how many hours will Jane's charges equal Gary's charges?

   F never

   G after 2 hours

   H after 5 hours

   J always

7. A tank filled with 75 liters of water loses 0.5 liter of water per hour. A tank filled with 50 liters of water loses 0.1 liter of water per hour. How would this system be classified?

   A inconsistent

   B dependent

   C consistent and independent

   D consistent and dependent

8. Simon is 3 years older than Renata. Five years ago, Renata was half as old as Simon is now. How old are Simon and Renata now?

   F Simon is 13 and Renata is 10.

   G Simon is 15 and Renata is 10.

   H Simon is 16 and Renata is 8.

   J Simon is 16 and Renata is 13.

© Houghton Mifflin Harcourt Publishing Company

Solving Linear Inequalities
Going Deeper

Essential question: *How do you graph a linear inequality in two variables?*

A **linear inequality in two variables**, such as $2x - 3y \geq 6$, results when you replace the $=$ sign in an equation by $<$, $>$, $\leq$, or $\geq$. A **solution of an inequality in two variables** x and y is any ordered pair (x, y) that makes the inequality true.

Video Tutor

MCC9–12.A.REI.12

1 EXAMPLE Graphing a Linear Inequality

Graph the solution set for $2x - 3y \geq 6$.

A Start by graphing $2x - 3y = 6$. The inequality is true for every point on this line because the inequality symbol is less than or equal to. The line is called the *boundary line* of the solution set.

x	y
0	
	0

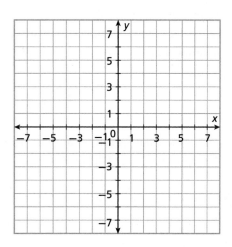

B Test several other points in the plane that are not on the boundary line to determine whether the inequality is true.

Point	Above or Below the Line?	Inequality	True or False?
(0, 0)	Above	$2(0) - 3(0) \geq 6$	False
(5, 0)			
(0, 3)			
(4, 2)			
(6, 1)			

The solutions of $2x - 3y \geq 6$ lie on or _____ $2x - 3y = 6$.

© Houghton Mifflin Harcourt Publishing Company

C Shade the set of solutions to the inequality $2x - 3y \geq 6$. The shaded region and the boundary line make up the graph of $2x - 3y \geq 6$. This area is referred to as a *half-plane*.

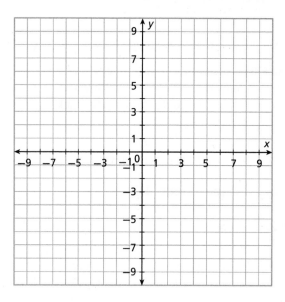

> **REFLECT**

1a. How would the graph of $2x - 3y \leq 6$ be like the graph of $2x - 3y \geq 6$? How would it be different?

_____

_____

1b. Would the points on the boundary line $2x - 3y = 6$ be included in the graph of the inequality $2x - 3y > 6$? Why or why not?

_____

_____

1c. **Error Analysis** A student says that you shade above the boundary line when the inequality is > or $\geq$ and you shade below it when the inequality is < or $\leq$. Use the example to explain why this is not always true.

_____

_____

To graph a linear inequality in the coordinate plane:

1. Graph the boundary line. If the symbol is $\leq$ or $\geq$, draw a solid line. If the symbol is < or >, draw a dashed line.

2. Choose a test point (x, y) that is not on the line. Substitute the values of x and y into the inequality and determine whether it is true or false.

3. If the inequality is true for the test point, shade the half-plane on the side of the boundary line that contains the test point. If not, shade the half-plane on the opposite side of the line.

© Houghton Mifflin Harcourt Publishing Company

2 **E X A M P L E** Graphing a Linear Inequality in Two Variables

Graph the inequality $7x - y < 13$.

A Write the equation of the boundary line. _____

B Graph the boundary line. The inequality symbol is >, so the line will be dashed.

C Test a point that is not on the line, such as (0, 0).

$$7\left(\boxed{}\right) - \boxed{} < 13 \qquad \text{True or false?} \underline{}$$

Shade the part of the plane on the correct side of the line.

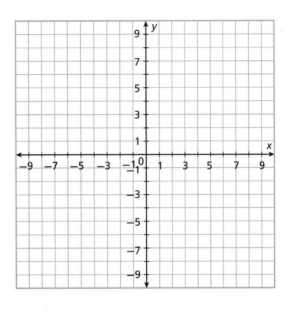

REFLECT

2a. Why is (0, 0) a good choice for a test point? When could you not use (0, 0)?

_____

_____

2b. For the graph of $x \geq 4$, the boundary line is the vertical line $x = 4$. Would you shade to the left or right of the boundary? Explain.

_____

_____

_____

_____

© Houghton Mifflin Harcourt Publishing Company

Graph the inequality.

1. $y \geq 2$

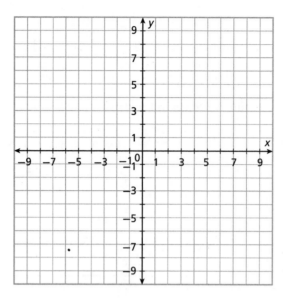

2. $x < -3$

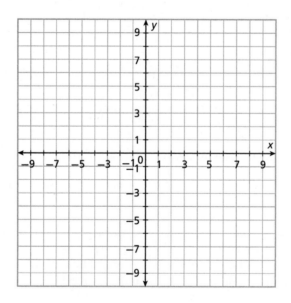

© Houghton Mifflin Harcourt Publishing Company

3. $x + 4y < 9$

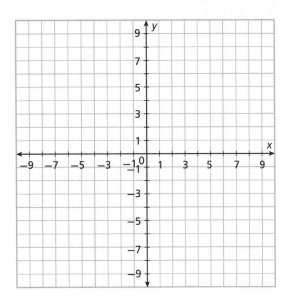

4. $2x - 2y \geq 5$

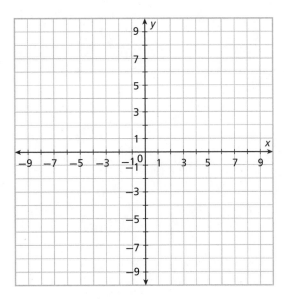

© Houghton Mifflin Harcourt Publishing Company

129

5. $-3x + 6y \geq 2$

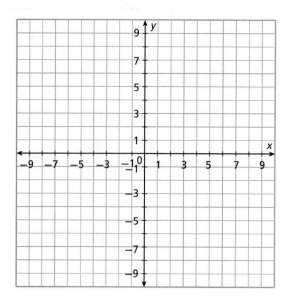

6. $7x - y > 13$

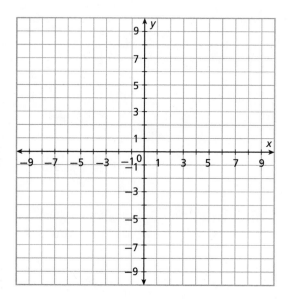

© Houghton Mifflin Harcourt Publishing Company

Additional Practice

Tell whether the ordered pair is a solution of the given inequality.

1. $(1, 6)$; $y < x + 6$

2. $(-3, -12)$; $y \geq 2x - 5$

3. $(5, -3)$; $y \leq -x + 2$

_____   _____   _____

Graph the solutions of each linear inequality.

4. $y \leq x + 4$

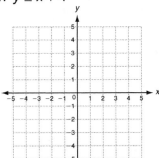

5. $2x + y > -2$

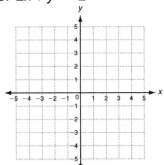

6. $x + y - 1 < 0$

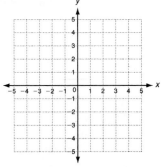

7. Clark is having a party at his house. His father has allowed him to spend at most $20 on snack food. He'd like to buy chips that cost $4 per bag, and pretzels that cost $2 per bag.

   a. Write an inequality to describe the situation.

   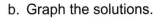
   _____

   b. Graph the solutions.

   c. Give two possible combinations of bags of chips and pretzels that Clark can buy.

   _____

   _____

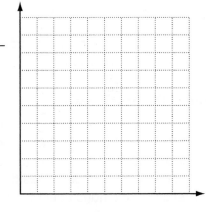

Write an inequality to represent each graph.

8.

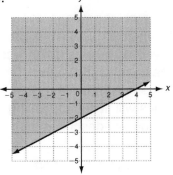

9.

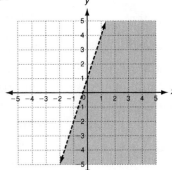

10.

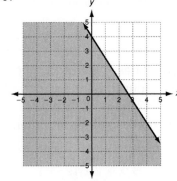

_____   _____   _____

© Houghton Mifflin Harcourt Publishing Company

Problem Solving

Write the correct answer.

1. Shania would like to give $5 gift cards and $4 teddy bears as party favors. Sixteen people have been invited to the party. Shania has $100 to spend on party favors. Write and graph an inequality to find the number of gift cards x and teddy bears y Shania could purchase.

_____

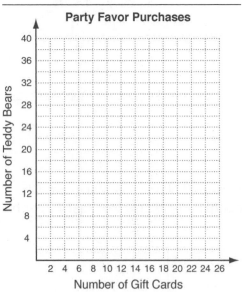
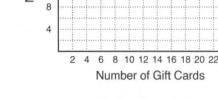

2. Hank has 20 yards of lumber that he can use to build a raised garden. Write and graph a linear inequality that describes the possible lengths and widths of the garden. If Hank wants the dimensions to be whole numbers only, what dimensions would produce the largest area?

_____

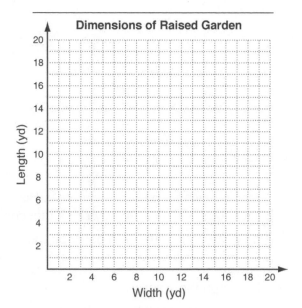

Select the best answer.

3. The royalties for the high school play are $250. Tickets to the play cost $5 for students and $8 for nonstudents. What linear inequality describes the number of student and nonstudent tickets that need to be sold so that the drama class can pay the royalties?

    A $5x + 8y \geq 250$ C $5xy + 8 < 250$

    B $5x + 8y > 250$ D $5xy + 8 \geq 250$

5. A baker is making chocolate and lemon pound cakes. He can make at most 12 cakes at one time. Which inequality describes the situation?

    A $x + y > 12$ C $x + y \leq 12$

    B $x + y \geq 12$ D $x + y < 12$

4. The inequality $x + y \leq 8$ describes the amounts of two juices Annette combines to make a smoothie. Which is a solution to the inequality?

    F (3, 6)   H (7, 2)

    G (6, 1)   J (0, 10)

6. Erasmus is the master gardener for a university. He wants to plant a mixture of purple and yellow pansies at the west entrance to the campus. From past experience, Erasmus knows that fewer than 350 pansies will fit in the planting area. Which inequality describes the situation?

    F $x + y \geq 350$ H $x + y \leq 350$

    G $x + y > 350$ J $x + y < 350$

© Houghton Mifflin Harcourt Publishing Company

Solving Systems of Linear Inequalities
Focus on Modeling

Essential question: *How can you use systems of linear equations or inequalities to model and solve contextual problems?*

GPS
COMMON
CORE

MCC9-12.N.Q.1*,
MCC9-12.N.Q.2*,
MCC9-12.A.CED.2*,
MCC9-12.A.CED.3*,
MCC9-12.A.REI.6,
MCC9-12.A.REI.12

Y ou are purchasing jeans and T-shirts. Jeans cost $35 and T-shirts cost $15. You plan on spending $115 and purchasing a total of 5 items. How many pairs of jeans and how many T-shirts can you buy?

1 **Write a system of linear equations to model the situation.**

A Write an expression to represent the amount you will pay for x pairs of jeans at $35 per pair.

_____

B Write an expression to represent the amount you will pay for y T-shirts at $15 per shirt.

_____

C The total amount spent for jeans and T-shirts is given below in words. Use this verbal model and your expressions from Steps 1A and 1B to write an equation for the total amount you will spend.

Amount Spent for Jeans	+	Amount Spent for T-shirts	=	Total Amount Spent
	+		=	

D What variable represents the number of pairs of jeans purchased?

_____

E What variable represents the number of T-shirts purchased?

_____

F Write an equation to represent the total number of items purchased.

_____

G Write a system of linear equations to model the situation.

_____

© Houghton Mifflin Harcourt Publishing Company

1a. What units are associated with the expressions that you wrote in 1A and 1B?

_____

_____

1b. When you add the units for the expressions representing the amounts spent on jeans and T-shirts, what units do you get for total amount spent? Are they the units you expect?

_____

_____

2 **Solve the system algebraically.**

A Solve an equation for one variable.

$x + y = 5$ Select one of the equations.

$y = $ ▢   Isolate the variable y on one side.

B Substitute the expression for y into the other equation and solve.

$35x + 15 \left(\right) = 115$ Substitute the expression for the variable y.

$35x + + 75 = 115$ Use the Distributive Property.

$ + 75 = 115$ Combine like terms.

$ = 40$ Subtract ____ from each side.

$x = $ Divide each side by _____.

C Substitute the value of the variable you found in Part B into one of the equations and solve for the other variable.

$ + y = 5$ Substitute the value you found into an equation.

$y = $ Subtract ____ from each side.

So, _____ is the solution of the system.

2a. In the solution, what does the x-value of the ordered pair represent in the context of the situation? What does the y-value represent?

_____

2b. Explain why substitution is a good method to use to solve this system.

_____

_____

© Houghton Mifflin Harcourt Publishing Company

3 Check the solution by graphing.

A Graph each equation.

Step 1: Find the intercepts for $35x + 15y = 115$ and graph the line.

x-intercept: _____   *y*-intercept: _____

Step 2: Find the intercepts for $x + y = 5$ and graph the line.

x-intercept: _____   *y*-intercept: _____

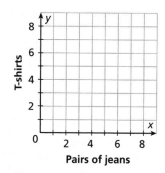

Pairs of jeans

B Find the point of intersection.

The two lines appear to intersect at _____ .

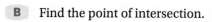

REFLECT

3a. What units are represented on the *x*-axis?

_____

3b. What units are represented on the *y*-axis?

_____

3c. Does the solution you found by graphing confirm that the solution you found algebraically was correct? Explain.

_____

_____

3d. Was it easier to solve the system algebraically or by graphing? Explain your reasoning.

_____

_____

4 Interpret the solution.

A What does the solution tell you about the number of pairs of jeans and the number of T-shirts you can purchase?

_____

B In the context of the problem, what could be the values of *x* and *y*?

_____

C Is the solution reasonable? Explain your reasoning.

_____

_____

_____

© Houghton Mifflin Harcourt Publishing Company

4a. Is the solution you found the only solution for this linear system? Explain how you know.

_____

_____

EXTEND

1. Suppose you want to buy at least 5 items and spend no more than $115. How can you modify the system of linear equations you wrote to model this new situation?

_____

_____

2. Write an inequality to represent buying at least 5 items.

_____

3. Write an inequality to represent spending no more than $115.

_____

4. Are there any other conditions on the system, based on the context of the problem? If so, what are they?

_____

_____

5. Write a system of linear inequalities to model the situation. Include any new conditions from Question 4.

_____

6. What constraints do the additional conditions based on the context of the problem place on where in the plane the solution region will be located?

_____

© Houghton Mifflin Harcourt Publishing Company

7. Graph the system of inequalities.

Step 1 Graph $x + y \geq 5$.

The equation of the boundary line is _____.

x-intercept: _____   **y-intercept:** _____

The inequality symbol is $\geq$, use a _____ line.

Shade _____ the boundary line, because $(0, 0)$ is *not* a solution of the inequality.

Step 2 Graph $35x + 15y \leq 115$.

The equation of the boundary line is _____.

x-intercept: _____   **y-intercept:** _____

The inequality symbol is $\leq$, use a _____ line.

Shade _____ the boundary line line, because $(0, 0)$ *is* a solution of the inequality.

Step 3 Identify the solutions.

The solutions of the system are represented by the _____ shaded regions that form a _____ to the _____ of the y-axis.

8. In the context of the situation, are all points in the overlapping shaded region possible solutions? Why or why not? Explain.

_____

_____

9. Is the ordered pair that was the solution of the system of linear equations for this situation a solution of this system of inequalities?

_____

_____

10. If you buy at least 5 items and spend no more than $115, what is the greatest number of jeans you can buy? Explain your reasoning.

_____

_____

11. If you buy at least 5 items and spend no more than $115, what is the greatest number of T-shirts you can buy? Explain your reasoning.

_____

_____

© Houghton Mifflin Harcourt Publishing Company

12. Use the graph to make a list of all the possible solutions for the number of pairs of jeans and number of T-shirts you can purchase if you buy at least 5 items and spend no more than $115.

Pairs of Jeans	T-Shirts	Total Items	Total Cost

© Houghton Mifflin Harcourt Publishing Company

Additional Practice

Tell whether the ordered pair is a solution of the given system.

1. $(2, -2); \begin{cases} y < x - 3 \\ y > -x + 1 \end{cases}$

2. $(2, 5); \begin{cases} y > 2x \\ y \geq x + 2 \end{cases}$

3. $(1, 3); \begin{cases} y \leq x + 2 \\ y > 4x - 1 \end{cases}$

_____   _____   _____

Graph the system of linear inequalities. a. Give two ordered pairs that are solutions. b. Give two ordered pairs that are not solutions.

4. $\begin{cases} y \leq x + 4 \\ y \geq -2x \end{cases}$

5. $\begin{cases} y \leq \frac{1}{2}x + 1 \\ x + y < 3 \end{cases}$

6. $\begin{cases} y > x - 4 \\ y < x + 2 \end{cases}$

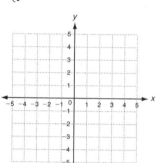
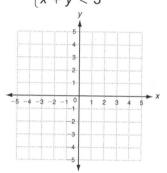
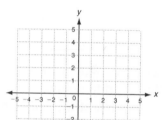

a. _____   a. _____   a. _____

b. _____   b. _____   b. _____

7. Charlene makes $10 per hour babysitting and $5 per hour gardening. She wants to make at least $80 a week, but can work no more than 12 hours a week.

   a. Write a system of linear equations.

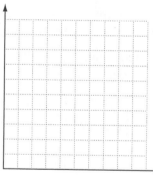

   _____

   b. Graph the solutions of the system.

   c. Describe all the possible combinations of hours that Charlene could work at each job.

   _____

   _____

   d. List two possible combinations. _____

   _____

© Houghton Mifflin Harcourt Publishing Company

Problem Solving

Write the correct answer.

1. Paul earns $7 per hour at the bagel shop and $12 per hour mowing lawns. Paul needs to earn at least $120 per week, but he must work less than 30 hours per week. Write and graph the system of linear inequalities that describes this situation.

_____

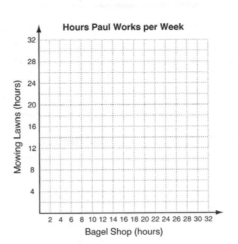

2. Zoe plans to knit a scarf. She wants the scarf to be more than 1 but less than 1.5 feet wide, and more than 6 but less than 8 feet long. Graph all possible dimensions of Zoe's scarf. List two possible combinations.

_____

_____

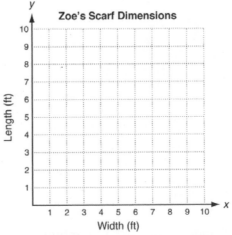

The graph shows the numbers of two types of custom wood tables that can be made to fit a client's needs. Select the best answer.

3. Which system of linear inequalities represents the graph?

A $\begin{cases} x + y \le 15 \\ y \ge 12 - \dfrac{4}{3}x \end{cases}$ C $\begin{cases} x + y \ge 15 \\ y \ge \dfrac{4}{3}x - 12 \end{cases}$

B $\begin{cases} y \le x + 15 \\ y \ge 12 - \dfrac{4}{3}x \end{cases}$ D $\begin{cases} y \le 15 - x \\ y \le \dfrac{4}{3}x - 12 \end{cases}$

4. If 6 buffet tables are built, which can NOT be the number of dining tables built?

F 4   H 8

G 6   J 10

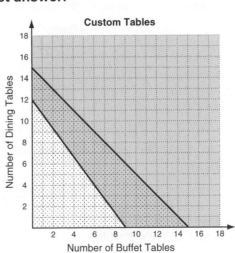

© Houghton Mifflin Harcourt Publishing Company

UNIT 2

Performance Tasks

GPS
COMMON
CORE

MCC9-12.A.CED.3
MCC9-12.A.CED.4
MCC9-12.A.REI.3
MCC9-12.A.REI.5

★ 1. Astronomers talk about the *luminosity* of a star, which is a measure of how much energy the star puts out, and the *brightness* of a star, which is a measure of how intense the star's light is. The formula $b = \frac{L}{4\pi d^2}$ relates the brightness b of a star to its luminosity L and its distance from the Earth, d.

a. Solve the equation for L.

b. If d is measured in meters and b is measured in watts per meter squared, what units is L measured in?

★ 2. Sariq's last four test scores in history were 87, 85, 91, and 88. What scores on his next test will give him an average of 90 or above? Write and solve an inequality. Show your work.

★ 3. A theater company put on a play, and charged the prices shown in the table for tickets.

Ticket Prices		
Child	Adult	Senior
$2.50	$6.00	$3.50

a. Write an equation for the total revenue R for C children, A adults, and S seniors.

b. There were 4 times as many adults as children, and half as many seniors as adults. Write expressions for the number of children and the number of seniors in terms of the number of adults.

c. Rewrite your equation from part **a** in terms of A, the number of adults.

© Houghton Mifflin Harcourt Publishing Company

d. If the company made a total of $301.50, how many children attended? Explain how you found your answer.

4. Students are raising money for a field trip by selling scented candles and specialty soap. The candles cost $0.75 each and will be sold for $1.75, and the soap costs $1.25 per bar and will be sold for $3.25. The students need to raise at least $200 to cover their trip costs.

a. Write an inequality that relates the number of candles c and the number of bars of soap s to the needed income.

b. The wholesaler can supply no more than 80 bars of soap and no more than 140 candles. Graph the inequality from part **a** and these constraints, using number of candles for the vertical axis.

c. What does the shaded area of your graph represent?

© Houghton Mifflin Harcourt Publishing Company

Name _____ Class _____ Date _____

SELECTED RESPONSE

1. Find the solution set for $8x - 3 = 2(x - \frac{1}{2})$.

   F. $\left\{-\frac{1}{3}\right\}$ **H.** $\left\{\frac{1}{3}\right\}$

   G. $\left\{\frac{1}{5}\right\}$ **J.** $\left\{\frac{2}{5}\right\}$

2. Tia spent $15 on skating. This included a $5 charge for renting skates and a $2.50 per hour fee for skating. Which equation can be solved to find the number of hours t that Tia spent skating?

   A. $5 = 2.5t + 15$

   B. $5 = 15t + 2.5$

   C. $15 = 2.5t + 5$

   D. $15 = 5t + 2.5$

3. Solve $q = \frac{r}{2}(s + t)$ for t.

   F. $t = \frac{qr}{2} - s$ **H.** $t = \frac{2q}{r} - s$

   G. $t = \frac{2q - s}{r}$ **J.** $t = \frac{q}{2r} - s$

4. Solve $V = \frac{1}{3}\pi r^2 h$ for h.

   A. $h = \frac{3V}{\pi r^2}$ **C.** $h = \frac{\pi V}{3r^2}$

   B. $h = \frac{3\pi V}{r^2}$ **D.** $h = r\sqrt{\frac{3V}{\pi}}$

5. Given $-\frac{1}{3}x - \frac{2}{3} \geq 7x + 3$, which property is used below?

   $$3\left(-\frac{1}{3}x - \frac{2}{3}\right) \geq 3(7x + 3)$$

   F. Distributive Property

   G. Multiplication Property of Inequality

   H. Subtraction Property of Inequality

   J. Associative Property of Multiplication

6. A 130-pound woman burns 9.83 Calories per minute while running. She burns 3.25 Calories per minute while walking during her cool-down. She runs for t minutes and exercises for a total of 45 minutes. Write an inequality to represent the amount of time she has to run to burn at least 100 Calories.

A. $100 \leq\, = 9.83t + 3.25(45 - t)$

B. $100 \leq\, = 9.83t + 3.25(t - 45)$

C. $100 \leq\, = 9.83t + 3.25t$

D. $100 \leq\, = 9.83(t - 45) + 3.25t$

7. Which graph represents the solution of the inequality $2x - 5 \leq -3$?

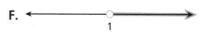

8. It costs $5 to have a tote bag monogrammed with up to 12 letters and $.50 for each additional letter. A club has a budget of $8 maximum per tote bag. Write an inequality for the number of additional letters that the club can have monogrammed on a tote bag.

   A. $5 + 0.5x > 8$ **C.** $5 + 0.5x < 8$

   B. $5 + 0.5x \geq 8$ **D.** $5 + 0.5x \leq 8$

9. Which system of linear equations is represented by the graph shown below?

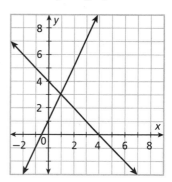

F. $\begin{cases} x + y = 4 \\ 2x + y = 1 \end{cases}$ **H.** $\begin{cases} x - y = 4 \\ 2x - y = -1 \end{cases}$

G. $\begin{cases} x + y = 4 \\ 2x - y = -1 \end{cases}$ **J.** $\begin{cases} x + y = 4 \\ x - 2y = 1 \end{cases}$

© Houghton Mifflin Harcourt Publishing Company

10. You are purchasing paint and paintbrushes for an art project. Tubes of paint cost $6 each and paintbrushes cost $8 each. You plan on spending $60 and purchasing a total of 9 items. Which linear system best represents the situation?

A. $\begin{cases} 6x + 8y = 9 \\ x + y = 60 \end{cases}$ C. $\begin{cases} 9x + 9y = 60 \\ 6x + 8y = 60 \end{cases}$

B. $\begin{cases} 6x + 9y = 60 \\ 9x + 8y = 60 \end{cases}$ D. $\begin{cases} x + y = 9 \\ 6x + 8y = 60 \end{cases}$

CONSTRUCTED RESPONSE

11. Keira is asked to solve the inequality $4a + 7 < -3$ and $4a + 7 > 2$. Using number sense she immediately answers that there is no solution. How can she tell that there is no solution without solving algebraically?

_____

_____

_____

_____

12. Pilar says that the two linear systems below have the same solution.

$\begin{cases} 3x + 2y = 2 \\ 5x + 4y = 6 \end{cases}$ $\begin{cases} 3x + 2y = 2 \\ 11x + 8y = 10 \end{cases}$

Is she correct? Explain.

_____

_____

_____

_____

_____

_____

13. Graph the solution to $3x - 4y \leq 1$.

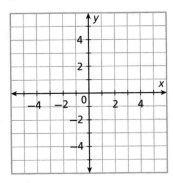

14. The art club at Lily's school has had 300 calendars printed to sell as a fundraiser. It costs the art club $4 per calendar to have the calendars printed and the club sells them for $10 per calendar. The art club's profit $P(n)$ is given by the following function, where n represents the number of calendars sold.

$$P(n) = 10n - 1200$$

a. What does the term "$10n$" represent? What are its units? Explain your reasoning using unit analysis.

_____

_____

_____

_____

b. What does the term "1200" represent? Explain your reasoning.

_____

_____

_____

_____

c. What is the maximum profit the art club can earn? Explain.

_____

_____

_____

_____

© Houghton Mifflin Harcourt Publishing Company

Linear and Exponential Functions

GPS
COMMON
CORE

© Houghton Mifflin Harcourt Publishing Company

Unpacking the Standards

Understanding the standards and the vocabulary terms in the standards will help you know exactly what you are expected to learn in this unit.

GPS COMMON CORE MCC9-12.F.IF.4

For a function that models a relationship between two quantities, interpret key features of graphs and tables in terms of the quantities, and sketch graphs showing key features given a verbal description of the relationship.

What It Means For You

Learning to interpret a graph enables a deep visual understanding of all sorts of relationships.

EXAMPLE
A group of friends walked to the town market, did some shopping there, then returned home

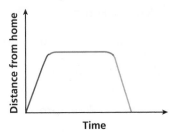

GPS COMMON CORE MCC9-12.F.IF.6

Calculate and interpret the average rate of change of a function (presented symbolically or as a table) over a specified interval. Estimate the rate of change from a graph.

Key Vocabulary
rate of change *(tasa de cambio)*
A ratio that compares the amount of change in a dependent variable to the amount of change in an independent variable.

What It Means For You

Average rate of change measures the change in the dependent variable against the change in the independent variable over a specific interval. This helps you understand how quickly the values in a function change.

EXAMPLE

Time (hours)	1	2	3	4
Distance (miles)	60	120	180	240

Average rate of change $= \frac{180 - 60}{3 - 1} = 60$ mi/h

© Houghton Mifflin Harcourt Publishing Company

© Houghton Mifflin Harcourt Publishing Company; Photo credit: © Comstock/Photolibrary/Getty Images

MCC9-12.F.BF.2

Write arithmetic and geometric sequences both recursively and with an explicit formula, use them to model situations, and translate between the two forms.

Key Vocabulary

arithmetic sequence *(sucesión aritmética)* A sequence whose successive terms differ by the same nonzero number *d*, called the *common difference*.

geometric sequence *(sucesión geométrica)* A sequence in which the ratio of successive terms is a constant *r*, called the *common ratio*, where $r \neq 0$ and $r \neq 1$.

recursive formula *(fórmula recurrente)* A formula for a sequence in which one or more previous terms are used to generate the next term.

What It Means For You

You can write rules for arithmetic and geometric sequences as a function of the term number or with respect to the previous term. You can use the form that is more useful for a particular situation.

EXAMPLE **Explicit and Recursive Formulas**

In the geometric sequence below, each term is twice the previous term. So, the common ratio is $r = 2$.

$$
\begin{array}{cccc}
1 & 2 & 3 & 4 \quad \leftarrow \text{Position, } n \\
\downarrow & \downarrow & \downarrow & \downarrow \\
3 & 6 & 12 & 24 \quad \leftarrow \text{Term, } a_n \\
a_1 & a_2 & a_3 & a_4
\end{array}
$$

Explicit formula: $a_n = a_1 r^{n-1}$, so $a_n = 3 \cdot 2^{n-1}$

Recursive formula: The recursive formula gives the first term and for finding successive terms:
$a_n = a_{n-1} r$, so $a_1 = 3$, $a_n = 2a_{n-1}$

MCC9-12.F.LE.2

Construct linear and exponential functions, including arithmetic and geometric sequences, given a graph, a description of a relationship, or two input-output pairs (include reading these from a table).

What It Means For You

You can construct a model of a linear or exponential function from different descriptions or displays of the same situation.

EXAMPLE **Geometric Sequence**

A ball is dropped 81 inches onto a hard surface. The table shows the ball's height on successive bounces. Write a model for the height reached as a function of the number of bounces.

Bounce	1	2	3	4
Height (in.)	54	36	24	16

Consecutive terms have a common ratio of $\frac{2}{3}$. You can write a model as an exponential function or as a geometric sequence:

Exponential function: $f(x) = 81\left(\frac{2}{3}\right)^x$, where *x* is the bounce number

Geometric sequence: $a_1 = 54$, $a_n = \frac{2}{3} a_{n-1}$, where *n* is the bounce number

UNIT 3

Key Vocabulary

arithmetic sequence *(sucesión aritmética)* A sequence whose successive terms differ by the same nonzero number d, called the *common difference*.

common difference *(diferencia común)* In an arithmetic sequence, the nonzero constant difference of any term and the previous term.

common ratio *(razón común)* In a geometric sequence, the constant ratio of any term and the previous term.

dependent variable *(variable dependiente)* The output of a function; a variable whose value depends on the value of the input, or independent variable.

direct variation *(variación directa)* A linear relationship between two variables, x and y, that can be written in the form $y = kx$, where k is a nonzero constant.

domain *(dominio)* The set of all first coordinates (or x-values) of a relation or function.

exponential decay *(decremento exponencial)* An exponential function of the form $f(x) = ab^x$ in which $0 < b < 1$. If r is the rate of decay, then the function can be written $y = a(1 - r)^t$, where a is the initial amount and t is the time.

exponential function *(función exponencial)* A function of the form $f(x) = ab^x$, where a and b are real numbers with $a \neq 0$, $b > 0$, and $b \neq 1$.

exponential growth *(crecimiento exponencial)* An exponential function of the form $f(x) = ab^x$ in which $b > 1$. If r is the rate of growth, then the function can be written $y = a(1 + r)^t$, where a is the initial amount and t is the time.

function *(función)* A relation in which every domain value is paired with exactly one range value.

function notation *(notación de función)* If x is the independent variable and y is the dependent variable, then the function notation for y is $f(x)$, read "f of x," where f names the function.

geometric sequence *(sucesión geométrica)* A sequence in which the ratio of successive terms is a constant r, called the *common ratio*, where $r \neq 0$ and $r \neq 1$.

independent variable *(variable independiente)* The input of a function; a variable whose value determines the value of the output, or dependent variable.

linear function *(función lineal)* A function that can be written in the form $y = mx + b$, where x is the independent variable and m and b are real numbers. Its graph is a line.

range of a function or relation *(rango de una función o relación)* The set of all second coordinates (or y-values) of a function or relation.

recursive formula *(fórmula recurrente)* A formula for a sequence in which one or more previous terms are used to generate the next term.

reflection *(reflexión)* A transformation that reflects, or "flips," a graph or figure across a line, called the line of reflection.

rotation *(rotación)* A transformation that rotates or turns a figure about a point called the center of rotation.

slope *(pendiente)* A measure of the steepness of a line. If (x_1, y_1) and (x_2, y_2) are any two points on the line, the slope of the line, known as m, is represented by the equation $m = \frac{y_2 - y_1}{x_2 - x_1}$.

translation *(traslación)* A transformation that shifts or slides every point of a figure or graph the same distance in the same direction.

Graphing Relationships
Going Deeper

Essential question: *How can you describe a relationship given a graph and sketch a graph given a description?*

Video Tutor

MCC9–12.F.IF.4

1 **EXPLORE** Interpreting Graphs

The outside temperature varies throughout the day. The graph shows the outside temperature for a day at one location from midnight to midnight.

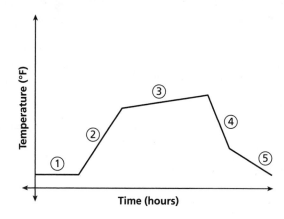

A Segment 1 shows that the temperature from midnight to sunrise stayed constant. Describe what Segment 2 shows.

_____

B Based on the time frame, give a possible explanation for the change in temperature represented by Segment 2.

_____

C Which segments of the graph show decreasing temperatures? Give a possible explanation.

_____

REFLECT

1a. Explain how the slope of each segment of the graph is related to whether the temperature increases or decreases.

_____
_____
_____
_____

© Houghton Mifflin Harcourt Publishing Company

2 EXPLORE   Match Graphs to Situations

On three days in September, Atlanta received the same amount of rainfall.

- On September 8, it rained very hard during the morning, but then rained less and less as the day went on.
- On September 19, it rained steadily all day.
- On September 27, it rained lightly during the morning, but then rained heavily for the rest of the day.

Match each day's rain with the correct graph.

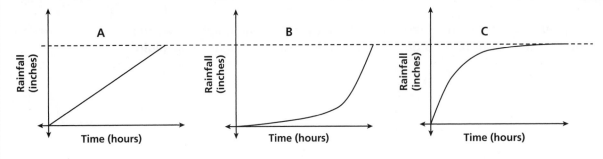

_____   _____   _____

A Describe the rainfall represented by Graph A.

_____

B Describe the rainfall represented by Graph B.

_____

_____

C Describe the rainfall represented by Graph C.

_____

_____

D Determine which graph represents each day's rainfall and write the dates under the appropriate graphs.

REFLECT

2a. Could a graph of rainfall throughout a day ever slant downward from left to right? Explain.

_____

_____

_____

© Houghton Mifflin Harcourt Publishing Company

3 EXPLORE   Sketching a Graph for a Situation

The pool in a community park is being filled for the summer. A water truck arrives early in the morning, but no water is put from it into the pool for one hour because a small repair must be made to the pool first. The spigot on the water truck is then opened partially to add water gradually to the pool during the next two hours.

A Sketch a graph showing the height of the water in the pool over the first three hours that the water truck is at the pool.

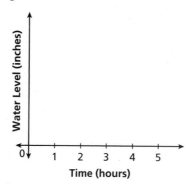

B The workers determine that the repair they made to the pool is working, so they completely open the spigot on the water truck to continue filling the pool. How do you think this will affect the water level in the pool?

_____

C Considering your answer to **B**, sketch a graph showing the height of the water in the pool during the first six hours that the water truck is at the pool.

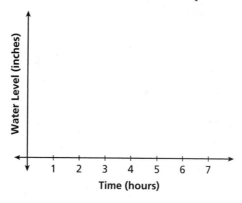

REFLECT

3a. Suppose a second water truck arrived at the end of 4 hours to also add water to the pool. How do you think this would affect the water level of the pool? How would it affect the water level if the second truck were the same type and size as the first truck?

_____

_____

3b. How would your answer to **3a** affect the graph?

_____

_____

© Houghton Mifflin Harcourt Publishing Company

PRACTICE

A hot air balloon rises as the air inside it is heated to a temperature greater than that of the surrounding air. During a balloon trip, the pilot controls the height of the balloon by adjusting the burning of propane fuel to change the temperature of the air inside the balloon. The graph shows the height of a balloon over time.

1. During which phase is the change in height greatest? Explain.

_____

_____

_____

2. What happens to to the balloon's height during Phase 4?

_____

_____

_____

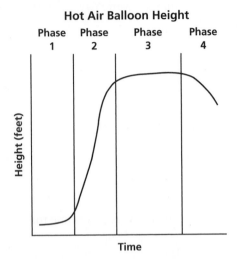

Hot Air Balloon Height

Phase 1 Phase 2 Phase 3 Phase 4

Height (feet)

Time

Scientists in a lab are conducting an experiment on a bacteria colony that causes its mass to fluctuate. The graph describes the changes in the colony's mass over time.

3. What happened to the bacteria colony's mass before time *t*?

_____

_____

_____

4. Suppose at time *t*, a second colony of bacteria is added to the first. Draw a new graph to show how this action might affect the mass of the bacteria colony after time *t*.

5. Suppose at some point after time *t*, scientists add a substance to the colony that destroys some of the bacteria. Describe how your graph from problem **4** might change.

_____

_____

_____

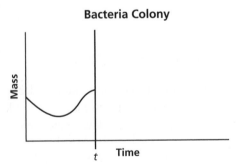

Bacteria Colony

Mass

Time

t

Bacteria Colony

Mass

t Time

© Houghton Mifflin Harcourt Publishing Company

Additional Practice

Choose the graph that best represents each situation.

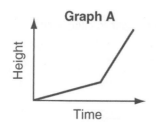

Graph A

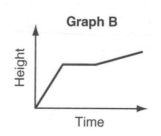

Graph B

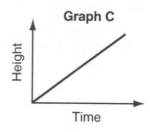

Graph C

1. A tomato plant grows taller at a steady pace.

_____

2. A tomato plant grows quickly at first, remains a constant height during a dry spell, then grows at a steady pace.

_____

3. A tomato plant grows at a slow pace, then grows rapidly with more sun and water.

_____

4. Lora has $15 to spend on movie rentals for the week. Each rental costs $3. Sketch a graph to show how much money she might spend on movies in a week. Tell whether the graph is continuous or discrete.

_____

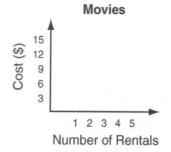

Write a possible situation for each graph.

5.

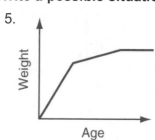

_____
_____
_____
_____

6.

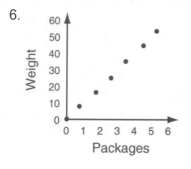

_____
_____
_____
_____

© Houghton Mifflin Harcourt Publishing Company

Problem Solving

Sketch a graph for the given situation. Tell whether the graph is discrete or continuous.

1. A giraffe is born 6 feet tall and continues to grow at a steady rate until it is fully grown.

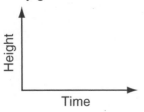

2. The price of a used car is discounted $200 each week.

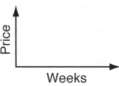

3. A city planner buys more buses as the population of her city grows.

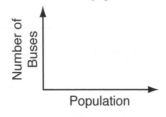

4. Joseph is sky-diving. At first, he is free-falling rapidly and then he releases his parachute to slow his descent until he reaches the ground.

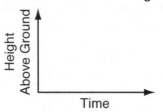

Choose the graph that best represents the situation.

5. Rebekah turns on the oven and sets it to 300 °F. She bakes a tray of cookies and then turns the oven off.

   A Graph 1   C Graph 3
   B Graph 2   D Graph 4

6. Leon puts ice cubes in his soup to cool it down before eating it.

   F Graph 1   H Graph 3
   G Graph 2   J Graph 4

7. Barlee has the flu and her temperature rises slowly until it reaches 101 °F.

   A Graph 1   C Graph 3
   B Graph 2   D Graph 4

8. On a hot day, Karin walks into and out of an air-conditioned building.

   F Graph 1   H Graph 3
   G Graph 2   J Graph 4

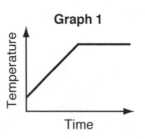

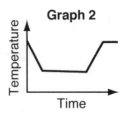

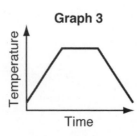

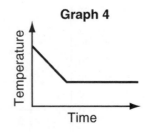

© Houghton Mifflin Harcourt Publishing Company

Relations and Functions
Going Deeper

Essential question: *How do you represent functions?*

MCC9–12.F.IF.1

1 ENGAGE   Understanding Functions

Video Tutor

A *set* is a collection of items called *elements*. A **function** pairs each element in one set, called the **domain**, with exactly one element in a second set, called the **range**. For example, the function below pairs each element in the domain with its square.

Domain   Range

A function can be described using **function notation**. The function f assigns the *output* value $f(x)$ in the range to the corresponding *input* value x from the domain. The notation $f(x)$ is read as "f of x." (It does not indicate the product "f times x.") For the function shown above, $f(3) = 9$.

REFLECT

1a. The domain of the function can be written using *set notation* as {0, 1, 2, 3, 4}. Write the range of the function using set notation.

_____

1b. Tell how to read the statement $f(4) = 16$. Then interpret what it means in terms of input and output values.

_____

1c. Suppose the 3 were paired with the 4 instead of the 9. Would the pairing of the two sets still be a function? Why or why not?

_____

1d. Suppose the 3 were paired with the 4 and the 9. Would the pairing of the two sets still be a function? Why or why not?

_____

1e. If you pair each month with all the possible numbers of days in the month, will you get a function? Why or why not?

_____

_____

© Houghton Mifflin Harcourt Publishing Company

Functions are often used to describe a relationship between two variables. The **independent variable** represents an input value of the function and the **dependent variable** represents an output value.

An algebraic expression that defines a function is a **function rule** . For example, x^2 is the function rule for the squaring function $f(x) = x^2$. If you know a value for the independent variable, you can use a function rule to find the corresponding value for the dependent variable.

MCC9–12.F.IF.2

2 EXAMPLE   Representing Discrete Linear Functions

The cost of sending m text messages at \$0.25 per message can be represented by the function $C(m) = 0.25m$.

A Complete the table for the given domain values. Write the results as ordered pairs in the form (independent variable, dependent variable).

Independent variable, *m*	Dependent variable, *C(m)* = 0.25*m*	(*m, C(m)*)
0	0.25(0) = 0	(0, 0)
1		
2		
3		
4		

B Choose a beginning, an end, and a scale for the vertical axis.

_____

C Graph the function by plotting the ordered pairs. The independent variable goes on the horizontal axis and the dependent variable on the vertical axis. Use scales that will make it easy to read points. Label the graph.

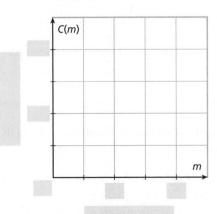

© Houghton Mifflin Harcourt Publishing Company

2a. Use function notation to represent the cost of sending 15 text messages. Evaluate the function for that value. Include units.

_____

2b. Suppose that the domain of the function is not limited as in the Example. Describe a reasonable domain of the function.

_____

_____

2c. Suppose that the domain of the function is not limited as in the Example. Describe a reasonable range of the function.

_____

_____

2d. Is the independent variable represented by the *horizontal axis* or the *vertical axis*? Why does this make sense?

_____

_____

_____

2e. Would it make sense to connect the points on the graph with a line? Why or why not?

_____

_____

2f. The figure below shows a representation of the function rule. Explain what is being shown in the context of the situation.

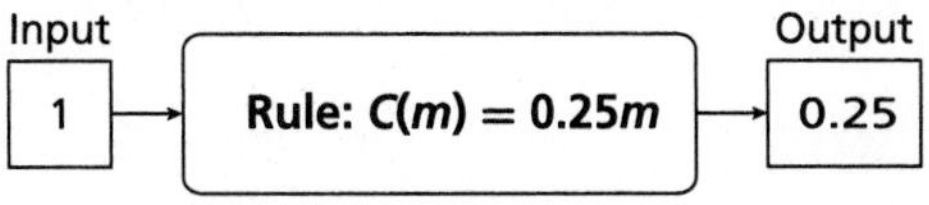

Input		Output
1	**Rule:** $C(m) = 0.25m$	0.25

_____

_____

_____

2g. Suppose the cost per text message were $0.20 instead of $0.25. Then the cost of sending m text messages could be represented by the function $C(m) = 0.2m$. Describe a reasonable domain and range for this function.

_____

_____

© Houghton Mifflin Harcourt Publishing Company

3 EXAMPLE   Representing Discrete Nonlinear Functions

Ben wants to tile part of a floor with 36 square tiles. The tiles come in whole-number side lengths from 2 to 6 inches. If s is the side length of a tile, the area that he can cover is $A(s) = 36s^2$.

A   Identify the domain of the function.

_____

B   Make a table of values for this domain. Write the results as ordered pairs in the form (independent variable, dependent variable).

Independent variable, s	Dependent variable, $A(s) = 36s^2$	$(s, A(s))$

C   Choose a beginning, an end, and a scale for the vertical axis.

_____

D   Graph the function by plotting the ordered pairs.

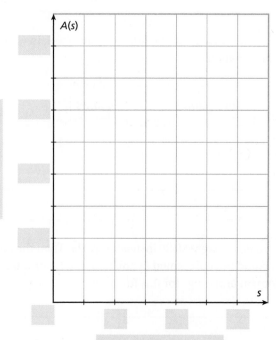

© Houghton Mifflin Harcourt Publishing Company

3a. Identify the range of the function.

_____

3b. What does $A(3) = 324$ mean in this context?

_____

_____

3c. Describe another reasonable beginning, end, and scale for the vertical axis. Include units.

_____

3d. Do the points appear to lie in a straight line?

_____

PRACTICE

Tell whether each pairing of numbers describes a function. If so, identify the domain and the range. If not, explain why not.

1. Each whole number from 0 to 9 is paired with its opposite.

_____

2. Each odd number from 3 to 9 is paired with the next greater whole number.

_____

3. The whole numbers from 10 to 12 are paired with their factors.

_____

_____

4. Each even number from 2 to 10 is paired with half the number.

_____

5. $\{(36, 6), (49, 7), (64, 8), (81, 9), (36, -6), (49, -7), (64, -8), (81, -9)\}$

_____

6. $\{(-64, -4), (-27, -3), (-8, -2), (-1, -1), (0, 0), (1, 1), (8, 2), (27, 3), (64, 4)\}$

_____

_____

© Houghton Mifflin Harcourt Publishing Company

7. Whitley has a $5 gift card for music downloads. Each song costs $1 to download. The amount of money left on the card can be represented by the function $M(d) = 5 - d$, where d is the number of songs she has downloaded.

a. Make a table and graph the function.

d	M(d)	(d, M(d))

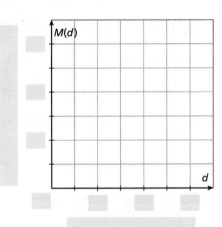

b. Identify the domain and range of the function and the units of the independent and dependent variables.

_____

_____

8. Ben wants to cover a table that has an area of 864 square inches. The function $T(s) = \frac{864}{s^2}$ gives the number of tiles he needs with side length s. The tiles come in side lengths of 1 in., 4 in., 6 in., and 12 in.

a. Make a table and graph the function.

s	T(s)	(s, T(s))

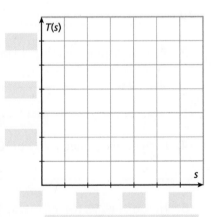

b. Identify the domain and range of the function and the units of the independent and dependent variables.

_____

_____

© Houghton Mifflin Harcourt Publishing Company

Additional Practice

Express each relation as a table, as a graph, and as a mapping diagram.

1. {(−5, 3), (−2, 1), (1, −1), (4, −3)}

x	y

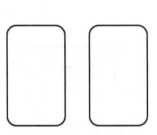

2. {(4, 0) (4, 1), (4, 2), (4, 3), (4, 4), (4, 5)}

x	y

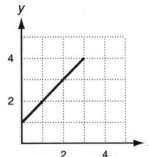

Give the domain and range of each relation. Tell whether the relation is a function. Explain.

3.

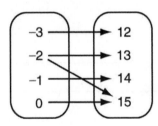

4.

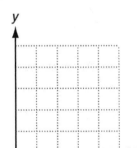

5.

x	y
8	8
6	6
4	4
2	6
0	8

D: _____   D: _____   D: _____

R: _____   R: _____   R: _____

Function? _____   Function? _____   Function? _____

Explain: _____   Explain: _____   Explain: _____

_____   _____   _____

_____   _____   _____

_____   _____   _____

© Houghton Mifflin Harcourt Publishing Company

Problem Solving

Give the domain and range of each relation and tell whether it is a function.

1. The mapping diagram shows the ages *x* and grade level *y* of four children.

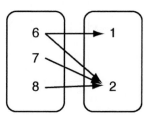

2.

Age *x*	Shoe Size *y*
6	8
9	10
12	10
15	10.5
18	11

_____

_____

_____

_____

_____

_____

3. The list represents the number of cars sold and the bonus received by the salespeople of a car dealership.

   {(1, 50), (2, 50), (3, 100), (4, 150)}

_____

_____

_____

4. A 2-inch-tall plant grows at a rate of 2.5 inches every week for 5 weeks. Let *x* represent the number of weeks and *y* represent the height of the plant.

_____

_____

_____

Use the graph below to answer questions 5–6. A conservation group has been working to increase the population of a herd of Asian elephants. The graph shows the results of their efforts. Select the correct answer.

5. Which relation represents the information in the graph?

   A {(1, 4.5), (2, 6), (3, 10), (4, 14.5)}

   B {(1, 5), (2, 6), (3, 10), (4, 15)}

   C {(4.5, 1), (6, 2), (10, 3), (14.5, 4)}

   D {(5, 1), (6, 2), (10, 3), (15, 4)}

6. What is the range of the relation shown in the graph?

   F {0, 1, 2, 3, 4, 5}

   G {1, 2, 3, 4}

   H {4.5, 6, 10, 14.5}

   J {5, 6, 10, 15}

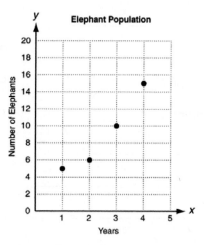

© Houghton Mifflin Harcourt Publishing Company

Writing Functions
Extension: Function Operations and Inverses

Essential question: *How can you use operations to combine functions and how can you find inverses of functions?*

Just as you can perform operations with numbers, you can perform operations with functions. In this lesson you will add and subtract linear functions as well as multiply a linear function by a nonzero constant function. Performing an operation on two functions $f(x)$ and $g(x)$ produces a new function $h(x)$.

Video Tutor

MCC9–12.F.BF.1b

1 EXAMPLE Performing Operations with Functions

A Given $f(x) = 3x - 1$ and $g(x) = -2x + 2$, find $h(x) = f(x) + g(x)$.

$h(x) = f(x) + g(x)$ Write the general form of $h(x)$.

$= (3x - 1) + \left(\boxed{}\right)$ Substitute the rules for $f(x)$ and $g(x)$.

$= \left(3x + \boxed{}\right) + \left(-1 + \boxed{}\right)$ Collect like terms for adding.

$= \boxed{} + \boxed{}$ Simplify.

B Given $f(x) = x + 5$ and $g(x) = 4x - 2$, find $h(x) = f(x) - g(x)$.

$h(x) = f(x) - g(x)$ Write the general form of $h(x)$.

$= (x + 5) - \left(\boxed{}\right)$ Substitute the rules for $f(x)$ and $g(x)$.

$= \left(x - \boxed{}\right) + \left(5 - \boxed{}\right)$ Collect like terms for subtracting.

$= \boxed{} + \boxed{}$ Simplify.

C Given $f(x) = 3$ and $g(x) = \frac{1}{3}x - 2$, find $h(x) = f(x) \cdot g(x)$.

$h(x) = f(x) \cdot g(x)$ Write the general form of $h(x)$.

$= \boxed{} \left(\frac{1}{3}x - 2\right)$ Substitute the rules for $f(x)$ and $g(x)$.

$= \boxed{} - \boxed{}$ Multiply using the distributive property.

REFLECT

1a. The table shows the values of the sum $f(x) + g(x)$ for several values of x using the functions $f(x)$ and $g(x)$ from part A. Use the rule that you found for $h(x)$ in part A to complete the third column of the table. What do you notice?

_____

x	$f(x) + g(x)$	$h(x)$
-2	$-7 + 6 = -1$	
-1	$-4 + 4 = 0$	
0	$-1 + 2 = 1$	
1	$2 + 0 = 2$	
2	$5 + (-2) = 3$	

© Houghton Mifflin Harcourt Publishing Company

1b. Error Analysis A student wrote the rule for $h(x)$ in part A as $5x + 1$. After letting $x = 0$ and observing that $f(0) + g(0) = -1 + 2 = 1$ and $h(0) = 1$, the student concluded that the rule must be correct. Describe what is incorrect about the student's reasoning, and describe what the student should have done to check the rule for $h(x)$.

_____

_____

_____

MCC9–12.F.BF.1b

2 EXAMPLE **Adding Linear Models**

For the initial year of a soccer camp, 44 girls and 56 boys enrolled. Each year thereafter, 5 more girls and 8 more boys enrolled in the camp. Let t be the time (in years) since the camp opened. Write a rule for each of the following functions:

- $g(t)$, the number of girls enrolled as a function of time t
- $b(t)$, the number of boys enrolled as a function of time t
- $T(t)$, the total enrollment as a function of time t

A For the function $g(t)$, the initial value is _____ and the rate of change is _____. So, $g(t) =$ _____.

B For the function $b(t)$, the initial value is _____ and the rate of change is _____. So, $b(t) =$ _____.

C The total enrollment is the sum of the functions $g(t)$ and $b(t)$.

$T(t) = g(t) + b(t)$ Write the general form of $T(t)$.

$=$ [   ] $+$ [   ] Substitute the rules for $g(t)$ and $b(t)$.

$=$ [   ] Simplify.

REFLECT

2a. Use unit analysis to show that the rule for $g(t)$ makes sense.

_____

_____

_____

© Houghton Mifflin Harcourt Publishing Company

3 EXAMPLE **Multiplying Linear Models**

For the soccer camp in the previous example, the cost per child each year was $200. Let t be the time (in years) since the camp opened. Write a rule for each of the following functions:

- $C(t)$, the cost per child of the camp as a function of time t
- $R(t)$, the revenue generated by the total enrollment as a function of time t

A For the function $C(t)$, the initial value is _____ and the rate of change

is _____. So, $C(t) = $ _____.

B The revenue generated by the total enrollment is the product of the cost function $C(t)$ and the total enrollment function $T(t)$, which was found in the previous example.

$R(t) = C(t) \cdot T(t)$ — Write the general form of $R(t)$.

$= $ _____ $\cdot ($ _____ $)$ — Substitute the rules for $C(t)$ and $T(t)$.

$= $ _____ — Multiply using the distributive property.

REFLECT

3a. Explain why $C(t)$ is a constant function.

_____

3b. Use unit analysis to explain why you multiply the cost function $C(t)$ and the enrollment function $T(t)$ to get the revenue function $R(t)$.

_____

_____

_____

3c. What was the initial revenue for the camp? What was the annual rate of change in the revenue?

_____

3d. The camp's organizer had initial expenses of $18,000, which increased each year by $2,500. Write a rule for the expenses function $E(t)$. Then write a rule for the profit function $P(t)$ based on the fact that profit is the difference between revenue and expenses.

_____

© Houghton Mifflin Harcourt Publishing Company

Recall that inverse operations are operations that undo each other. Similarly, the **inverse of a function** is another function that undoes everything that the original function does.

MCC9–12.F.BF.4a

4 EXPLORE Using Inverse Operations to Find Inverse Functions

Find the inverse of $f(x) = 2x + 1$ using inverse operations.

A List the operations that the function performs on an input value x in the order that the function performs them. Illustrate these steps using $x = 3$.

x ⟶ Multiply by 2. ⟶ _____

3 ⟶ $2 \cdot 3 = 6$ ⟶ _____

B List the *inverse operations* in the *reverse order*. Illustrate these steps using $x = 7$.

x ⟶ Subtract 1. ⟶ _____

7 ⟶ $7 - 1 = 6$ ⟶ _____

C Write a rule for the function $g(x)$ that performs the inverse operations in the reverse order. Check your rule by finding $g(7)$.

$$g(x) = \frac{x - \boxed{}}{\boxed{}}, \text{ so } g(7) = \frac{7 - \boxed{}}{\boxed{}} = \boxed{}$$

REFLECT

4a. The first table at the right shows some input-output pairs for the function f. The outputs of f are then listed as inputs for the function g in the second table. Complete the second table.

4b. The function g is the inverse of the function f. If $f(a) = b$, then what is $g(b)$?

_____

4c. Is it reasonable to describe f as the inverse of g? Explain.

_____

x	f(x)
−2	−3
0	1
2	5

x	g(x)
−3	
1	
5	

© Houghton Mifflin Harcourt Publishing Company

To find the rule for the inverse of a linear function f, let $y = f(x)$ and solve for x in terms of y. Whatever sequence of operations f performs on x to obtain y, the process of solving for x will introduce the inverse operations in the reverse order. You now have a function g where $g(y) = x$. Since x is commonly used as a function's input variable and y as its output variable, as a final step switch x and y to obtain $g(x) = y$.

MCC9–12.F.BF.4a

5 EXAMPLE   Finding the Inverse by Solving $y = f(x)$ for x

Find the inverse of $f(x) = \frac{1}{2}x - 1$.

A Let $y = f(x)$. Solve for x in terms of y.

$$y = \boxed{} \qquad\qquad \text{Write } y = f(x).$$

$$y + \boxed{} = \boxed{} \qquad\qquad \text{Add 1 to both sides.}$$

$$\boxed{}\left(y + \boxed{}\right) = \boxed{} \qquad\qquad \text{Multiply both sides by 2.}$$

$$\boxed{}\,y + \boxed{} = \boxed{} \qquad\qquad \text{Distribute.}$$

B Switch x and y and then write the rule for the inverse function g.

$$\boxed{}\,x + \boxed{} = \boxed{} \qquad\qquad \text{Switch } x \text{ and } y.$$

The inverse of $f(x) = \frac{1}{2}x - 1$ is $g(x) = $ _____.

REFLECT

5a. Find $f(4)$. Then use this value as the input x for $g(x)$. What output value do you get? Why is this expected?

_____

_____

5b. When solving $y = f(x)$ for x, you multiplied both sides by 2 instead of dividing both sides by $\frac{1}{2}$. In other words, instead of using an *inverse operation*, you used a *multiplicative inverse*. Why is this acceptable?

_____

_____

5c. When you switch x and y to find the inverse function, are you solving the function for y? Why or why not?

_____

_____

© Houghton Mifflin Harcourt Publishing Company

5d. The graph of $f(x) = \frac{1}{2}x - 1$ is shown. Graph the inverse function g. Also graph $y = x$ as a dashed line. How are the graphs of f and g related to the line $y = x$?

_____

_____

$f(x) = \frac{1}{2}x - 1$

5e. The point $(4, 1)$ is on the graph of f. What is the corresponding point on the graph of g? In general, if (a, b) is a point on the graph of f, what is the corresponding point on the graph of g?

_____

MCC9–12.F.BF.4a

6 **EXAMPLE** **Finding Inverses of Real-World Functions**

The function $A(r) = 2r + 30$ gives the total amount A that you will spend at an amusement park if you spend \$30 on admission and food and you go on r rides that cost \$2 each. Find the inverse function.

$A = 2r + 30$ Write the function using A for $A(r)$.

$A - \boxed{} = \boxed{}$ Subtract 30 from both sides.

$\dfrac{A - \boxed{}}{\boxed{}} = r$ Divide both sides by 2.

REFLECT

6a. Write the inverse function using function notation.

_____

6b. Explain how the inverse function would be useful if you have a fixed amount of money that you can spend at the amusement park.

_____

_____

_____

6c. When finding the inverse of a real-world function, why shouldn't you switch the variables as the final step?

_____

_____

© Houghton Mifflin Harcourt Publishing Company

1. Given $f(x) = -2x$ and $g(x) = 4x - 8$, find $h(x) = f(x) + g(x)$.

_____

2. Given $f(x) = 3x - 5$ and $g(x) = -2x + 1$, find $h(x) = f(x) - g(x)$.

_____

3. Given $f(x) = -2$ and $g(x) = 5x - 6$, find $h(x) = f(x) \cdot g(x)$.

_____

4. Given $f(x) = 4$, $g(x) = x + 1$, and $h(x) = x$, find $j(x) = f(x) \cdot [g(x) + h(x)]$.

_____

5. To raise funds, a club is publishing and selling a calendar. The club has sold $500 in advertising and will sell copies of the calendar for $20 each. The cost of printing each calendar is $6. Let c be the number of calendars to be printed and sold.

  a. Write a rule for the function $R(c)$, which gives the revenue generated by the sale of the calendars.

  _____

  b. Write a rule for the function $E(c)$, which gives the expense of printing the calendars.

  _____

  c. Describe how the function $P(c)$, which gives the club's profit from the sale of the calendars, is related to $R(c)$ and $E(c)$. Then write a rule for $P(c)$.

  _____

6. The five winners of a radio station contest will spend a day at an amusement park with all expenses paid. The per-person admission cost is $10, and each person can spend $20 on food. The radio station will pay for all rides, which cost $2 each. Assume that each person takes the same number r of rides.

  a. Write a rule for the function $C(r)$, which gives the cost per person.

  _____

  b. Write a rule for the function $P(r)$, which gives the number of people.

  _____

  c. Describe how the function $T(r)$, which gives the radio station's total cost, is related to $C(r)$ and $P(r)$. Then write a rule for $T(r)$.

  _____

© Houghton Mifflin Harcourt Publishing Company

Find the inverse g(x) of each function.

7. $f(x) = x - 1$

8. $f(x) = -x + 4$

9. $f(x) = 2x - 3$

_____

_____

_____

10. $f(x) = \frac{2}{3}x + 6$

11. $f(x) = 3x - \frac{3}{4}$

12. $f(x) = -\frac{5}{2}x - \frac{15}{2}$

_____

_____

_____

13. The formula to convert a temperature F measured in degrees Fahrenheit to a temperature C measured in degrees Celsius is $C = \frac{9}{5}(F - 32)$. You can think of this formula as function $C(F)$. Find the inverse function $F(C)$ and describe what it does.

_____

14. A cylindrical candle 10 inches tall burns at rate of 0.5 inch per hour.

a. Write a rule for the function $h(t)$, the height (in inches) of the candle at time t (in hours since the candle was lit). State the domain and range of the function.

_____

b. Find the inverse function $t(h)$. State the domain and range of the function.

_____

c. Explain how the inverse function is useful.

_____

_____

15. Prove that the inverse of a non-constant linear function is another non-constant linear function by starting with the general linear function $f(x) = mx + b$ where $m \neq 0$ and showing that the inverse function $g(x)$ is also linear. Identify the slope and y-intercept of the graph of $g(x)$.

_____

16. Can a constant function have an inverse function? Why or why not?

_____

_____

© Houghton Mifflin Harcourt Publishing Company

Additional Practice

For each pair of functions, find $f(x) + g(x)$ and $f(x) - g(x)$.

1. $f(x) = 3x + 2$, $g(x) = 2x + 5$

2. $f(x) = 4x - 1$, $g(x) = 3x - 4$

3. $f(x) = -5x + 3$, $g(x) = 2x - 4$

4. $f(x) = 3x - 4$, $g(x) = -2x + 3$

For each pair of functions, find $f(x) \cdot g(x)$.

5. $f(x) = -x + 7$, $g(x) = -2$

6. $f(x) = -5$, $g(x) = 2x - 7$

Find the inverse of the function.

7. $f(x) = 3x + 9$

8. $f(x) = 5x - 2$

9. $f(x) = -x + 2$

10. $f(x) = -4x + 3$

11. $f(x) = 0.5x - 2$

12. $f(x) = -0.25x + 6$

© Houghton Mifflin Harcourt Publishing Company

Problem Solving

Write the correct answer.

1. Over time, the enrollment at one high school in a city can be modeled by $f(t) = 32t + 1255$. The enrollment at the city's other high school can be modeled by $g(t) = 27t + 1380$. Write a rule for the total enrollment as a function of time.

   _____

2. Use the functions from Problem 1 to find the difference in the enrollments between the two high schools. Write the answer using two different functions.

   _____

   _____

3. The function $f(x) = 50x + 6500$ represents the amount of money in a bank account over time. The function $g(x) = -25x + 9300$ represents the amount of money in another account over time. Write a rule for the total amount of money in the two accounts over time.

   _____

4. Use the functions from Problem 3 to find the difference in the amounts of money between the two accounts. Write the answer using two different functions.

   _____

   _____

Select the best answer.

5. The enrollment at a summer camp over time can be represented by $f(x) = 24x + 465$. The cost to attend the camp is $500 per summer. Write a rule for the amount of money the camp makes over time.

   A $g(x) = 24x + 965$

   B $g(x) = 24x + 232{,}500$

   C $g(x) = 12{,}000x + 465$

   D $g(x) = 12{,}000x + 232{,}500$

6. Find the inverse of the function $f(x) = 0.25x + 12$.

   F $g(x) = -0.25x - 12$

   G $g(x) = -4x - 12$

   H $g(x) = 4x - 48$

   J $g(x) = 4x + 48$

7. Four friends go to an amusement arcade. The cost to get in is $5 per person and the cost of each game is $2. The cost per person can be represented by the function $c(x) = 2x + 5$. Write a rule for the total cost for the four friends if they all play the same number of games.

   A $T(x) = 5x + 8$

   B $T(x) = 8x + 20$

   C $T(x) = 2x + 20$

   D $T(x) = 20x + 5$

8. Find the inverse of the function $f(x) = -\dfrac{2}{3}x - 18$.

   F $g(x) = \dfrac{3}{2}x + 27$

   G $g(x) = -\dfrac{3}{2}x + 27$

   H $g(x) = -\dfrac{3}{2}x - 27$

   J $g(x) = \dfrac{3}{2}x - 27$

© Houghton Mifflin Harcourt Publishing Company

Graphing Functions
Extension: Piecewise Functions

Essential question: *How are piecewise functions and their graphs different from other functions?*

A **piecewise function** has different rules for different parts of its domain. The **greatest integer function** is a piecewise function whose rule is denoted by $[\![x]\!]$, which represents the greatest integer less than or equal to x. To evaluate a piecewise function for a given value of x, substitute the value of x into the rule for the part of the domain that includes x.

Video Tutor

MCC9–12.F.IF.2

1 **EXAMPLE** **Evaluating Piecewise Functions**

A Find $f(-3), f(-0.2), f(0)$, and $f(2)$ for $f(x) = \begin{cases} -x & \text{if } x < 0 \\ x+1 & \text{if } x \geq 0 \end{cases}$.

$-3 < 0$, so use the rule $f(x) = -x$: $\qquad f(-3) = -(-3) = $ _____

$-0.2 < 0$, so use the rule _____: $\qquad f(-0.2) = -(-0.2) = $ _____

$0 \geq 0$, so use the rule $f(x) = x + 1$: $\qquad f(0) = 0 + 1 = $ _____

$2 \geq 0$, so use the rule _____: $\qquad f(2) = $ _____ = _____

B Find $f(-3), f(-2.9), f(0.7)$, and $f(1.06)$ for $f(x) = [\![x]\!]$.

The greatest integer function $f(x) = [\![x]\!]$ can also be written as shown below. Complete the rules for the function before evaluating it.

$$f(x) = \begin{cases} \vdots \\ -3 & \text{if } -3 \leq x < -2 \\ \boxed{} & \text{if } -2 \leq x < -1 \\ -1 & \text{if } \boxed{} \leq x < \boxed{} \\ \boxed{} & \text{if } 0 \leq x < 1 \\ 1 & \text{if } \boxed{} \leq x < \boxed{} \\ 2 & \text{if } \boxed{} \leq x < \boxed{} \\ \vdots \end{cases}$$

← For any number x that is less than -2 and greater than or equal to -3, the greatest of the integers less than or equal to x is -3.

-3 is in the interval $-3 \leq x < -2$, so $f(-3) = -3$.

-2.9 is in the interval $-3 \leq x < -2$, so $f(-2.9) = $ _____.

0.7 is in the interval _____, so $f(0.7) = $ _____.

1.06 is in the interval _____, so $f(1.06) = $ _____.

© Houghton Mifflin Harcourt Publishing Company

REFLECT

1a. Why should the parts of the domain of a piecewise function $f(x)$ have no common x-values?

_____

_____

1b. For positive numbers, how is applying the greatest integer function different from the method of rounding to the nearest whole number?

_____

_____

_____

MCC9–12.F.IF.7b

2 EXAMPLE **Graphing Piecewise Functions**

Graph each function.

A $f(x) = \begin{cases} -x & \text{if } x < 0 \\ x + 1 & \text{if } x \geq 0 \end{cases}$

Complete the table. Use the values to help you complete the graph. Extend the pattern to cover the entire domain on the grid.

x	−3	−2	−1	−0.9	−0.1
f(x)	3	2		0.9	

x	0	0.1	0.9	1	2
f(x)	1	1.1			3

The transition from one rule, $-x$, to the other, $x + 1$, occurs at $x = 0$. Show an open dot at $(0, 0)$ because the point is not part of the graph. Show a closed dot at $(0, 1)$ because the point is part of the graph.

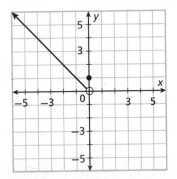

B $f(x) = [\![x]\!]$

Complete the table. Use the values to help you complete the graph. Extend the pattern to cover the entire domain on the grid.

x	−4	−3.9	−3.1	−3	−2.9
f(x)	−4	−4		−3	

x	−2.1	−2	−1.5	−1	0
f(x)		−2			0

x	1	1.5	2	3	4
f(x)					4

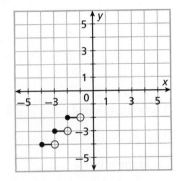

© Houghton Mifflin Harcourt Publishing Company

Lesson 1

2a. Why does the first graph use rays and not lines?

_____

_____

2b. The greatest integer function is an example of a **step function**, a piecewise function that is constant for each rule. Use the graph of the greatest integer function to explain why such a function is called a step function.

_____

_____

2c. Does the greatest integer function have a maximum or minimum value? Explain.

_____

_____

MCC9–12.A.CED.2

3 EXAMPLE Writing and Graphing a Piecewise Function

On his way to class from his dorm room, a college student walks at a speed of 0.05 mile per minute for 3 minutes, stops to talk to a friend for 1 minute, and then to avoid being late for class, runs at a speed of 0.10 mile per minute for 2 minutes. Write a piecewise function for the student's distance from his dorm room during this time. Then graph the function.

A Express the student's distance traveled d (in miles) as a function of time t (in minutes). Write an equation for the function $d(t)$.

$$d(t) = \begin{cases} \boxed{}\, t & \text{if } 0 \le t \le 3 \\ 0.15 & \text{if } 3 < t \le \boxed{} \\ 0.15 + 0.10\,(t-4) & \text{if } 4 < t \le \boxed{} \end{cases}$$

←He travels at 0.05 mile per minute for 3 minutes.

←Distance traveled is constant for 1 minute.

←Add the distance traveled at 0.10 mile per minute to the distance already traveled.

B Complete the table.

t	0	1	2	3
$d(t)$				

t	4	5	6
$d(t)$			

C Complete the graph.

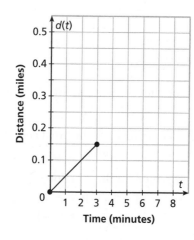

© Houghton Mifflin Harcourt Publishing Company

REFLECT

3a. Why is the second rule for the function $d(t) = 0.15$ instead of $d(t) = 0$?

____

3b. Why is the third rule for the function $d(t) = 0.15 + 0.10(t - 4)$?

____

____

MCC9–12.F.BF.1

4 EXAMPLE Writing a Function When Given a Graph

Write the equation for each function whose graph is shown.

A

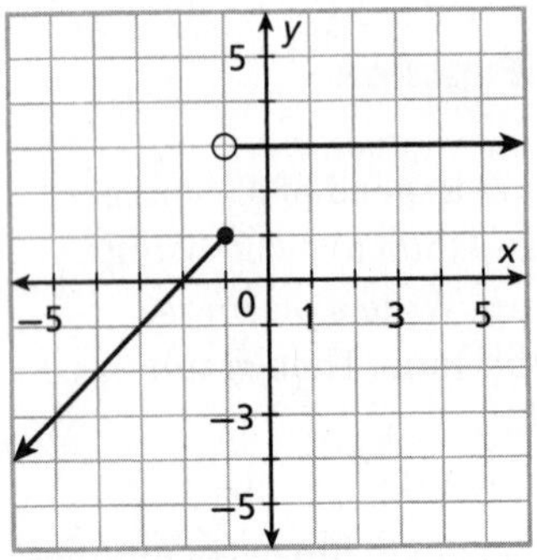

Find the equation for each ray:

- Make a table of values for the ray on the left.

x	y
−1	
−2	
−3	
−4	
−5	

The value of y is ____ more than the value of x. The equation is ____.

- The equation of the line that contains the horizontal ray is $y =$ ____.

The equation for the function is:

$$f(x) = \begin{cases} ____ & \text{if } x \le -1 \\ ____ & \text{if } x > -1 \end{cases}$$

B

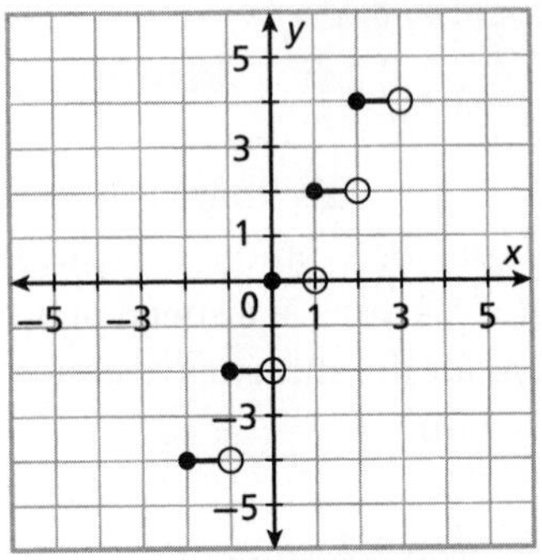

Write a rule for each horizontal line segment.

$$f(x) = \begin{cases} -4 & \text{if } -2 \le x < -1 \\ ____ & \text{if } -1 \le x < 0 \\ 0 & \text{if } 0 \le x < 1 \\ ____ & \text{if } 1 \le x < 2 \\ ____ & \text{if } 2 \le x < 3 \end{cases}$$

Although the graph shows the function's domain to be $-2 \le x < 3$, assume that the domain consists of all real numbers and that the graph continues its stair-step pattern for $x < -2$ and $x \ge 3$.

Notice that each function value is ________ times the corresponding value of the greatest integer function.

The equation for the function is:

$$f(x) = ____ [\![x]\!]$$

© Houghton Mifflin Harcourt Publishing Company

4a. When writing a piecewise function from a graph, how do you determine the domain of each rule?

_____

_____

4b. How can you use y-intercepts to check that your answer in part A is reasonable?

_____

_____

PRACTICE

Graph each function.

1. $f(x) = \begin{cases} -x + 1 & \text{if } x < 0 \\ x & \text{if } x \geq 0 \end{cases}$

2. $f(x) = \begin{cases} -1 & \text{if } x < 1 \\ 2x - 2 & \text{if } x \geq 1 \end{cases}$

3. $f(x) = [\![x]\!] + 1$

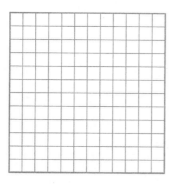

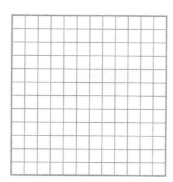

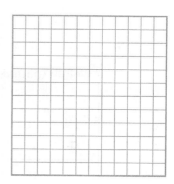

Write the equation for each function whose graph is shown.

4.

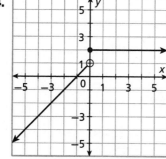

5.

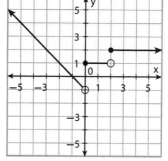

6.

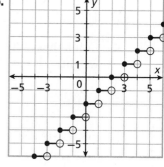

© Houghton Mifflin Harcourt Publishing Company

7. A garage charges the following rates for parking (with an 8 hour limit):

$3 per hour for the first 6 hours

No additional charge for the next 2 hours

a. Write a piecewise function that gives the parking cost *C* (in dollars) in terms of the time *t* (in hours) that a car is parked in the garage.

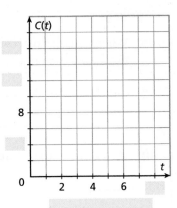

_____

b. Graph the function. Include labels to show what the axes represent and to show the scales on the axes.

8. The cost to send a package between two cities is $8.00 for any weight less than 1 pound. The cost increases by $4.00 when the weight reaches 1 pound and again each time the weight reaches a whole number of pounds after that.

a. For a package having weight *w* (in pounds), write a function in terms of $[\![w]\!]$ to represent the shipping cost *C* (in dollars).

_____

b. Complete the table.

Weight (pounds) *w*	Cost (dollars) *C(w)*
0.5	
1	
1.5	
2	
2.5	

c. Graph the function. Show the costs for all weights less than 5 pounds.

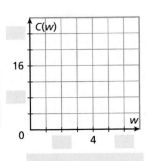

© Houghton Mifflin Harcourt Publishing Company

Additional Practice

Graph the function for the given domain.

1. $f(x) = \begin{cases} 2x + 1 \text{ if } x \le 0 \\ x - 3 \text{ if } x > 0 \end{cases}$

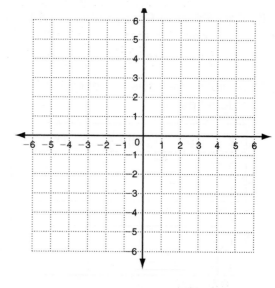

Graph the function.

2. $f(x) = \begin{cases} 3x - 2 \text{ if } x \le 3 \\ -2x + 5 \text{ if } x > 3 \end{cases}$

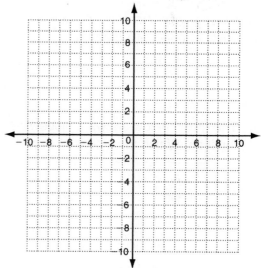

3. The cost for shipping a package is given by the step function $C(w) = [[\, w \,]] + 2$, where w is the weight of the package in pounds. Graph this function. Use the graph to find the cost of shipping a 6 pound package.

_____

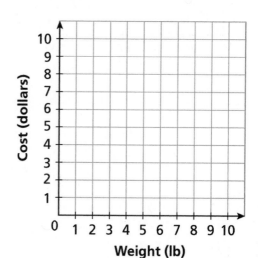

© Houghton Mifflin Harcourt Publishing Company

Problem Solving

City Park Parking Garage charges $4 per hour or part of an hour to park your car. The step function $C(x) = 4[[x]] + 4$ represents the cost of parking in the garage for x hours.

1. Complete the table by generating ordered pairs.

x	$C(x) = 4[[x]] + 4$	(x, y)
0		
1		
2		
3		
4		

2. Graph the function $C(x) = 4[[x]] + 4$.

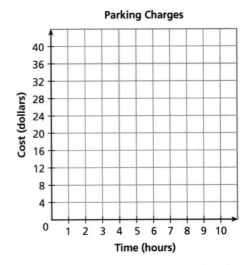

Parking Charges

3. Use the graph to estimate how much it costs to park for 3.5 hours.

_____

Select the correct answer.

4. The graph below shows a piecewise function. Which function is shown?

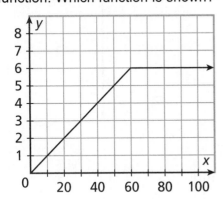

A $f(x) = \begin{cases} 0.1x \text{ if } 0 \le x < 6 \\ 6x \text{ if } x \ge 6 \end{cases}$

B $f(x) = \begin{cases} 0.1x \text{ if } 0 \le x < 6 \\ 6 \text{ if } x \ge 6 \end{cases}$

C $f(x) = \begin{cases} 10x \text{ if } 0 \le x < 6 \\ 6 \text{ if } x \ge 6 \end{cases}$

D $f(x) = \begin{cases} 10x \text{ if } 0 \le x < 6 \\ 6x \text{ if } x \ge 6 \end{cases}$

© Houghton Mifflin Harcourt Publishing Company

Exploring Transformations
Going Deeper

Essential question: *What patterns govern transformations of functions?*

MCC9–12.F.BF.3

1 EXPLORE   Translating Points

Translate the point (−2, 5) three units to the left and two units down.

To translate three units to the left, _____ 3 from the _____ -coordinate.

To translate two units down, _____ 2 from the _____ -coordinate.

Translating (−2, 5) three units to the left and two units down results in the

point _____.

REFLECT

1a. When you translate a point left or right, how do you change the coordinates of the point?

_____

1b. When you translate up or down, how do you change the coordinates of the point?

_____

MCC9–12.F.BF.3

2 EXAMPLE   Translating a Function

Translate the graph of *f(x)* three units to the left.

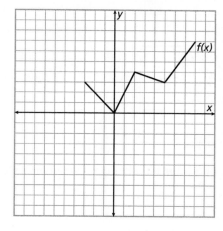

© Houghton Mifflin Harcourt Publishing Company

9-2

Video Tutor

2a. How do the x-coordinates of the points on the graph change after being shifted to the left?

_____

2b. How do the y-coordinates change after being shifted to the left?

_____

MCC9–12.F.IF.5

3 **EXAMPLE** **Reflecting a Function**

Reflect the graph of f(x) across the x-axis.

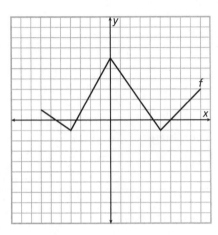

REFLECT

3a. Fill in the table to show how points on the graph of change after the graph is reflected over the x-axis.

Original Function	Transformation
(−7, 1)	
(−4, −1)	
(0, 6)	
(5, −1)	

3b. How do the y-coordinates of the points change after being reflected over the x-axis?

_____

3c. How do the x-coordinates of the points change after being reflected over the x-axis?

_____

© Houghton Mifflin Harcourt Publishing Company

4 EXAMPLE Stretching or Compressing a Function

Consider the transformations $(x, y) \rightarrow (2x, y)$ and $(x, y) \rightarrow \left(\frac{1}{2}x, y\right)$. You will use the tables below to see the effects of these transformations on the graph of $f(x) = x^2$. Complete the table with values of $2x$ and $\frac{1}{2}x$ that correspond to the given values of x.

$2x$	x	$y = x^2$	$\frac{1}{2}x$	x	$y = x^2$
	−2	4		−2	4
	−1	1		−1	1
	0	0		0	0
	1	1		1	1
	2	4		2	4

The graph of $f(x) = x^2$ is shown on the grids. Plot the points $(2x, y)$ from your table on the coordinate grid on the left. Connect them with a smooth curve. Do the same for the points $\left(\frac{1}{2}x, y\right)$ on the coordinate grid on the right.

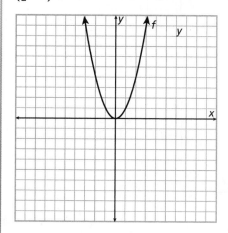 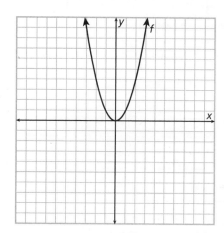

REFLECT

4a. A transformation of the form $(x, y) \rightarrow (ax, y)$ is a horizontal stretch or compression. Based on the graphs above, for what kinds of numbers a do you think that the transformation $(x, y) \rightarrow (ax, y)$ is a horizontal compression?

_____

4b. For what kinds of numbers a do you think that the transformation $(x, y) \rightarrow (ax, y)$ is a horizontal stretch?

_____

© Houghton Mifflin Harcourt Publishing Company

Perform the given translation on the point (5, −3) and give the coordinates of the translated point.

1. 6 units right

2. 2 units up

3. 1 unit right, 7 units down

_____

_____

_____

Use a table to perform each transformation of y = f(x).

4. translation 4 units up

Original Function	Transformation
(−5, 2)	
(−4, −1)	
(1, −1)	
(3, 3)	
(7, 3)	

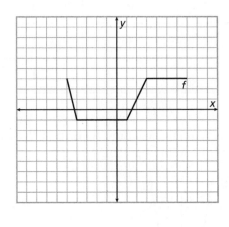

5. reflection across the y-axis

Original Function	Transformation
(−5, 0)	
(−3, 3)	
(0, 0)	
(2, −2)	
(6, 2)	

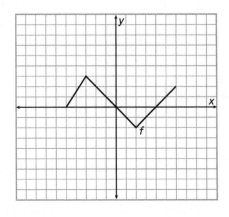

6. horizontal stretch by a factor of 4

Original Function	Transformation
(−4, 8)	
(−1, 2)	
(0, 0)	
(2, 2)	
(4, 4)	

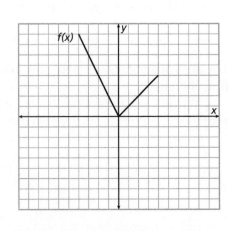

© Houghton Mifflin Harcourt Publishing Company

Additional Practice

Perform the given translation on the point (2, 5) and give the coordinates of the translated point.

1. left 3 units

2. down 6 units

3. right 4 units, up 2 units

_____ _____ _____

Use the table to perform each transformation of $y = f(x)$. Use the same coordinate plane as the original function.

4. translation left 1 unit, down 5 units

	x	y	
	−3	3	
	−1	1	
	1	2	
	2	1	
	3	2	

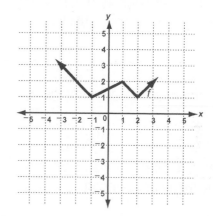

5. vertical stretch factor of $\dfrac{3}{2}$

	x	y	
	−3	3	
	−1	1	
	1	2	
	2	1	
	3	2	

6. horizontal compression factor of $\dfrac{1}{2}$

	x	y	
	−3	3	
	−1	1	
	1	2	
	2	1	
	3	2	

7. reflection across x-axis

	x	y	
	−3	3	
	−1	1	
	1	2	
	2	1	
	3	2	

Solve.

8. George has a goal for the number of computers he wants to sell each month for the next 6 months at his computer store. He draws a graph to show his projected profits for that period. Then he decides to discount the prices by 10%. How will this affect his profits? Identify the transformation to his graph and describe how to find the ordered pairs for the transformation.

_____

© Houghton Mifflin Harcourt Publishing Company

Problem Solving

Harry is working on a budget for a concert. The graph shows the total cost of renting the hall. A cleaning fee of $40 for each rental is included in the graph. Use the graph for Exercises 1–6.

1. What is the cost of renting the hall for 2 hours? for 3 hours? for 6 hours? for 7 hours?

_____

2. What is the rate per hour not including the cleaning fee if Harry rents the hall for up to 3 hours?

_____

3. What is the rate per hour after the first 3 hours?

_____

4. Describe the effect on the graph if the cleaning fee were changed to $25.

_____

5. The managers decide that the minimum time for which the hall can be rented is 3 hours. Describe the effect this change would have on the graph above. How would the range change?

_____

_____

Concert Hall Rental

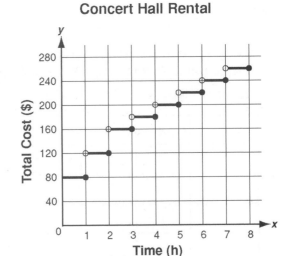

6. The Art Center gives Harry a graph showing its charges. This graph is the same shape as the graph above, but every point has been translated up 10 units. What would be the effect on Harry's budget if he chose to have the concert at the Art Center?

_____

_____

Choose the letter for the best answer.

7. Martha's profits from her bagel store last year were $0.35 per dozen bagels sold. This year her profits decreased 10%. What kind of transformation does this represent?

   A vertical compression

   B vertical stretch

   C horizontal compression

   D none of the above

8. Shana drew the graph for a quadratic function. Then she did a horizontal stretch of the curve. Which transformation did she perform?

   F $(x, y) \rightarrow (x, ay); |a| > 1$

   G $(x, y) \rightarrow (bx, y); 0 < |b| < 1$

   H $(x, y) \rightarrow (x, ay); 0 < |a| < 1$

   J $(x, y) \rightarrow (bx, y); |b| > 1$

© Houghton Mifflin Harcourt Publishing Company

9-3

Arithmetic Sequences
Going Deeper

Essential question: *Why is a sequence a function and how can you write a rule for an arithmetic sequence?*

MCC9–12.F.IF.3

1 ENGAGE   Understanding Sequences

Video Tutor

A **sequence** is an ordered list of numbers or other items. Each element in a sequence is called a **term**. For instance, in the sequence 1, 3, 5, 7, 9, ..., the second term is 3.

Each term in a sequence can be paired with a position number, and these pairings establish a function whose domain is the set of position numbers and whose range is the set of terms, as illustrated below. The position numbers are consecutive integers that typically start at either 1 or 0.

Position number	n	1	2	3	4	5	Domain
Term of sequence	$f(n)$	1	3	5	7	9	Range

For the sequence shown in the table, you can write $f(4) = 7$, which can be interpreted as "the fourth term of the sequence is 7."

REFLECT

1a. The domain of the function f defining the sequence 2, 5, 8, 11, 14, ... is the set of consecutive integers starting with 0. What is $f(4)$? Explain how you determined your answer.

_____

_____

1b. How does your answer to Question 1a change if the domain of the function is the set of consecutive integers starting with 1?

_____

1c. Predict the next term in the sequence 48, 42, 36, 30, 24, ... Explain your reasoning.

_____

_____

1d. Why is the relationship between the position numbers and the terms of a sequence a function?

_____

1e. Give an example of a sequence from your everyday life. Explain why your example represents a sequence.

_____

_____

© Houghton Mifflin Harcourt Publishing Company

Some numerical sequences can be described by using algebraic rules. An **explicit rule** for a sequence defines the nth term as a function of n.

MCC9–12.F.BF.2

2 EXAMPLE Using an Explicit Rule to Generate a Sequence

Write the first 4 terms of the sequence $f(n) = n^2 + 1$. Assume that the domain of the function is the set of consecutive integers starting with 1.

n	$n^2 + 1$	$f(n)$
1	$\boxed{}^2 + 1 = \boxed{} + 1$	$\boxed{}$
2	$\boxed{}^2 + 1 = \boxed{} + 1$	$\boxed{}$
3	$\boxed{}^2 + 1 = \boxed{} + 1$	$\boxed{}$
4	$\boxed{}^2 + 1 = \boxed{} + 1$	$\boxed{}$

The first 4 terms are _____.

REFLECT

2a. How could you use a graphing calculator to check your answer?

_____

2b. Explain how to find the 20th term of the sequence.

_____

A **recursive rule** for a sequence defines the nth term by relating it to one or more previous terms.

MCC9–12.F.BF.2

3 EXAMPLE Using a Recursive Rule to Generate a Sequence

Write the first 4 terms of the sequence with $f(1) = 3$ and $f(n) = f(n - 1) + 2$ for $n \geq 2$. Assume that the domain of the function is the set of consecutive integers starting with 1.

The first term is given: $f(1) = 3$. Use $f(1)$ to find $f(2)$, $f(2)$ to find $f(3)$, and so on. In general, $f(n - 1)$ refers to the term that precedes $f(n)$.

n	$f(n - 1) + 2$	$f(n)$
2	$f(2 - 1) + 2 = f(1) + 2 = 3 + 2$	$\boxed{}$
3	$f\left(\boxed{} - 1\right) + 2 = f\left(\boxed{}\right) + 2 = \boxed{} + 2$	$\boxed{}$
4	$f\left(\boxed{} - 1\right) + 2 = f\left(\boxed{}\right) + 2 = \boxed{} + 2$	$\boxed{}$

The first 4 terms are _____.

© Houghton Mifflin Harcourt Publishing Company

3a. Describe how to find the 12th term of the sequence.

_____

3b. Suppose you want to find the 50th term of a sequence. Would you rather use a recursive rule or an explicit rule? Explain your reasoning.

_____

_____

_____

In an **arithmetic sequence**, the difference between consecutive terms is constant. The constant difference is called the **common difference**, often written as d.

4 **E X A M P L E**   **Writing Rules for an Arithmetic Sequence**

The table shows end-of-month balances in a bank account that does not earn interest. Write a recursive and an explicit rule for the arithmetic sequence described by the table.

Month	n	1	2	3	4	5
Account Balance ($)	$f(n)$	60	80	100	120	140

A Find the common difference by calculating the differences between consecutive terms.

$80 - 60 =$ ⬜

$100 - 80 =$ ⬜

$120 - 100 =$ ⬜

$140 - 120 =$ ⬜

The common difference, d, is _____.

B Write a recursive rule for the sequence.

$f(1) =$ ⬜ and   The first term is _____.

$f(n) =$ ⬜ $+$ ⬜ for $n \geq 2$ Every other term is the _____ of the previous term and the common difference.

© Houghton Mifflin Harcourt Publishing Company

C Write an explicit rule for the sequence by writing each term as the sum of the first term and a multiple of the common difference.

n	$f(n)$
1	$60 + 20(0) = 60$
2	$60 + 20(1) = 80$
3	$60 + 20\left(\right) = 100$
4	$60 + 20\left(\right) = 120$
5	$60 + 20\left(\right) = 140$

Generalize the results from the table: $f(n) = \boxed{} + 20\left(n - \boxed{}\right)$

REFLECT

4a. Explain how you know that the sequence 1, 2, 4, 8, 16, … is not an arithmetic sequence.

_____

4b. An arithmetic sequence has a common difference of 3. If you know that the third term of the sequence is 15, how can you find the fourth term?

_____

MCC9–12.F.BF.2

5 EXPLORE   **Writing General Rules for Arithmetic Sequences**

Use the arithmetic sequence 6, 9, 12, 15, 18, … to help you write a recursive rule and an explicit rule for any arithmetic sequence. For the general rules, the values of n are consecutive integers starting with 1.

A Find the common difference.

Numbers

6, 9, 12, 15, 18, …

Common difference = $\boxed{}$

Algebra

$f(1), f(2), f(3), \boxed{}, \boxed{}, \ldots$

Common difference = d

B Write a recursive rule.

Numbers

$f(1) = \boxed{}$ and

$f(n) = f(n-1) + \boxed{}$ for $n \geq 2$

Algebra

Given $f(1)$,

$f(n) = f(n-1) + \boxed{}$ for $n \geq 2$

C Write an explicit rule.

Numbers

$f(n) = \boxed{} + \boxed{} (n-1)$

Algebra

$f(n) = \boxed{} + \boxed{} (n-1)$

© Houghton Mifflin Harcourt Publishing Company

REFLECT

5a. The first term of an arithmetic sequence is 4 and the common difference is 10. Explain how you can find the 6th term of the sequence.

_____

_____

5b. What information do you need to know in order to find the 8th term of an arithmetic sequence by using its recursive rule?

_____

5c. What is the recursive rule for the sequence $f(n) = 2 + (-3)(n - 1)$?

_____

MCC9–12.F.LE.2

6 EXAMPLE   Relating Arithmetic Sequences and Functions

The graph shows how the cost of a rafting trip depends on the number of passengers. Write an explicit rule for the sequence of costs.

Whitewater Rafting

Cost (dollars)

- (4, 150)
- (3, 125)
- (2, 100)
- (1, 75)

Passengers

A   Represent the sequence in a table.

n	1	2	3	4
$f(n)$				

B   Examine the sequence.

Is the sequence arithmetic? Explain how you know.

_____

What is the common difference? _____

C   Write an explicit rule for the sequence.

$f(n) = f(1) + d(n - 1)$ Write the general rule.

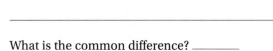   Substitute _____ for $f(1)$ and _____ for d.

So, the sequence has the rule _____, where n is the number of

passengers and $f(n)$ is the _____.

© Houghton Mifflin Harcourt Publishing Company

6a. An arithmetic sequence is equivalent to a function with a restricted domain. On the graph above, draw the line that passes through the given points. Then write a function of the form $f(n) = mn + b$ for the line that you drew and give the function's domain.

_____

6b. Show that the explicit rule for the sequence is equivalent to the function. Justify the steps you take.

_____

_____

_____

6c. A function of the form $f(n) = mn + b$ is called a *linear function* because its graph is a line. Using the line you drew, what is the relationship between m and the common difference of the arithmetic sequence?

_____

PRACTICE

Write the first four terms of each sequence. Assume that the domain of the function is the set of consecutive integers starting with 1.

1. $f(n) = (n - 1)^2$

_____

2. $f(n) = \dfrac{n + 1}{n + 3}$

_____

3. $f(n) = 4(0.5)^n$

_____

4. $f(n) = \sqrt{n - 1}$

_____

5. $f(1) = 2$ and $f(n) = f(n - 1) + 10$ for $n \geq 2$ _____

6. $f(1) = 16$ and $f(n) = \dfrac{1}{2} f(n - 1)$ for $n \geq 2$ _____

7. $f(1) = 1$ and $f(n) = 2f(n - 1) + 1$ for $n \geq 2$ _____

8. $f(1) = f(2) = 1$ and $f(n) = f(n - 2) - f(n - 1)$ for $n \geq 3$ _____

Write the 12th term of each sequence. Assume that the domain of the function is the set of consecutive integers starting with 1.

9. $f(n) = 3n - 2$ _____

10. $f(n) = 2n(n + 1)$ _____

© Houghton Mifflin Harcourt Publishing Company

Write an explicit rule for each sequence. Assume that the domain of the function is the set of consecutive integers starting with 1.

11.

n	f(n)
1	6
2	7
3	8
4	9
5	10

12.

n	f(n)
1	3
2	6
3	9
4	12
5	15

13.

n	f(n)
1	1
2	$\frac{1}{2}$
3	$\frac{1}{3}$
4	$\frac{1}{4}$
5	$\frac{1}{5}$

_____   _____   _____

Write a recursive rule for each sequence. Assume that the domain of the function is the set of consecutive integers starting with 1.

14.

n	f(n)
1	8
2	9
3	10
4	11
5	12

15.

n	f(n)
1	2
2	4
3	8
4	16
5	32

16.

n	f(n)
1	27
2	24
3	21
4	18
5	15

_____   _____   _____

_____   _____   _____

Write a recursive rule and an explicit rule for each arithmetic sequence.

17. 3, 7, 11, 15, …

_____

18. 19, 9, −1, −11, …

_____

19. 1, $\frac{5}{2}$, 4, $\frac{11}{2}$, …

_____

© Houghton Mifflin Harcourt Publishing Company

20. Carrie borrowed money interest-free to pay for a car repair. She is repaying the loan in equal monthly payments.

Monthly Payment Number	n	1	2	3	4	5
Loan Balance ($)	$f(n)$	840	720	600	480	360

   a. Explain how you know that the sequence of loan balances is arithmetic.

   _____

   b. Write recursive and explicit rules for the sequence of loan balances.

   _____

   c. How many months will it take Carrie to pay off the loan? Explain.

   _____

   d. How much did Carrie borrow? Explain.

   _____

21. The graph shows the lengths of the rows formed by various numbers of grocery carts when they are nested together.

   a. Write an explicit rule for the sequence of row lengths.

   _____

   b. What is the length of a row of 25 nested carts?

   _____

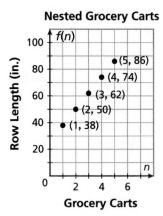

Nested Grocery Carts

22. Each stair on a staircase has a height of 7.5 inches.

   a. Write an explicit rule for an arithmetic sequence that gives the height (in inches) of the nth stair above the base of the staircase.

   _____

   b. What is the fourth term of the sequence, and what does it represent in this situation?

   _____

© Houghton Mifflin Harcourt Publishing Company

Additional Practice

Determine whether each sequence is an arithmetic sequence. If so, find the common difference and the next three terms.

1. −10, −7, −4, −1, …

2. 0, 1.5, 3, 4.5, …

_____

3. 5, 8, 12, 17, …

4. −20, −20.5, −21, −21.5, …

_____

Find the indicated term of each arithmetic sequence.

5. 28th term: 0, −4, −8, −12, …

6. 15th term: 2, 3.5, 5, 6.5, …

_____

7. 37th term: $a_1 = -3$; $d = 2.8$

8. 14th term: $a_1 = 4.2$; $d = -5$

_____

9. 17th term; $a_1 = 2.3$; $d = -2.3$

10. 92nd term; $a_1 = 1$; $d = 0.8$

_____

11. A movie rental club charges $4.95 for the first month's rentals. The club charges $18.95 for each additional month. How much is the total cost for one year? _____

12. A carnival game awards a prize if Kasey can shoot a basket. The charge is $5.00 for the first shot, then $2.00 for each additional shot. Kasey needed 11 shots to win a prize. What is the total amount Kasey spent to win a prize? _____

© Houghton Mifflin Harcourt Publishing Company

Problem Solving

Find the indicated term of each arithmetic sequence.

1. Darnell has a job and his saving his paychecks each week.

Weeks	1	2	3	4
Savings	$130	$260	$390	$520

   How much will Darnell have saved after 11 weeks?

   _____

3. A new car costs $13,000 and is depreciating by $900 each year. How much will the car be worth after 4 years?

   _____

2. A tube containing 3 ounces of toothpaste is being used at a rate of 0.15 ounces per day. How much toothpaste will be in the tube after one week?

   _____

4. Jessie is playing an arcade game that costs 50¢ for the first game and 25¢ to continue if she loses. How much will she spend on the game if she continues 9 times?

   _____

Use the graph below to answer questions 5–9. The graph shows the size of Ivor's ant colony over the first four weeks. Assume the ant population will continue to grow at the same rate. Select the best answer.

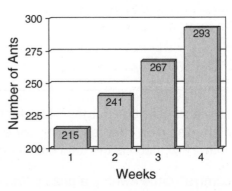

Ivor's Ant Farm

5. Which of the following shows how many ants Ivor will have in the next three weeks?

   A 315, 341, 367

   B 317, 343, 369

   C 318, 334, 350

   D 319, 345, 371

6. Which rule can be used to find how large the colony will be in *n* weeks?

   F $a_n = 215 + 26n$

   G $a_n = 215n + 26$

   H $a_n = 215(n - 1) + 26$

   J $a_n = 215 + 26(n - 1)$

7. How many ants will Ivor have in 27 weeks?

   A 891   C 5616

   B 917   D 5831

8. Ivor's ants weigh 1.5 grams each. How many grams do all of his ants weigh in 13 weeks?

   F 660.5   H 722

   G 683   J 790.5

9. When the colony reaches 1385 ants, Ivor's ant farm will not be big enough for all of them. In how many weeks will the ant population be too large?

   A 45   C 47

   B 46   D 48

© Houghton Mifflin Harcourt Publishing Company

Identifying Linear Functions
Extension: Discrete and Continuous Functions

Essential question: *What is a discrete linear function and how are discrete and continuous linear functions alike and how are they different?*

MCC9–12.F.IF.5

1 EXPLORE Analyzing a Discrete Real-World Function

Video Tutor

You buy a printer for $80 and then pay $15 for each ink cartridge that you use. A function relating the cost, C (in dollars), of operating the printer to the number of cartridges used, n, is $C(n) = 15n + 80$.

A Complete the table to represent the total cost for 0 to 4 cartridges.

Number of cartridges, n	Cost, C (dollars)
0	
1	
2	
3	
4	

B Graph the function from Part A. Specify the scale you use.

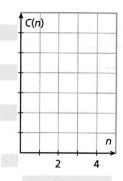

C What is the initial value of the cost function? What does it represent? What number of cartridges corresponds to the initial cost?

_____

D Compare the differences in cost with each unit increase in the number of cartridges purchased.

_____

_____

REFLECT

1a. Identify the domain and range for the function $C(n)$ using set notation.

Domain: _____   Range: _____

1b. Describe the pattern formed by the points in the graph.

_____

© Houghton Mifflin Harcourt Publishing Company

1c. How do your answers change if the price of the printer is $90?

_____

_____

_____

MCC9–12.F.IF.3

2 ENGAGE   Recognizing Linear Functions

A function whose output values have a *common difference* for each unit increase in the input values is a *linear function*. A **linear function** can be represented by the equation $f(x) = mx + b$, where m and b are constants. The graph of a linear function forms a straight line.

When a linear function is *discrete*, its graph consists of isolated points along a straight line. If a discrete linear function has inputs that are a set of equally spaced integers, then its outputs form an arithmetic sequence.

REFLECT

2a. Give three reasons why the cost function in the Explore is linear.

_____

_____

_____

2b. What are m and b and what do they represent for the cost function?

_____

MCC9–12.F.IF.2

3 EXPLORE   Comparing Linear Functions

A   Avocados cost $1.50 each. Green beans cost $1.50 per pound. The total cost of a avocados is $C(a) = 1.5a$ and the total cost of g pounds of green beans is $C(g) = 1.5g$. Complete the tables to find a few values.

Cost of Avocados		
a	$C(a) = 1.5a$	$(a, C(a))$
0	0	(0, 0)
1		
2		
3		

Cost of Green Beans		
g	$C(g) = 1.5g$	$(g, C(g))$
0	0	(0, 0)
1		
2		
3		

B   What is a reasonable domain for $C(a)$? for $C(g)$? Explain.

_____

_____

© Houghton Mifflin Harcourt Publishing Company

C Graph the two cost functions for all appropriate domain values from the given scales below.

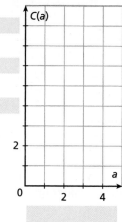

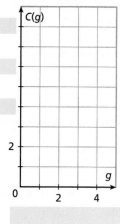

D Compare the graphs. How are they alike? How are they different?

_____

_____

_____

_____

REFLECT

3a. Describe the range for $C(a)$ and for $C(g)$.

_____

_____

3b. How do the units of a and g imply that their graphs will be different?

_____

_____

_____

3c. A function whose graph is unbroken is a *continuous* function. Tell which cost function is *continuous* and which is *discrete*.

_____

MCC9–12.F.IF.9

4 **E X A M P L E**   **Comparing Functions Given a Table and a Rule**

The functions $f(x)$ and $g(x)$ below are linear. Find the initial value and the range of each function. Then compare the functions.

- The table gives the values of the function $f(x)$. The domain of $f(x)$ is $\{4, 5, 6, 7\}$.
- Let the domain of the function $g(x) = 2x + 3$ be all real numbers such that $4 \leq x \leq 7$.

x	f(x)
4	8
5	10
6	12
7	14

© Houghton Mifflin Harcourt Publishing Company

A The initial value is the output that is paired with the least input.

The initial value of $f(x)$ is $f($_____$) = $_____.

The initial value of $g(x)$ is $g($_____$) = $_____.

B The range of $f(x)$ is _____.

Because $g(x)$ is a continuous linear function the range is

$g(4) \le g(x) \le g(7)$, or $\{g(x) \mid$ _____ $\le g(x) \le$ _____$\}$.

C How are the functions alike? How are they different? Consider their domains, initial values, and ranges.

_____

_____

_____

_____

_____

_____

REFLECT

4a. Find and compare the common differences per unit increase in the input values for the functions $f(x)$ and $g(x)$ in the Example.

_____

_____

4b. How can you tell that $f(x)$ and $g(x)$ in the Example are linear?

_____

_____

_____

© Houghton Mifflin Harcourt Publishing Company

MCC9–12.F.IF.9

5 **EXAMPLE** **Comparing Descriptions and Graphs of Functions**

Compare the following functions.

- A heavy rainstorm lasted for 2.5 hours during which time it rained at a steady rate of 0.5 inches per hour. The function $A_h(t)$ represents the amount of rain that fell in t hours.

- The graph at the right shows the amount of rain that fell during a violent rainstorm $A_v(t)$ (in inches) as a function of time t (in hours).

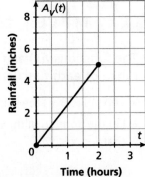

A How long did each storm last? Explain your reasoning.

_____

_____

B Calculate the amount of rainfall during the heavy storm. Then compare the amounts of rainfall for the two storms.

Heavy rainfall: (_____ inches per hour) · (_____ hours) = _____ inches of rain

_____

_____

C Calculate how many inches of rain fell per hour during the violent rainstorm. Then compare the rainfall rates for the two storms.

Violent rainfall rate: (_____ inches) ÷ (_____ hours) = _____ inches per hour

_____

REFLECT

5a. How would the graphs of $A_h(t)$ and $A_v(t)$ compare with one another?

_____

_____

PRACTICE

1. Andrea receives a $40 gift card to use a town pool. It costs her $8 per visit to swim. A function relating the value of the gift card, v, to the number of visits, n, is $v(n) = 40 - 8n$.

  a. Graph the function. Label axes and scales.

  b. What is the initial value?

  _____

  c. What is the difference between a given card value and the previous card value?

  _____

  d. Identify the domain and the range of the function using set notation.

  _____

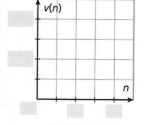

© Houghton Mifflin Harcourt Publishing Company

e. Is the function a discrete linear function? Are its outputs an arithmetic sequence? Why or why not?

_____

_____

_____

_____

2. The functions $f(x)$ and $g(x)$ are defined by the table and graph below.

x	f(x)
0	−2
1	1
2	4
3	7
4	10
5	13

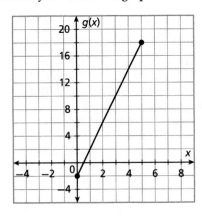

a. Compare the domains, initial values, and ranges of the functions.

_____

_____

_____

b. Explain why the functions are linear. Tell whether each function is _discrete_ or _continuous._

_____

_____

_____

_____

3. Grace works between 10 and 20 hours per week while attending college. She earns $9.00 per hour. Her hours are rounded to the nearest quarter hour. Her roommate Frances also has a job. Her pay for t hours is given by the function $f(t) = 10t$, where $5 \leq t \leq 15$. Her hours are not rounded.

a. Find the domain and range of each function.

_____

_____

_____

b. Compare their hourly wages and the amount they each earn per week.

_____

_____

© Houghton Mifflin Harcourt Publishing Company

Additional Practice

Identify whether each graph represents a function. Explain. If the
graph does represent a function, is the function linear?

1.
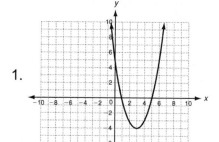
_____

_____

_____

2.
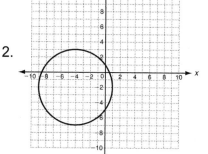
_____

_____

_____

3. Compare the functions represented by the ordered pairs.

Set A: {(5, 1), (4, 4), (3, 9), (2, 16), (1, 25)}   _____

Set B: {(1, −5), (2, −3), (3, −1), (4, 1), (5, 3)}   _____

4. Graph $y = -2x$. Give the domain and range. Is the function
discrete or continuous?

_____

_____

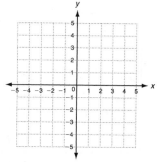

5. In 2005, the Shabelle River in Somalia rose an
estimated 5.25 inches every hour for 15 hours. The
increase in water level is represented by the function
$f(x) = 5.25x$, where x is the number of hours. Graph
this function and give its domain and range. Is the
function discrete or continuous?

_____

_____

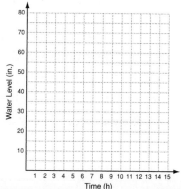

© Houghton Mifflin Harcourt Publishing Company

Problem Solving

Write the correct answer.

1. A daycare center charges a $75 enrollment fee plus $100 per week. The function $f(x) = 100x + 75$ gives the cost of daycare for x weeks. Graph this function and give its domain and range. Is the function discrete or continuous?

_____

_____

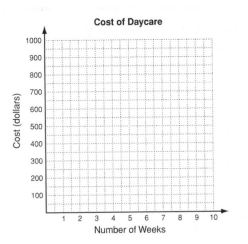

2. A family swimming pool holds 60 m³ of water. The function $f(x) = 60 - 0.18x$ gives the cubic meters of water in the pool, taking into account water lost to evaporation over x days. Graph this function and give its domain and range. Is the function discrete or continuous?

_____

_____

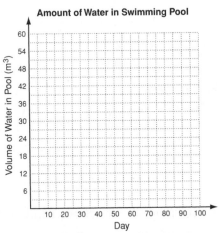

Elijah is using a rowing machine. The table shows how many Calories he can burn for certain lengths of time. Select the best answer.

Time (min)	Calories
2	24
4	48
6	72
8	96
10	120

3. Which function could be used to describe the number of Calories burned after x minutes?

   F $y = 12 + x$ H $xy = 12$

   G $x + y = 12$ J $y = 12x$

4. What is the domain of the function?

   A $\{0, 1, 2, 3, ...\}$ C $x \geq 0$

   B $\{2, 4, 6, ...\}$ D $x \geq 2$

5. What is the range of the function?

   F $\{0, 12, 24, 36, ...\}$ H $y \geq 0$

   G $\{24, 48, 72, ...\}$ J $y \geq 24$

6. Elijah graphed the function in problem 3. Which best describes the graph?

   A Line increasing from left to right.

   B Line decreasing from left to right.

   C Five points increasing from left to right.

   D Five points decreasing from left to right.

© Houghton Mifflin Harcourt Publishing Company

Using Intercepts
Going Deeper

Essential question: *How can you use intercepts to graph the solutions to a linear equation in two variables?*

An equation in two variables x and y that can be written in the form $Ax + By = C$ for real numbers A, B, and C is a **linear equation in two variables**.

The form $Ax + By = C$ where A and B are not both 0 is called the **standard form of a linear equation**.

A **solution of an equation in two variables** x and y is any ordered pair (x, y) that makes the equation true.

MCC9–12.A.REI.10

1 EXPLORE Definition of a Linear Equation in Two Variables

   A Complete the table of values to find solutions of the linear equation $x + y = 5$.

   B Plot the ordered pairs on a coordinate grid.

x_1	y_1	(x_1, y_1)
−2		
−1		
0		
1		
2		
3		
4		
5		
6		
7		

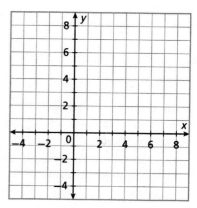

REFLECT

1a. What appears to be true about the points that are solutions of a linear equation?

_____

1b. What is the minimum number of points you would need to plot to graph a linear equation? Explain. Why should you graph more than the minimum number of points?

_____

_____

_____

© Houghton Mifflin Harcourt Publishing Company

To determine whether an ordered pair (x_1, y_1) is a solution of a linear equation, substitute the values of x_1 and y_1 into the linear equation. If the two sides of the equation are equal, then the ordered pair is a solution.

MCC9–12.A.REI.10

2 EXAMPLE Determining Whether an Ordered Pair is a Solution

Which ordered pair is a solution to $3x + 5y = 15$?

A (0, 3)

$3(0) + 5(3) = 15$

_____

B (8, 1)

_____

_____

(0, 3) _____ a solution to $3x + 5y = 15$.

(8, 1) _____ a solution to $3x + 5y = 15$.

REFLECT

2a. What do you know about the point (0, 3) and its relationship to the graph of $3x + 5y = 15$?

_____

2b. Explain how you know that $3x + 5y = 15$ is a linear equation.

_____

The graph of a linear equation is a line. To graph a line, it is necessary to plot only two points. However, it is a good idea to plot a third point as a check. For linear equations written in standard form, two good points to plot are where the line crosses each axis. The x-coordinate of the point where the line crosses the x-axis is called the **x-intercept** and is found by substituting 0 for y in the equation of the line. The y-coordinate of the point where the line crosses the y-axis is called the **y-intercept** and is found by substituting 0 for x in the equation of the line.

MCC9–12.A.REI.10

3 EXAMPLE Graphing a Linear Equation in Standard Form

Graph $2x + y = 4$.

A Make a table of values. Each row in the table of values makes an ordered pair (x, y).

B Substitute 0 for x in the equation and solve for y.

$2(0) + y = 4$

$y = \boxed{}$

Write the value for y next to the 0 in the first row of the table.

x	y
0	
	0
1	

© Houghton Mifflin Harcourt Publishing Company

C Next substitute 0 for y in the equation and solve for x.

$$2x + (0) = 4$$

$$2x = 4$$

$$x = \boxed{}$$

Write the value for x before the 0 in the second row of the table.

D Choose another value for x and solve for y. It is usually easiest to choose a simple value such as 1.

$$2(1) + y = 4$$

$$\boxed{} + y = 4$$

$$y = \boxed{}$$

Write the value for y after the 1 in the third row of the table.

E Plot the first two points on the coordinate grid. Then plot the third point. If you have done your calculations correctly, all three points should lie on a straight line. Draw a line through the points.

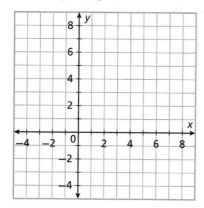

REFLECT

3a. List three other solutions to $2x + y = 4$.

_____

3b. Why should you find the x- and y-intercepts when making a table of values to graph a linear equation?

_____

_____

3c. Suppose that in part E the three points did not lie on a straight line. What would this tell you and what should you do?

_____

_____

© Houghton Mifflin Harcourt Publishing Company

4 EXAMPLE Vertical and Horizontal Lines

Graph $x = 3$ and $y = -4$.

Note that the equation $x = 3$ can be written as $1x + 0y = 3$.
All points with an x-value of 3 are solutions to the equation.
These points lie on a vertical line that passes through $(3, 0)$.

Note that the equation $y = -4$ can be written as $0x + 1y = -4$.
All points with a y-value of -4 are solutions to the equation.
These points lie on a horizontal line that passes through $(0, -4)$.

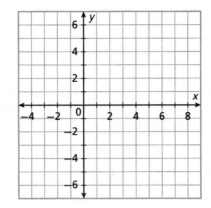

REFLECT

4a. Describe the graph of the line $y = 1$.

_____

4b. Describe the graph of the line $x = -2$.

_____

A linear equation in the form $Ax + By = C$ where $C = 0$ has a special property. To see
what this property is, look below at the table and graph of the equation $-4x + 3y = 0$.

x	y
0	0
0	0
3	4

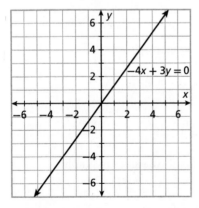

Notice that the table gives the same point for the x-intercept and for the y-intercept,
namely the point $(0, 0)$. Notice also that the graph passes through the origin. This is true
for any linear equation of the form $Ax + By = C$ where $C = 0$. Consequently, you cannot
use the x- and y-intercepts to draw their graphs. For these equations, first plot a point at
the origin. Then substitute two other values for x to locate two more points.

© Houghton Mifflin Harcourt Publishing Company

5 EXAMPLE   Lines Through the Origin

Graph $2x - 3y = 0$.

A   Complete the table of values.

B   Plot the points on the coordinate grid.

C   Check that all three points are collinear.

D   Draw a line through the points.

x	y
0	0
1	
2	

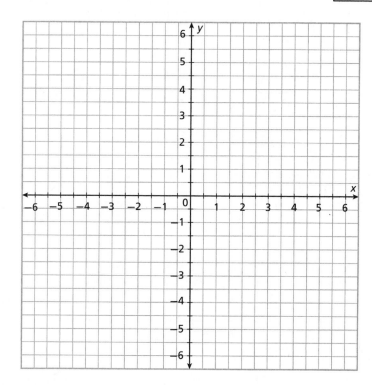

REFLECT

5a. Would it have been easier to use x-values of 3 and -3 to graph the line? Why or why not?

_____

_____

5b. If C does not equal 0, can the graph of $Ax + By = C$ pass through the origin? Why or why not?

_____

_____

© Houghton Mifflin Harcourt Publishing Company

Tell whether the ordered pair is a solution to the equation.

1. $-5x + 2y = 4;\ (4, 8)$

2. $2x - 7y = 1;\ (11, 3)$

_____

_____

Complete the table and graph the equation.

3. $-2x + y = 3$

x	y

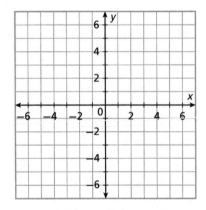

4. $3x = -6$

x	y

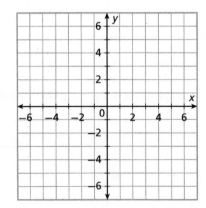

5. $4x + 5y = 0$

x	y
0	
	−4
−5	

© Houghton Mifflin Harcourt Publishing Company

Additional Practice

Find the *x*- and *y*-intercepts.

1.

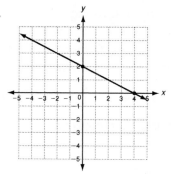

_____

_____

2.

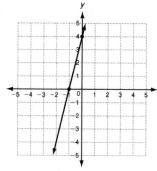

_____

_____

3.

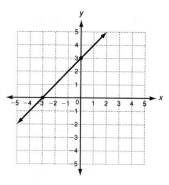

_____

_____

Use intercepts to graph the line described by each equation.

4. $3x + 2y = -6$

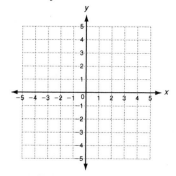

5. $x - 4y = 4$

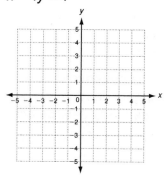

6. At a fair, hamburgers sell for $3.00 each and hot dogs sell for $1.50 each. The equation $3x + 1.5y = 30$ describes the number of hamburgers and hot dogs a family can buy with $30.

   a. Find the intercepts and graph the function.

   _____

   b. What does each intercept represent?

   _____

   _____

   _____

   _____

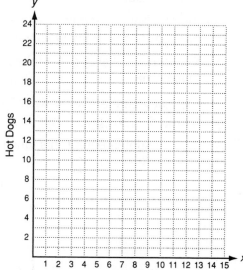

© Houghton Mifflin Harcourt Publishing Company

Problem Solving

Write the correct answer.

1. Naima has $40 to spend on refreshments for herself and her friends at the movie theater. The equation $5x + 2y = 40$ describes the number of large popcorns x and small drinks y she can buy. Graph this function and find its intercepts.

2. Turner is reading a 400-page book. He reads 4 pages every 5 minutes. The number of pages Turner has left to read after x minutes is represented by the function $f(x) = 400 - \frac{4}{5}x$. Graph this function and find its intercepts.

_____

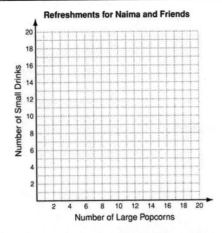

_____

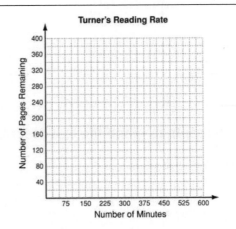

The graph shows the distance of an elevator at Chimney Rock, North Carolina, from its destination as a function of time. Use the graph to answer questions 3–6. Select the best answer.

3. What is the x-intercept of this function?

   A 0

   B 30

   C 258

   D 300

4. What does the x-intercept represent?

   F the total distance the elevator travels

   G the number of seconds that have passed for any given distance

   H the number of seconds it takes the elevator to reach its destination

   J the distance that the elevator has traveled at any given time

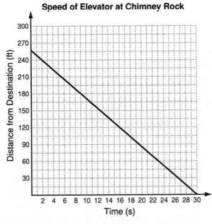

5. What is the y-intercept for this function?

   A 0

   B 30

   C 258

   D 300

6. What does the y-intercept represent?

   F the total distance the elevator travels

   G the number of seconds that have passed for any given distance

   H the number of seconds it takes the elevator to reach its destination

   J the distance that the elevator has traveled at any given time

© Houghton Mifflin Harcourt Publishing Company

10-3

Rate of Change and Slope
Going Deeper

Essential question: *What is the slope of a linear function and how can you use it to graph the function?*

If $f(x)$ is a linear function, then its graph is a line. The ordered pairs $(x_1, f(x_1))$ and $(x_2, f(x_2))$ can be used to name two points on the line. The change in the independent variables between these points is $x_2 - x_1$. The change in the dependent variables is $f(x_2) - f(x_1)$.

QR code: Video Tutor

MCC9–12.F.IF.6

1 EXPLORE Changes in Independent and Dependent Variables

A Use the function $f(x) = 2x + 1$ to complete the table for each interval.

Interval	From $x = 1$ to $x = 2$	From $x = 1$ to $x = 3$	From $x = 1$ to $x = 4$
Change in x, the independent variable	$2 - 1 = 1$		
Change in $f(x)$, the dependent variable	$f(2) - f(1) =$ $5 - 3 = 2$		
$\dfrac{\text{Change in } f(x)}{\text{Change in } x}$	$\dfrac{2}{1} = 2$	⬚/⬚ = ⬚	⬚/⬚ = ⬚

B The ratio $\dfrac{f(x_2) - f(x_1)}{x_2 - x_1}$ over each interval simplifies to _____.

REFLECT

1a. What is the relationship between the ratio of $f(x_2) - f(x_1)$ to $x_2 - x_1$ and the function rule?

_____

1b. Is the ratio of $f(x_2) - f(x_1)$ to $x_2 - x_1$ the same over the interval from $x = 2$ to $x = 4$? Explain.

_____

1c. Suppose the function rule was $f(x) = 2x + 5$ instead of $f(x) = 2x + 1$. Would the ratio of $f(x_2) - f(x_1)$ to $x_2 - x_1$ remain the same? Explain.

_____

_____

_____

© Houghton Mifflin Harcourt Publishing Company

The ratio of $f(x_2) - f(x_1)$ to $x_2 - x_1$ for a linear function $f(x)$ is the **rate of change** of $f(x)$ with respect to x. The rate of change is the same for any two points on the graph of a given linear function.

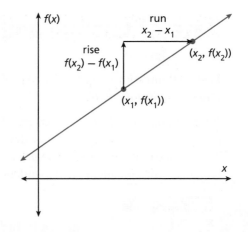

You can interpret the rate of change of a linear function $f(x)$ geometrically as the *slope* of its graph. The diagram at the right shows the graph of $f(x)$, where the vertical axis represents the function values. The **rise** is the change in function values, $f(x_2) - f(x_1)$, and the **run** is the change in x-values, $x_2 - x_1$. The **slope** of the line is the ratio of the rise to the run.

Several ways of expressing the slope of a line are given below.

$$\text{slope} = \frac{\text{rise}}{\text{run}} = \frac{f(x_2) - f(x_1)}{x_2 - x_1} = \frac{\text{change in } f(x)}{\text{change in } x}$$

REFLECT

2a. Complete the following to show that the y-intercept of the graph of a linear function $f(x)$ is the value of b in the equation $f(x) = mx + b$.

The y-intercept of the graph of an equation occurs where $x = 0$.

So, the y-intercept of the graph of $f(x) = mx + b$ is as follows.

$$f(0) = m \cdot \boxed{} + b$$

$$f(0) = \boxed{} + b$$

$$f(0) = b$$

2b. Complete the following to show that the slope of the graph of a linear function $f(x)$ is the value of m in the equation $f(x) = mx + b$.

To find the slope of the graph of $f(x) = mx + b$, choose any two points on the line. Two convenient points are $(x_1, f(x_1)) = (0, b)$ and $(x_2, f(x_2)) = (1, m + b)$.

$$\frac{f(x_2) - f(x_1)}{x_2 - x_1} = \frac{\boxed{} - \boxed{}}{\boxed{} - \boxed{}} = \frac{\boxed{}}{\boxed{}} = m$$

2c. Show that the y-intercept of the graph of the function $f(x) = 4x + 1$ is 1 and that the rate of change of $f(x)$ with respect to x is 4.

_____

_____

© Houghton Mifflin Harcourt Publishing Company

3 ENGAGE   **Classifying Slopes of Lines**

The slope of a line, can be positive, negative, 0, or undefined. If the slope is undefined, the line is not the graph of a function.

   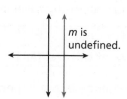

| The line rises from left to right. | The line falls from left to right. | The line is horizontal. | The line is vertical. |

REFLECT

3a. When you move from left to right between two points on a line with a positive slope, is the rise *positive*, *negative*, or 0? Is the run *positive*, *negative*, or 0? Use your answers to explain why the slope of a line that rises from left to right is positive.

_____

_____

3b. When you move from left to right between two points on a line with a negative slope, is the rise *positive*, *negative*, or 0? Is the run *positive*, *negative*, or 0? Use your answers to explain why the slope of a line that falls from left to right is negative.

_____

_____

3c. When you move from left to right between two points on a horizontal line, is the rise *positive*, *negative*, or 0? Is the run *positive*, *negative*, or 0? Use your answers to explain why the slope of a horizontal line is 0.

_____

3d. When you move up from one point to another on a vertical line, is the rise *positive*, *negative*, or 0? Is the run *positive*, *negative*, or 0? Use your answers to explain why the slope of a vertical line is undefined.

_____

_____

3e. A **constant function** is a function that has a rate of change of 0. Describe the graph of a constant function and the form of its equation.

_____

_____

© Houghton Mifflin Harcourt Publishing Company

1. Calculate the rate of change of the function in the table. _____

Tickets for rides	10	12	14	16
Total cost of carnival ($)	12.50	14.00	15.50	17.00

Estimate the change in the dependent variable over the given interval from the domain of the independent variable. Estimate the rate of change.

2.

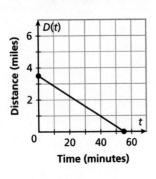

Given interval: $20 \le t \le 40$

Change in $D(t)$: _____

Rate of change: _____

3.

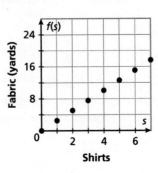

Given interval: $3 \le s \le 5$

Change in $f(s)$: _____

Rate of change: _____

Find the slope of the line that passes through the two given points. Classify each slope and tell whether the line represents a function.

4. $(-3, 2)$ and $(5, -3)$

_____

5. $(0, -4)$ and $(7, 5)$

_____

6. $(-4, 5)$ and $(-4, -8)$

_____

7. $(-3, 0)$ and $(7, 0)$

_____

8. $(-5, 0)$ and $(0, -10)$

_____

9. $(-2, -7)$ and $(4, -1)$

_____

© Houghton Mifflin Harcourt Publishing Company

Additional Practice

Find the rise and run between each set of points. Then, write the slope of the line.

1.
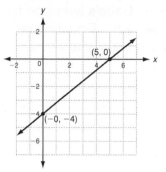

rise = _____ run = _____

slope = _____

2.
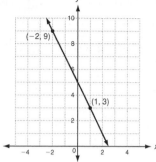

rise = _____ run = _____

slope = _____

3.
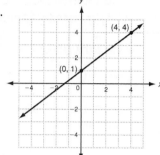

rise = _____ run = _____

slope = _____

4.
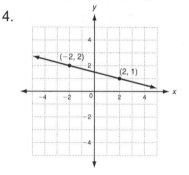

rise = _____ run = _____

slope = _____

5.
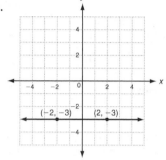

rise = _____ run = _____

slope = _____

6.
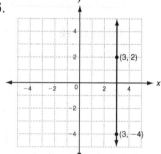

rise = _____ run = _____

slope = _____

Tell whether the slope of each line is positive, negative, zero, or undefined.

7.
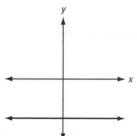

_____

8.
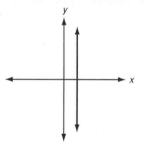

_____

9.
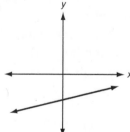

_____

10. The table shows the amount of water in a pitcher at different times. Graph the data and show the rates of change. Between which two hours is the rate of change the greatest? _____

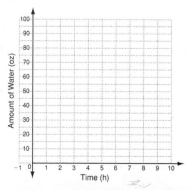

Time (h)	0	1	2	3	4	5	6	7
Amount (oz)	60	50	25	80	65	65	65	50

© Houghton Mifflin Harcourt Publishing Company

Problem Solving

Write the correct answer.

1. The table shows the cost per pound of Granny Smith apples.

Weight (lb)	1	2	3	4
Cost ($)	1.49	2.98	4.47	5.96

Describe the rate(s) of change shown by the data.

_____

_____

2. The table shows Gabe's height on his birthday for five years. Find the rate of change during each time interval.

Age	9	11	12	13	15
Height (in.)	58	59.5	61.5	65	69

_____

_____

When did the greatest rate of change occur? _____

When was the rate of change the least?

_____

During which two time periods were the rates of change the same?

_____

3. The table shows the distance of a courier from her destination.

Time (p.m.)	2:15	2:30	2:45	3:00
Distance (mi)	5.4	5.4	5.0	0.5

What is the rate of change from 2:15 p.m. to 2:30 p.m.? What does this rate of change mean?

_____

_____

The graph below tracks regular gasoline prices from July 2004 to December 2004. Use the graph to answer questions 5–7. Select the best answer.

4. What is the slope of the line from November to December?

   A −4   C −0.04

   B −1   D −0.01

5. During which time interval did the cost decrease at the greatest rate?

   F Jul to Aug   H Sep to Oct

   G Aug to Sep   J Oct to Nov

6. During which time interval was the slope positive?

   A Jul to Aug   C Sep to Oct

   B Aug to Sep   D Oct to Nov

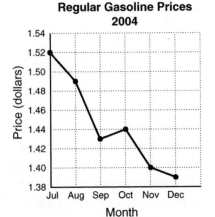

Regular Gasoline Prices 2004

7. What was the rate of change from October to December?

   F −0.05   H 0.025

   G −0.025   J 0.05

© Houghton Mifflin Harcourt Publishing Company

The Slope Formula

Extension: Estimating Average Rate of Change

Essential Question: *How can you estimate the average rate of change of a function from a graph?*

The slope of a line is the ratio of the difference in y-values to the difference in x-values between any two points on the line. This is represented by $m = \dfrac{y_2 - y_1}{x_2 - x_1}$.

Video Tutor

MCC9–12.F.IF.6

1 EXPLORE Finding the Slope of a Linear Function

Find the slope of the linear function represented by the graph.

A Use points A and B to find the slope of the line. Let the coordinates of A be (x_1, y_1) and the coordinates of B be (x_2, y_2).

$m = \dfrac{y_2 - y_1}{x_2 - x_1}$ Use the slope formula.

$m = \dfrac{\boxed{} - \left(\boxed{}\right)}{\boxed{} - \left(\boxed{}\right)}$ Substitute.

$m = \dfrac{\boxed{}}{\boxed{}} = \boxed{}$ Simplify.

B Use points A and C to find the slope of the line. Let the coordinates of A be (x_1, y_1) and the coordinates of C be (x_2, y_2).

$m = \dfrac{y_2 - y_1}{x_2 - x_1}$ Use the slope formula.

$m = \dfrac{\boxed{} - \left(\boxed{}\right)}{\boxed{} - \left(\boxed{}\right)}$ Substitute.

$m = \dfrac{\boxed{}}{\boxed{}} = \boxed{}$ Simplify.

C Use points B and C to find the slope of the line. Let the coordinates of B be (x_1, y_1) and the coordinates of C be (x_2, y_2).

$m = \dfrac{y_2 - y_1}{x_2 - x_1}$ Use the slope formula.

$m = \dfrac{\boxed{} - \boxed{}}{\boxed{} - \boxed{}}$ Substitute.

$m = \dfrac{\boxed{}}{\boxed{}} = \boxed{}$ Simplify.

© Houghton Mifflin Harcourt Publishing Company

1a. Is the slope of the linear function constant? Explain.

_____

_____

MCC9–12.F.IF.6

2 EXPLORE   **Estimating the Slope of Sections of a Quadratic Function**

Estimate the average slope of particular sections of the quadratic function $y = x^2$ represented by the graph at the right.

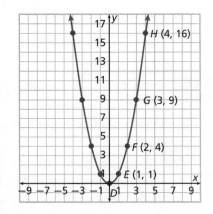

A Use the slope formula to complete the table below.

x-coordinate of D	x-coordinate of E	x-coordinate of F	x-coordinate of G

y-coordinate of D	y-coordinate of E	y-coordinate of F	y-coordinate of G

average slope between D and E	average slope between E and F	average slope between F and G	average slope between G and H

B How are the x-coordinates of each pair of points given in the table related?

_____

_____

C For $y = x^2$, make a conjecture about how the average slope between two points whose x-coordinates are 1 unit apart is related to the x-coordinate of the point with the lesser x-coordinate. [*Hint*: Write and simplify an algebraic expression for the slope between (x, x^2) and $(x + 1, (x + 1)^2)$.] Is the slope of a quadratic function constant?

_____

_____

D Use your conjecture to estimate the average slope between $(8, 64)$ and $(9, 81)$ in $y = x^2$. Explain your work. Then use the slope formula to check your estimate.

_____

© Houghton Mifflin Harcourt Publishing Company

2a. Will your conjecture hold for negative x-coordinates? Give an example or counterexample to support your answer.

_____

_____

2b. Find the average slopes of pairs of points with negative x-coordinates that are 1 unit apart. Arrange them in order from least to greatest with the slopes from Part A. What do you notice about the average slopes as the x-coordinates increase? Will the average slope ever be zero? Why or why not?

_____

_____

MCC9–12.F.IF.6

3 EXPLORE **Estimating the Slope of Sections of an Exponential Function**

Estimate the average slope of particular sections of the exponential function $y = 2^x$ represented by the graph at the right.

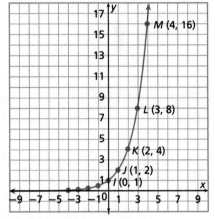

A Use the slope formula to complete the table below.

x-coordinate of I	x-coordinate of J	x-coordinate of K	x-coordinate of L
average slope between I and J	average slope between J and K	average slope between K and L	average slope between L and M

B How are the x-coordinates of each pair of points given in the table related?

_____

_____

C For $y = 2^x$, make a conjecture about how the average slope between two points whose x-coordinates are 1 unit apart is related to the x-coordinate of the point with the lesser x-coordinate?

_____

_____

© Houghton Mifflin Harcourt Publishing Company

D Use your conjecture to estimate the average slope between (8, 256) and (9, 512) in $y = 2^x$. Explain your work. Then use the slope formula to check your estimate.

_____

3a. Will your conjecture hold for negative x-coordinates? Give an example or counterexample to support your answer.

_____

_____

3b. Find the average slopes of pairs of points with negative x-coordinates that are 1 unit apart. Arrange them in order from least to greatest with the slopes from Part A. What do you notice about the average slopes as the x-coordinates increase? Do you think the average slope will ever be negative? Why or why not?

_____

_____

_____

PRACTICE

Make a conjecture about the average slope of various sections of each graph. Use sections that have endpoints in which the x-coordinates are 1 unit apart.

1. $y = 2x^2$

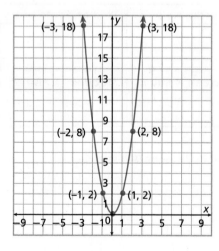

2. $y = 3^x$

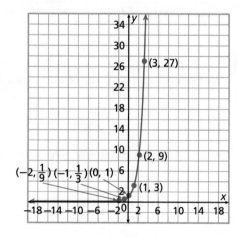

_____

_____

_____

_____

_____

_____

© Houghton Mifflin Harcourt Publishing Company

Additional Practice

Find the slope of the line that contains each pair of points.

1. (2, 8) and (1, −3)

$$m = \frac{y_2 - y_1}{x_2 - x_1}$$

$$= \frac{\boxed{} - \boxed{}}{\boxed{} - \boxed{}}$$

$$= \frac{\boxed{}}{\boxed{}} = \boxed{}$$

2. (−4, 0) and (−6, −2)

$$m = \frac{y_2 - y_1}{x_2 - x_1}$$

$$= \frac{\boxed{} - \boxed{}}{\boxed{} - \boxed{}}$$

$$= \frac{\boxed{}}{\boxed{}} = \boxed{}$$

3. (0, −2) and (4, −7)

$$m = \frac{y_2 - y_1}{x_2 - x_1}$$

$$= \frac{\boxed{} - \boxed{}}{\boxed{} - \boxed{}}$$

$$= \frac{\boxed{}}{\boxed{}}$$

Each graph or table shows a linear relationship. Find the slope.

4.

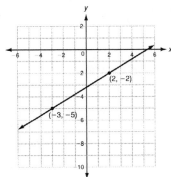

5.

x	y
1	3.75
2	5
3	6.25
4	7.50
5	8.75

_____

6.

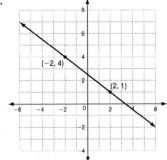

_____

_____

Find the slope of each line.

7.

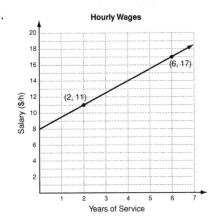

_____

_____

8.

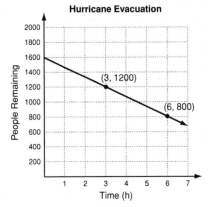

_____

_____

For each equation, find the slope between the given points.

9. $y = 3x^2$; (0, 0) and (1, 3); (1, 3) and (2, 12)

10. $y = 4^x$; (0, 1) and (1, 4); (1, 4) and (2, 16)

_____

_____

© Houghton Mifflin Harcourt Publishing Company

Problem Solving

Write the correct answer.

1. The graph shows the number of emergency kits assembled by volunteers over a period of days. Find the slope of the line.

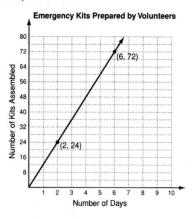

_____

_____

2. The graph shows how much flour is in a bag at different times. Find the slope of the line.

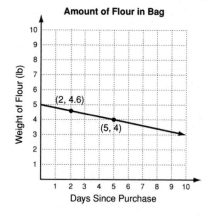

_____

_____

3. The function $y = 10^x$ represents a population of amoebas each day. Is the slope of this function increasing or decreasing as x increases?

_____

The graph below shows the cost of membership at Fabulously Fit. Use the graph to answer questions 4–7. Select the best answer.

4. What is the slope of the line?

   A 24   C 50

   B 35   D 70

5. What happens to the slope as the line rises?

   F It increases.

   G It decreases.

   H It becomes 0.

   J It remains constant.

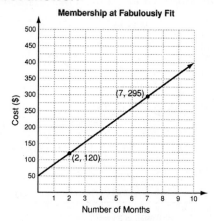

6. A second line is graphed that shows the cost of membership at The Fitness Studio. The line contains (0, 35) and (5, 85). What is the slope of this line?

   A 10   C 45

   B 20   D 50

7. How much greater is the monthly fee at Fabulously Fit than The Fitness Studio?

   F $15   H $35

   G $25   J $40

© Houghton Mifflin Harcourt Publishing Company

Direct Variation
Extension: Transformations of $f(x) = mx$ and $g(x) = a|x|$

Essential question: *How does changing the values of m and a affect the graphs of $f(x) = mx$ and $g(x) = a|x|$?*

Video Tutor

MCC9–12.F.BF.3

1 EXPLORE Changing the Value of *m* in $f(x) = mx$

Investigate what happens to the graph of $f(x) = mx$ when you change the value of *m*.

A Use a graphing calculator. Start with the standard viewing window, which you can obtain by pressing **ZOOM** and selecting ZStandard. Because the distances between consecutive tick marks on the *x*-axis and on the *y*-axis are not equal, you can make them equal by pressing **ZOOM** again and selecting ZSquare.

What interval on each axis does the viewing window now show? (Press **WINDOW** to find out.)

_____

B Graph the function $f(x) = x$ by pressing **Y=** and entering the function's rule next to $Y_1 =$. As shown, the graph of the function is a line that makes a 45° angle with each axis.

What are the slope and *y*-intercept of the graph of $f(x) = x$?

_____

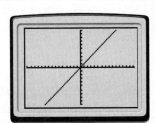

C Press **Y=** and graph other functions of the form $f(x) = mx$ by entering their rules next to $Y_2 =$, $Y_3 =$, and so on. Use only values of *m* that are greater than 1. For instance, graph $f(x) = 2x$ and $f(x) = 6x$.

What do the graphs have in common? How are they different?

_____

As the value of *m* increases from 1, does the graph become more vertical or more horizontal?

_____

D Again press **Y=** and clear out all but the function $f(x) = x$. Then graph other functions of the form $f(x) = mx$ by entering their rules next to $Y_2 =$, $Y_3 =$, and so on. This time use only values of *m* that are less than 1 but greater than 0. For instance, graph $f(x) = 0.5x$ and $f(x) = 0.2x$.

As the value of *m* decreases from 1 toward 0, does the graph become more vertical or more horizontal?

_____

© Houghton Mifflin Harcourt Publishing Company

E Again press [Y=] and clear out all but the function $f(x) = x$. Then graph the function $f(x) = -x$ by entering its rule next to $Y_2 =$.

What are the slope and y-intercept of the graph of $f(x) = -x$?

_____

How are the graphs of $f(x) = x$ and $f(x) = -x$ geometrically related?

_____

F Again press [Y=] and clear out all the functions. Graph $f(x) = -x$ by entering its rule next to $Y_1 =$. Then graph other functions of the form $f(x) = mx$ where $m < 0$ by entering their rules next to $Y_2 =$, $Y_3 =$, and so on. Be sure to choose values of m less than -1 as well as values of m between -1 and 0.

Describe what happens to the graph of $f(x) = mx$ as the value of m decreases from -1 and as it increases from -1 to 0.

_____

REFLECT

1a. A function $f(x)$ is called an *increasing function* when the value of $f(x)$ always increases as the value of x increases. For what values of m is the function $f(x) = mx$ an increasing function? How can you tell from the graph of a linear function that it is an increasing function?

_____

1b. A function $f(x)$ is called a *decreasing function* when the value of $f(x)$ always decreases as the value of x increases. For what values of m is the function $f(x) = mx$ a decreasing function? How can you tell from the graph of a linear function that is a decreasing function?

_____

1c. When $m > 0$, increasing the value of m results in an increasing linear function that increases *faster*. What effect does increasing m have on the graph of the function?

_____

1d. When $m > 0$, decreasing the value of m toward 0 results in an increasing linear function that increases *slower*. What effect does decreasing m have on the graph of the function?

_____

1e. When $m < 0$, decreasing the value of m results in a decreasing linear function that decreases *faster*. What effect does decreasing m have on the graph of the function?

_____

1f. When $m < 0$, increasing the value of m toward 0 results in a decreasing linear function that decreases *slower*. What effect does increasing m have on the graph of the function?

_____

© Houghton Mifflin Harcourt Publishing Company

1g. The *steepness* of a line refers to the absolute value of its slope. A steeper line is more vertical; a less steep line is more horizontal. Complete the table to summarize, in terms of steepness, the effect of changing the value of m on the graph of $f(x) = mx$.

How the Value of *m* Changes	Effect on the Graph of *f(x) = mx*
Increase m when $m > 0$.	
Decrease m toward 0 when $m > 0$.	
Decrease m when $m < 0$.	
Increase m toward 0 when $m < 0$.	

As you have seen, changing the value of m in the function $f(x) = mx$ makes the graph more or less steep compared to the graph of $f(x) = x$ and reflects it over the x-axis if $m < 0$. Changing the value of a in the *absolute value function* $g(x) = a|x|$ has a similar effect on its graph compared to the graph of the parent function $g(x) = |x|$.

MCC9–12.F.IF.7b

2 ENGAGE   **Understanding the Parent Absolute Value Function**

The most basic **absolute value function** is a piecewise function given by the following rule.

$$f(x) = |x| = \begin{cases} x & \text{if } x \geq 0 \\ -x & \text{if } x < 0 \end{cases}$$

This function is sometimes called the *parent* absolute value function.

To graph the function, you can make a table of values like the one shown below, plot the ordered pairs, and draw the graph.

x	f(x) = |x|
−3	3
−2	2
−1	1
0	0
1	1
2	2
3	3

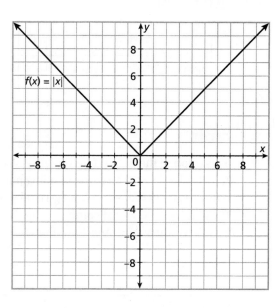

As shown at the right, the function's V-shaped graph consists of two rays with a common endpoint at $(0, 0)$. This point is called the *vertex* of the graph.

© Houghton Mifflin Harcourt Publishing Company

2a. What is the domain of $f(x) = |x|$? What is the range?

_____

2b. If you fold the graph of $f(x) = |x|$ over the y-axis, the two halves of the graph match up perfectly. The graph is said to be *symmetric* about the y-axis. Explain why it makes sense that the graph of $f(x) = |x|$ is symmetric about the y-axis.

_____

2c. For what values of x is the function $f(x) = |x|$ increasing? decreasing?

_____

To understand the effect of the constant a on the graph of $g(x) = a|x|$, you will graph the function using various values of a.

MCC9–12.F.BF.3

3 EXAMPLE   Graphing $g(x) = a|x|$ when $|a| > 1$

Graph each absolute value function using the same coordinate plane. (The graph of the parent function $f(x) = |x|$ is shown in gray.)

A $g(x) = 2|x|$

x	−3	−2	−1	0	1	2	3
g(x) = 2|x|							

B $g(x) = -2|x|$

x	−3	−2	−1	0	1	2	3
g(x) = −2|x|							

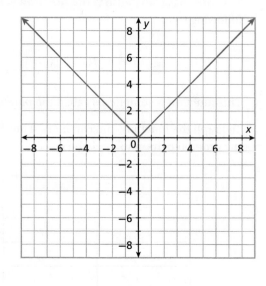

REFLECT

3a. The graph of the parent function $f(x) = |x|$ includes the point $(-1, 1)$ because $f(-1) = |-1| = 1$. The corresponding point on the graph of $g(x) = 2|x|$ is $(-1, 2)$ because $g(-1) = 2|-1| = 2$. In general, how does the y-coordinate of a point on the graph of $g(x) = 2|x|$ compare with the y-coordinate of a point on the graph of $f(x) = |x|$ when the points have the same x-coordinate?

_____

_____

3b. Describe how the graph of $g(x) = 2|x|$ compares with the graph of $f(x) = |x|$. Use either the word *stretch* or *shrink*, and include the direction of the movement.

_____

© Houghton Mifflin Harcourt Publishing Company

3c. What other transformation occurs when the value of a in $g(x) = a|x|$ is negative?

_____

MCC9–12.F.BF.3

4 **E X A M P L E** Graphing $g(x) = a|x|$ when $|a| < 1$

Graph each absolute value function using the same coordinate plane. (The graph of the parent function $f(x) = |x|$ is shown in gray.)

A $g(x) = \frac{1}{4}|x|$

x	-8	-4	0	4	8
$g(x) = \frac{1}{4}|x|$					

B $g(x) = -\frac{1}{4}|x|$

x	-8	-4	0	4	8
$g(x) = -\frac{1}{4}|x|$					

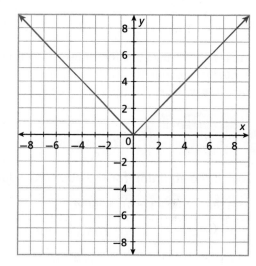

REFLECT

4a. How does the y-coordinate of a point on the graph of $g(x) = \frac{1}{4}|x|$ compare with the y-coordinate of a point on the graph of $f(x) = |x|$ when the points have the same x-coordinate?

_____

_____

4b. Describe how the graph of $g(x) = \frac{1}{4}|x|$ compares with the graph of $f(x) = |x|$. Use either the word _stretch_ or _shrink,_ and include the direction of the movement.

_____

4c. What other transformation occurs when the value of a in $g(x) = a|x|$ is negative?

_____

4d. Compare the domain and range of $g(x) = a|x|$ when $a > 0$ and when $a < 0$.

_____

_____

_____

© Houghton Mifflin Harcourt Publishing Company

4e. Summarize your observations about the graph of $g(x) = a|x|$.

Value of a	Vertical stretch or shrink?	Reflection across x-axis?
$a > 1$	Vertical stretch	No
$0 < a < 1$		
$-1 < a < 0$		
$a < -1$		

An absolute value function whose graph's vertex is at $(0, 0)$ has the form $g(x) = a|x|$. To write the equation for the function, you can use the coordinates of a point (x_1, y_1) on the graph to write $g(x_1) = a|x_1| = y_1$ and then solve for a.

MCC9–12.F.BF.1

5 EXAMPLE Writing the Equation for an Absolute Value Function

Write the equation for the absolute value function whose graph is shown.

Use the point $(-4, -3)$ to find a.

$g(x) = a|x|$ \qquad Function form

$g(-4) = a\left|\right| = $ \qquad Substitute.

$a\left(\right) = $ \qquad Simplify.

$a = \dfrac{}{}$ \qquad Solve for a.

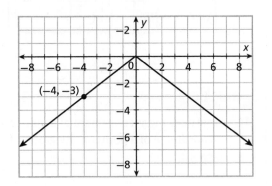

The equation for the function is _____.

REFLECT

5a. The fact that the given graph lies on or below the x-axis tells you what about the value of a? Does this agree with the value of a that you found? Explain.

_____

5b. The angle between the two rays that make up the graph of the parent function $f(x) = |x|$ is a right angle. What happens to this angle when the graph is vertically stretched? When the graph is vertically shrunk?

_____

5c. Based on your answer to Question 5b, does the given graph represent a vertical stretch or a vertical shrink of the graph of the parent function? Does this fact agree with the value of a that you found? Explain.

_____

© Houghton Mifflin Harcourt Publishing Company

Modeling with Absolute Value Functions When a rolling ball, such as a billiard ball, strikes a flat surface, such as an edge of the billiard table, the ball bounces off the surface at the same angle at which the ball hit the surface. (The angles are measured off a line perpendicular to the surface, as shown in the diagram.) A ray of light striking a mirror behaves in the same way.

The symmetry of the graph of an absolute value function makes the graph a perfect model for the path of a rolling ball or a ray of light.

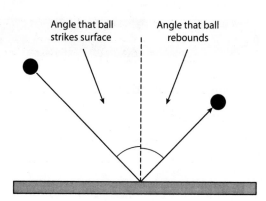

Angle that ball strikes surface   Angle that ball rebounds

6 EXAMPLE Modeling a Real-World Situation

Inez is playing miniature golf. Her ball is at point $A(-4, 6)$. She wants to putt the ball into the hole at $C(2, 3)$ with a bank shot, as shown. If the ball hits the edge at $B(0, 0)$, find the equation for the absolute value function whose graph models the path of the ball. How does the equation tell you whether the ball will go into the hole (if the ball is hit with sufficient force)?

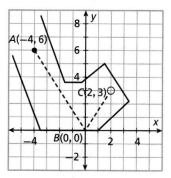

A Use the point $A(-4, 6)$ to write the equation for a function of the form $g(x) = a|x|$.

$$g(x) = a|x|$$ Function form

$$g(-4) = a\left|\ \rule{1.5em}{0pt}\ \right| = \rule{1.5em}{0pt}$$ Substitute.

$$a\left(\ \rule{1.5em}{0pt}\ \right) = \rule{1.5em}{0pt}$$ Simplify.

$$a = \frac{\rule{1.5em}{0pt}}{\rule{1.5em}{0pt}}$$ Solve for a.

So, the equation for the function is _____.

B Check to see whether the point $C(2, 3)$ lies on the path of the ball.

$g(2) = \frac{3}{2}|2| = \rule{1.5em}{0pt}$, so the ball _____ go into the hole.

REFLECT

6a. If you reflect point C in the x-axis, what do you notice about points A, B, and the reflection of C? Explain why this is so.

_____

_____

_____

_____

© Houghton Mifflin Harcourt Publishing Company

Graph each function.

1. $g(x) = 3x$

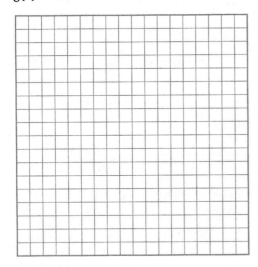

2. $g(x) = -2.5|x|$

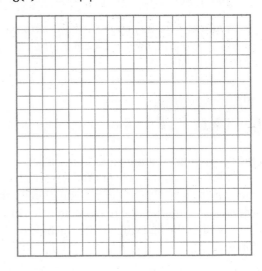

3. $g(x) = \frac{1}{2}|x|$

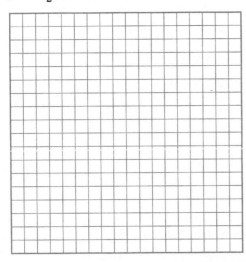

4. $g(x) = -\frac{2}{3}|x|$

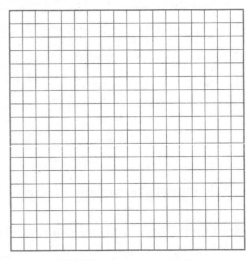

5. a. Complete the table and graph all the functions on the same coordinate plane.

x	-6	-3	0	3	6
$g(x) = \frac{1}{3}|x|$					
$g(x) = \left|\frac{1}{3}x\right|$					
$g(x) = -\frac{1}{3}|x|$					
$g(x) = \left|-\frac{1}{3}x\right|$					

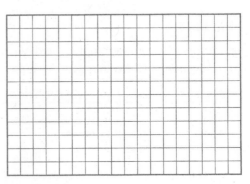

b. How do the graphs of $f(x) = a|x|$ and $g(x) = |ax|$ compare?

© Houghton Mifflin Harcourt Publishing Company

Write the equation of each function whose graph is shown.

6.

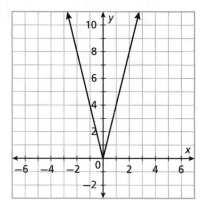

_____

7.

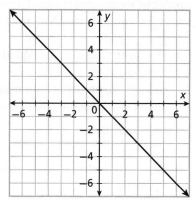

_____

8.

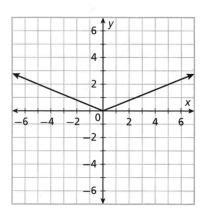

_____

9.

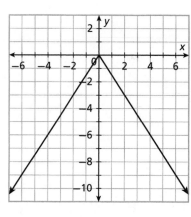

_____

10.

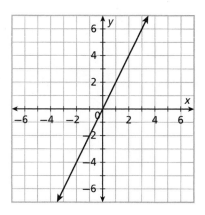

_____

11.

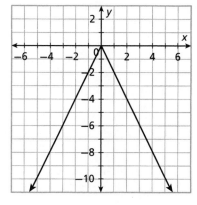

_____

© Houghton Mifflin Harcourt Publishing Company

12. From his driveway at point P, Mr. Carey's direct view of the traffic signal at point Q is blocked. In order to see the traffic signal, he places a mirror at point R and aligns it with the x-axis as shown.

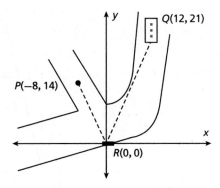

   a. Use point Q to write an equation for a function of the form $g(x) = a|x|$ whose graph models the path that light from the traffic signal takes when it strikes the mirror at R.

   _____

   b. Explain why the mirror is positioned correctly.

   _____

   _____

© Houghton Mifflin Harcourt Publishing Company

Additional Practice

Graph *f(x)* and *g(x)*. Then describe the transformation from the graph of *f(x)* to the graph of *g(x)*.

1. $f(x) = x$; $g(x) = 0.25x$

_____

_____

_____

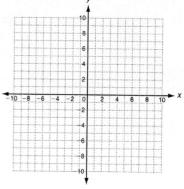

2. $f(x) = x$; $g(x) = -5x$

_____

_____

_____

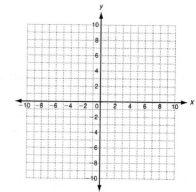

3. $f(x) = |x|$; $g(x) = 2|x|$

_____

_____

_____

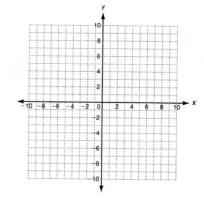

4. $f(x) = |x|$; $g(x) = -3|x|$

_____

_____

_____

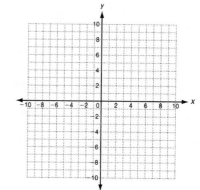

© Houghton Mifflin Harcourt Publishing Company

Problem Solving

Graph $f(x)$ and $g(x)$ given in Problems 1 and 2. Then describe the transformation from the graph of $f(x)$ to the graph of $g(x)$.

1. Sam is designing a target for a game called X Marks the Spot. One line of the X is given by $f(x) = 2x$. The other line is given by $g(x) = -2x$.

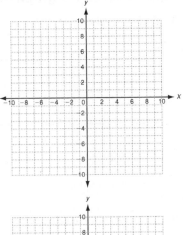

_____

_____

_____

2. The X Marks the Spot game needs two different X's for targets. For the second X Sam uses $f(x) = 0.5|x|$ and $g(x) = -0.5|x|$.

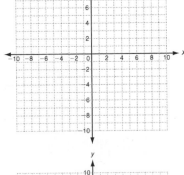

_____

_____

_____

3. You are asked to graph an increasing linear function $g(x)$ whose slope is steeper than the slope of $f(x) = x$. Choose the correct function and graph it at the right.

   A $g(x) = 0.3x$ C $g(x) = 3x$

   B $g(x) = -0.3x$ D $g(x) = -3x$

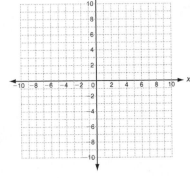

4. You are asked to graph an absolute value function $g(x)$ whose graph is a reflection over the x-axis of $f(x) = 5|x|$. Choose the correct function and graph it at the right.

   F $g(x) = -0.5|x|$ H $g(x) = 0.2|x|$

   G $g(x) = -0.2|x|$ J $g(x) = -5|x|$

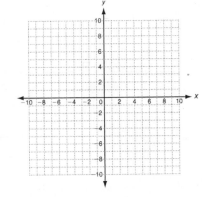

© Houghton Mifflin Harcourt Publishing Company

Slope-Intercept Form
Going Deeper

Essential question: *How can you represent relationships using linear functions?*

Graphing Lines You can graph the linear function $f(x) = mx + b$ using only the slope m and the y-intercept b. First, locate the point $(0, b)$ on the y-axis. Next, use the rise and run of the slope to locate another point on the line. Draw the line through the two points.

Video Tutor

When using m to locate a second point, bear in mind that m is a ratio, so many values of rise and run are possible. For instance, if $m = \frac{1}{2}$, then you could use a rise of $\frac{1}{2}$ and a run of 1, a rise of 1 and run of 2, a rise of -2 and a run of -4, and so on. Your choice of rise and run often depends on the scales used on the coordinate plane's axes.

MCC9–12.F.IF.7a

1 EXAMPLE Graphing a Line Using the Slope and *y*-Intercept

Graph each function.

A $f(x) = -\frac{2}{3}x + 4$

- The y-intercept is _____. Plot the point that corresponds to the y-intercept.

- The slope is _____. If you use -2 as the rise, then the run is _____.

- Use the slope to move from the first point to a second point. Begin by moving down _____ units, because the rise is negative. Then move right _____ units, because the run is positive. Plot a second point.

- Draw the line through the two points.

- The domain is the set of _____ numbers.

  The range is the set of _____ numbers.

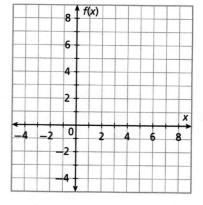

B A pitcher with a maximum capacity of 4 cups contains 1 cup of apple juice concentrate. A faucet is turned on filling the pitcher at a rate of 0.25 cup per second. The amount of liquid in the pitcher (in cups) is a function $A(t)$ of the time t (in seconds) that the water is running.

- The y-intercept is the initial amount in the pitcher at time 0, or _____ cup. Plot the point that corresponds to the y-intercept.

- The slope is the rate of change: _____ cup per second, or 1 cup in _____ seconds. So, the rise is _____ and the run is _____.

- Use the rise and run to move from the first point to a second point on the line by moving up _____ unit and right _____ units. Plot a second point.

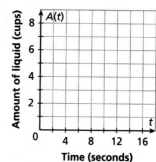

Amount of liquid (cups) — Time (seconds)

continued

© Houghton Mifflin Harcourt Publishing Company

- Connect the points and extend the line to the maximum value of the function, where $A(t) = $ _____ cups.

- The domain is the set of numbers _____ $\le t \le$ _____.

  The range is the set of numbers _____ $\le A(t) \le$ _____.

REFLECT

1a. How could you use the slope and y-intercept to graph the function $f(x) = 3$?

_____

_____

1b. What are the units of the rise in Part B? What are the units of the run?

_____

1c. How long does it take to fill the pitcher? Explain.

_____

1d. Why is the function rule $A(t) = \frac{1}{4}t + 1$? Use units to justify your answer.

_____

_____

_____

_____

MCC9–12.F.LE.2

2 EXAMPLE   **Writing a Linear Function**

Write the linear function f using the given information.

A   The graph of the function has a slope of 3 and a y-intercept of -1.

A linear function has the form $f(x) = mx + b$ where m is the slope and

b is the y-intercept. Substitute _____ for m and _____ for b.

So, the function is $f(x) = $

B   A different function has the values shown in the table.

First calculate the slope using any two ordered pairs from the table. For instance, let $(x_1, f(x_1)) = (-1, 5)$ and $(x_2, f(x_2)) = (3, -3)$.

x	$f(x)$
-1	5
3	-3
7	-11

$m = \dfrac{f(x_2) - f(x_1)}{x_2 - x_1}$ Write the slope formula.

$= \dfrac{\boxed{} - \boxed{}}{\boxed{} - \left(\boxed{}\right)}$ Substitute values.

© Houghton Mifflin Harcourt Publishing Company

$$= \frac{\boxed{}}{\boxed{}}$$ Simplify numerator and denominator.

$$= \boxed{}$$ Simplify fraction.

Then find the value of b using the fact that $m =$ _____ and $f(-1) = 5$.

$f(x) = \boxed{} \; x + b$ Write the function with the known value of m.

$\boxed{} = \boxed{} \left(\boxed{} \right) + b$ Substitute -1 for x and 5 for $f(x)$.

$\boxed{} = \boxed{} + b$ Simplify the right side of the equation.

$\boxed{} = b$ Solve for b.

So, the function is $f(x) = \boxed{}$.

> ### REFLECT

2a. In Part B, use the ordered pair $(7, -11)$ to check your answer.

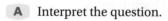

MCC9–12.F.LE.2

3 EXAMPLE   Writing a Linear Function from a Graph

The graph shows the increase in pressure (measured in pounds per square inch) as a scuba diver descends from a depth of 10 feet to a depth of 30 feet.

Pressure is the result of the weight of the column of water above the diver as well as the weight of the column of Earth's atmosphere above the water. Pressure is a linear function of depth.

What is the pressure on the diver at the water's surface?

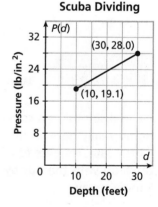

Scuba Dividing

A Interpret the question.

Let d represent depth and P represent pressure. At the water's surface,

$d =$ _____. For this value of d, what meaning does $P(d)$ have in terms of the line that contains the line segment shown on the graph?

B Find the value of m in $P(d) = md + b$. Use the fact that $P(10) = 19.1$ and $P(30) = 28.0$.

$$m = \frac{P(d_2) - P(d_1)}{d_2 - d_1}$$ Write the slope formula.

$$= \frac{\boxed{} - \boxed{}}{30 - 10}$$ Substitute values.

continued

$$= \frac{\boxed{}}{\boxed{}}$$ Simplify numerator and denominator.

$$= \boxed{}$$ Write in decimal form.

C Find the value of b in $P(d) = md + b$. Use the value of m from Part B as well as the fact that $P(10) = 19.1$.

$P(d) = \boxed{} d + b$ Write the function with the known value of m.

$\boxed{} = \boxed{} \left(\boxed{} \right) + b$ Substitute 10 for d and 19.1 for $P(d)$.

$\boxed{} = \boxed{} + b$ Simplify the right side of the equation.

$\boxed{} \approx b$ Solve for b. Round to the nearest tenth.

So, the pressure at the water's surface is $P(0) = b \approx$ _____ lb/in.^{2}

REFLECT

3a. Interpret the value of m in the context of the problem.

_____

3b. Write the function $P(d) = md + b$ using the calculated values of m and b. Use the function to find the pressure on the diver at a depth of 20 feet.

_____

MCC9–12.A.REI.11

4 E X A M P L E   **Writing and Solving a System of Equations**

Mr. Jackson takes a commuter bus from his suburban home to his job in the city. He normally gets on the bus in the town where he lives, but today he is running a little late. He gets to the bus stop 2 minutes after the bus has left. He wants to catch up with the bus by the time it gets to the next stop in a neighboring town 5 miles away.

The speed limit on the road connecting the two stops is 40 miles per hour, but Mr. Jackson knows that the bus travels the road at 30 miles per hour. He decides to drive at 40 miles per hour to the next stop. Does he successfully catch the bus there?

A Identify the independent and dependent variables, how they are measured, and how you will represent them.

The independent variable is _____, measured in minutes. Let t represent the time since Mr. Jackson began driving to the next bus stop.

The dependent variable is _____, measured in miles. Let d represent the distance traveled. Since you need to track the distances traveled by both Mr. Jackson and the bus, use subscripts: d_J will represent the distance traveled by Mr. Jackson, and d_B will represent the distance traveled by the bus.

© Houghton Mifflin Harcourt Publishing Company

B Write a distance-traveled function for Mr. Jackson and for the bus.

Each function has the form $d(t) = rt + d_0$ where r is the rate of travel and d_0 is any initial distance. Although you know the rates of travel, they are given in miles per hour, which is incompatible with the unit of time (minutes). So, you need to convert miles per hour to miles per minute. In the conversions below, express the miles as simplified fractions.

Mr. Jackson: $\dfrac{40 \text{ miles}}{\text{hour}} \cdot \dfrac{1 \text{ hour}}{60 \text{ minutes}} = \boxed{}$ mile per minute

Bus: $\dfrac{30 \text{ miles}}{\text{hour}} \cdot \dfrac{1 \text{ hour}}{60 \text{ minutes}} = \boxed{}$ mile per minute

At the moment Mr. Jackson begins driving to the next bus stop, the bus has traveled for 2 minutes. If you use Mr. Jackson's position as the starting point, then the initial distance for Mr. Jackson is 0 miles, and the

initial distance for the bus is $\boxed{} \cdot 2 = \boxed{}$.

So, the distance-traveled functions are:

Mr. Jackson: $d_J(t) = \boxed{}\, t + \boxed{}$ Bus: $d_B(t) = \boxed{}\, t + \boxed{}$

C Determine the value of t for which $d_J(t) = d_B(t)$. You can do this by graphing the two functions and seeing where the graphs intersect. Carefully draw the graphs on the coordinate plane below, and label the intersection point.

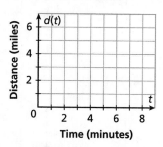

The t-coordinate of the point of intersection is _____, so

Mr. Jackson catches up with the bus in _____.

D Check the result against the conditions of the problem, and then answer the problem's question.

The problem states that the next bus stop is _____ miles away, and the

graph shows that Mr. Jackson catches up with the bus in _____ miles.

So, does Mr. Jackson successfully catch the bus? _____

REFLECT

4a. Explain how you can use algebra rather than a graph to find the time when Mr. Jackson catches up with the bus. Then show that you get the same result.

© Houghton Mifflin Harcourt Publishing Company

4b. In terms of the context of the problem, explain why the *t*-coordinate of the intersection point (and not some other point) determines how long it takes Mr. Jackson to catch up with the bus.

_____

_____

_____

PRACTICE

Graph each linear function.

1. $f(x) = 3x - 4$

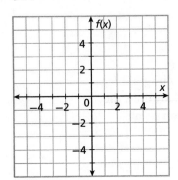

2. $f(x) = \frac{1}{2}x + 2$

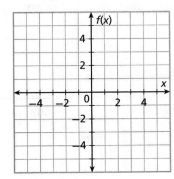

3. $f(x) = -1$

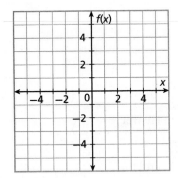

4. $f(x) = \frac{4}{3}x$

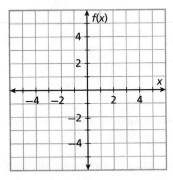

5. $f(x) = \frac{1}{4}x - 3$

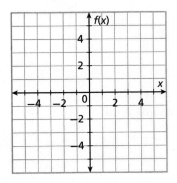

6. $f(x) = -5x + 1$

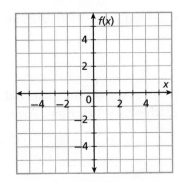

© Houghton Mifflin Harcourt Publishing Company

Graph each linear function and answer the question. Explain your answer.

7. A plumber charges $50 for a service call plus $75 per hour. The total of these costs (in dollars) is a function $C(t)$ of the time t (in hours) on the job. For how many hours will the cost be $200? $300?

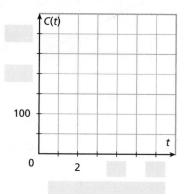

8. A bamboo plant is 10 centimeters tall at noon and grows at a rate of 5 centimeters every 2 hours. The height (in centimeters) is a function $h(t)$ of the time t it grows. When will the plant be 20 centimeters tall?

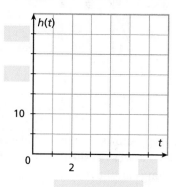

_____

_____

_____

_____

Write the linear function f using the given information.

9. The graph of the function has a slope of 4 and a y-intercept of 1.

_____

10. The graph of the function has a slope of 0 and a y-intercept of 6.

_____

11. The graph of the function has a slope of $-\frac{2}{3}$ and a y-intercept of 5.

_____

12. The graph of the function has a slope of $\frac{7}{4}$ and a y-intercept of 0.

_____

13.

x	f(x)
−3	8
0	5
3	2

14.

x	f(x)
0	−3
2	0
4	3

15.

x	f(x)
1	−1
2	5
3	11

16.

x	f(x)
5	−2
10	−6
15	−10

© Houghton Mifflin Harcourt Publishing Company

Write the linear function *f* using the given information.

17.

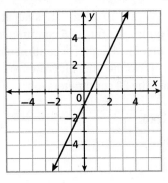

_____

18.

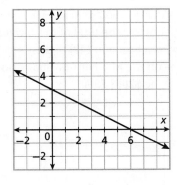

_____

19. The graph shows the amount of gas remaining in the gas tank of Mrs. Liu's car as she drives at a steady speed for 2 hours. How long can she drive before her car runs out of gas?

Fuel Consumption

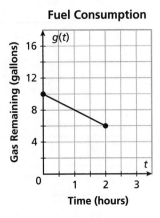

a. Interpret the question by describing what aspect of the graph would answer the question.

_____

_____

b. Write a linear function whose graph includes the segment shown.

_____

c. Tell how to use the function to answer the question; then find the answer.

_____

20. Jamal and Nathan exercise by running one circuit of a basically circular route that is 5 miles long and takes them past each other's home. The two boys run in the same direction, and Jamal passes Nathan's home 12 minutes into his run. Jamal runs at a rate of 7.5 miles per hour while Nathan runs at a rate of 6 miles per hour. If the two boys start running at the same time, when, if ever, will Jamal catch up with Nathan before completing his run?

a. Identify the independent and dependent variables, how they are measured, and how you will represent them.

_____

_____

_____

b. Write distance-run functions for Jamal and Nathan.

_____

c. Graph the functions, find the intersection point, and check the point against the conditions of the problem to answer the question.

_____

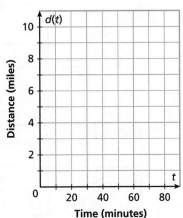

© Houghton Mifflin Harcourt Publishing Company

Additional Practice

Write the equation that describes each line in slope-intercept form.

1. slope = 4; y-intercept = –3

   y = _____

2. slope = –2; y-intercept = 0

   y = _____

3. slope = $-\dfrac{1}{3}$; y-intercept = 6

   y = _____

4. slope = $\dfrac{2}{5}$, (10, 3) is on the line.

   Find the y-intercept $y = mx + b$

   ____ = (____) ____ + b

   ____ = ____ + b

   ____ = b

   Write the equation: y = _____

Write each equation in slope-intercept form. Then graph the line described by the equation.

5. $y + x = 3$

6. $y + 4 = \dfrac{4}{3}x$

7. $5x - 2y = 10$

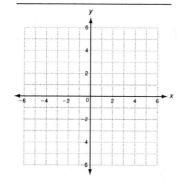

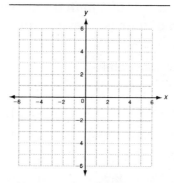

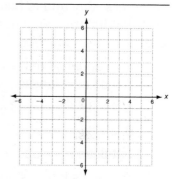

8. Daniel works as a volunteer in a homeless shelter. So far, he has worked 22 hours, and he plans to continue working 3 hours per week. His hours worked as a function of time is shown in the graph.

   a. Write an equation that represents the hours Daniel will work as a function of time. _____

   b. Identify the slope and y-intercept and describe their meanings. _____

   _____

   c. Find the number of hours worked after 16 weeks.

   _____

Volunteer Hours

(graph with y-axis "Hours Worked" 10–100 and x-axis "Time (weeks)" 2–20)

© Houghton Mifflin Harcourt Publishing Company

Problem Solving

The cost of food for an honor roll dinner is $300 plus $10 per student. The cost of the food as a function of the number of students is shown in the graph. Write the correct answer.

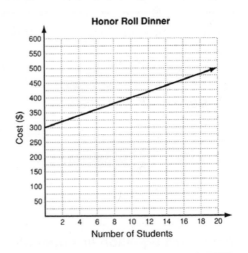

Honor Roll Dinner

1. Write an equation that represents the cost as a function of the number of students.

   _____

2. Identify the slope and y-intercept and describe their meanings.

   _____

   _____

3. Find the cost of the food for 50 students. _____

Laura is on a two-day hike in the Smoky Mountains. She hiked 8 miles on the first day and is hiking at a rate of 3 mi/h on the second day. Her total distance as a function of time is shown in the graph. Select the best answer.

4. Which equation represents Laura's total distance as a function of time?

   A $y = 3x$ C $y = 3x + 8$

   B $y = 8x$ D $y = 8x + 3$

5. What does the slope represent?

   F Laura's total distance after one day

   G Laura's total distance after two days

   H the number of miles Laura hiked per hour on the first day

   J the number of miles Laura hikes per hour on the second day

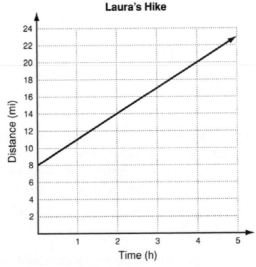

Laura's Hike

6. What does the y-intercept represent?

   A Laura's total distance after one day

   B Laura's total distance after two days

   C the number of miles Laura hiked per hour on the first day

   D the number of miles Laura hikes per hour on the second day

7. What will be Laura's total distance if she hikes for 6 hours on the second day?

   F 14 miles   H 26 miles

   G 18 miles   J 28 miles

© Houghton Mifflin Harcourt Publishing Company

Video Tutor

Point-Slope Form

Connection: Relating Slope-Intercept, Point-Slope, and Standard Forms

Essential question: *What properties of linear functions does each linear function form illustrate?*

MCC9–12.F.IF.8

1 EXAMPLE Writing Equations in Slope-Intercept Form

Write an equation for $-4x + 5y = 10$ in slope-intercept form. Then use that form to identify the slope and y-intercept.

A Rewrite the equation in slope-intercept form by solving for y.

$-4x + 5y = 10$ Standard form of the equation

$5y = \boxed{} + 10$ Add $4x$ to each side.

$y = \boxed{} + \frac{10}{5}$ Divide each side by 5.

$y = \boxed{}$ Simplify.

B Identify the slope and y-intercept of the line.

The equation is in the form $y = mx + b$, where m is the slope and b is the y-intercept. So, the slope of the line is $\boxed{}$ and the y-intercept is $\boxed{}$.

REFLECT

1a. In the Example, which equation form would you use to graph the equation? Explain.

_____

_____

_____

1b. Rewrite $Ax + By = C$ in slope-intercept form. Explain how you can use this form to identify the slope and y-intercept of a line when its equation is given in standard form.

_____

_____

_____

© Houghton Mifflin Harcourt Publishing Company

2 EXAMPLE   Writing Equations in Standard Form

Write an equation for $y - 4 = \frac{2}{3}(x - 9)$ in standard form. Then use that form to identify the x- and y-intercepts.

A Rewrite the equation in standard form by collecting the x- and y-terms on one side of the equation.

$$y - 4 = \frac{2}{3}(x - 9) \qquad \text{Point-slope form of the equation}$$

$$\boxed{} = \boxed{} \cdot \frac{2}{3}(x - 9) \qquad \text{Multiply each side by 3.}$$

$$3y - 12 = \boxed{} \qquad \text{Simplify.}$$

$$3y = \boxed{} \qquad \text{Add 12 to each side.}$$

$$\boxed{} = \boxed{} \qquad \text{Subtract } 2x \text{ from each side.}$$

B Find the x-intercept by substituting 0 for y and solving for x.

$$-2x + 3\left(\boxed{}\right) = -6 \qquad \text{Substitute 0 for } y.$$

$$\boxed{} = -6 \qquad \text{Simplify.}$$

$$x = \boxed{} \qquad \text{Solve for } x.$$

The x-intercept is $\boxed{}$.

C Find the y-intercept by substituting 0 for x and solving for y.

$$-2\left(\boxed{}\right) + 3y = -6 \qquad \text{Substitute 0 for } x.$$

$$\boxed{} = -6 \qquad \text{Simplify.}$$

$$y = \boxed{} \qquad \text{Solve for } y.$$

The y-intercept is $\boxed{}$.

REFLECT

2a. Find the x-intercept of the line in the Example by substituting 0 for y and solving for x in the point-slope form of the equation. Is it easier to find the x-intercept using the standard form or the point-slope form? Explain your answer.

_____

_____

2b. Explain why you substitute 0 for x in the equation to find the y-intercept.

_____

_____

_____

© Houghton Mifflin Harcourt Publishing Company

3 EXAMPLE   Choosing an Appropriate Form of a Linear Equation

Determine which form of a linear equation to use to write an equation for the line that passes through (−4, 9) and (8, 6). Then write an equation for the line.

A   To determine which form to use, identify the given information.

Two points on the line are given, and neither of them is the *y*-intercept. So, write the equation using _____ form.

B   Find the slope of the line using the two points.

$$m = \frac{y_2 - y_1}{x_2 - x_1} = \frac{6 - \boxed{}}{\boxed{} - (-4)} = \boxed{} = \boxed{}$$

C   Write the equation in _____ form using the point (8, 6).

$$y - y_1 = m(x - x_1) \qquad \text{General form of the equation}$$

$$y - \boxed{} = \boxed{} \left(x - \boxed{}\right) \qquad \text{Substitute values for } x_1, y_1, \text{ and } m.$$

REFLECT

3a. Could (−4, 9) have been used to write an equation of the line in Part C? Explain.

_____

_____

3b. Suppose you are given the *y*-intercept and the slope of a line. Which linear equation form would you use to write an equation for the line? Explain your reasoning.

_____

_____

The following table provides a summary of the information presented in the Examples above.

Form	Equation	Information	When to Use
slope-intercept	$y = mx + b$	• *m* is the slope. • *b* is the *y*-intercept.	• When given the slope and the *y*-intercept
point-slope	$y - y_1 = m(x - x_1)$	• *m* is the slope. • (x_1, y_1) lies on the line.	• When given the slope and one point on the line • When given two points on the line
standard	$Ax + By = C$	• *A*, *B*, and *C* are real numbers. • *A* and *B* are not both 0.	• When given a horizontal or vertical line and one point on the line

© Houghton Mifflin Harcourt Publishing Company

Rewrite the equation to find the characteristics of the line.

1. Rewrite $y = -\frac{3}{2}x + 6$ in standard form. Identify the x-intercept of the line.

_____

2. Rewrite $-7x + 9y = 18$ in slope-intercept form. Identify the slope and y-intercept of the line.

_____

3. Rewrite $y + 1 = 4(x + 3)$ in slope-intercept form. Identify the y-intercept of the line.

_____

4. Rewrite $y + 25 = -\frac{5}{3}(x - 12)$ in standard form. Identify the x- and y-intercepts of the line.

_____

Determine which form of a linear equation to use to write an equation for the line with the given characteristics. Then write an equation for the line in that form.

5. passes through $(-5, -4), (7, 5)$

_____

6. slope $= -\frac{2}{7}$; y-intercept $= 9$

_____

7. vertical line through $(8, 1)$

_____

8. slope $= \frac{11}{13}$; passes through $(-3, 6)$

_____

9. You are asked to rewrite $-9x + 4y = 14$ to find the slope of the line. Would you rewrite the equation in slope-intercept form or point-slope form? Explain.

_____

_____

10. Find the x- and y-intercepts of the graph of $Ax + By = C$. Explain how you can use these intercepts to find the x- and y-intercepts of any line in standard form.

_____

_____

_____

© Houghton Mifflin Harcourt Publishing Company

Additional Practice

Write an equation in point-slope form for the line with the given slope that contains the given point.

1. slope = 3; (−4, 2)

2. slope = −1; (6, −1)

_____   _____

Graph the line described by each equation.

3. $y + 2 = -\dfrac{2}{3}(x - 6)$

4. $y + 3 = -2(x - 4)$

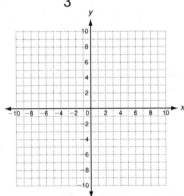   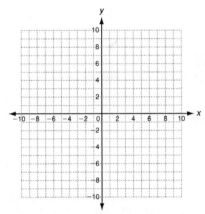

Write the equation that describes the line in slope-intercept form.

5. slope = −4; (1, −3) is on the line

6. slope = $\dfrac{1}{2}$; (−8, −5) is on the line

_____   _____

7. (2, 1) and (0, −7) are on the line

8. (−6, −6) and (2, −2) are on the line

_____   _____

Find the intercepts of the line that contains each pair of points.

9. (−1, −4) and (6, 10) _____

10. (3, 4) and (−6, 16) _____

11. The cost of internet access at a cafe is a function of time. The costs for 8, 25, and 40 minutes are shown. Write an equation in slope-intercept form that represents the function. Then find the cost of surfing the web at the cafe for one hour.

Time (min)	8	25	40
Cost ($)	4.36	7.25	9.80

_____

© Houghton Mifflin Harcourt Publishing Company

Problem Solving

Write the correct answer.

1. The number of students in a school has been increasing at a constant rate. The table shows the number of students in the school for certain numbers of years since 1995.

Years Since 1995	Number of Students
0	118
5	124
10	130

Write an equation in point-slope form that represents this linear function.

_____

Write the equation in slope-intercept form.

_____

Assuming the rate of change remains constant, how many students will be in the school in 2010?

_____

2. Toni is finishing a scarf at a constant rate. The table shows the number of hours Toni has spent knitting this week and the corresponding number of rows in the scarf.

Toni's Knitting	
Hours	**Rows of Knitting**
2	38
4	44
6	50

Write an equation in slope-intercept form that represents this linear function.

_____

3. A photo lab manager graphed the cost of having photos developed as a function of the number of photos in the order. The graph is a line with a slope of $\frac{1}{10}$ that passes through (10, 6). Write an equation in slope-intercept form that describes the cost to have photos developed. How much does it cost to have 25 photos developed?

_____

The cost of a cell phone for one month is a linear function of the number of minutes used. The total cost for 20, 35, and 40 additional minutes are shown. Select the best answer.

4. What is the slope of the line represented in the table?

   A 0.1   C 2

   B 0.4   D 2.5

5. What would be the monthly cost if 60 additional minutes were used?

   F $64   H $84

   G $72   J $150

Cell-Phone Costs			
Number of Additional Minutes	20	35	40
Total Cost	$48	$54	$56

6. What does the y-intercept of the function represent?

   A total cost of the bill

   B cost per additional minute

   C number of additional minutes used

   D cost with no additional minutes used

© Houghton Mifflin Harcourt Publishing Company

Transforming Linear Functions
Going Deeper

Essential question: *How can a linear function be understood as the transformation of another linear function?*

Given a linear function, you can find the related function that results from shifting the graph of the given function vertically or horizontally, reflecting it across the *x*- or *y*-axis, stretching or compressing it.

Video Tutor

MCC9–12.F.BF.3

1 EXPLORE   Translating Linear Functions Vertically

A Complete the table of values for the function $f(x) = \frac{1}{2}x - 2$. Then graph the function.

x	−4	−2	0	2	4
f(x)	−4	−3			

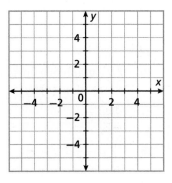

B For each point that you graphed, plot a new point 5 units above the first. Do not translate the points horizontally. Draw a line connecting the 5 new points and label it *g*.

C Find the slope and *y*-intercept of the new line. What is the equation of the line?

_____

REFLECT

1a. Compare *f*(*x*) and *g*(*x*). How do you account for the difference(s) in the functions?

_____

_____

_____

1b. Find *k* if $g(x) = f(x) + k$.

_____

1c. Suppose *f* is translated 3 units down to produce the function *h*. What is the equation of *h*? Explain your reasoning.

_____

_____

_____

_____

© Houghton Mifflin Harcourt Publishing Company

2 EXPLORE — Translating Linear Functions Horizontally

A Complete the table of values for the function $f(x) = x + 2$. Then graph the function.

x	−4	−2	0	2	4
f(x)	−2	0			

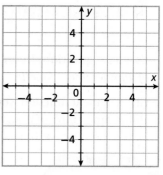

B For each point that you graphed, plot a new point 2 units to the right of the first. Do not translate the points vertically. Draw a line connecting the 5 new points and label it *g*.

C Find the slope and *y*-intercept of the new line. What is the equation of the line?

_____

REFLECT

2a. If the graph of a linear function *f* is translated horizontally, the resulting function *g* is related to *f(x)* by $g(x) = f(x − k)$. Find *k* for the transformation graphed.

_____

2b. If $f(x) = x + 2$ is shifted 5 units to the left, the resulting function is $g(x) = x + 7$. The shift is horizontal, so $g(x) = f(x − k)$. Find *k* for this transformation.

_____

2c. What is the relationship between *k* in the equation for the horizontal translation of a linear function $g(x) = f(x − k)$ and how far and in what direction the function is translated?

_____

_____

3 EXPLORE — Reflecting Linear Functions

A Complete the table of values for the function $f(x) = x + 2$. Then graph the function.

x	−2	−1	0	1	2
f(x)	0	1			

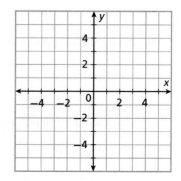

B Reflect each of the points that you graphed across the *y*-axis. Draw a line connecting the 5 new points and label it *g*.

C Use the graphs and the table of values to complete the equations:

$g(-2) = f()$ $g(-1) = f()$ $g(0) = f()$ $g(1) = f()$ $g(2) = f()$

$g(x) = f()$

© Houghton Mifflin Harcourt Publishing Company

3a. The graph of $f(x) = x + 2$ is reflected across the x-axis. The image, h, is shown in the graph. Use the graph to write the order pairs $(x, f(x))$ and $(x, h(x))$ for $x = -3, -2, -1, 0, 1, 2,$ and 3.

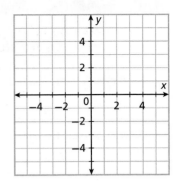

_____

_____

_____

3b. Write $h(x)$ in terms of $f(x)$: $h(x) = $ [____]

MCC9–12.F.BF.3

4 EXPLORE **Compressing or Stretching Functions Vertically**

A The graph of $f(x) = x$ is shown. For each of the values $x = 0, 2, 4,$ 6, and 8, plot the point that is halfway between the x-axis and the point (x, x). That is, compress the graph of f vertically. Then draw a line through the points and label the graph h.

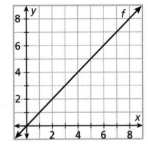

B Explain how the y-coordinate of each point $(x, h(x))$ is related to the y-coordinate of the point $(x, f(x))$. Then write a rule for h in terms of $f(x)$.

_____

4a. Compare the segments of the graphs of f and h for which the endpoints have x-coordinates 2 and 8. How do the two segments show that h is a vertical compression of f?

_____

4b. The graph of h appears to be a counterclockwise rotation of the graph of f. Tell how you know that this is not true.

_____

4c. Explain why the vertical compression $h(x) = \frac{1}{2}f(x) = \frac{1}{2}x$ is also a horizontal stretch.

_____

4d. Give a value of k for which $h(x) = k\,f(x)$ is a vertical stretch of f. Explain your reasoning.

_____

_____

© Houghton Mifflin Harcourt Publishing Company

Linear function f is transformed to produce g. Write $g(x)$ in terms of $f(x)$.

1. $f(x) = 3x$ is translated 6 units up.

2. $f(x) = x - 6$ is translated 3 units down.

3. $f(x) = -x$ is translated 2 units up.

4. $f(x) = -4x + 5$ is translated 6 units down.

5. $f(x) = 4x + 3$ is translated 2 units left.

6. $f(x) = -3x$ is translated 5 units right.

7. $f(x) = 13x$ is translated 3 units to the left.

8. $f(x) = 2x + 9$ is translated 7 units right.

9. $f(x) = 2x$ is reflected across the y-axis.

10. $f(x) = x - 7$ is reflected across the x-axis.

11. $f(x) = -x + 5$ is reflected across the y-axis.

12. $f(x) = -2x + 11$ is reflected across the x-axis.

Choose from the following phrases the appropriate description(s) of g as a transformation of f: *vertical compression, vertical stretch, horizontal compression, horizontal stretch*.

13. $g(x) = \frac{3}{4}f(x)$

14. $g(x) = 3f(x)$

Linear function f is transformed twice to produce g. Write $g(x)$ in terms of $f(x)$. You can use a graphing calculator to check your answers.

15. f is translated 5 units down, then 4 units right.

16. f is translated 5 units right, then 4 units down.

17. f is reflected across the x-axis, then across the y-axis.

18. f is translated 6 units up, then reflected across the x-axis.

19. f is translated 4 units right, then reflected across the y-axis.

© Houghton Mifflin Harcourt Publishing Company

Additional Practice

Let _g(x)_ be the indicated transformation of _f(x)_. Write the rule for _g(x)_.

1.

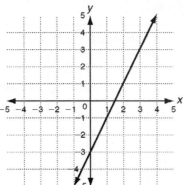

horizontal translation

left 3 units

_____

2.

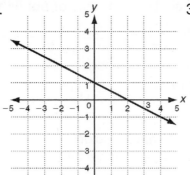

vertical compression by

a factor of $\frac{1}{5}$

_____

3.

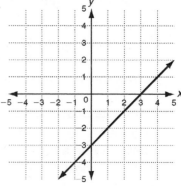

reflection across the

_y_-axis

_____

4. linear function defined by the table; horizontal stretch by
   a factor of 2.3

   _____

x	−5	0	7
y	−3	7	21

5. $f(x) = 1.7x - 3$; vertical compression by a factor of 0.7   _____

**Let _g(x)_ be the indicated combined transformation of _f(x) = x_. Write
the rule for _g(x)_.**

6. vertical translation down 2 units followed by a

   horizontal compression by a factor of $\frac{2}{5}$ _____

7. horizontal stretch by a factor of 3.2 followed by
   a horizontal translation right 3 units   _____

Solve.

8. The Red Cab Taxi Service used to charge $1.00 for the first $\frac{1}{5}$ mile and $0.75 for each

   additional $\frac{1}{5}$ mile. The company just raised its rates by a factor of 1.5.

   a. Write a new price function _g(x)_ for a taxi ride.

   _____

   b. Describe the transformation(s) that have been applied.

   _____

© Houghton Mifflin Harcourt Publishing Company

The students in Ms. Hari's English class are planning to print a booklet of their creative writings. Use the table of publishing prices.

1. The students decide to print a booklet containing black and white text only. Write a function, $C(p)$, to show the cost of printing a booklet of p pages with a cover that also has text only.

   _____

Publishing Prices		
	Text Only	**Color Graphic**
Per page	$0.55	$1.25
Cover	$2.25	$3.50

2. Julie wants the booklet cover to have a color graphic. Write a new function, $J(p)$, to show this cost for a booklet of p pages.

   _____

3. What is the slope of each function? What does the slope tell you about the relationship of the lines?

   _____

4. What is the y-intercept of each function? What is represented by the y-intercept?

   _____

5. Describe the transformation that has been applied to the graph by the decision to change the cover.

   _____

6. Oscar suggests that the booklet have 30 pages, one for each person in the class. What is the cost of printing 50 booklets, using the function $J(p)$?

   _____

Choose the letter for the best answer.

7. Lee writes a function for the cost of p pages, all in color, with a plain text cover. What transformation does this apply to the graph of $C(p)$?

   A Horizontal stretch

   B Horizontal compression

   C Vertical stretch

   D Vertical compression

8. Tina finds a printer who will print text pages at $0.25 a page, with a color cover for $2.00. Using this printer, what is the cost of 50 booklets of 30 pages each?

   A $950

   B $725

   C $600

   D $475

© Houghton Mifflin Harcourt Publishing Company

Geometric Sequences

Essential question: *How can you write a rule for a geometric sequence?*

In a **geometric sequence**, the ratio of consecutive terms is constant.
The constant ratio is called the **common ratio**, often written as *r*.

MCC9–12.F.BF.1a

1 EXAMPLE Writing Rules for a Geometric Sequence

Makers of Japanese swords in the 1400s repeatedly folded and hammered the metal to form layers. The folding process increased the strength of the sword.

The table shows how the number of layers depends on the number of folds. Write a recursive rule and an explicit rule for the geometric sequence described by the table.

Number of Folds	*n*	1	2	3	4	5
Number of Layers	*f(n)*	2	4	8	16	32

A Find the common ratio by calculating the ratios of consecutive terms.

$\frac{4}{2} = $ [　] $\frac{8}{4} = $ [　]

$\frac{16}{8} = $ [　] $\frac{32}{16} = $ [　]

The common ratio, *r*, is _____.

B Write a recursive rule for the sequence.

$f(1) = $ [　] and

The first term is _____.

$f(n) = $ [　] · [　] for $n \geq 2$

Every other term is the _____ of the previous term and the common ratio.

C Write an explicit rule for the sequence by writing each term as the product of the first term and a power of the common ratio.

n	*f(n)*
1	$2(2)^0 = 2$
2	$2(2)^1 = 4$
3	$2(2)^{[　]} = 8$
4	$2(2)^{[　]} = 16$
5	$2(2)^{[　]} = 32$

Generalize the results from the table: $f(n) = $ [　] $\cdot 2^{n-[　]}$

© Houghton Mifflin Harcourt Publishing Company

1a. Explain how you know that the sequence 4, 12, 36, 108, 324, ... is a geometric sequence.

_____

1b. A geometric sequence has a common ratio of 5. If you know that the 6th term of the sequence is 30, how could you find the 7th term?

_____

MCC9–12.F.BF.1a

2 EXPLORE   Writing General Rules for Geometric Sequences

Use the geometric sequence 6, 24, 96, 384, 1536, ... to help you write a recursive rule and an explicit rule for any geometric sequence. For the general rules, the values of _n_ are consecutive integers starting with 1.

A Find the common ratio.

Numbers

6, 24, 96, 384, 1536, ...

Common ratio = ☐

Algebra

$f(1), f(2), f(3),$ ☐ , ☐ , ...

Common ratio = r

B Write a recursive rule.

Numbers

$f(1) =$ ☐ and

$f(n) = f(n-1) \cdot$ ☐ for $n \geq 2$

Algebra

Given $f(1)$,

$f(n) = f(n-1) \cdot$ ☐ for $n \geq 2$

C Write an explicit rule.

Numbers

$f(n) =$ ☐ $\cdot$ ☐$^{n-1}$

Algebra

$f(n) =$ ☐ $\cdot$ ☐$^{n-1}$

REFLECT

2a. The first term of a geometric sequence is 81 and the common ratio is $\frac{1}{3}$. Explain how you could find the 4th term of the sequence.

_____

2b. What information do you need to know in order to find the 5th term of a geometric sequence by using its explicit rule?

_____

2c. What is the recursive rule for the sequence $f(n) = 5(4)^{n-1}$?

_____

© Houghton Mifflin Harcourt Publishing Company

3 EXAMPLE Relating Geometric Sequences and Exponential Functions

The graph shows the heights to which a ball bounces after it is dropped. Write an explicit rule for the sequence of bounce heights.

A Represent the sequence in a table.

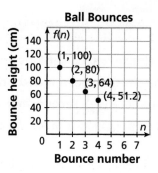

Ball Bounces

n	1	2	3	4
$f(n)$				

B Examine the sequence.

Is the sequence geometric? Explain.

_____

What is the common ratio? _____

C Write an explicit rule for the sequence.

$f(n) = f(1) \cdot r^{n-1}$ Write the general rule.

$f(n) = \boxed{} \cdot \boxed{}^{\,n-1}$ Substitute _____ for $f(1)$ and _____ for r.

So, the sequence has the rule _____ where n is the bounce

number and $f(n)$ is the _____.

REFLECT

3a. A geometric sequence is equivalent to an exponential function with a restricted domain. On the graph above, draw an exponential curve that passes through the given points. Then write an exponential function of the form $f(n) = ab^n$, where a is the initial amount (or y-intercept) and b is the common ratio, for the curve that you drew and give the function's domain.

_____

3b. Show that the explicit rule for the sequence is equivalent to the exponential function. Justify the steps you take.

_____

_____

_____

© Houghton Mifflin Harcourt Publishing Company

The explicit and recursive rules for a geometric sequence can also be written in subscript notation.

Explicit: $a^n = a_1 \cdot r^{n-1}$

Recursive: a_1 is given and $a_n = a_{n-1} \cdot r$ for $n \geq 2$

MCC9–12.F.LE.2

4 EXAMPLE Writing a Geometric Sequence Given Two Terms

The shutter speed settings on a camera form a geometric sequence where a_n is the shutter speed in seconds and n is the setting number. The fifth setting on the camera is $\frac{1}{60}$ second, and the seventh setting on the camera is $\frac{1}{15}$ second. Write an explicit rule for the sequence using subscript notation.

A Identify the given terms in the sequence.

$a_5 = \boxed{}$

The fifth setting is $\frac{1}{60}$ second, so the 5th term of the sequence is $\frac{1}{60}$.

$a_{\boxed{}} = \boxed{}$

The seventh setting is $\frac{1}{15}$ second, so the _____ term of the sequence is _____.

B Find the common ratio.

$a_7 = a_6 \cdot r$ Write the recursive rule for a_7.

$a_6 = \boxed{} \cdot r$ Write the recursive rule for a_6.

$a_7 = \boxed{} \cdot \boxed{} \cdot r$ Substitute the expression for a_6 into the rule for a_7.

$\boxed{} = \boxed{} \cdot r^2$ Substitute $\frac{1}{15}$ for a_7 and _____ for a_5.

$\boxed{} = r^2$ Multiply both sides by 60.

$\boxed{} = r$ Definition of positive square root

C Find the first term of the sequence.

$a_n = a_1 \cdot r^{n-1}$ Write the explicit rule.

$\boxed{} = a_1 \cdot \boxed{}^{\boxed{}-1}$ Substitute $\frac{1}{60}$ for a_n, _____ for r, and 5 for n.

$\frac{1}{60} = a_1 \cdot \boxed{}$ Simplify.

$\boxed{} = a_1$ Divide both sides by 16.

D Write the explicit rule.

$a_n = a_1 \cdot r^{n-1}$ Write the general rule.

$a_n = \boxed{} \cdot \boxed{}^{\,n-1}$ Substitute _____ for a_1 and _____ for r.

© Houghton Mifflin Harcourt Publishing Company

REFLECT

4a. When finding the common ratio, why can you ignore the negative square root of 4 when solving the equation $4 = r^2$?

_____

_____

_____

4b. If you graphed the explicit rule for the sequence, what would the graph look like?

_____

PRACTICE

Write a recursive rule and an explicit rule for each geometric sequence.

1. 9, 27, 81, 243, ...

_____

2. 5, −5, 5, −5, ...

_____

3. $12, 3, \dfrac{3}{4}, \dfrac{3}{16}, \ldots$

_____

4. The table shows the beginning-of-month balances, rounded to the nearest cent, in Marla's savings account for the first few months after she made an initial deposit in the account.

Month	n	1	2	3	4
Account Balance ($)	$f(n)$	2010.00	2020.05	2030.15	2040.30

a. Explain how you know that the sequence of account balances is geometric.

_____

b. Write recursive and explicit rules for the sequence of account balances.

_____

c. What amount did Marla deposit initially? Explain.

_____

© Houghton Mifflin Harcourt Publishing Company

5. The graph shows the number of players in the first four rounds of the U.S. Open women's singles tennis tournament.

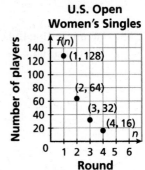

U.S. Open Women's Singles

(graph showing Number of players vs Round with points (1, 128), (2, 64), (3, 32), (4, 16))

a. Write an explicit rule for the sequence of players in each round.

_____

b. How many rounds are there in the tournament? (*Hint:* In the last round, only 2 players are left.)

_____

6. The numbers of points that a player must accumulate to reach the next level of a video game form a geometric sequence, where a_n is the number of points needed to complete level n.

a. A player needs 1000 points to complete level 2 and 8,000,000 points to complete level 5. Write an explicit rule for the sequence using subscript notation.

_____

b. How many points are needed for level 7? _____

Write an explicit rule for each geometric sequence based on the given terms from the sequence. Assume that the common ratio r is positive.

7. $a_2 = 12$ and $a_4 = 192$

_____

8. $a_5 = 0.32$ and $a_7 = 0.0128$

_____

Each rule represents a geometric sequence. If the given rule is recursive, write it as an explicit rule. If the given rule is explicit, write it as a recursive rule. Assume that $f(1)$ is the first term of the sequence.

9. $f(n) = 6(3)^{n-1}$

_____

10. $f(1) = 10; f(n) = f(n-1) \cdot 8$ for $n \geq 2$

_____

11. An economist predicts that the cost of food will increase by 4% per year for the next several years.

a. Use the economist's prediction to write an explicit rule for a geometric sequence that gives the cost in dollars of a box of cereal in year n given that it costs $3.20 in year 1.

_____

b. What is the fourth term of the sequence, and what does it represent in this situation?

_____

© Houghton Mifflin Harcourt Publishing Company

Additional Practice

Find the next three terms in each geometric sequence.

1. −5, −10, −20, −40, …

   _____

3. −10, 40, −160, 640, …

   _____

2. 7, 56, 448, 3584…

   $r = .8$

   _____

4. 40, 10, $\dfrac{5}{2}$, $\dfrac{5}{8}$, …

   _____

5. The first term of a geometric sequence is 6 and the common ratio is −8. Find the 7th term.

   _____

6. The first term of a geometric sequence is −3 and the common ratio is $\dfrac{1}{2}$. Find the 6th term.

   _____

7. The first term of a geometric sequence is −0.25 and the common ratio is −3. Find the 10th term.

   _____

8. What is the 12th term of the geometric sequence −4, −12, −36, …?

   _____

9. What is the 10th term of the geometric sequence 2, −6, 18, …?

   _____

10. What is the 6th term of the geometric sequence 50, 10, 2, …?

   _____

11. A shoe store is discounting shoes each month. A pair of shoes cost $80. The table shows the discount prices for several months. Find the cost of the shoes after 8 months. Round your answer to the nearest cent.

Month	Price
1	$80.00
2	$72.00
3	$64.80

_____

© Houghton Mifflin Harcourt Publishing Company

Problem Solving

Write the correct answer.

1. A ball is dropped from 400 feet. The table shows the height of each bounce.

Bounce	Height (ft)
1	280
2	196
3	137.2

Find the height of the ball on the 6th bounce. Round your answer to the nearest tenth of a foot.

_____

3. Jeanette started selling bagels to offices in her area. Her sales for the first 3 months are shown in the table.

Month	Sales ($)
1	$200.00
2	$230.00
3	$264.50

If this trend continues, find the amount of Jeanette's sales in Month 8.

_____

2. A plant starts with 1 branch. Every year, each branch becomes 3 branches. A sketch of the plant for the first 3 years is shown. How many branches will the plant have in year 10?

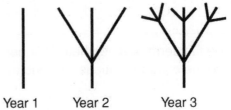

Year 1   Year 2   Year 3

_____

How many branches would the plant have in year 10 if the plant had 5 branches the first year? (Each branch still becomes 3 branches every year.)

_____

The table shows the number of houses in a new subdivision. Use the table to answer questions 4–7. Select the best answer.

Month	Houses
1	3
2	6
3	12
4	24

4. The number of houses forms a geometric sequence. What is r?

   A 0.5   C 3

   B 2   D 6

5. Assuming that the trend continues, how many houses would be in the subdivision in Month 6?

   F 36   H 60

   G 48   J 96

6. Management decides the subdivision is complete when the number of houses reaches 48. When will this happen?

   A Month 5   C Month 7

   B Month 6   D Month 8

7. Suppose the number of houses tripled every month. How many more houses would be in the subdivision in Month 4? (The number of houses in Month 1 is still 3.)

   F 48   H 72

   G 57   J 81

© Houghton Mifflin Harcourt Publishing Company

Exponential Functions
Going Deeper

Essential question: *How does changing the values of a, h, and k affect the graph of an exponential function?*

A general exponential growth function has the form $f(x) = ab^{x-h} + k$ where $b > 0$ and a, h, and k are real numbers with $a > 0$. Every value of b represents a different family of functions that can be transformed by changing the values of a, h, and k. The general exponential decay function has the same form, but $0 < b < 1$.

Video Tutor

MCC9–12.F.BF.3

1 EXPLORE Changing *h* and *k*

Use your graphing calculator to help you with this activity.

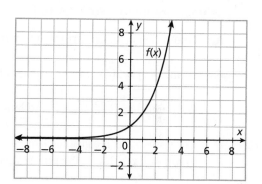

A Graph $f(x) = 2^x$. Confirm that it matches the graph shown at right.

B Graph $g(x) = 2^{x-4}$. Sketch and label $g(x)$ at right.

C Graph $h(x) = 2^{x+6}$. Sketch and label $h(x)$ at right.

D Compare the three graphs. How is the graph of $g(x)$ related to the graph of $f(x)$? How is the graph of $h(x)$ related to the graph of $f(x)$?

_____

_____

_____

E Delete all equations from the equation editor. Then graph $f(x) = 3^x$. Confirm that it matches the graph shown at right.

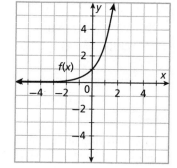

F Graph $g(x) = 3^x + 3$. Sketch and label $g(x)$ at right.

G Graph $h(x) = 3^x - 5$. Sketch and label $h(x)$ at right.

H Compare the three graphs. How is the graph of $g(x)$ related to the graph of $f(x)$? How is the graph of $h(x)$ related to the graph of $f(x)$?

_____

_____

_____

© Houghton Mifflin Harcourt Publishing Company

1a. How do you think the value of h affects the graph of $g(x) = b^{x-h}$?

_____

_____

1b. How do you think the value of k affects the graph of $g(x) = b^x + k$?

_____

_____

MCC9–12.F.BF.3

2 EXPLORE · Changing a

Use your graphing calculator to help you with this activity.

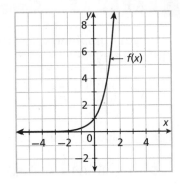

A Graph $f(x) = 4^x$. Confirm that it matches the graph shown.

B Graph $g(x) = 3(4)^x$. Sketch and label $g(x)$ at right.

C Graph $h(x) = \frac{1}{2}(4)^x$. Sketch and label $h(x)$ at right.

D Compare the three graphs. How is the graph of $g(x)$ related to the graph of $f(x)$? How is the graph of $h(x)$ related to the graph of $f(x)$?

_____

_____

REFLECT

2a. For $a > 0$, how do you think the value of a affects the graph of $g(x) = ab^x$?

_____

_____

2b. Without graphing, explain how the graph of $g(x) = 4(2)^{x+1} - 7$ compares to the graph of $f(x) = 2^x$.

_____

_____

The following table summarizes how the values of the parameters a, h, and k affect the graph of an exponential growth function or an exponential decay function.

$f(x) = ab^{x-h} + k$	
Parameter	**Effect**
h	If $h > 0$, the graph of the parent function is translated $|h|$ units to the right. If $h < 0$, the graph of the parent function is translated $|h|$ units to the left.
k	If $k > 0$, the graph of the parent function is translated $|k|$ units up. If $k < 0$, the graph of the parent function is translated $|k|$ units down.
a	If $a > 1$, the graph of the parent function is stretched vertically by a factor of a. If $0 < a < 1$, the graph of the parent function is shrunk vertically by a factor of a.

© Houghton Mifflin Harcourt Publishing Company

3 EXAMPLE Graphing $f(x) = b^{x-h} + k$

Graph each exponential decay function.

A $g(x) = \left(\frac{1}{2}\right)^x - 5$

- First graph the parent function, $f(x) = \left(\frac{1}{2}\right)^x$. The graph of $f(x)$ is shown at right.

- The graph of $g(x)$ is a translation of the graph of $f(x)$ by how many units and in which direction?

  _____

- Use this transformation to sketch the graph of $g(x)$ at right.

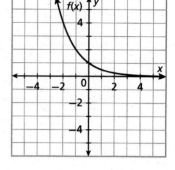

B $g(x) = \left(\frac{1}{3}\right)^{x+2} + 1$

- The parent function $f(x)$ is _____. The graph of $f(x)$ is shown at right.

- The graph of $g(x)$ is a translation of the graph of $f(x)$ by how many units and in which direction or directions?

  _____

- Use this transformation to sketch the graph of $g(x)$ at right.

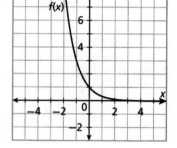

REFLECT

3a. How is the graph of $g(x) = 0.25^{x-3}$ related to the graph of $f(x) = 0.25^x$?

_____

3b. How is the graph of $h(x) = 0.25^{x+3}$ related to the graph of $f(x) = 0.25^x$?

_____

3c. How is the graph of $g(x) = 0.25^{x-3}$ related to the graph of $h(x) = 0.25^{x+3}$?

_____

4 EXAMPLE Graphing $f(x) = ab^x$

Graph each exponential decay function.

A $g(x) = 4(0.25)^x$

- First graph the parent function, $f(x) = 0.25^x$. The graph of $f(x)$ is shown at right.

- The graph of $g(x)$ is a vertical stretch of the graph of $f(x)$ by

  a factor of _____.

- Use this transformation to sketch the graph of $g(x)$ at right.

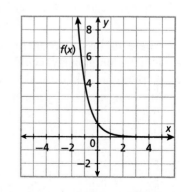

© Houghton Mifflin Harcourt Publishing Company

B $g(x) = \frac{1}{2}\left(\frac{1}{2}\right)^x$

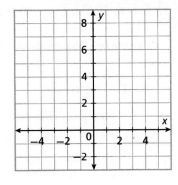

- The parent function $f(x)$ is _____. Graph $f(x)$ on the coordinate plane at right.

- How is the graph of $g(x)$ related to the graph of $f(x)$?

  _____

  _____

- Use this transformation to sketch the graph of $g(x)$ at right.

REFLECT

4a. How is the graph of $g(x) = 9\left(\frac{2}{3}\right)^x$ related to the graph of $f(x) = \left(\frac{2}{3}\right)^x$?

_____

_____

4b. How is the graph of $h(x) = \frac{1}{3}\left(\frac{2}{3}\right)^x$ related to the graph of $f(x) = \left(\frac{2}{3}\right)^x$?

_____

_____

4c. How is the graph of $h(x) = \frac{1}{3}\left(\frac{2}{3}\right)^x$ related to the graph of $g(x) = 9\left(\frac{2}{3}\right)^x$?

_____

_____

4d. Use properties of exponents to explain why the graph of $g(x) = \left(\frac{1}{2}\right)^{x-3}$ may be considered a vertical stretch of the graph of $f(x) = \left(\frac{1}{2}\right)^x$. What is the factor of the vertical stretch?

_____

_____

Using the properties of exponents, you can rewrite the expression $ab^{x-h} + k$ as follows:

$$ab^{x-h} + k = ab^x \cdot b^{-h} + k = \left(ab^{-h}\right)b^x + k$$

where ab^{-h} is a constant because a, b, and h are constants. This means that the parameter h in the function $f(x) = ab^{x-h} + k$ can be eliminated by combining it with the parameter a. Therefore, when you are asked to find the equation of an exponential growth or decay function, you can assume that it has the form $f(x) = ab^x + k$.

© Houghton Mifflin Harcourt Publishing Company

Lesson 2

5 **E X A M P L E** Writing an Equation from a Graph

Write an equation of the exponential growth function $g(x)$ whose graph is shown.

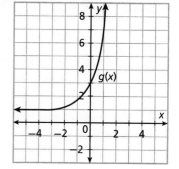

A Let $g(x) = ab^x + k$. First find the value of k.

Since the graph has the line $y = 1$ as a horizontal asymptote, there is a vertical translation of the parent function.

So, $k =$ _____ .

B Find the value of a.

The y-intercept of the graph of $g(x)$ is _____ .

If the graph of $g(x)$ is translated so that the x-axis is the asymptote, then the y-intercept of the graph will be _____ .

The y-intercept of the parent exponential growth function $f(x) = b^x$ is _____ .

This means the graph of the parent function is stretched vertically by a factor of _____ .

So, $a =$ _____ .

C Find the value of b.

The graph of $g(x)$ passes through $(1, 7)$.

If the graph is translated as in part A, then it passes through $(1, \underline{\quad})$.

Shrinking produces the graph of the parent function passing through $(1, \underline{\quad})$.

The graph of the parent function passes through $(1, b)$, so $b =$ _____ .

D Write the equation.

Using the values of the parameters from above, $g(x) =$ _____ .

REFLECT

5a. How did you use the fact that $g(x)$ passes through $(1, 7)$ to find a point through which the parent function passes?

_____

_____

5b. How can you check that you wrote a correct equation?

_____

© Houghton Mifflin Harcourt Publishing Company

The graph of $f(x) = 2.5^x$ is shown. Write the function rules for $g(x)$ and $h(x)$ based on the descriptions given. Then sketch and label the graphs of $g(x)$ and $h(x)$ on the same coordinate plane.

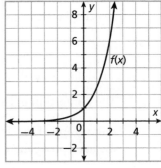

1. The graph of $g(x)$ is the translation of the graph of $f(x)$ to the left 3 units.

_____

2. The graph of $h(x)$ is the translation of the graph of $f(x)$ up 2 units.

_____

The graph of $f(x) = 3^x$ is shown. Write the function rules for $g(x)$ and $h(x)$ based on the descriptions given. Then sketch and label the graphs of $g(x)$ and $h(x)$ on the same coordinate plane.

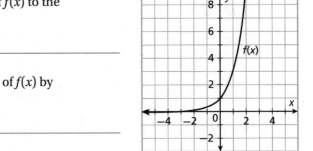

3. The graph of $g(x)$ is the translation of the graph of $f(x)$ to the right 2 units and down 1 unit.

_____

4. The graph of $h(x)$ is a vertical stretch of the graph of $f(x)$ by a factor of 2.5.

_____

Given $f(x) = 2^x$, write the function rules for $g(x)$, $h(x)$, $j(x)$, and $k(x)$ based on the descriptions given. Then give the range of each function.

5. The graph of $g(x)$ is a vertical shrink of the graph of $f(x)$ by a factor of $\frac{1}{3}$ and a vertical translation 6 units up.

_____

6. The graph of $h(x)$ is a vertical stretch of the graph of $f(x)$ by a factor of 5 and a horizontal translation 4 units left.

_____

7. The graph of $j(x)$ is a vertical stretch of the graph of $f(x)$ by a factor of 1.2, a horizontal translation 2 units right, and a vertical translation 4 units down.

_____

8. The graph of $k(x)$ is a vertical shrink of the graph of $f(x)$ by a factor of 0.1, a horizontal translation 1 unit left, and a vertical translation 3 units up.

_____

© Houghton Mifflin Harcourt Publishing Company

9. Error Analysis A student is told that the graph shown at right is a vertical translation of $f(x) = 1.5^x$ and determines that the equation of the function must be $f(x) = 1.5^x - 3$ because the y-intercept is -3. Explain and correct the error in the student's reasoning.

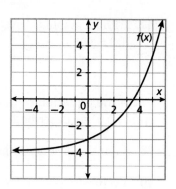

_____

_____

_____

Write an equation of the exponential function $g(x)$ whose graph is shown.

10.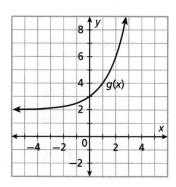

11.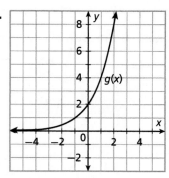

12.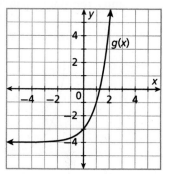

_____   _____   _____

Graph each exponential decay function.

13. $f(x) = \left(\frac{1}{4}\right)^x + 1$

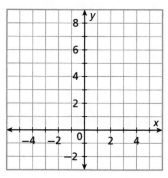

14. $f(x) = 0.5^{x-2} - 1$

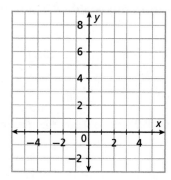

15. $f(x) = 3\left(\frac{1}{3}\right)^x$

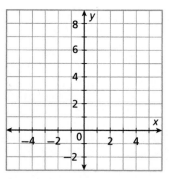

16. $f(x) = 2(0.5)^{x+1}$

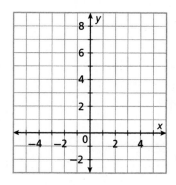

© Houghton Mifflin Harcourt Publishing Company

17. Without graphing, give the *y*-intercept and the horizontal asymptote of the graph of
$f(x) = 7(0.2)^x - 4$.

_____

**Write the equation of *g(x)* given that *g(x)* is a transformation of the graph of
f(x) = 0.6^x as described.**

18. A translation 2 units right and 1 unit up   _____

19. A vertical stretch by a factor of 3.5   _____

20. A vertical shrink by a factor of 0.1
and a translation 5 units left   _____

Write an equation of the exponential function *g(x)* whose graph is shown.

21.

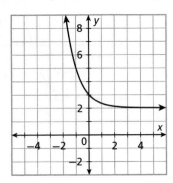

22.

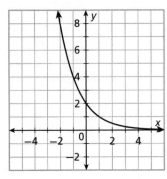

23.

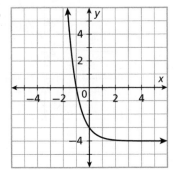

_____   _____   _____

**Rewrite the function $f(x) = ab^{x-h} + k$ in the form $f(x) = ab^x + k$ to eliminate the
parameter *h*.**

24. $f(x) = 100(5^{x-2}) + 8$ **25.** $f(x) = 216(3^{x-3}) - 4$ **26.** $f(x) = 32(2^{x-5}) + 1$

_____   _____   _____

27. $f(x) = 3(4^{x+3}) + 6$ **28.** $f(x) = 0.4(5^{x+3}) + 9$ **29.** $f(x) = 0.5(2^{x+5}) - 11$

_____   _____   _____

© Houghton Mifflin Harcourt Publishing Company

Additional Practice

Given $f(x) = 3^x$, write function rules for $g(x)$, $h(x)$, $j(x)$, $k(x)$, and $m(x)$ based on the descriptions given.

1. The graph of $g(x)$ is a translation of the graph of $f(x)$ to the right 5 units.

   _____

2. The graph of $h(x)$ is a translation of the graph of $f(x)$ down 7 units.

   _____

3. The graph of $j(x)$ is a translation of the graph of $f(x)$ to the right 2 units and up 4 units.

   _____

4. The graph of $k(x)$ is a vertical stretch of the graph of $f(x)$ by a factor of 4.5.

   _____

5. The graph of $m(x)$ is a vertical shrink of the graph of $f(x)$ by a factor of 0.5 and a translation 6 units to the left.

   _____

Graph each exponential function.

6. $y = 5(2)^x$

7. $y = -2(3)^x$

8. $y = 3\left(\dfrac{1}{2}\right)^x$

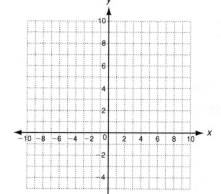
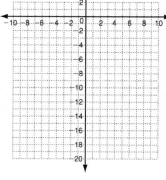

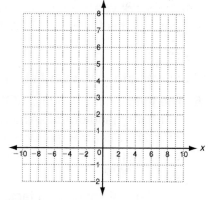

In the year 2000, the population of Virginia was about 7,400,000. Between the years 2000 and 2004, the population in Virginia grew at a rate of 5.4%. At this growth rate, the function $f(x) = 7,400,000(1.054)^x$ gives the population x years after 2000.

9. In what year will the population reach 15,000,000? _____

10. In what year will the population reach 20,000,000? _____

© Houghton Mifflin Harcourt Publishing Company

Problem Solving

Write the correct answer.

1. The function $f(x) = 6(1.5)^x$ models the length of a photograph in inches after the photo has been enlarged by 50% x times. Graph the function.

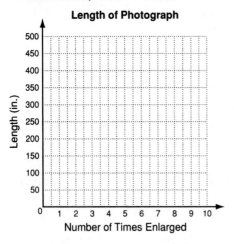

Length of Photograph

Length (in.) vs. Number of Times Enlarged

2. A population of 550 rabbits is increasing by 2.5% each year. The function $y = 5.5(1.025)^x$ gives the population of rabbits, in hundreds, x years from now. How is the graph of this function related to the graph of $y = 1.025^x$?

_____

_____

3. The function $y = 0.2(1.0004)^x$ models the balance, in thousands of dollars on a customer's line of credit x days after the end of the grace period (the time when no interest accumulates). How is the graph of this function related to the graph of $y = 1.0004^x$?

_____

_____

4. The function $f(x) = 2300(0.995)^x$ models enrollment in a high school, where x is the number of years after 2005. How is the graph of this function related to the graph of $y = 0.995^x$?

_____

_____

A lake was stocked with fish in early April. Select the best answer.

5. The function $f(x) = 300(0.85)^x$ models the number of landlocked salmon in the lake x months after the lake was stocked. How is the graph of $f(x)$ related to the graph of $g(x) = 0.85^x$?

   A Vertical shrink by a factor of 0.85

   B Vertical stretch by a factor of 300

   C Translation to the right by 0.85 units

   D Translation to the right by 300 units

6. The function $f(x) = 0.075(1.2)^x$ models the number of rainbow trout, in thousands, in the lake x years after 2005. How is the graph of $f(x)$ related to the graph of $g(x) = 1.2^x$?

   F Translation to the left by 0.075 units

   G Translation to the left by 1.2 units

   H Vertical shrink by a factor of 0.075

   J Vertical stretch by a factor of 1.2

© Houghton Mifflin Harcourt Publishing Company

Exponential Growth and Decay
Going Deeper

Essential question: *How do you write, graph, and interpret exponential growth and decay functions?*

Video Tutor

When you graph a function $f(x)$ in a coordinate plane, the x-axis represents the independent variable and the y-axis represents the dependent variable. Therefore, the graph of $f(x)$ is the same as the graph of the equation $y = f(x)$. You will use this form when you use a calculator to graph functions.

MCC9–12.F.IF.7e

1 EXPLORE Describing End Behavior of a Growth Function

A Use a graphing calculator to graph the exponential growth function $f(x) = 200(1.10)^x$ using Y_1 for $f(x)$. Use a viewing window from -20 to 20 for x, with a scale of 2, and from -100 to 1000 for y, with a scale of 50. Make a copy of the curve below.

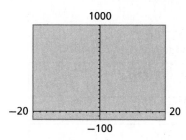

B To describe the *end behavior* of a function, you describe the function values as x increases or decreases without bound. Using the TRACE feature, move the cursor to the right along the curve. Describe the end behavior as x increases without bound.

_____

C Using the TRACE feature, move the cursor to the left along the curve. Describe the end behavior as x decreases without bound.

_____

REFLECT

1a. Describe the domain and the range of the function.

_____

1b. Identify the y-intercept of the graph of the function. _____

1c. An *asymptote* of a graph is a line the graph approaches more and more closely. Identify an asymptote of this graph _____

1d. Why is the value of the function always greater than 0?

_____

© Houghton Mifflin Harcourt Publishing Company

Recall that a function of the form $y = ab^x$ represents exponential growth when $a > 0$ and $b > 1$. If b is replaced by $1 + r$ and x is replaced by t, then the function is the **exponential growth model** $y = a(1 + r)^t$, where a is the *initial amount*, the base $(1 + r)$ is the *growth factor*, r is the *growth rate*, and t is the *time interval*. The value of the model increases with time.

MCC9–12.F.LE.2

2 EXAMPLE   Modeling Exponential Growth

Alex buys a rare trading card for $4. The value of the card increases 40% per year for four years.

A   Identify the initial amount and the growth rate.

$a = $ _____

$r = $ _____

B   Write an exponential growth equation for this situation:

$$y = \boxed{}\left(1 + \boxed{}\right)^t$$

C   Copy and complete the table. Round to the nearest cent.

Time (years) t	Value ($) y
0	
1	
2	
3	
4	

D   Graph the points from the table using appropriate scales. Draw a smooth curve connecting the points. Label the axes.

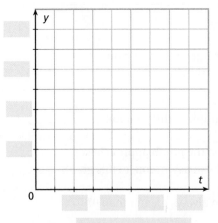

© Houghton Mifflin Harcourt Publishing Company

REFLECT

2a. Identify the *y*-intercept of the graph. What does it represent?

_____

2b. What is the growth factor $(1 + r)$ written as a percent? _____

2c. Use the graph to estimate the value of the card in 3.5 years. Then explain why it makes sense to connect the points from the table with a smooth curve when graphing this function.

_____

_____

2d. Describe the domain and range of the function $y = 4(1.4)^t$ outside of the context of this problem. Do all of these values make sense in the context of this situation? Why or why not?

_____

_____

_____

MCC9–12.F.IF.7e

3 EXPLORE   **Describing End Behavior of a Decay Function**

A   Use a graphing calculator to graph the exponential decay function $f(x) = 500(0.8)^x$ using Y_1 for $f(x)$. Use a viewing window from -10 to 10 for *x*, with a scale of 1, and from -500 to 5,000 for *y*, with a scale of 500. Make a copy of the curve below.

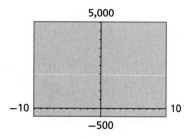

B   Using the TRACE feature, move the cursor to the right along the curve. Describe the end behavior as *x* increases without bound.

_____

C   Using the TRACE feature, move the cursor to the left along the curve. Describe the end behavior as *x* decreases without bound.

_____

© Houghton Mifflin Harcourt Publishing Company

REFLECT

3a. Describe the domain and the range of the function.

_____

3b. Identify the *y*-intercept of the graph of the function. _____

3c. Identify an asymptote of this graph. Why is this line an asymptote?

_____

Recall that a function of the form $f(x) = ab^x$ represents exponential decay when $a > 0$ and $0 < b < 1$. If b is replaced by $1 - r$ and x is replaced by t, then the function is the **exponential decay model** $y = a(1 - r)^t$, where a is the *initial amount*, the base $(1 - r)$ is the *decay factor*, r is the *decay rate*, and t is the *time interval*.

MCC9–12.F.LE.2

4 **E X A M P L E** **Modeling Exponential Decay**

You pay $12,000 for a car. The value then depreciates at a rate of 15% per year. That is, the car loses 15% of its value each year.

A Write an exponential decay equation for this situation.

$$y = \boxed{}\left(1 - \boxed{}\right)^t$$

B Complete the table. Round to the nearest dollar.

C Graph the points and connect them with a smooth curve. Label the axes.

Time (years) t	Value ($) y
0	
1	
2	
3	
4	
5	
6	

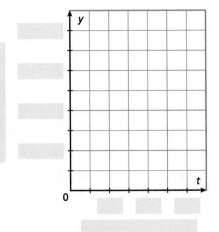

REFLECT

4a. Identify the *y*-intercept of the graph. What does it represent?

_____

4b. What is the decay factor $(1 - r)$ written as a percent?

_____

© Houghton Mifflin Harcourt Publishing Company

4c. What values make sense for the domain and range of this function?

_____

_____

4d. Predict the value of the car after 10 years.

_____

4e. In how many years was the value of the car $8000?

_____

4f. Explain why exponential functions of this type are referred to as exponential _decay_ functions.

_____

MCC9–12.F.LE.1c

5 **E X A M P L E** **Comparing Exponential Growth and Exponential Decay**

The graph shows the value of two different shares of stock over the period of four years since they were purchased. The values have been changing exponentially. Describe and compare the behaviors of the two stocks.

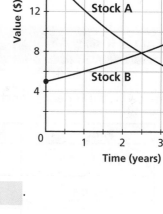

A The model for the graph representing Stock A is an exponential _____ model.

The initial value is _____ and the

decay factor is ☐ ÷ ☐ = ☐ .

B The model for the graph representing Stock B is an exponential _____ model. The initial

value is _____ and the growth factor is ☐ ÷ ☐ = ☐ .

C The value of Stock A is going _____ over time. The value of Stock B is going

_____ over time. The initial value of Stock A is _____ than the initial value

of Stock B. However, after about _____ years, the value of Stock A becomes less

than the value of Stock B.

© Houghton Mifflin Harcourt Publishing Company

5a. What is the growth rate for the increasing function above? Explain your reasoning.

_____

5b. What is the decay rate for the decreasing function above? Explain your reasoning.

_____

5c. How did the values of the stocks compare initially? after four years?

_____

_____

5d. In how many years was the value of Stock A about equal to the value of Stock B? Explain your reasoning.

_____

5e. In how many years was the value of Stock A about twice the value of Stock B? Explain your reasoning.

_____

_____

PRACTICE

Complete the table for each function.

Function	Initial Amount	Growth Rate	Growth Factor
1. $y = 1250(1 + 0.02)^t$			
2. $y = 40(1 + 0.5)^t$			
3. $y = 50(1.06)^t$			

Write an equation for each exponential growth function.

4. Eva deposits $1500 in an account that earns 4% interest each year.

_____

5. Lamont buys a house for $255,000. The value of the house increases 6% each year.

_____

6. Brian invests $2000. His investment grows at a rate of 16% per year.

_____

© Houghton Mifflin Harcourt Publishing Company

7. Sue is a coin collector. At the end of 2005 she bought a coin for $2.50 whose value had been growing 20% per year for 3 years. The value continued to grow at this rate until she sold the coin 4 years later.

    a. Write an exponential growth equation for this situation, using the amount Sue paid as the value at time 0. _____

    b. Complete the table.

                                               c. Graph and connect the points.

Time (years) t	Value ($) y
−3	
−2	
−1	
0	
1	
2	
3	
4	

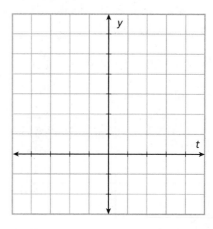

    d. Describe the domain and range for this situation.

    _____

    _____

    e. Identify the y-intercept. What does it represent?

    _____

    f. What was the value of the coin at the end of 2003? at the time Sue sold the coin? Explain your reasoning.

    _____

    _____

    _____

8. Suppose you invest $1600 on your 16th birthday and your investment earns 8% interest each year. What will be the value of the investment on your 30th birthday? Explain your reasoning.

_____

© Houghton Mifflin Harcourt Publishing Company

9. Identify the initial amount, the decay factor, and the decay rate for the function $y = 2.50(0.4)^t$. Explain how you found the decay rate.

_____

10. Mr. Nevin buys a car for $18,500. The value depreciates 9% per year. Write an equation for this function

_____

11. You are given a gift of $2,500 in stock on your 16th birthday. The value of the stock declines 10% per year.

  a. Write an exponential decay equation for this situation.   _____

  b. Complete the table.

Time (years), t	Value ($), y
0	
1	
2	
3	
4	
5	

  c. Graph and connect the points. Label the axes.

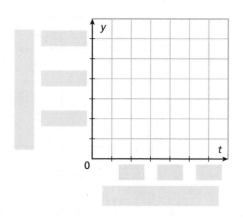

  d. Predict the value of the stock on your 22nd birthday.   _____

12. The value of two parcels of land has been changing exponentially in the years since they were purchased, as shown in the graph. Describe and compare the values of the two parcels of land.

_____

_____

_____

_____

_____

_____

_____

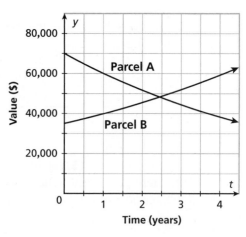

© Houghton Mifflin Harcourt Publishing Company

Additional Practice

Write an exponential growth function to model each situation. Then find the value of the function after the given amount of time.

1. Annual sales for a fast food restaurant are $650,000 and are increasing at a rate of 4% per year; 5 years

_____

2. The population of a school is 800 students and is increasing at a rate of 2% per year; 6 years

_____

3. During a certain period of time, about 70 northern sea otters had an annual growth rate of 18%; 4 years

_____

Write a compound interest function to model each situation. Then find the balance after the given number of years.

4. $50,000 invested at a rate of 3% compounded monthly; 6 years

_____

5. $43,000 invested at a rate of 5% compounded annually; 3 years

_____

6. $65,000 invested at a rate of 6% compounded quarterly; 12 years

_____

Write an exponential decay function to model each situation. Then find the value of the function after the given amount of time.

7. The population of a town is 2500 and is decreasing at a rate of 3% per year; 5 years

_____

8. The value of a company's equipment is $25,000 and decreases at a rate of 15% per year; 8 years

_____

9. The half-life of Iodine-131 is approximately 8 days. Find the amount of Iodine-131 left from a 35 gram sample after 32 days. _____

© Houghton Mifflin Harcourt Publishing Company

Problem Solving

Write the correct answer.

1. A condo in Austin, Texas, was worth $80,000 in 1990. The value of the condo increased by an average of 3% each year. Write an exponential growth function to model this situation. Then find the value of the condominium in 2005.

_____

_____

2. Markiya deposited $500 in a savings account. The annual interest rate is 2%, and the interest is compounded monthly. Write a compound interest function to model this situation. Then find the balance in Markiya's account after 4 years.

_____

_____

3. The population of a small Midwestern town is 4500. The population is decreasing at a rate of 1.5% per year. Write an exponential decay function to model this situation. Then find the number of people in the town after 25 years.

_____

_____

4. Twelve students at a particular high school passed an advanced placement test in 2000. The number of students who passed the test increased by 16.4% each year thereafter. Find the number of students who passed the test in 2004.

_____

_____

Half-lives range from less than a second to billions of years. The table below shows the half-lives of several substances. Select the best answer.

5. About how many grams of a 500 g sample of Technetium-99 is left after 2 days?

   A 1.95 g   C 31.25 g

   B 7.81 g   D 62.5 g

6. Which equation can be used to find how much of a 50 g sample of Nitrogen-16 is left after 7 minutes?

   F $A = 50(0.5)^1$ H $A = 50(0.5)^{42}$

   G $A = 50(0.5)^7$ J $A = 50(0.5)^{60}$

7. How many billions of years will it take 1000 grams of Uranium-238 to decay to just 125 grams?

   A 0.125   C 9

   B 3   D 13.5

Half-Lives	
Nitrogen-16	7 s
Technetium-99	6 h
Sulfur-35	87 days
Tritium	12.3 yr
Uranium-238	4.5 billion yrs

8. A researcher had 37.5 g left from a 600 g sample of Sulfer-35. How many half-lives passed during that time?

   F 4   H 7

   G 5   J 16

9. Look at problem 8. How many days passed during that time?

   A 7   C 348

   B 16   D 435

© Houghton Mifflin Harcourt Publishing Company

Linear, Quadratic, and Exponential Models

Extension: Exponential models and regression

Essential question: *How can you model and solve problems involving exponential data?*

Video Tutor

You can apply the properties of equations you already know to solve equations involving exponents. You will also need the following property.

Equating Exponents when Solving Equations		
Words	**Algebra**	**Example**
Two powers with the same positive base other than 1 are equal if and only if the exponents are equal.	If $b > 0$ and $b \neq 1$, then $b^x = b^y$ if and only if $x = y$.	If $2^x = 2^9$, then $x = 9$. If $x = 9$, then $2^x = 2^9$.

MCC9–12.A.REI.1

1 **EXAMPLE** Solving Equations by Equating Exponents

Solve each equation.

A $\frac{5}{2}(2)^x = 80$

$\boxed{} \cdot \frac{5}{2}(2)^x = \boxed{} \cdot 80$ Multiply to isolate the power $(2)^x$.

$(2)^x = 32$ Simplify.

$(2)^{\boxed{}} = 2^{\boxed{}}$ Write 32 as a power of 2.

$x = \boxed{}$ $b^x = b^y$ if and only if $x = y$.

B $4\left(\frac{5}{3}\right)^x = \frac{500}{27}$

$\boxed{} \cdot 4\left(\frac{5}{3}\right)^x = \boxed{} \cdot \frac{500}{27}$ Multiply to isolate the power.

$\left(\frac{5}{3}\right)^x = \frac{125}{27}$ Simplify.

$\left(\frac{5}{3}\right)^x = \left(\frac{5}{3}\right)^{\boxed{}}$ Write the fraction as a power of $\frac{5}{3}$.

$x = \boxed{}$ $b^x = b^y$ if and only if $x = y$.

© Houghton Mifflin Harcourt Publishing Company

1a. How can you check a solution?

_____

1b. How can you work backward to write $\frac{125}{27}$ as a power of $\frac{5}{3}$?

_____

1c. Is it possible to solve the equation $2^x = 96$ using the method in the Example? Why or why not?

_____

Some equations can't be solved using the method in the Example because it isn't possible to write both sides of the equation as a whole number power of the same base. Instead, you can consider the expressions on either side of the equation as the rules for two different functions. You can then solve the original equation in one variable by graphing the two functions. The solution is the input value for the point where the two graphs intersect.

MCC9–12.A.REI.11

2 EXAMPLE   **Writing an Equation and Solving by Graphing**

A town has 78,918 residents. The population is increasing at a rate of 6% per year. The town council is offering a prize for the best prediction of how long it will take for the population to reach 100,000. Make a prediction.

A   Write an exponential model to represent the situation. Let y represent the population and x represent time (in years).

$$y = 78{,}918\left(1 + \boxed{}\right)^{x}$$

B   Write an equation in one variable to represent the time, x, when the population reaches 100,000.

$$\boxed{} = 78{,}918\left(1 + \boxed{}\right)^{x}$$

C   Write functions for the expressions on either side of the equation.

$$f(x) = \boxed{}$$

$$g(x) = 78{,}918\left(1 + \boxed{}\right)^{x}$$

D   What type of function is $f(x)$? What type of function is $g(x)$?

_____

© Houghton Mifflin Harcourt Publishing Company

E Graph the functions on a graphing calculator. Let $Y_1 = f(x)$ and $Y_2 = g(x)$. Sketch the graph of Y_2 below. (Y_1 is already graphed for you.) Include the missing window values.

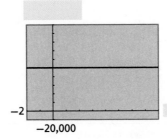

-2

$-20{,}000$

F Use the intersect feature on the CALC menu to find the input value where the graphs intersect. (Do not round.)

_____

G Make a prediction as to the number of years until the population reaches 100,000.

_____

REFLECT

2a. Suppose the contest is announced on January 1, and the town has 78,918 residents on that date. Explain how to predict *the date* on which the population will be 100,000.

_____

_____

_____

2b. Explain why the *x*-coordinate of the point where the graphs of $Y_1 = f(x)$ and $Y_2 = g(x)$ intersect is the solution of the equation in Part B.

_____

_____

_____

_____

_____

_____

© Houghton Mifflin Harcourt Publishing Company

In the previous Example you knew the growth rate and were able to write an exponential model for the situation. However, in many real-world situations you only may have data points with which to create a model. For situations that can be modeled exponentially, you can use the exponential regression feature on a graphing calculator to create a model for the data.

MCC9–12.S.ID.6a

3 EXAMPLE Fitting a Function to Data

The table shows the number of internet hosts from 2001 to 2007.

Number of Internet Hosts							
Years since 2001	0	1	2	3	4	5	6
Number (millions)	110	147	172	233	318	395	490

A Enter the data from the table on a graphing calculator, with years since 2001 in List 1 and number of internet hosts in List 2. Then set up a scatter plot of the data, as shown, and graph it. Copy the points below.

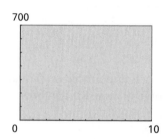

B The data fall along a curve, so an exponential function might fit the data. Use your calculator's statistical calculation features to find the exponential regression model. Record the results rounded to three significant digits.

Function $y =$ _____ Correlation coefficient $r =$ _____

REFLECT

3a. What does the correlation coefficient suggest about the model?

_____

3b. Use your rounded function model to predict the number of internet hosts in 2010 and in 2020. Round to three significant digits.

2010: _____ 2020: _____

3c. Are these predictions likely to be accurate? Explain.

_____

_____

© Houghton Mifflin Harcourt Publishing Company

Residuals You have used residuals to assess how well a linear model fits a data set. You can also use residuals for exponential and other models. Remember that if (x, y_d) is a data point and the corresponding point on the model is (x, y_m), then the corresponding *residual* is the difference $y_d - y_m$.

Recall that a model is a good fit for the data when the following are true:

- The numbers of positive and negative residuals are roughly equal.
- The residuals are randomly distributed about the *x*-axis, with no pattern.
- The absolute values of the residuals are small relative to the data.

MCC9–12.S.ID.6b

4 EXAMPLE Plotting and Analyzing Residuals

Continue working with the data from the first Example to plot and analyze the residuals.

A Enter the regression equation from your calculator as the rule for equation Y_1. (It can be found with the statistical variables on the variables menu.) Then view the table to find the function values y_m for the model. Record the results in the table at the right. Round to three significant digits.

B Use the results of Part A to complete the residuals column of the table.

Number of Internet Hosts (millions)			
x	**y_d**	**y_m**	**Residual $y_d - y_m$**
0	110	110	0
1	147	142	5
2	172		
3	233		
4	318		
5	395		
6	490		

C Set up a residual scatter plot of the data, as shown, and graph it. Adjust the viewing window as needed. Copy the points below.

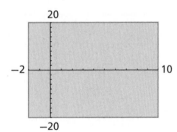

D At first glance, does the model fit the data well? Explain.

_____

_____

© Houghton Mifflin Harcourt Publishing Company

4a. Use the model $y = 110(1.29)^x$ from Part B of the first Example to find the function value for $x = 4$. Round to three significant digits. Compare the result with the value in the table above and with the actual value.

_____

_____

4b. Are the residuals in the calculator plotted on the residual plot exactly the same as the residuals in the table? Why or why not?

_____

_____

4c. One reason the model is a good fit for the data is that the absolute values of the residuals are small relative to the data. What does this claim mean? Give examples from the table to support this claim.

_____

_____

4d. Another reason the model fits the data well is that the residuals are randomly distributed about the x-axis with no pattern. Use a graphing calculator to find a _linear_ regression model for these data. Describe the residual plot. What does it tell you about the model?

_____

_____

_____

4e. Describe what the parameters a and b in the model represent. Is the number of internet hosts growing or decaying? Explain your reasoning. What is the growth or decay rate?

_____

_____

_____

© Houghton Mifflin Harcourt Publishing Company

Solve each equation without graphing.

1. $5(3)^x = 405$

$x =$ _____

2. $\frac{1}{5}(5)^x = 5$

$x =$ _____

3. $10(4)^x = 640$

$x =$ _____

4. $7\left(\frac{1}{2}\right)^x = \frac{7}{8}$

$x =$ _____

5. $\frac{3}{4}\left(\frac{2}{3}\right)^x = \frac{4}{27}$

$x =$ _____

6. $3\left(\frac{3}{10}\right)^x = \frac{27}{100}$

$x =$ _____

Solve each equation by graphing. Round to the nearest hundredth.

7. $6^x = 150$

$x \approx$ _____

8. $5^x = 20$

$x \approx$ _____

9. $(2.5)^x = 40$

$x \approx$ _____

10. Last year a debate club sold 972 fundraiser tickets on their most successful day. This year the 4 club officers plan to match that number on a single day as follows:

To start off, on Day 0, each of the 4 officers of the club will sell 3 tickets and ask each buyer to sell 3 more tickets the next day. Every time a ticket is sold, the buyer of the ticket will be asked to sell 3 more tickets the next day.

If the plan works, on what day will the number of tickets sold be 972?

a. Write an equation in one variable to model the situation. _____

b. If the plan works, on what day will the number sold be 972? _____

11. There are 175 deer in a state park. The population is increasing at the rate of 12% per year. At this rate, when will the population reach 300?

a. Write an equation in one variable to model the situation. _____

b. How long will it take for the population to reach 300?

_____

c. Suppose there are 200 deer in another state park and that the deer population is increasing at a rate of 10% per year. Which park's deer population will reach 300 sooner? Explain.

_____

_____

12. A city has 642,000 residents on July 1, 2011. The population is decreasing at the rate of 2% per year. At that rate, in what month and year will the population reach 500,000? Explain how you found your answer.

_____

_____

© Houghton Mifflin Harcourt Publishing Company

The first two columns of the table show the population of Arizona (in thousands) in census years from 1900 to 2000.

13. Find an exponential function model for the data. Round to four significant digits.

_____

14. Identify the parameters in the model, including the growth or decay rate, and explain what they represent.

_____

_____

_____

15. Use the more precise model stored on your calculator to complete the third column of the table with population values based on the model. Round to three significant digits.

16. Use the results of Exercise 15 to complete the residuals column of the table.

17. Use your model from Exercise 13 to predict the population of Arizona in 1975 and in 2030, to the nearest thousand. Discuss the accuracy of the results. Which result is likely to be more accurate? Why?

_____

_____

_____

18. Make a residual plot. Does the model fit the data well? Explain.

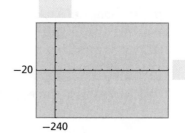

Arizona Population y (in thousands) in Years x Since 1900			
x	y_d	y_m	$y_d - y_m$
0	123		
10	204		
20	334		
30	436		
40	499		
50	750		
60	1,302		
70	1,771		
80	2,718		
90	3,665		
100	5,131		

© Houghton Mifflin Harcourt Publishing Company

Additional Practice

Solve each equation without graphing.

1. $3(2)^x = 384$

_____

2. $6(5)^x = 750$

_____

3. $0.25(6)^x = 324$

_____

4. $4\left(\dfrac{1}{5}\right)^x = \dfrac{4}{125}$

_____

5. $\dfrac{2}{5}\left(\dfrac{2}{3}\right)^x = \dfrac{32}{405}$

_____

6. $\dfrac{1}{2}\left(\dfrac{5}{8}\right)^x = \dfrac{3125}{65,536}$

_____

Solve each equation by graphing. Round to the nearest hundredth.

7. $6^x = 100$

_____

8. $7^x = 420$

_____

9. $5^x = 280$

_____

10. $(2.5)^x = 130$

_____

11. $(5.5)^x = 1525$

_____

12. $(1.5)^x = 50$

_____

There are 225 trout in a lake. The population is increasing at the rate of 15% per year. At this rate, when will the population reach 500 trout?

13. Write an equation in one variable to represent this situation.

_____

14. How long will it take for the trout population to reach 500? Round the answer to the nearest tenth of a year.

_____

15. Suppose there are 150 trout in another lake. The population of trout in that lake is increasing at a rate of 20% per year. Which lake's trout population will reach 500 sooner? Explain.

_____

_____

_____

_____

© Houghton Mifflin Harcourt Publishing Company

Problem Solving

Write the correct answer.

1. There are 250 wolves in a national park. The wolf population is increasing at a rate of 16% per year. Write an exponential model to represent the situation.

   _____

2. Use the model from Problem 1 to determine how long it will take the wolf population in the national park to reach 1000. Round the answer to the nearest hundredth.

   _____

3. A city has a population of 350,000 residents. The population is decreasing at the rate of 5% per year. Write an exponential model to represent the situation.

   _____

4. Use the model from Problem 3 to determine how long it will take the population of the city to reach 275,000 residents. Round the answer to the nearest hundredth.

   _____

A city has a population of 175,000 residents. The population of the city is increasing at the rate of 4% per year.

5. Write an exponential model to represent the situation.

   A $y = 175,000(1.04)x$

   B $y = 175,000(0.96)^x$

   C $y = 175,000(1.04)^x$

   D $y = 1.04(175,000)^x$

6. Use the model from Problem 5 to determine how long it will take the population of the city to reach 250,000 residents. Round the answer to the nearest tenth.

   F 9.1 years   H 0.1 year

   G 3.4 years   J 1.0 year

7. Another city has a population of 300,000 residents. The population of that city is decreasing at a rate of 2% per year. Write an exponential model to represent the situation.

   A $y = 300,000(1.02)^x$

   B $y = 300,000(0.98)x$

   C $y = 300,000(0.98)^x$

   D $y = 0.98(300,000)^x$

8. Use the model from Problem 7 to determine how long it will take the population of the second city to reach 250,000 residents. Round the answer to the nearest tenth.

   F 0.9 year   H 3.4 years

   G 1.0 year   J 9.0 years

© Houghton Mifflin Harcourt Publishing Company

Comparing Functions
Going Deeper

Essential question: *How can you recognize, describe, and compare linear and exponential functions?*

MCC9–12.F.LE.1

1 ENGAGE | **Comparing Constant Change and Constant Percent Change**

Suppose you are offered a job that pays $1000 the first month with a raise every month after that. You can choose a $100 raise or a 10% raise. Which option would you choose? What if the raise were 8%, 6%, or 4%?

A Work in groups and use multiple calculators to find the monthly salaries by following the steps described below. For the first three months, record the results in the table below, rounded to the nearest dollar.

- For the $100 raise, enter 1000, press **ENTER** , enter +100, press **ENTER** , and then press **ENTER** repeatedly.

- For the 10% raise, enter 1000, press **ENTER** , enter ×1.10, press **ENTER** , and then press **ENTER** repeatedly.

- For the other raises, replace 1.10 with these factors: 1.08, 1.06, and 1.04.

	Monthly Salary After Indicated Monthly Raise				
Month	$100	10%	8%	6%	4%
0	$1000	$1000	$1000	$1000	$1000
1	$1100	$1100	$1080	$1060	$1040
2					
3					

B Continue until you find the number of months it takes for each salary with a percent raise to exceed that month's salary with the $100 raise. Record the number of months in the table below.

	Number of Months Until Salary with Percent Raise Exceeds Salary with $100 Raise			
$100	10%	8%	6%	4%
---------	2			

© Houghton Mifflin Harcourt Publishing Company

1a. What is the change per unit interval in monthly salary for each option? Which of these is a constant rate of change in dollars per month? Explain your reasoning.

_____

_____

1b. Why are the differences from row to row in each percent column not constant? What *is* constant about the changes from row to row?

_____

_____

_____

MCC9–12.F.LE.3

2 **EXAMPLE**　**Comparing Linear and Exponential Functions**

Compare these two salary plans:

- Job A: $1000 for the first month with a $100 raise every month thereafter
- Job B: $1000 for the first month with a 1% raise every month thereafter

Will Job B ever have a higher monthly salary than Job A?

A　Write functions that represent the monthly salaries. Let t represent the number of elapsed months. Then tell whether the function is *linear* or *exponential*.

Job A:　$S_A(t) = $ ____ $ + $ ____ t　　　S_A is a/an _____ function.

Job B:　$S_B(t) = $ ____ $ \cdot $ ____ ^{t}　　　S_B is a/an _____ function.

B　Graph the functions on a calculator and sketch them below. Label the functions and include the scale.

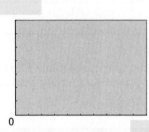

0

C　Will Job B ever have a higher monthly salary than Job A? If so, after how many months will this happen? Explain your reasoning.

_____

_____

© Houghton Mifflin Harcourt Publishing Company

2a. Revise $S_B(t)$ and use the Table feature on your graphing calculator to find the interval in which the monthly salary for Job B finally exceeds that for Job A if the growth rate is 0.1%. Use intervals of 1,000. Repeat for a growth rate of 0.01%, using intervals of 10,000.

_____

2b. Why does a quantity increasing exponentially eventually exceed a quantity increasing linearly?

_____

_____

_____

2c. The table shows values for the monthly salary functions in four-month intervals rather than one-month intervals.

t	$S_A(t)$	$S_B(t)$
0	1000	1000.00
4	1400	1040.60
8	1800	1082.86
12	2200	1126.83
16	2600	1172.58
20	3000	1220.19

- Does $S_A(t)$ grow by equal differences over each four-month interval? Explain your reasoning.

_____

_____

- Does $S_A(t)$ grow by the same difference over the first eight-month interval as it does over the first four-month interval? Explain your reasoning.

_____

- Does $S_B(t)$ grow by equal factors over each four-month interval? Explain your reasoning.

_____

- Does $S_B(t)$ grow by the same factor over the first eight-month interval as it does over the first four-month interval? Explain your reasoning.

_____

Later you will prove that linear functions grow by the same difference over equal intervals and that exponential functions grow by equal factors over equal intervals.

Tell whether each quantity is changing at a *constant rate* per unit of time, at a *constant percent rate* per unit of time, or *neither*.

1. Amy's salary is $40,000 in her first year on a job with a $2,000 raise every year thereafter. _____

2. Carla's salary is $50,000 in her first year on a job plus a 1% commission on all sales. _____

3. Enrollment at a school is 976 students initially and then it declines 2.5% each year thereafter. _____

4. Companies X and Y each have 50 employees. If Company X increases its workforce by 2 employees per month, and Company Y increases its workforce by 2% per month, will Company Y ever have more employees than Company X? If so, when?

_____

5. Centerville and Easton each have 2500 residents. Centerville's population decreases by 80 people per year, and Easton's population decreases by 3% per year. Will Centerville ever have a greater population than Easton? If so, when? Explain your reasoning.

_____

_____

_____

Complete each statement with the correct function from the table at the right.

6. _____ grows at a constant rate per unit interval.

7. _____ grows at a constant percent rate per unit interval.

8. An equation for the linear function is as follows:

_____

9. An equation for the exponential function is as follows:

_____

x	f(x)	g(x)
0	50	100
1	54	104
2	58	108
3	63	112
4	68	116
5	73	120

© Houghton Mifflin Harcourt Publishing Company

10. In 1970, the populations of both Marston and Denton were 5000. The population of Marston increased by 5000 each decade from 1970 until 2010, while the population of Denton doubled each decade during the same period. Consider the ordered pairs (n, p) for each city where n is the number of decades since 1970 and p is the population of the city.

a. Tell whether the data for each city can be represented by a linear function or an exponential function. Explain your reasoning.

_____

_____

b. Complete the table for each city. Use the tables to justify your answers in part a.

Decades since 1970	Marston's population
0	5000
1	
2	
3	
4	

Decades since 1970	Denton's population
0	5000
1	
2	
3	
4	

_____

_____

c. Write a function that models the population for each town. Then use the model to predict each town's population in 2030.

_____

_____

© Houghton Mifflin Harcourt Publishing Company

11. Complete the proof that linear functions grow by equal differences over equal intervals.

Given: $x_2 - x_1 = x_4 - x_3$,
             f is a linear function of the form $f(x) = mx + b$.

Prove: $f(x_2) - f(x_1) = f(x_4) - f(x_3)$

Proof:

$x_2 - x_1 = x_4 - x_3$	Given
$m(x_2 - x_1) = \boxed{} (x_4 - x_3)$	Mult. Prop. of Equality
$mx_2 - \boxed{} = mx_4 - \boxed{}$	Distributive Property
$mx_2 + b - mx_1 - b = mx_4 + \boxed{} - mx_3 - \boxed{}$	Add. and Subt. Prop. of Equality
$(mx_2 + b) - (mx_1 + b) = \underline{}$	Distributive Property
$f(x_2) - f(x_1) = \underline{}$	Definition of $f(x)$

12. Complete the proof that exponential functions grow by equal factors over equal intervals.

Given: $x_2 - x_1 = x_4 - x_3$
             f is an exponential function of the form $f(x) = ab^x$.

Prove: $\dfrac{f(x_2)}{f(x_1)} = \dfrac{f(x_4)}{f(x_3)}$

Proof:

$x_2 - x_1 = x_4 - x_3$	Given
$b^{x_2 - x_1} = b^{x_4 - x_3}$	If $x = y$, then $b^x = b^y$.
$\dfrac{b^{x_2}}{b^{x_1}} = \dfrac{b^{x_4}}{\boxed{}}$	Quotient of Powers Prop.
$\dfrac{ab^{x_2}}{ab^{x_1}} = \dfrac{ab^{x_4}}{\boxed{}}$	Mult. Prop. of Equality
$\dfrac{f(x_2)}{f(x_1)} = \dfrac{\boxed{}}{\boxed{}}$	Definition of $f(x)$

© Houghton Mifflin Harcourt Publishing Company

Additional Practice

1. Two functions are given below. Complete the tables and find the rate of change over [0, 3] for each function. Then graph both functions on the same coordinate plane.

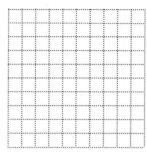

$y = 4x + 10$	
x	**y**
0	
1	
2	
3	
4	

$y = 1 + 4^x$	
x	**y**
0	
1	
2	
3	
4	

Rate of
change _____ _____

a. Compare the rates of change. _____
_____

b. How do the y-values at $x = 0$ and $x = 3$ relate to the rates of change over [0, 3]? _____
_____

2. An engineer designs reflector surfaces. Equations for the shapes of two of his designs are shown below. Complete the tables for each function. Compare the designs by finding and comparing average rates of change, minimums, and maximums over the interval [0, 3]. Then graph the functions on the same coordinate plane.

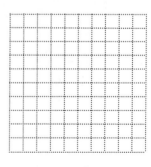

Design A: $y = 5 + 5x$	
x	**y**
0	
1	
2	
3	
4	

Design B: $y = 5 + 5^x$	
x	**y**
0	
1	
2	
3	
4	

Rate of
change _____   _____

Minimum
value on [0, 3] _____   _____

Maximum
value on [0, 3] _____   _____

© Houghton Mifflin Harcourt Publishing Company

Problem Solving

1. George and Julie each deposit money into their savings accounts monthly. Compare the accounts by finding slopes and *y*-intercepts.

   George's Account

Month	0	1	2	3
Balance ($)	125	175	225	275

   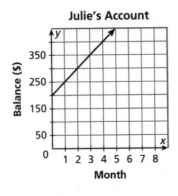

   Julie's Account

2. Miguel tracked the weekly spread of two strains of flu virus. His data are shown below. Compare the number of cases of flu by finding and interpreting average rates of change from week 0 to week 4.

   Strain 1

Week	0	1	2	3	4	5
Cases	15	25	40	60	85	115

   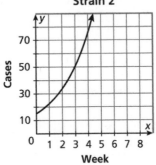

   Strain 2

_____

_____

The table and graph below show functions used to model the changing population of the United States. Use the table or graph to select the best answers for 3 and 4.

Year (2000 = 0)	Population (millions)
0	282
2	288
4	293
6	298
8	304

www.census.gov/popest/geographic/NST-EST2008-01

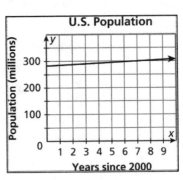

U.S. Population

3. What is the rate of change in the table from the year 2000 to the year 2008?

   A 1.75

   B 2.75

   C 22

   D 73.25

4. What is the rate of change in the graph from the year 2000 to the year 2008?

   F about 7.5 million people/year

   G about 3.5 million people/year

   H about 3 million people/year

   J about 2.5 million people/year

© Houghton Mifflin Harcourt Publishing Company

Performance Tasks

GPS
COMMON
CORE

MCC9-12.F.IF.2
MCC9-12.F.IF.5
MCC9-12.F.IF.6
MCC9-12.F.BF.1
MCC9-12.F.BF.3
MCC9-12.F.LE.5

★ **1.** A gym charges a one-time sign-up fee and then a regular monthly fee. The cost of a membership as a function of the number of months as a member is shown for 2010 and 2011 on the graph.

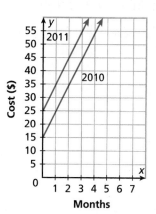

   a. What characteristics of the graph represent the sign-up fee and the monthly fee? What are those values for the 2010 line?

   b. How did the membership costs change from 2010 to 2011? Explain how you can tell from the graphs.

★ **2.** Seymour invests in a 5-year CD. Over the 5-year period, the CD earns a fixed annual interest rate, compounded once per year.

   a. The equation $V(t) = 3000(1.049)^t$ gives the value $V(t)$, in dollars, of the CD after t years. What do the parameters 3000 and 1.049 represent?

   b. What is the value of the CD after 5 years?

© Houghton Mifflin Harcourt Publishing Company

3. The weight in pounds that can be supported by a diving board is given by the function $w(x) = \frac{5000}{x}$, where x is the distance in feet from the base of the diving board to a point along the length of the board.

a. What is the domain of the function? Can the domain include zero? Explain.

b. Make a table of values and generate five ordered pairs to represent the function.

c. Plot the ordered pairs and draw a smooth curve connecting the points.

4. George goes out for a run. The graph shows the function $g(t)$, which gives his distance traveled m in miles t minutes after he starts running. The graphs $f(t)$ and $h(t)$ represent the distances his friends, Francine and Hector, have traveled t minutes after George started running.

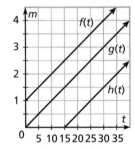

a. Who is running the fastest? Who started running first? Explain using the graph.

b. Write the rule for the function $g(t)$. Then write rules for $f(t)$ and $h(t)$ in terms of $g(t)$.

c. Interpret the transformation that produces $h(t)$ from $g(t)$ in the context of the problem.

© Houghton Mifflin Harcourt Publishing Company

Name _____ Class _____ Date _____

SELECTED RESPONSE

1. Which set of ordered pairs represents a function?

   A. $\{(-1, 1), (0, 0), (1, 1), (2, 2)\}$

   B. $\{(3, -3), (2, -2), (1, -1), (1, 1)\}$

   C. $\{(4, 2), (4, -2), (9, 3), (9, -3)\}$

   D. $\{(-2, -1), (-2, 0), (-2, 1), (-2, 2)\}$

2. Pat pays $250 to be a gym member for 2 months and $550 to be a member for 6 months. What is the monthly cost of a gym membership?

   F. $50   **H.** $150

   G. $75   **J.** $300

3. Which statement is **NOT** true about the functions $f(x) = 1.2(1.05)^x$ and $g(x) = 1.2(1.07)^x$?

   A. As x increases without bound, $f(x)$ and $g(x)$ both increase without bound.

   B. As x increases to the right of 0, the value of $g(x)$ is greater than the value of $f(x)$ for every value of x.

   C. The y-intercept of $g(x)$ is greater than the y-intercept of $f(x)$.

   D. The y-intercept of $g(x)$ is equal to the y-intercept of $f(x)$.

4. The graph of which function is stretched vertically and reflected in the x-axis as compared to the parent function $f(x) = x^3$?

   F. $g(x) = 3x^3$ **H.** $g(x) = \frac{1}{3}x^3$

   G. $g(x) = -3x^3$ **J.** $g(x) = -\frac{1}{3}x^3$

5. Given $f(x) = 3x + 2$ and $g(x) = -2x - 4$, find $h(x) = f(x) - g(x)$.

   A. $h(x) = x - 2$

   B. $h(x) = x + 6$

   C. $h(x) = 5x + 6$

   D. $h(x) = 5x - 2$

6. The graph of $g(x) = (x + 4)^2 - 1$ can be obtained from the graph of $f(x) = x^2$ using which transformations?

   F. Translate 4 units up and 1 unit left.

   G. Translate 4 units up and 1 unit right.

   H. Translate 4 units left and 1 unit down.

   J. Translate 4 units right and 1 unit down.

7. For $f(x) = -\frac{2}{5}x + 3$, find the slope and y-intercept, and determine whether the graph is increasing or decreasing.

   A. $m = -\frac{2}{5}$, $b = 3$, decreasing

   B. $m = -\frac{2}{5}$, $b = 3$, increasing

   C. $m = 3$, $b = -\frac{2}{5}$, decreasing

   D. $m = 3$, $b = -\frac{2}{5}$, increasing

8. Amber buys a car for $17,500. The car depreciates (loses value) 8% each year. Which function shows y, the value of the car (in dollars) in t years?

   F. $y = 17,500(0.08)^t$

   G. $y = 17,500(0.8)^t$

   H. $y = 17,500(0.92)^t$

   J. $y = 17,500(1.08)^t$

CONSTRUCTED RESPONSE

9. a. Graph $g(x) = -2x + 1$.

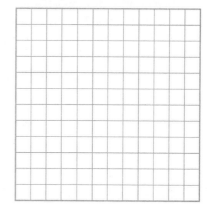

© Houghton Mifflin Harcourt Publishing Company

b. Describe transformations that you could have to perform on the graph of $f(x) = x$ to obtain the graph of g.

_____

_____

_____

c. If the graph of g is translated 3 units to the right to obtain the graph of h, what is the equation for h?

_____

10. Emily walks to meet her brother and one of his classmates after kindergarten and walks them home.

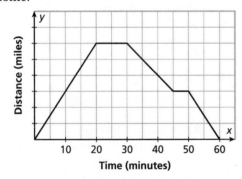

a. During which interval(s) is Emily's distance from home increasing?

_____

b. During which interval(s) is Emily's distance from home decreasing?

_____

_____

c. Which interval do you think represents the time when Emily is dropping her brother's classmate at his house? Justify your answer.

_____

_____

_____

_____

_____

11. Henry purchased a roll of 100 stamps. He uses 5 stamps each week.

a. The number of stamps at the end of each week is a function $S(w)$ of the number of weeks. Write an equation for the function.

_____

b. What types of numbers are reasonable for the domain and the range?

_____

_____

_____

c. Complete the table using selected domain values. Then graph the function.

w	S(w)	(w, S(w))

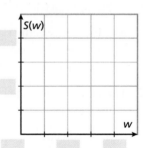

d. At the end of how many weeks will Henry have one quarter of the stamps left? Explain your reasoning.

_____

_____

© Houghton Mifflin Harcourt Publishing Company

Describing Data

© Houghton Mifflin Harcourt Publishing Company

Unpacking the Standards

Understanding the standards and the vocabulary terms in the standards will help you know exactly what you are expected to learn in this unit.

 MCC9-12.S.ID.1

Represent data with plots on the real number line (dot plots, histograms, and box plots).

Key Vocabulary
histogram *(histograma)* A bar graph used to display data grouped in intervals.
box-and-whisker plot *(gráfica de mediana y rango)* A method of showing how data are distributed by using the median, quartiles, and minimum and maximum values; also called a box plot.

What It Means For You

Displaying numerical data on the real number line gives you an instant visual image of how the data are distributed, and helps you draw conclusions about the center and spread of the data.

EXAMPLE   **Histogram**

A histogram gives you an overall picture of how data are distributed, but does not indicate any particular values or statistics.

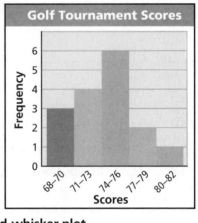

EXAMPLE   **Box-and-whisker plot**

A box-and-whisker plot includes five statistical values.

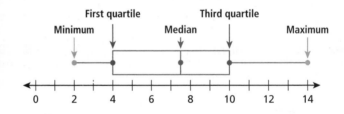

 MCC9-12.S.ID.3

Interpret differences in shape, center, and spread in the context of the data sets, accounting for possible effects of extreme data points (outliers).

Key Vocabulary
outlier *(valor extremo)* A data value that is far removed from the rest of the data.

What It Means For You

Always examine the displays and statistics for a data set in its own particular context so that you can draw valid conclusions.

EXAMPLE   **Outliers**

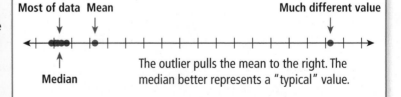

The outlier pulls the mean to the right. The median better represents a "typical" value.

© Houghton Mifflin Harcourt Publishing Company; Photo credit: © Corbis

© Houghton Mifflin Harcourt Publishing Company; Photo credit: © Corbis

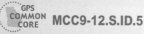

MCC9-12.S.ID.5

Summarize categorical data for two categories in two-way frequency tables. Interpret relative frequencies in the context of the data (including joint, marginal, and conditional relative frequencies). Recognize possible associations and trends in the data.

Key Vocabulary

frequency table *(tabla de frequencia)* A table that lists the number of times, or frequency, that each data value occurs.

joint relative frequency *(frecuencia relativa conjunta)* The ratio of the frequency in a particular category divided by the total number of data values.

marginal relative frequency *(frecuencia relativa marginal)* The sum of the joint relative frequencies in a row or column of a two-way table.

conditional relative frequency *(frecuencia relativa condicional)* The ratio of a joint relative frequency to a related marginal relative frequency in a two-way table.

What It Means For You

Two-way frequency tables give you a visual way to organize data categorized by two different variables so that you can more easily identify relationships.

EXAMPLE **A two-way relative frequency table**

The table shows the portions of households in a study that own a dog, a cat, both, or neither.

Joint relative frequencies

	Owns a cat		
Owns a dog	Yes	No	Total
Yes	0.15	0.24	0.39
No	0.18	0.43	0.61
Total	0.33	0.67	1

Marginal relative frequencies

Here are a few conclusions you can draw from the table:

- 39% own a dog, and 33% own a cat.
- 15% own a dog and a cat, and 43% own neither.
- Of dog owners, $\frac{15}{39}$% ≈ 38% also own a cat.
- Of cat owners, $\frac{15}{33}$% ≈ 45% also own a dog.

UNIT 4

MCC9-12.S.ID.6

Represent data on two quantitative variables on a scatter plot, and describe how the variables are related.

Key Vocabulary

scatter plot *(diagrama de dispersion)* A graph with points plotted to show a possible relationship between two sets of data.

What It Means For You

You can graph ordered pairs of data on a scatter plot to help you identify any pattern in the relationship between the data sets.

EXAMPLE

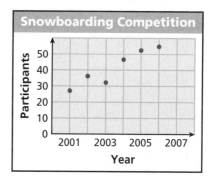

Participation in the snowboarding competition generally increased during the years shown.

Key Vocabulary

box-and-whisker plot *(gráfica de mediana y rango)* A method of showing how data are distributed by using the median, quartiles, and minimum and maximum values; also called a box plot.

correlation *(correlación)* A measure of the strength and direction of the relationship between two variables or data sets.

correlation coefficient *(coeficiente de correlación)* A number r, where $-1 \leq r \leq 1$, that describes how closely the points in a scatter plot cluster around the least-squares line.

first quartile *(primer cuartil)* The median of the lower half of a data set, denoted Q_1. Also called *lower quartile*.

histogram *(histograma)* A bar graph used to display data grouped in intervals

interquartile range (IQR) *(rango entre cuartiles)* The difference of the third (upper) and first (lower) quartiles in a data set, representing the middle half of the data.

least-squares line *(línea de mínimos cuadrados)* The line of fit for which the sum of the squares of the residuals is as small as possible.

line of best fit *(línea de mejor ajuste)* The line that comes closest to all of the points in a data set.

linear regression *(regresión lineal)* A statistical method used to fit a linear model to a given data set.

mean *(media)* The sum of all the values in a data set divided by the number of data values. Also called the *average*.

median *(mediana)* For an ordered data set with an odd number of values, the median is the middle value. For an ordered data set with an even number of values, the median is the average of the two middle values.

outlier *(valor extremo)* A data value that is far removed from the rest of the data.

range of a data set *(rango de un conjunto de datos)* The difference of the greatest and least values in the data set.

residual *(residuo)* The signed vertical distance between a data point and a line of fit.

scatter plot *(diagrama de dispersion)* A graph with points plotted to show a possible relationship between two sets of data.

third quartile *(tercer cuartil)* The median of the upper half of a data set. Also called *upper quartile*.

14-1

Organizing and Displaying Data
Extension: Two-Way Frequency Tables

Essential question: *How can categorical data be organized and analyzed?*

In previous lessons, you worked with numerical data involving variables such as age and height. In this lesson, you will analyze *categorical* data that involve variables such as pet preference and gender. The **frequency** of a data value is the number of times it occurs. A **frequency table** shows the frequency of each data value.

Video Tutor

MCC9–12.S.ID.5

1 EXAMPLE Creating a Relative Frequency Table

The frequency table below shows the results of a survey that Jenna took at her school. She asked 40 randomly selected students whether they preferred dogs, cats, or other pets. Convert this table to a *relative frequency* table that uses decimals as well as one that uses percents.

Preferred Pet	Dog	Cat	Other	Total
Frequency	18	12	10	40

A Divide the numbers in the frequency table by the total to obtain relative frequencies as decimals. Record the results in the table below.

Preferred Pet	Dog	Cat	Other	Total
Relative Frequency	$\frac{18}{40} = 0.45$			

B Write the decimals as percents in the table below.

Preferred Pet	Dog	Cat	Other	Total
Relative Frequency	45%			

REFLECT

1a. How can you check that you have correctly converted frequencies to relative frequencies?

_____

_____

1b. Explain why the number in the Total column of a relative frequency table is always 1 or 100%.

_____

_____

© Houghton Mifflin Harcourt Publishing Company

In the previous example, the categorical variable was pet preference, and the variable had three possible data values: dog, cat, and other. The frequency table listed the frequency for each value of that single variable. If you have two categorical variables whose values have been paired, you list the frequencies of the paired values in a **two-way frequency table**.

MCC9–12.S.ID.5

2 EXAMPLE   Creating a Two-Way Frequency Table

For her survey, Jenna also recorded the gender of each student. The results are shown in the two-way frequency table below. Each entry is the frequency of students who prefer a certain pet *and* are a certain gender. For instance, 8 girls prefer dogs as pets. Complete the table.

Preferred Pet / Gender	Dog	Cat	Other	Total
Girl	8	7	1	
Boy	10	5	9	
Total				

A Find the total for each gender by adding the frequencies in each row. Write the row totals in the Total column.

B Find the total for each preferred pet by adding the frequencies in each column. Write the column totals in the Total row.

C Find the grand total, which is the sum of the row totals as well as the sum of the column totals. Write the grand total in the lower-right corner of the table (the intersection of the Total column and the Total row).

REFLECT

2a. Where have you seen the numbers in the Total row before?

_____

2b. In terms of Jenna's survey, what does the grand total represent?

_____

You can obtain the following *relative* frequencies from a two-way frequency table:

- A **joint relative frequency** is found by dividing a frequency that is not in the Total row or the Total column by the grand total.
- A **marginal relative frequency** is found by dividing a row total or a column total by the grand total.

© Houghton Mifflin Harcourt Publishing Company

A **two-way relative frequency table** displays both joint relative frequencies and marginal relative frequencies.

MCC9–12.S.ID.5

3 E X A M P L E Creating a Two-Way Relative Frequency Table

Create a two-way relative frequency table for Jenna's data.

A Divide each number in the two-way frequency table from the previous example by the grand total. Write the quotients as decimals.

Preferred Pet / Gender	Dog	Cat	Other	Total
Girl	$\frac{8}{40} = 0.2$			
Boy				
Total	$\frac{18}{40} = 0.45$			$\frac{40}{40} = 1$

B Check by adding the joint relative frequencies in a row or column to see if the sum equals the row or column's marginal relative frequency.

Girl row: $0.2 + \quad\quad + \quad\quad = \quad\quad$

Boy row: $\quad\quad + \quad\quad + \quad\quad = \quad\quad$

Dog column: $0.2 + \quad\quad = 0.45$

Cat column: $\quad\quad + \quad\quad = \quad\quad$

Other column: $\quad\quad + \quad\quad = \quad\quad$

REFLECT

3a. A joint relative frequency in a two-way relative frequency table tells you what portion of the entire data set falls into the intersection of a particular value of one variable and a particular value of the other variable. For instance, the joint relative frequency of students surveyed who are girls *and* prefer dogs as pets is 0.2, or 20%. What is the joint relative frequency of students surveyed who are boys and prefer cats as pets?

_____

3b. A marginal relative frequency in a two-way relative frequency table tells you what portion of the entire data set represents a particular value of just one of the variables. For instance, the marginal relative frequency of students surveyed who prefer dogs as pets is 0.45, or 45%. What is the marginal relative frequency of students surveyed who are girls?

_____

© Houghton Mifflin Harcourt Publishing Company

One other type of relative frequency that you can obtain from a two-way frequency table is a *conditional relative frequency.* A **conditional relative frequency** is found by dividing a frequency that is not in the Total row or the Total column by the frequency's row total or column total.

4 EXAMPLE   Calculating Conditional Relative Frequencies

From Jenna's two-way frequency table you know that 16 students surveyed are girls and 12 students surveyed prefer cats as pets. You also know that 7 students surveyed are girls who prefer cats as pets. Use this information to find each conditional relative frequency.

A   Find the conditional relative frequency that a student surveyed prefers cats as pets, given that the student is a girl.

Divide the number of girls who prefer cats as pets by the number of girls. Express your answer as a decimal and as a percent.

_____

B   Find the conditional relative frequency that a student surveyed is a girl, given that the student prefers cats as pets.

Divide the number of girls who prefer cats as pets by the number of students who prefer cats as pets. Express your answer as a decimal and as a percent.

_____

REFLECT

4a.   When calculating a conditional relative frequency, why do you divide by a row total or a column total and not by the grand total?

_____

_____

_____

_____

4b.   You can obtain conditional relative frequencies from a two-way *relative* frequency table. For instance, in Jenna's survey, the relative frequency of girls who prefer cats as pets is 0.175, and the relative frequency of girls is 0.4. Find the conditional relative frequency that a student surveyed prefers cats as pets, given that the student is a girl.

_____

© Houghton Mifflin Harcourt Publishing Company

5 EXAMPLE   Finding Possible Associations Between Variables

Jenna conducted her survey because she was interested in the question, "Does gender influence what type of pet people prefer?" If there is no influence, then the distribution of gender within each subgroup of pet preference should roughly equal the distribution of gender within the whole group. Use the results of Jenna's survey to investigate possible influences of gender on pet preference.

A   Identify the percent of all students surveyed who are girls: _____

B   Determine each conditional relative frequency.

Of the 18 students who prefer dogs as pets, 8 are girls.
Percent who are girls, given a preference for dogs as pets: _____

Of the 12 students who prefer cats as pets, 7 are girls.
Percent who are girls, given a preference for cats as pets: _____

Of the 10 students who prefer other pets, 1 is a girl.
Percent who are girls, given a preference for other pets: _____

C   Interpret the results by comparing each conditional relative frequency to the percent of all students surveyed who are girls.

The percent of girls among students who prefer dogs is fairly close to 40%, so gender does not appear to influence preference for dogs.

The percent of girls among students who prefer cats is much greater than 40%. What conclusion might you draw in this case?

_____

The percent of girls among students who prefer other pets is much less than 40%. What conclusion might you draw in this case?

_____

REFLECT

5a. Suppose you analyzed the data by focusing on boys rather than girls. How would the percent in Part A change? How would the percents in Part B change? How would the conclusions in Part C change?

_____

_____

5b. For pet preference to be completely uninfluenced by gender, about how many girls would have to prefer each type of pet? Explain.

_____

_____

© Houghton Mifflin Harcourt Publishing Company

Antonio surveyed 60 of his classmates about their participation in school activities as well as whether they have a part-time job. The results are shown in the two-way frequency table below. Use the table to complete the exercises.

1. Complete the table by finding the row totals, column totals, and grand total.

Activity / Job	Clubs Only	Sports Only	Both	Neither	Total
Yes	12	13	16	4	
No	3	5	5	2	
Total					

2. Create a two-way relative frequency table using decimals.

Activity / Job	Clubs Only	Sports Only	Both	Neither	Total
Yes					
No					
Total					

3. Give each relative frequency as a percent.

   a. The joint relative frequency of students surveyed who participate in school clubs only and have part-time jobs: _____

   b. The marginal relative frequency of students surveyed who do not have a part-time job: _____

   c. The conditional relative frequency that a student surveyed participates in both school clubs and sports, given that the student has a part-time job: _____

4. Discuss possible influences of having a part-time job on participation in school activities. Support your response with an analysis of the data.

_____

_____

_____

© Houghton Mifflin Harcourt Publishing Company

Additional Practice

The owner of an ice cream shop conducted a survey regarding customers' favorite flavors. The owner asked 80 randomly selected customers whether they preferred vanilla, chocolate, or strawberry. The results are shown in the frequency table below.

Flavor	Vanilla	Chocolate	Strawberry	Total
Frequency	22	34	24	80

1. Convert this table to a relative frequency table that uses decimals.

Flavor	Vanilla	Chocolate	Strawberry	Total
Relative Frequency				

2. Convert this table to a relative frequency table that uses percents.

Flavor	Vanilla	Chocolate	Strawberry	Total
Relative Frequency				

3. The owner also recorded the gender of each customer. The results are shown in the two-way frequency table below. Complete the table.

Gender/ Flavor	Vanilla	Chocolate	Strawberry	Total
Male	10	20	16	
Female	12	14	8	
Total				

4. Create a two-way relative frequency table for the data in Exercise 3.

Gender/ Flavor	Vanilla	Chocolate	Strawberry	Total
Male				
Female				
Total				

© Houghton Mifflin Harcourt Publishing Company

Problem Solving

A mobile phone company conducted a survey regarding how people communicate with their friends. The company asked 200 randomly selected customers whether they preferred texting, talking, or emailing. The results are shown in the frequency table below.

Communication	Text	Talk	Email	Total
Frequency	116	54	30	200

1. Convert this table to a relative frequency table that uses decimals.

Communication	Text	Talk	Email	Total
Relative Frequency				

2. The company also recorded the gender of each customer. The results are shown in the two-way frequency table below. Complete the table.

Gender/Communication	Text	Talk	Email	Total
Male	75	36	14	
Female	41	18	16	
Total				

3. Create a two-way relative frequency table for the data in Problem 2.

Gender/Communication	Text	Talk	Email	Total
Male				
Female				
Total				

Select the best answer.

4. Find the conditional relative frequency that a person surveyed prefers talking, given that the person is male.

    A 0.6   C 0.288

    B 0.112   D 0.24

5. Find the conditional relative frequency that a person surveyed is female, given that the person prefers texting.

    F $\frac{1}{3}$ H $\frac{75}{116}$

    G $\frac{8}{15}$ J $\frac{41}{116}$

© Houghton Mifflin Harcourt Publishing Company

Frequency and Histograms
Going Deeper

Essential question: *How can you estimate statistics from data displayed in a histogram?*

Like a line plot, a histogram uses a number line to display data. Rather than display the data values individually as a line plot does, a histogram groups the data values into adjoining intervals of equal width and uses the heights of bars to indicate the number of data values that occur in each interval.

The number of data values in an interval is called the *frequency* of the interval. A histogram has a vertical frequency axis so that you can read the frequency for each interval. In the histogram at the right, you can see that 3 students had test scores in the interval 60–69, 9 students had test scores in the interval 70–79, and so on.

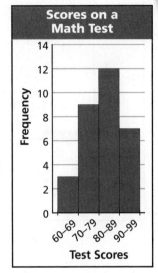

MCC9–12.S.ID.1

1 EXAMPLE   Creating a Histogram

Listed below are the ages of the 100 U.S. senators at the time that the 112th Congress began on January 3, 2011. Create a histogram for this data set.

39, 39, 42, 44, 46, 47, 47, 47, 48, 49, 49, 49, 50, 50, 51, 51, 52, 52, 53, 53, 54, 54, 55, 55, 55, 55, 55, 55, 56, 56, 57, 57, 57, 58, 58, 58, 58, 58, 59, 59, 59, 59, 60, 60, 60, 60, 60, 60, 60, 61, 61, 62, 62, 62, 63, 63, 63, 63, 64, 64, 64, 64, 66, 66, 66, 67, 67, 67, 67, 67, 67, 67, 68, 68, 68, 68, 69, 69, 69, 70, 70, 70, 71, 71, 73, 73, 74, 74, 74, 75, 76, 76, 76, 76, 77, 77, 78, 86, 86, 86

A Create a frequency table. To do so, you must decide what the interval width will be and where to start the first interval. Since the data are ages that run from 39 to 86, you might decide to use an interval width of 10 and start the first interval at 30. So, the first interval includes any Senator who is in his or her 30s.

Use the data to complete the table at the right. When done, be sure to check that the sum of the frequencies is 100.

Age Interval	Frequency
30–39	2

© Houghton Mifflin Harcourt Publishing Company

B Use the frequency table to complete the histogram.

Ages of U.S. Senators at the Start of the 112th Congress

(histogram with y-axis labeled 0, 5, 10, 15, 20, 25, 30, 35, 40; first bar labeled 30–39)

REFLECT

1a. Describe the shape of the distribution. Is it approximately symmetric, or does it have more data points to the right or to the left of its center? Explain.

_____

_____

_____

1b. Estimate the center of the distribution. Explain your reasoning.

_____

_____

1c. Using the histogram alone, and not the data values on the first page of this lesson, estimate the maximum possible range and the minimum possible range. Explain your reasoning.

_____

_____

_____

_____

_____

© Houghton Mifflin Harcourt Publishing Company

2 EXAMPLE Estimating Statistics from a Histogram

Although the first page of this lesson listed the ages all 100 senators, suppose you have only the histogram on the second page as a reference. Show how to estimate the mean and the median ages from the histogram.

A Estimate the mean. You know the frequency of each interval, but you don't know the individual data values. Use the midpoint of the interval as a substitute for each of those values. So, for the interval 30–39, you can estimate the sum of the data values by multiplying the midpoint, 35, by the frequency, 2. Complete the calculation below, rounding the final result to the nearest whole number.

$$\text{Mean} \approx \frac{35 \cdot 2 + \boxed{} \cdot \boxed{} + \boxed{} \cdot \boxed{} + \boxed{} \cdot \boxed{} + \boxed{} \cdot \boxed{} + \boxed{} \cdot \boxed{}}{\boxed{}}$$

$$= \frac{\boxed{}}{\boxed{}} \approx \boxed{}$$

B Estimate the median. The median is the average of the 50th and 51st data values. In what interval do these values fall? Explain.

_____

_____

The median is the average of the 8th and 9th values in an interval with 37 values, so you can estimate that the median is the sum of the interval's least value and $\frac{8.5}{37} \approx 20\%$ of the interval width, 10. So, what is the estimate?

_____

REFLECT

2a. How do the estimates of the mean and median support the observation that the distribution is approximately symmetric?

_____

_____

_____

2b. Is it possible to estimate the mode from the histogram? If so, give the mode. If not, explain why not.

_____

_____

_____

_____

_____

© Houghton Mifflin Harcourt Publishing Company

The ages of the first 44 U.S. presidents on the date of their first inauguration are listed below.

42, 43, 46, 46, 47, 47, 48, 49, 49, 50, 51, 51, 51, 51, 51, 52, 52, 54, 54, 54, 54, 54, 55, 55, 55, 55, 56, 56, 56, 57, 57, 57, 57, 58, 60, 61, 61, 61, 62, 64, 64, 65, 68, 69

1. Complete the frequency table by organizing the data into six equal intervals.

Age Interval	Frequency
41–45	2

2. Use the frequency table to complete the histogram.

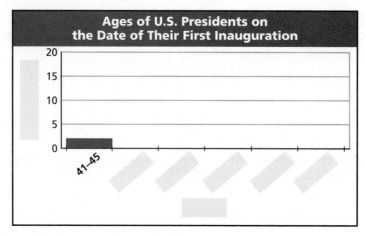

Ages of U.S. Presidents on the Date of Their First Inauguration

3. Describe the shape of the distribution. What measures of center would you use to characterize the data? Why?

_____

_____

4. Use the histogram to estimate the median.

_____

© Houghton Mifflin Harcourt Publishing Company

Name_____ Class_____ Date_____

Additional Practice

1. The heights, in centimeters, of various plants two weeks after planting are given below. Use the data to make a frequency table with intervals.

Plant Height (cm)						
12	24	23	33	38	41	33
35	37	35	39	48	41	50

Plant Height	
Height in cm	Frequency

2. Use the frequency table in Exercise 1 to make a histogram.

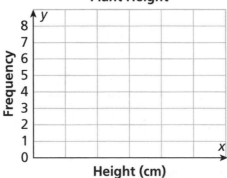

Plant Height

3. The number of calls per day received by a traveling Vet Van service for three weeks is given below. Use the data to make a frequency table with intervals.

Number of Calls						
18	22	13	15	16	21	22
26	17	14	12	13	18	14
16	22	23	20	21	18	22

Vet Van	
Number of Calls	Frequency

4. Use the frequency table in Exercise 3 to make a histogram.

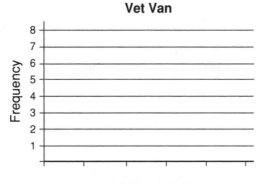

Vet Van

© Houghton Mifflin Harcourt Publishing Company

Problem Solving

The heights in inches of the 2005 NBA All-Star Game players are given below.

Players' Heights (in.)											
75	78	80	87	72	80	81	83	85	78	76	81
77	78	83	83	78	82	79	80	75	84	82	90

1. Use the data to make a frequency table with intervals. Use an interval of 5.

Players' Heights

Heights (in.)	Frequency

2. Use your frequency table to make a histogram for the data.

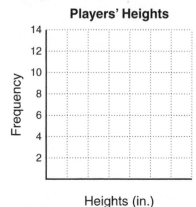

Select the best answer.

3. The file sizes, in megabytes, of 30 songs on an MP3 player are given below. If you create a histogram using intervals of 50-59, 60-69, 70-79, 80-89, and 90-99, which interval has the greatest bar?

50, 99, 98, 58, 61, 70, 86, 51, 65, 73, 81, 97, 50, 66, 76, 83, 55, 67, 78, 90, 54, 52, 63, 73, 77, 92, 76, 55, 60, 66

A 50-59   C 70-79

B 60-69   D 80-89

4. Using the file sizes and intervals from Problem 3, which interval has the shortest bar?

F 50-59   H 70-79

G 60-69   J 80-89

5. The frequency table below gives the scores of 100 students on a standardized mathematics test. How many students scored below 600?

Standardized Test Scores	
Scores	Cumulative Frequency
200–299	1
300–399	2
400–499	16
500–599	31
600–699	35
700–799	15

A 31   C 35

B 50   D 599

© Houghton Mifflin Harcourt Publishing Company

Two-Way Frequency Tables
Going Deeper

Essential question: *How do you calculate a conditional probability?*

The probability that event *B* occurs given that event *A* has already occurred is called the **conditional probability** of *B* given *A* and is written $P(B \mid A)$.

Video Tutor

MCC9–12.S.CP.6

1 EXAMPLE Finding Conditional Probabilities

One hundred people who frequently get migraine headaches were chosen to participate in a study of a new anti-headache medicine. Some of the particpants were given the medicine; others were not. After one week, the participants were asked if they got a headache during the week. The two-way table summarizes the results.

	Took Medicine	No Medicine	TOTAL
Headache	12	15	27
No Headache	48	25	73
TOTAL	60	40	100

A **To the nearest percent, what is the probability that a participant who took the medicine did not get a headache?**

Let event *A* be the event that a participant took the medicine. Let event *B* be the event that a participant did not get a headache.

To find the probability that a participant who took the medicine did not get a headache, you must find $P(B \mid A)$. You are only concerned with participants who took the medicine, so look at the data in the "Took Medicine" column.

There were _____ participants who took the medicine.

Of these participants, _____ participants did not get a headache.

So, $P(B \mid A) = \dfrac{}{} = \text{_____}$.

B **To the nearest percent, what is the probability that a participant who did not get a headache took the medicine?**

To find the probability that a participant who did not get a headache took the medicine, you must find $P(A \mid B)$. You are only concerned with participants who did not get a headache, so look at the data in the "No headache" row.

There were _____ participants who did not get a headache.

Of these participants, _____ participants took the medicine.

So, $P(A \mid B) = \dfrac{}{} \approx \text{_____}$.

© Houghton Mifflin Harcourt Publishing Company

REFLECT

1a. In general, do you think $P(B \mid A) = P(A \mid B)$? Why or why not?

_____

1b. How can you use set notation to represent the event that a participant took the medicine and did not get a headache? Is the probability that a participant took the medicine and did not get a headache equal to either of the conditional probabilities you calculated in the example?

_____

_____

MCC9–12.S.CP.3

2 **EXPLORE** Developing a Formula for Conditional Probability

You can generalize your work from the previous example to develop a formula for finding conditional probabilities.

A Recall how you calculated $P(B \mid A)$, the probability that a participant who took the medicine did not get a headache.

You found that $P(B \mid A) = \frac{48}{60}$.

Use the table shown here to help you write this quotient in terms of events A and B.

		Event A		
		Took Medicine	**No Medicine**	**TOTAL**
	Headache	12	15	27
Event B	**No Headache**	$48 = n(A \cap B)$	25	$73 = n(B)$
	TOTAL	$60 = n(A)$	40	100

$P(B \mid A) = \dfrac{\quad\quad}{\quad\quad}$

B Now divide the numerator and denominator of the quotient by $n(S)$, the number of outcomes in the sample space. This converts the counts to probabilities.

$$P(B \mid A) = \dfrac{\Big/ n(S)}{\Big/ n(S)} = \dfrac{\quad\quad}{\quad\quad}$$

REFLECT

2a. Write a formula for $P(A \mid B)$ in terms of $n(A \cap B)$ and $n(B)$.

_____

2b. Write a formula for $P(A \mid B)$ in terms of $P(A \cap B)$ and $P(B)$.

_____

© Houghton Mifflin Harcourt Publishing Company

You may have discovered the following formula for conditional probability.

Conditional Probability

The conditional probability of B given A (the probability that event B occurs given that event A occurs) is given by the following formula:

$$P(B \mid A) = \frac{P(A \cap B)}{P(A)}$$

MCC9–12.S.CP.3

3 EXAMPLE Using the Conditional Probability Formula

In a standard deck of playing cards, find the probability that a red card is a queen.

A Let event Q be the event that a card is a queen. Let event R be the event that a card is red. You are asked to find $P(Q \mid R)$. First find $P(R \cap Q)$ and $P(R)$.

$R \cap Q$ represents cards that are both red and a queen; that is, red queens.

There are _____ red queens in the deck of 52 cards, so $P(R \cap Q) =$ _____.

There are _____ red cards in the deck, so $P(R) =$ _____.

B Use the formula for conditional probability.

$P(Q \mid R) = \dfrac{P(Q \cap R)}{P(R)} = $ Substitute probabilities from above.

$ = $ ____   Multiply numerator and denominator by 52.

$ = $ ____   Simplify.

So, the probability that a red card is a queen is _____.

REFLECT

3a. How can you interpret the probability you calculated above?

_____

_____

3b. Is the probability that a red card is a queen equal to the probability that a queen is red? Explain.

_____

© Houghton Mifflin Harcourt Publishing Company

1. In order to study the connection between the amount of sleep a student gets and his or her school performance, data was collected about 120 students. The two-way table shows the number of students who passed and failed an exam and the number of students who got more or less than 6 hours of sleep the night before.

	Passed Exam	Failed Exam	TOTAL
Less than 6 hours of sleep	12	10	22
More than 6 hours of sleep	90	8	98
TOTAL	102	18	120

a. To the nearest percent, what is the probability that a student who failed the exam got less than 6 hours of sleep? _____

b. To the nearest percent, what is the probability that a student who got less than 6 hours of sleep failed the exam? _____

c. To the nearest percent, what is the probability that a student got less than 6 hours of sleep and failed the exam? _____

2. A botanist studied the effect of a new fertilizer by choosing 100 orchids and giving 70% of these plants the fertilizer. Of the plants that got the fertilizer, 40% produced flowers within a month. Of the plants that did not get the fertilizer, 10% produced flowers within a month. Find each probability to the nearest percent. (*Hint:* Construct a two-way table.)

a. Find the probability that a plant that produced flowers got the fertilizer. _____

b. Find the probability that a plant that got the fertilizer produced flowers. _____

3. At a school fair, a box contains 24 yellow balls and 76 red balls. One-fourth of the balls of each color are labeled "Win a prize." Find each probability as a percent.

a. Find the probability that a ball labeled "Win a prize" is yellow. _____

b. Find the probability that a ball labeled "Win a prize" is red. _____

c. Find the probability that a ball is labeled "Win a prize" and is red. _____

d. Find the probability that a yellow ball is labeled "Win a prize." _____

In Exercises 4–9, consider a standard deck of playing cards and the following events: *A*: the card is an ace; *B*: the card is black; *C*: the card is a club. Find each probability as a fraction.

4. $P(A \mid B)$

5. $P(B \mid A)$

6. $P(A \mid C)$

_____

_____

_____

7. $P(C \mid A)$

8. $P(B \mid C)$

9. $P(C \mid B)$

_____

_____

_____

© Houghton Mifflin Harcourt Publishing Company

Additional Practice

1. The table shows the results of a customer satisfaction survey of 100 randomly selected shoppers at the mall who were asked if they would shop at an earlier time if the mall opened earlier. Make a table of joint and marginal relative frequencies.

	Ages 10–20	Ages 21–45	Ages 46–65	65 and Older
Yes	13	2	8	24
No	25	10	15	3

	Ages 10–20	Ages 21–45	Ages 46–65	65 and Older	Total
Yes					
No					
Total					

2. Jerrod collected data on 100 randomly selected students, and summarized the results in a table.

Owns an MP3 Player

		Yes	No
Owns a Smart phone	**Yes**	28	12
	No	34	26

a. Make a table of the joint relative frequencies and marginal relative frequencies. Round to the nearest hundredth where appropriate.

Owns an MP3 player

		Yes	No	Total
Owns a Smart Phone	**Yes**			
	No			
	Total			

b. If you are given that a student owns an MP3 player, what is the probability that the student also owns a smart phone? Round your answer to the nearest hundredth.

_____

c. If you are given that a student owns a smart phone, what is the probability that the student also owns an MP3 player? Round your answer to the nearest hundredth.

_____

© Houghton Mifflin Harcourt Publishing Company

1. The table shows the number of students who would drive to school if the school provided parking spaces. Make a table of joint relative frequencies and marginal relative frequencies.

	Lowerclassmates	Upperclassmates
Always	32	122
Sometimes	58	44
Never	24	120

	Lowerclassmates	Upperclassmates	Total
Always			
Sometimes			
Never			
Total			

2. Gerry collected data and made a table of marginal relative frequencies on the number of students who participate in chorus and the number who participate in band.

		Chorus		
		Yes	**No**	**Total**
Band	**Yes**	0.38	0.29	0.67
	No	0.09	0.24	0.33
	Total	0.47	0.53	1.0

a. If you are given that a student is in chorus, what is the probability that the student also is in band? Round your answer to the nearest hundredth.

_____

b. If you are given that a student is not in band, what is the probability that the student is in chorus? Round your answer to the nearest hundredth.

_____

Select the best answer.

3. What is the probability if a student is not in chorus, then that student is in band?

  A 0.29   B 0.38

  C 0.43   D 0.55

4. What is the probability that if a student is not in band, then that student is not in chorus?

  F 0.09   G 0.33

  H 0.44   J 0.73

© Houghton Mifflin Harcourt Publishing Company

Data Distributions
Going Deeper

Essential question: *How can you characterize and compare the center and spread of data sets?*

Two commonly used measures of the center of a set of numerical data are the *mean* and *median*. Let n be the number of data values. The **mean** is the sum of the data values divided by n. When the data values are ordered from least to greatest, the **median** is either the middle value if n is odd or the average of the two middle values if n is even. The median divides the data set into two halves. The **first quartile** (Q_1) of a data set is the median of the lower half of the data. The **third quartile** (Q_3) is the median of the upper half.

Two commonly used measures of the spread of a set of numerical data are the *range* and *interquartile range*. The **range** is the difference between the greatest data value and the least data value. The **interquartile range** (IQR) is the difference between the third quartile and first quartile: $IQR = Q_3 - Q_1$.

MCC9–12.S.ID.2

1 EXAMPLE Finding Mean, Median, Range, and Interquartile Range

The April high temperatures (in degrees Fahrenheit) for five consecutive years in Boston are listed below. Find the mean, median, range, and interquartile range for this data set.

$$77 \quad 86 \quad 84 \quad 93 \quad 90$$

A Find the mean.

$$\text{Mean} = \frac{77 + 86 + 84 + 93 + 90}{\boxed{}} = \frac{\boxed{}}{} = \boxed{}$$

B Find the median.

Write the data values from least to greatest: _____

Identify the middle value: _____

C Find the range.

$$\text{Range} = 93 - \boxed{} = \boxed{}$$

D Find the interquartile range.

Find the first and third quartiles. Do not include the median as part of either the lower half or the upper half of the data.

$$Q_1 = \frac{\boxed{} + \boxed{}}{2} = \boxed{} \quad \text{and} \quad Q_3 = \frac{\boxed{} + \boxed{}}{2} = \boxed{}$$

Find the difference between Q_3 and Q_1: $IQR = \boxed{} - \boxed{} = \boxed{}$

© Houghton Mifflin Harcourt Publishing Company

1a. If 90°F is replaced with 92°F, will the median or mean change? Explain.

_____

_____

1b. Why is the IQR less than the range?

_____

_____

Standard Deviation Another measure of spread is **standard deviation**. It is found by squaring the deviations of the data values from the mean of the data values, then finding the mean of those squared deviations, and finally taking the square root of the mean of the squared deviations. The steps for calculating standard deviation are listed below.

1. Calculate the mean, $\bar{x}$.

2. Calculate each data value's deviation from the mean by finding $x - \bar{x}$ for each data value x.

3. Find $(x - \bar{x})^2$, the square of each deviation.

4. Find the mean of the squared deviations.

5. Take the square root of the mean of the squared deviations.

MCC9–12.S.ID.2

2 EXAMPLE Calculating the Standard Deviation

Calculate the standard deviation for the data from the previous example.

A Complete the table using the fact that the mean of the data is $\bar{x} = 86$.

Data value, x	Deviation from mean, $x - \bar{x}$	Squared deviation, $(x - \bar{x})^2$
77	$77 - 86 = -9$	$(-9)^2 = 81$
86		
84		
93		
90		

B Find the mean of the squared deviations.

$$\text{Mean} = \frac{81 + \boxed{} + \boxed{} + \boxed{} + \boxed{}}{\boxed{}} = \frac{\boxed{}}{\boxed{}} = \boxed{}$$

C Take the square root of the mean of the squared deviations. Use a calculator, and round to the nearest tenth.

$$\text{Square root of mean} = \sqrt{\boxed{}} \approx \boxed{}$$

© Houghton Mifflin Harcourt Publishing Company

REFLECT

2a. What is the mean of the deviations *before* squaring? Use your answer to explain why squaring the deviations is reasonable.

_____

_____

2b. In terms of the data values used, what makes calculating the standard deviation different from calculating the range?

_____

2c. What must be true about a data set if the standard deviation is 0? Explain.

_____

_____

Numbers that characterize a data set, such as measures of center and spread, are called **statistics**. They are useful when comparing large sets of data.

MCC9–12.S.ID.2

3 EXAMPLE Comparing Statistics for Related Data Sets

The tables below list the average ages of players on 15 teams randomly selected from the 2010 teams in the National Football League (NFL) and Major League Baseball (MLB). Compare the average ages of NFL players to the average ages of MLB players.

NFL Players' Average Ages	
Team	**Average Age**
Bears	25.8
Bengals	26.0
Broncos	26.3
Chiefs	25.7
Colts	25.1
Eagles	25.2
Jets	26.1
Lions	26.4
Packers	25.9
Patriots	26.6
Saints	26.3
Seahawks	26.2
Steelers	26.8
Texans	25.6
Titans	25.7

MLB Players' Average Ages	
Team	**Average Age**
Astros	28.5
Cardinals	29.0
Cubs	28.0
Diamondbacks	27.8
Dodgers	29.5
Giants	29.1
Marlins	26.9
Mets	28.9
Nationals	28.6
Padres	28.7
Pirates	26.9
Phillies	30.5
Reds	28.7
Rockies	28.9
Yankees	29.3

© Houghton Mifflin Harcourt Publishing Company

A On a graphing calculator, enter the two sets of data into two lists, L_1 and L_2. Examine the data as you enter the values, and record your general impressions about how the data sets compare before calculating any statistics.

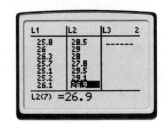

_____

_____

_____

B Calculate the statistics for the NFL data in list L_1. Then do the same for the MLB data in L_2. Record the results in the table below. Your calculator may use the following notations and abbreviations for the statistics you're interested in.

Mean: $\bar{x}$

Median: Med

IQR: May not be reported directly, but can be obtained by subtracting Q_1 from Q_3

Standard deviation: σx

	Center		Spread	
	Mean	**Median**	**IQR** $(Q_3 - Q_1)$	**Standard Deviation**
NFL				
MLB				

C Compare the corresponding statistics for the NFL data and the MLB data. Are your comparisons consistent for the two measures of center and the two measures of spread? Do your comparisons agree with your general impressions from Part A?

_____

_____

_____

_____

_____

_____

_____

© Houghton Mifflin Harcourt Publishing Company

3a. Based on a comparison of the measures of center, what conclusion can you draw about the typical age of an NFL player and of an MLB player?

_____

3b. Based on a comparison of the measures of spread, what conclusion can you draw about variation in the ages of NFL players and of MLB players?

_____

3c. What do you notice about the mean and median for the NFL? For the MLB?

_____

3d. What do you notice about the IQR and standard deviation for the NFL? For the MLB?

_____

Sets of data can be graphed on a box plot. A box plot allows you to see the range, the minimum and maximum values, the median, and the first and third quartiles easily on a number line plot. A box plot also allows you to visually compare two sets of data, including *outliers*. An **outlier** is a value in a data set that is much greater or much less than the other values. A data value x is an outlier if $x < Q_1 - 1.5(IQR)$ or $x > Q_3 + 1.5(IQR)$.

MCC9–12.S.ID.1

4 **EXAMPLE** Interpreting a Box Plot

The table lists the total number of home runs hit at home games by each team in Major League Baseball (MLB) during the 2010 season. The data are displayed in the box plot below the table. Identify the statistics that are represented in the box plot, and describe the distribution of the data.

Home Runs in 2010 MLB Games Played at Home					
Team	Home Runs	Team	Home Runs	Team	Home Runs
Toronto	146	Tampa Bay	78	Cleveland	64
NY Yankees	115	San Francisco	75	Pittsburgh	64
Chicago Sox	111	Atlanta	74	Houston	63
Colorado	108	Chicago Cubs	74	NY Mets	63
Cincinnati	102	Washington	74	LA Dodgers	61
Milwaukee	100	Baltimore	72	Kansas City	60
Boston	98	Detroit	70	San Diego	59
Arizona	98	LA Angels	69	Minnesota	52
Philadelphia	94	Florida	69	Oakland	46
Texas	93	St. Louis	67	Seattle	35

Home Runs in 2010 MLB Games Played at Home

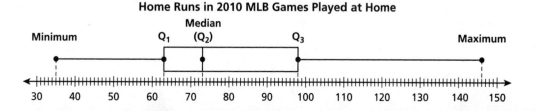

© Houghton Mifflin Harcourt Publishing Company

A A box plot displays a five-number summary of a data set. The five numbers are the statistics listed below. Use the box plot to determine each statistic.

Minimum	First Quartile	Median	Third Quartile	Maximum

B A box plot also shows the distribution of the data. Find the range of the lower half and the upper half of the data.

Range of lower half: _____   Range of upper half: _____

The data are more spread out in the upper half of the distribution than in the lower half.

REFLECT

4a. The lines that extend from the box in a box plot are sometimes called "whiskers." What *part* (lower, middle, or upper) and about what *percent* of the data does the box represent? What part and about what percent does each whisker represent?

_____

_____

4b. Which measures of spread can be determined from the box plot, and how are they found? Calculate each measure.

_____

_____

_____

4c. In the table, the data value 146 appears to be much greater than the other data values. Determine whether 146 is an outlier.

_____

_____

4d. The mean of the data is about 78.5. Use the shape of the distribution to explain why the mean is greater than the median.

_____

_____

_____

_____

© Houghton Mifflin Harcourt Publishing Company

5 EXAMPLE   Comparing Data Using Box Plots

The table lists the total number of home runs hit at away games by each team in Major League Baseball (MLB) during the 2010 season. Display the data in a box plot.

Home Runs in 2010 MLB Games Played Away					
Team	**Home Runs**	**Team**	**Home Runs**	**Team**	**Home Runs**
Boston	113	Milwaukee	82	Atlanta	65
Toronto	111	Arizona	82	NY Mets	65
Minnesota	90	Tampa Bay	82	Colorado	65
San Francisco	87	Chicago Cubs	75	Cleveland	64
LA Angels	86	Washington	75	Oakland	63
NY Yankees	86	San Diego	73	Pittsburgh	62
Cincinnati	86	Philadelphia	72	Baltimore	61
St. Louis	83	Texas	69	Kansas City	61
Florida	83	Chicago Sox	66	LA Dodgers	59
Detroit	82	Seattle	66	Houston	45

A Find the values for the five-number summary.

Minimum	First Quartile	Median	Third Quartile	Maximum

B Determine whether the data set includes any outliers. Begin by finding the value of each expression below using the fact that the IQR = $Q_3 - Q_1 = 83 - 65 = 18$.

$Q_1 - 1.5(\text{IQR}) = $ _____ $Q_3 + 1.5(\text{IQR}) = $ _____

These values are sometimes called *fences* because they form the boundaries outside of which a data value is considered to be an outlier. Which data values, if any, are outliers for the away-game data? Why?

_____

C The box plot shown below displays the number of home runs hit at home games during the 2010 MLB season. Draw a second box plot that displays the data for away games. The whiskers should extend only to the least and greatest data values that lie within the fences established in Part B. Show any outliers as individual dots.

Home Runs in 2010 MLB Games
Home games

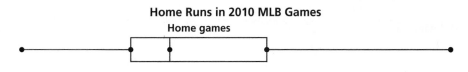

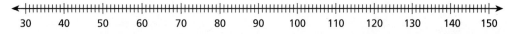

© Houghton Mifflin Harcourt Publishing Company

5a. Use the box plots to compare the center, spread, and shape of the two data distributions. Ignore any outliers.

_____

_____

_____

_____

PRACTICE

The numbers of students in each of a school's six Algebra 1 classes are listed below. Find each statistic for this data set.

$$28 \quad 30 \quad 29 \quad 26 \quad 31 \quad 30$$

1. Mean = _____   **2.** Median = _____

3. Range = _____   **4.** IQR = _____

5. Find the standard deviation of the Algebra 1 class data by completing the table and doing the calculations below it.

Data value, x	Deviation from mean, $x - \overline{x}$	Squared deviation, $(x - \overline{x})^2$
28		
30		
29		
26		
31		
30		

Mean of squared deviations = _____

Standard deviation ≈ _____

© Houghton Mifflin Harcourt Publishing Company

6. Error Analysis Suppose a student in the Algebra 1 class with 31 students transfers to the class with 26 students. The student claims that the measures of center and the measures of spread will all change. Correct the student's error.

_____

_____

_____

_____

7. The table lists the heights (in centimeters) of 8 males and 8 females on the U.S. Olympic swim team, all randomly selected from swimmers on the team who participated in the 2008 Olympic Games held in Beijing, China.

Heights of Olympic male swimmers	196	188	196	185	203	183	183	196
Heights of Olympic female swimmers	173	170	178	175	173	180	180	175

a. Use a graphing calculator to complete the table below.

	Center		Spread	
	Mean	Median	IQR ($Q_3 - Q_1$)	Standard deviation
Olympic male swimmers				
Olympic female swimmers				

b. Discuss the consistency of the measures of center for male swimmers and the measures of center for female swimmers, and then compare the measures of center for male and female swimmers.

_____

_____

_____

_____

c. What do the measures of spread tell you about the variation in the heights of the male and female swimmers?

_____

_____

_____

© Houghton Mifflin Harcourt Publishing Company

8. The table shows the 2010 average salary for an MLB player by team for both the American League (AL) and the National League (NL).

a. Find the values for the five-number summary for each league.

	AL	NL
Min.		
Q₁		
Median		
Q₃		
Max.		

MLB Players' Average 2010 Salaries (in Millions of Dollars)			
American League		**National League**	
Team	**Salary**	**Team**	**Salary**
New York	8.3	Chicago	5.4
Boston	5.6	Philadelphia	5.1
Detroit	4.6	New York	5.1
Chicago	4.2	St. Louis	3.7
Los Angeles	3.6	Los Angeles	3.7
Seattle	3.5	San Francisco	3.5
Minnesota	3.5	Houston	3.3
Baltimore	3.1	Atlanta	3.1
Tampa Bay	2.7	Colorado	2.9
Kansas City	2.5	Milwaukee	2.8
Cleveland	2.1	Cincinnati	2.8
Toronto	2.1	Arizona	2.3
Texas	1.9	Florida	2.1
Oakland	1.7	Washington	2.0
		San Diego	1.5
		Pittsburgh	1.3

b. Complete the scale on the number line below. Then use the number line to create two box plots, one for each league. Show any outliers as individual dots.

MLB Player's Average 2010 Salaries (in Millions of Dollars)

1.0

c. Compare the center, spread, and shape of the two data distributions. Ignore any outliers.

_____

_____

_____

_____

_____

_____

_____

© Houghton Mifflin Harcourt Publishing Company

Additional Practice

Find the mean, median, mode, and range of each data set.

1. 22, 45, 30, 18, 22

2. 8, 10, 8, 14, 8, 15

_____

_____

3. 1.25, 0.5, 3.25, 0.75, 1.75

4. 95, 92, 96, 93, 94, 95, 93

_____

_____

Identify the outlier in each data set, and determine how the outlier affects the mean, median, mode, and range of the data.

5. 31, 35, 41, 40, 40, 98

6. 82, 24, 100, 96, 79, 93, 86

_____

_____

_____

_____

7. The amounts of Cathy's last six clothing purchases were $109, $72, $99, $15, $99, and $89. For each question, choose the mean, median, or mode, and give its value.

   a. Which value describes the average of Cathy's purchases? _____

   b. Which value would Cathy tell her parents to convince them that she is not spending too much money on clothes? Explain.

   _____

   c. Which value would Cathy tell her parents to convince them that she needs an increase in her allowance? Explain.

   _____

Use the data to make a box-and-whisker plot.

8. 71, 79, 56, 24, 35, 37, 81, 63, 75

9. 210, 195, 350, 250, 260, 300

The finishing times of two runners for several one-mile races, in minutes, are shown in the box-and-whisker plots.

10. Who has the faster median time? _____

11. Who has the slowest time? _____

12. Overall, who is the faster runner? Explain.

_____

© Houghton Mifflin Harcourt Publishing Company

Problem Solving

Write the correct answer.

1. While window shopping, Sandra recorded the prices of shoes she would like to try on. The prices were $48, $63, $52, $99, and $58. Find the mean, median, and mode of the prices. Which best represents the typical shoe she looked at? Why?

_____

_____

2. The number of cans Xavier recycled each week for eight weeks is 24, 33, 76, 42, 35, 33, 45, and 33. Find the mean, median, and mode of the numbers of cans. How do the mean and median change when the outlier is removed?

_____

_____

3. The amounts due on the Harvey's electric bill, rounded to the nearest dollar, for the past six months were $64, $83, $76, $134, $76, and $71. Find the mean, median, and mode of the amounts. Which value should Mr. Harvey tell his family to convince them to cut down on electric use?

_____

4. A manager at a bowling alley surveys adult patrons about their shoes sizes. He records sizes 11, 12, 8, 4, 8, 5, 8, 7, 9, 10, 8, 9, 8, and 10. Find the mean, median, and mode of the sizes. Which is most important to the manager when ordering new rental shoes?

_____

The number of traffic citations given daily by two police departments over a two-week period is shown in the box-and-whisker plots. Choose the letter of the best answer.

5. What is the best estimate of the difference in the greatest number of citations given by each department in one day?

   A 10   B 20

   C 30   D 35

6. What is the difference in the median number of citations between the two departments?

   F about 8

   G about 15

   H about 22

   J about 40

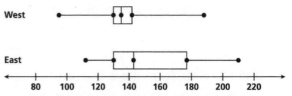

7. Which statement is NOT true?

   A The East department gave the greatest number of citations in one day.

   B The East department gave the least number of citations in one day.

   C The East department has a greater IQR than the West department.

   D The East department has the greater median number of citations in one day.

© Houghton Mifflin Harcourt Publishing Company

Video Tutor

Scatter Plots and Trend Lines
Extension: Correlation, Lines of Fit, and Predictions

Essential question: *How can you decide whether a correlation exists between paired numerical data and, if so, what is the line of fit for that data?*

MCC9–12.S.ID.8

1 ENGAGE   Understanding Correlation

When two real-world variables (such as height and weight or latitude and average temperature) are measured from the same things (the same people, places, etc.), you obtain a set of paired numerical data that you can plot as points in the coordinate plane to create a data display called a *scatter plot*. Sometimes the scatter plot will show a linear pattern. When it does, the linear pattern may be tight (that is, the points lie very close to a line), or it may be loose (that is, the points are more dispersed about a line). The degree to which a scatter plot shows a linear pattern is an indicator of the strength of a **correlation** between the two variables.

Mathematicians have defined a measure of the direction and magnitude of a correlation. This measure is called the **correlation coefficient** and is denoted by r. When the points in a scatter plot all lie on a line that is not horizontal, r has a value of 1 if the line rises from left to right and a value of -1 if the line falls from left to right. The correlation coefficient takes on values between -1 and 1 in cases where the points are not perfectly linear.

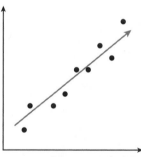

Strong positive correlation
r is close to 1.

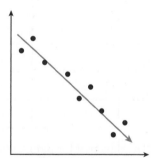

Strong negative correlation
r is close to -1.

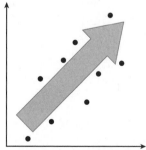

Weak positive correlation
r is closer to 0.5 than to 0 or 1.

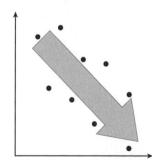

Weak negative correlation
r is closer to -0.5 than to 0 or -1.

© Houghton Mifflin Harcourt Publishing Company

1a. What conclusion would you draw about the value of *r* for the scatter plot shown at the right? Why?

_____

_____

1b. If the variables *x* and *y* have a strong positive correlation, what generally happens to *y* as *x* increases? What if *x* and *y* have a strong negative correlation?

_____

MCC9–12.S.ID.8

2 EXAMPLE   Estimating Correlation Coefficients

The table lists the latitude and average annual temperature for various cities in the Northern Hemisphere. Describe the correlation and estimate the correlation coefficient.

City	Latitude	Avg. Annual Temperature
Bangkok, Thailand	13.7°N	82.6°F
Cairo, Egypt	30.1°N	71.4°F
London, England	51.5°N	51.8°F
Moscow, Russia	55.8°N	39.4°F
New Delhi, India	28.6°N	77.0°F
Tokyo, Japan	35.7°N	58.1°F
Vancouver, Canada	49.2°N	49.6°F

A   Make a scatter plot. The data pair for Bangkok has been plotted.

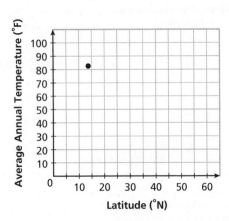

B   Describe the correlation, and estimate the correlation coefficient.

Because the plotted points appear to lie very close to a line that slants _____ from left to right, the scatter plot shows a _____ correlation. So, the correlation coefficient is close to _____.

© Houghton Mifflin Harcourt Publishing Company

2a. Mexico City, Mexico, is at latitude 19.4°N and has an average annual temperature of 60.8°F. If you include this data pair in the data set, how would it affect the correlation? Why?

_____

_____

Correlation and Causation In the preceding example, you would expect that a city's latitude has an effect on the city's average annual temperature. While it does, there are other factors that contribute to a city's weather, such as whether a city is located on a coast or inland.

A common error when interpreting paired data is confusing correlation and causation. If a correlation exists between two variables, this does not necessarily mean that one variable causes the other. When one variable increases, the other variable may increase (or decrease) as a result of other variables not being considered. Such variables are sometimes called *lurking variables*.

MCC9–12.S.ID.9

3 EXAMPLE Distinguishing Causation from Correlation

Read the article. Decide whether correlation implies causation in this case.

A Identify the two variables that the scientists correlated. Was the correlation positive or negative?

_____

_____

B Decide whether correlation implies causation in this case. Explain your reasoning.

_____

_____

_____

_____

_____

_____

_____

_____

BRAIN'S AMYGDALA CONNECTED TO SOCIAL BEHAVIOR

An almond-shaped part of the brain called the amygdala has long been known to play a role in people's emotional states. Now scientists studying the amygdala have discovered a connection between its size and the size of a person's social network. The scientists used a brain scanner to determine the size of the amygdala in the brains of 58 adults. They also gave each person a survey that measured the size of the person's social network. Their analysis of the data found that there is a correlation between the two: People with larger amygdalas tend to have larger social networks.

© Houghton Mifflin Harcourt Publishing Company

3a. Suppose scientists study a group of people over time and find that those who increased the size of their social networks also had an increase in the size of their amygdalas. Does this result establish a cause-and-effect relationship? Explain.

_____

_____

When paired numerical data have a strong positive or negative correlation, you can find a linear model for the data. The process is called *fitting a line to the data* or *finding a line of fit for the data.*

MCC9–12.S.ID.6c

4 EXAMPLE   Finding a Line of Fit for Data

The table lists the median age of females living in the United States based on the results of the U.S. Census over the past few decades. Determine whether a linear model is reasonable for the data. If so, find a linear model for the data.

Year	Median Age of Females
1970	29.2
1980	31.3
1990	34.0
2000	36.5
2010	38.2

A Identify the independent and dependent variables, and specify how you will represent them.

The independent variable is time, so use the variable t. Rather than let t take on the values 1970, 1980, and so on, define t as the number of years since 1970.

The dependent variable is the median age of females. Although you could simply use the variable a, you can use F as a subscript to remind yourself that only median *female* ages are being considered. So, the dependent variable is a_F.

B Make a table of paired values of t and a_F. Then draw a scatter plot.

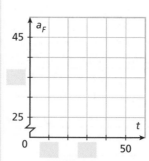

t	a_F

Time (years since 1970)

C Draw a line of fit on the scatter plot.

Using a ruler, draw a line that passes as close as possible to the plotted points. Your line does not necessarily have to pass through any of the points, but you should try to balance points above and below the line.

© Houghton Mifflin Harcourt Publishing Company

© Houghton Mifflin Harcourt Publishing Company

REFLECT

4a. What type of correlation does the scatter plot show?

_____

4b. Before you placed a ruler on the scatter plot to draw a line of fit, you may have thought that the plotted points were perfectly linear. How does the table tell you that they are not?

_____

_____

_____

_____

Making Predictions A linear model establishes the dependent variable as a linear function of the independent variable, and you can use the function to make predictions. The accuracy of a prediction depends not only on the model's goodness of fit but also on the value of the independent variable for which you're making the prediction.

A model's domain is determined by the least and greatest values of the independent variable found in the data set. For instance, the least and greatest t-values for the median age data are 0 (for 1970) and 40 (for 2010), so the domain of any model for the data is $\{t \mid 0 \leq t \leq 40\}$. Making a prediction using a value of the independent variable from *within* the model's domain is called **interpolation**. Making a prediction using a value from *outside* the domain is called **extrapolation**. As you might expect, you can have greater confidence in an interpolation than in an extrapolation.

MCC9–12.S.ID.6a

5 EXAMPLE Making Predictions Using a Linear Model

A linear equation that models the data from the previous example is $a_F = 0.25t + 29$. Use this model to predict the median age of females in 1995 and in 2015. Identify each prediction as an interpolation or as an extrapolation.

A To make a prediction about 1995, let $t =$ _____. Then to the nearest

tenth, the predicted value of a_F is $a_F = 0.25 \left(\right) + 29 \approx $.

Because the t-value falls _____ the model's domain,

the prediction is an _____.

B To make a prediction about 2015, let $t =$ _____. Then to the nearest

tenth, the predicted value of a_F is $a_F = 0.25 \left(\right) + 29 \approx $.

Because the t-value falls _____ the model's domain, the

prediction is an _____.

5a. Use the linear model to predict the median age of females in 1995 and 2015.

_____

_____

5b. The Census Bureau gives 35.5 as the median age of females for 1995 and an estimate of 38.4 for 2015. Which of your predictions using the linear model was more accurate? Explain.

_____

_____

PRACTICE

1. The table lists the heights and weights of the six wide receivers who played for the New Orleans Saints during the 2010 football season.

Wide Receiver	Height (inches)	Weight (pounds)
Arrington	75	192
Colston	76	225
Henderson	71	200
Meachem	74	210
Moore	69	190
Roby	72	189

  a. Make a scatter plot.

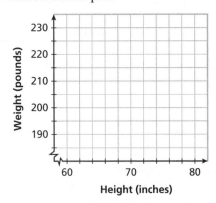

  b. Describe the correlation, and estimate the correlation coefficient using one of these values: −1, −0.5, 0, 0.5, 1.

_____

2. Read the article shown at the right. Describe the correlation and decide whether correlation implies causation in this case. Explain your reasoning.

_____

_____

_____

_____

_____

_____

WALKING SPEED MAY PREDICT LIFE SPAN

Researchers who looked at data from nearly 35,000 senior citizens discovered that an elderly person's walking speed is correlated to that person's chance of living 10 more years. For instance, the researchers found that only 19 percent of the slowest-walking 75-year-old men lived for 10 more years compared with 87 percent of the fastest-walking 75-year-old men. Similar results were found for elderly women.

© Houghton Mifflin Harcourt Publishing Company

3. The table lists the median age of males living in the United States based on the results of the U.S. Census over the past few decades.

Year	1970	1980	1990	2000	2010
Median Age of Males	26.8	28.8	31.6	34.0	35.5

a. Let t represent time (in years since 1970), and let a_M represent the median age of males. Make a table of paired values of t and a_M. Then draw a scatter plot.

t	a_M

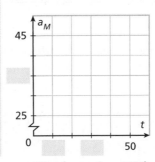

Time (years since 1970)

b. Draw a line of fit on the scatter plot.

c. A linear equation that models the data from parts (a) and (b) is $a_M = 0.24t + 26.6$. Use this model to predict the median age of males in 1995 and 2015. Identify each prediction as an interpolation or an extrapolation, and then compare the predictions with these median ages of males from the Census Bureau: 33.2 in 1995 and an estimated 35.9 in 2015.

_____

_____

_____

4. Compare the equations of the lines of fit for the median age of females and the median age of males. When referring to any constants in those equations, be sure to interpret them in the context of the data.

_____

_____

_____

_____

5. Explain why it isn't reasonable to use linear models to predict the median age of females or males far into the future.

_____

_____

_____

_____

© Houghton Mifflin Harcourt Publishing Company

6. The table lists, for various lengths (in centimeters), the median weight (in kilograms) of male infants and female infants (ages 0–36 months) in the United States.

Length (cm)	50	60	70	80	90	100
Median Weight (kg) of Male Infants	3.4	5.9	8.4	10.8	13.0	15.5
Median Weight (kg) of Female Infants	3.4	5.8	8.3	10.6	12.8	15.2

a. Let l represent an infant's length in excess of 50 centimeters. (For instance, for an infant whose length is 60 cm, $l = 10$.) Let w_M represent the median weight of male infants, and let w_F represent the median weight of female infants. Make a table of paired values of l and either w_M or w_F (whichever you prefer).

l						
w						

b. Draw a scatter plot of the paired data.

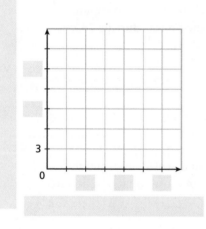

c. Draw a line of fit on the scatter plot.

d. A linear equation that models the data for the median weight of male infants is $w_M = 0.244l + 3.4$. A linear equation that models the data for the median weight of female infants is $w_F = 0.238l + 3.4$. According to these models, at what rate does weight change with respect to height?

_____

_____

© Houghton Mifflin Harcourt Publishing Company

Additional Practice

Graph a scatter plot using the given data.

1. The table shows the percent of people ages 18–24 who reported they voted in the presidential elections. Graph a scatter plot using the given data.

Year	1988	1992	1996	2000	2004
% of 18-24 year olds	36	43	32	32	42

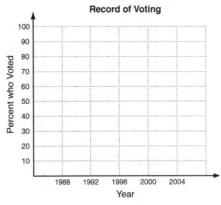

Write *positive*, *negative*, or *none* to describe the correlation illustrated by each scatter plot.

2.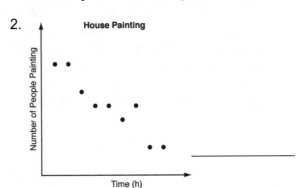

3.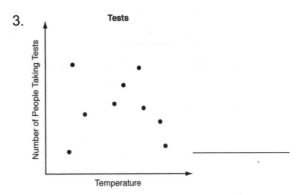

4. Identify the correlation you would expect to see between the number of pets a person has and the number of times they go to a pet store. Explain.

_____

_____

Neal kept track of the number of minutes it took him to assemble sandwiches at his restaurant. The information is in the table below.

Number of sandwiches	1	2	4	6	7
Minutes	3	4	5	6	7

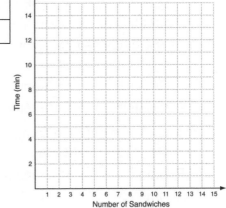

5. Graph a scatter plot of the data.

6. Draw a trend line.

7. Describe the correlation.

_____

8. Based on the trend line you drew, predict the amount of time it will take Neal to assemble 12 sandwiches.

_____

© Houghton Mifflin Harcourt Publishing Company

Problem Solving

Fawn is trying to improve her reading skills by taking a speed-reading class. She is measuring how many words per minute (wpm) she can read after each week of the class.

1. Graph a scatter plot using the given data.

Weeks	1	2	3	4	5
wpm	220	230	260	260	280

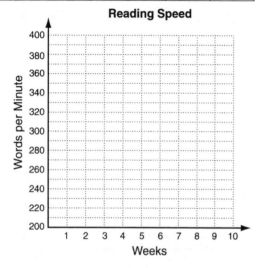

2. Describe the correlation illustrated by the scatter plot.

_____

_____

3. Draw a trend line and use it to predict the number of words per minute that Fawn will read after 8 weeks of this class.

_____

4. Fawn is paying for this class each week out of her savings account. Identify the correlation between the number of classes and Fawn's account balance.

_____

_____

Choose the scatter plot that best represents the described relationship.

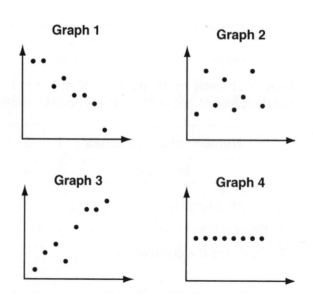

5. the distance a person runs and how physically tired that person is

    A Graph 1   C Graph 3

    B Graph 2   D Graph 4

6. the price of a new car and the number of hours in a day

    F Graph 1   H Graph 3

    G Graph 2   J Graph 4

7. a person's age and the amount of broccoli the person eats

    A Graph 1   C Graph 3

    B Graph 2   D Graph 4

8. the number of cats in a barn and the number of mice in that barn

    F Graph 1   H Graph 3

    G Graph 2   J Graph 4

© Houghton Mifflin Harcourt Publishing Company

Line of Best Fit
Going Deeper

Video Tutor

Essential question: *How can you use residuals and linear regression to fit a line to data?*

Residuals You can evaluate a linear model's goodness of fit using *residuals*. A **residual** is the difference between an actual value of the dependent variable and the value predicted by the linear model. After calculating residuals, you can draw a **residual plot**, which is a scatter plot of points whose *x*-coordinates are the values of the independent variable and whose *y*-coordinates are the corresponding residuals.

Whether the fit of a line to data is suitable and good depends on the distribution of the residuals, as illustrated below.

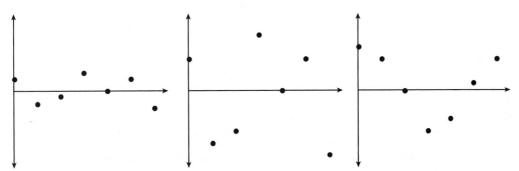

Distribution of residuals about the *x*-axis is random and tight. A linear fit to the data is suitable and strong.

Distribution of residuals about the *x*-axis is random but loose. A linear fit to the data is suitable but weak.

Distribution of residuals about the *x*-axis is not random. A linear fit to the data may not be suitable.

MCC9–12.S.ID.6b

1 EXAMPLE Creating a Residual Plot and Evaluating Fit

Using t as the years since 1970 and a_F as the median age of females, a student fit the line $a_F = 0.25t + 29$ to the data shown in the table. Make a residual plot and evaluate the goodness of fit.

Year	Median Age of Females
1970	29.2
1980	31.3
1990	34.0
2000	36.5
2010	38.2

A Calculate the residuals. Substitute each value of t into the equation to find the value predicted for a_F by the linear model. Then subtract predicted from actual to find the residual.

t	a_F actual	a_F predicted	Residual
0	29.2	29.0	0.2
10	31.3		
20	34.0		
30	36.5		
40	38.2		

© Houghton Mifflin Harcourt Publishing Company

B Plot the residuals.

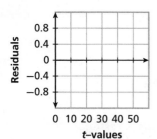

C Evaluate the suitability of a linear fit and the goodness of the fit.

- Is there a balance between positive and negative residuals?

  _____

  _____

  _____

- Is there a pattern to the residuals? If so, describe it.

  _____

  _____

- Is the absolute value of each residual small relative to a_F (actual)? For instance, when $t = 0$, the residual is 0.2 and the value of a_F is 29.2, so the relative size of the residual is $\frac{0.2}{29.2} \approx 0.7\%$, which is quite small.

  _____

  _____

- What is your overall evaluation of the suitability and goodness of the linear fit?

  _____

  _____

REFLECT

1a. Suppose the line of fit with equation $a_F = 0.25t + 29$ is changed to $a_F = 0.25t + 28.8$. What effect does this change have on the residuals? On the residual plot? Is the new line a better fit to the data? Explain.

_____

_____

_____

© Houghton Mifflin Harcourt Publishing Company

You can use a graphing calculator to fit a line to a set of paired numerical data that have a strong positive or negative correlation. The calculator uses a method called **linear regression**, which involves minimizing the sum of the squares of the residuals.

MCC9–12.S.ID.6c

2 EXPLORE   Comparing Sums of Squared Residuals

Suppose in the first Example one person came up with the equation $a_F = 0.25t + 29.0$ while another came up with $a_F = 0.25t + 28.8$ where, in each case, t is the time in years since 1970 and a_F is the median age of females.

A Complete each table below in order to calculate the squares of the residuals for each line of fit.

Table for $a_F = 0.25t + 29.0$

$a_F = 0.25t + 29.0$				
t	a_F (actual)	a_F (predicted)	Residuals	Square of Residuals
0	29.2	29.0	0.2	0.04
10	31.3			
20	34.0			
30	36.5			
40	38.2			

Table for $a_F = 0.25t + 28.8$

$a_F = 0.25t + 28.8$				
t	a_F (actual)	a_F (predicted)	Residuals	Square of Residuals
0	29.2	28.8	0.4	0.16
10	31.3			
20	34.0			
30	36.5			
40	38.2			

© Houghton Mifflin Harcourt Publishing Company

B Find the sum of the squared residuals for each line of fit.

Sum of squared residuals for $a_F = 0.25t + 29.0$: _____

Sum of squared residuals for $a_F = 0.25t + 28.8$: _____

C Identify the line that has the smaller sum of the squared residuals.

_____

_____

_____

REFLECT

2a. If you use a graphing calculator to perform linear regression on the data, you obtain the equation $a_F = 0.232t + 29.2$. Complete the table to calculate the squares of the residuals and then the sum of the squares for this line of fit.

	$a_F = 0.232t + 29.2$			
t	a_F (actual)	a_F (predicted)	Residuals	Square of Residuals
0	29.2	29.2	0	0
10	31.3			
20	34.0			
30	36.5			
40	38.2			

Sum of squared residuals: _____

2b. Explain why the model $a_F = 0.232t + 29.2$ is a better fit to the data than $a_F = 0.25t + 29.0$ or $a_F = 0.25t + 28.8$.

_____

_____

_____

© Houghton Mifflin Harcourt Publishing Company

Because linear regression produces an equation for which the sum of the squared residuals is as small as possible, the line obtained from linear regression is sometimes called the *least-squares regression line*. It is also called the *line of best fit*. Not only will a graphing calculator automatically find the equation of the line of best fit, but it will also give you the correlation coefficient and display the residual plot.

MCC9–12.S.ID.6c

3 EXAMPLE   Performing Linear Regression on a Graphing Calculator

The table gives the distances (in meters) that a discus was thrown by men to win the gold medal at the Olympic Games from 1920 to 1964. (No Olympic Games were held during World War II.) Use a graphing calculator to find the line of best fit, to find the correlation coefficient, and to evaluate the goodness of fit.

A Identify the independent and dependent variables, and specify how you will represent them.

The independent variable is time. Since the graphing calculator uses the variables x and y, let x represent time. To simplify the values of x, define x as years since 1920 so that, for instance, $x = 0$ represents 1920 and $x = 44$ represents 1964. Then $x =$ _____ represents 1924, $x =$ _____ represents 1928, $x =$ _____ represents 1932, and so on.

The dependent variable is the distance that won the gold medal for the men's discus throw. Let y represent that distance.

Year of Olympic Games	Men's Gold Medal Discus Throw (meters)
1920	44.685
1924	46.155
1928	47.32
1932	49.49
1936	50.48
1940	No Olympics
1944	No Olympics
1948	52.78
1952	55.03
1956	56.36
1960	59.18
1964	61.00

B Enter the paired data into two lists, L_1 and L_2, on your graphing calculator after pressing STAT .

Do the distances increase or decrease over time? What does this mean for the correlation?

_____

_____

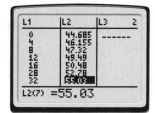

© Houghton Mifflin Harcourt Publishing Company

C Create a scatter plot of the paired data using STAT PLOT. The calculator will choose a good viewing window and plot the points automatically if you press ZOOM and select ZoomStat.

Describe the correlation.

_____

_____

_____

D Perform linear regression by pressing STAT and selecting LinReg $(ax + b)$ from the CALC menu. The calculator reports the slope a and y-intercept b of the line of best fit. It also reports the correlation coefficient r.

Does the correlation coefficient agree with your description of the correlation in Part C? Explain.

_____

_____

_____

E Graph the line of best fit by pressing Y= , entering the equation of the line of best fit, and then pressing GRAPH . You should round the values of a and b when entering them so that each has at most 4 significant digits.

What is the equation of the line of best fit?

_____

F Create a residual plot by replacing L_2 with RESID in STAT PLOT as the choice for Ylist. (You can select RESID from the NAMES menu after pressing 2nd STAT .)

Evaluate the suitability and goodness of the fit.

_____

_____

_____

© Houghton Mifflin Harcourt Publishing Company

3a. Interpret the slope and y-intercept of the line of best fit in the context of the data.

_____

_____

3b. Use the line of best fit to make predictions about the distances that would have won gold medals if the Olympic Games had been held in 1940 and 1944. Are the predictions interpolations or extrapolations?

_____

3c. Several Olympic Games were held prior to 1920. Use the line of best fit to make a prediction about the distance that would have won a gold medal in the 1908 Olympics. What value of x must you use? Is the prediction an interpolation or an extrapolation? How does the prediction compare with the actual value of 40.89 meters?

_____

_____

PRACTICE

Throughout these exercises, use a graphing calculator.

1. The table gives the distances (in meters) that a discus was thrown by men to win the gold medal at the Olympic Games from 1968 to 2008.

Year of Olympic Games	Men's Gold Medal Discus Throw (meters)
1968	64.78
1972	64.40
1976	67.50
1980	66.64
1984	66.60
1988	68.82
1992	65.12
1996	69.40
2000	69.30
2004	69.89
2008	68.82

a. Find the equation of the line of best fit.

_____

b. Find the correlation coefficient.

_____

c. Evaluate the suitability and goodness of the fit.

_____

_____

d. Does the slope of the line of best fit for the 1968–2008 data equal the slope of the line of best fit for the 1920–1964 data? If not, speculate about why this is so.

_____

_____

© Houghton Mifflin Harcourt Publishing Company

2. Women began competing in the discus throw in the 1928 Olympic Games. The table gives the distances (in meters) that a discus was thrown by women to win the gold medal at the Olympic Games from 1928 to 1964.

Year of Olympic Games	Women's Gold Medal Discus Throw (meters)
1928	39.62
1932	40.58
1936	47.63
1940	No Olympics
1944	No Olympics
1948	41.92
1952	51.42
1956	53.69
1962	55.10
1964	57.27

  a. Find the equation of the line of best fit.

    _____

  b. Find the correlation coefficient.

    _____

  c. Evaluate the suitability and goodness of the fit.

    _____

    _____

    _____

3. Research the distances that a discus was thrown by women to win the gold medal at the Olympic Games from 1968 to 2008. Explain why a linear model is not appropriate for the data.

_____

4. The table lists the median heights (in centimeters) of girls and boys from age 2 to age 10. Choose either the data for girls or the data for boys.

Age (years)	Median Height (cm) of Girls	Median Height (cm) of Boys
2	84.98	86.45
3	93.92	94.96
4	100.75	102.22
5	107.66	108.90
6	114.71	115.39
7	121.49	121.77
8	127.59	128.88
9	132.92	133.51
10	137.99	138.62

  a. Identify the real-world variables that x and y will represent.

    _____

  b. Find the equation of the line of best fit.

    _____

    _____

  c. Find the correlation coefficient.

    _____

  d. Evaluate the suitability and goodness of the fit.

    _____

    _____

© Houghton Mifflin Harcourt Publishing Company

Additional Practice

1. The data in the table are graphed at right along with two lines of fit.

x	0	2	4	6
y	7	3	4	6

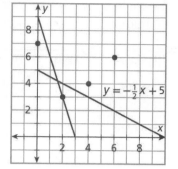

$y = -\frac{1}{2}x + 5$

a. Find the sum of the squares of the residuals for $y = -3x + 9$._____

b. Find the sum of the squares of the residuals for $y = -\frac{1}{2}x + 5$._____

c. Which line is a better fit for the data?_____

2. Use the data in the table to answer the questions that follow.

x	5	6	6.5	7.5	9
y	0	−1	3	−2	4

a. Find an equation for a line of best fit. _____

b. What is the correlation coefficient? _____

c. How well does the line represent the data? _____

d. Describe the correlation. _____

3. Use the data in the table to answer the questions that follow.

x	10	8	6	4	2
y	1	1.1	1.2	1.3	1.5

a. Find an equation for a line of best fit. _____

b. What is the correlation coefficient? _____

c. How well does the line represent the data? _____

d. Describe the correlation. _____

4. The table shows the number of pickles four students ate during the week versus their grades on a test. The equation of the least-squares line is $y \approx 2.11x + 79.28$, and $r \approx 0.97$. Discuss correlation and causation for the data set.

Pickles Eaten	0	2	5	10
Test Score	77	85	92	99

_____

_____

© Houghton Mifflin Harcourt Publishing Company

1. The table shows the number of hours different players practice basketball each week and the number of baskets each player scored during a game.

Player	Alan	Brenda	Caleb	Shawna	Fernando	Gabriela
Hours Practiced	5	10	7	2	0	21
Baskets Scored	6	11	8	4	2	19

a. Find an equation for a line of best fit. Round decimals to the nearest tenth.

   _____

b. Interpret the meaning of the slope and *y*-intercept.

   _____

   _____

c. Find the correlation coefficient. _____

Select the best answer.

2. Use your equation above to predict the number of baskets scored by a player who practices 40 hours a week. Round to the nearest whole number.

   A 32 baskets

   B 33 baskets

   C 34 baskets

   D 35 baskets

3. Which is the best description of the correlation?

   F strong positive

   G weak positive

   H weak negative

   J strong negative

4. Given the data, what advice can you give to a player who wants to increase the number of baskets he or she scores during a game?

   A Practice more hours per week.

   B Practice fewer hours per week.

   C Practice the same hours per week.

   D There is no way to increase baskets.

5. Do the data support causation, correlation, or chance?

   F correlation

   G causation

   H chance

   J chance and correlation

© Houghton Mifflin Harcourt Publishing Company

Performance Tasks

UNIT 4

GPS
COMMON
CORE

MCC9-12.S.ID.1
MCC9-12.S.ID.2
MCC9-12.S.ID.5
MCC9-12.S.ID.6

⭐ **1.** Jeremy had these scores on his weekly quizzes in History class.

93, 85, 88, 100, 84, 82, 95, 95, 91, 92, 98, 100, 68, 67, 80

Use the data to make a frequency table. Then draw a histogram based on your frequency table.

⭐ **2.** The relationship between the number of hours students spend watching TV every week and the number of hours they spend playing video games is shown in the scatter plot. Based on the data, what is the approximate number of hours of video games for a student who watches 5 hours of TV per week? Explain how you found your answer.

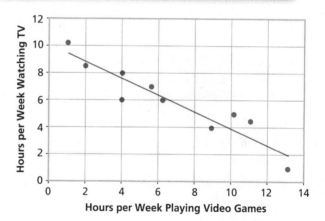

⭐⭐ **3.** Gail counted the number of cars passing a certain store on Tuesday from 4 P.M. to 4:05 P.M. and on Saturday from 4 P.M. to 4:05 P.M. for 6 weeks. Her data sets are shown below.

Week	1	2	3	4	5	6
Cars on Tuesday	10	8	12	3	9	15
Cars on Saturday	24	8	31	36	29	32

continued

© Houghton Mifflin Harcourt Publishing Company

a. Choose the measure of center that best describes both data sets. Calculate that measure for both data sets, and use them to compare the data sets. Explain why the measure you chose is the best representation.

b. Draw two box-and-whisker plots on the same number line to represent the data.

c. The store owner is considering closing on Saturday afternoons. Do you think this would be a good idea? Explain why or why not.

4. A total of 82 ninth graders and 63 tenth graders were surveyed. They were asked if they currently ate lunch in the cafeteria, and if they did not, they were asked if they would eat lunch in the cafeteria if it had a salad bar. The results are shown in the table.

	Currently eat in cafeteria	Do not eat in cafeteria, but would with salad bar
9th graders	36	14
10th graders	25	10

a. What category of responses is not included in the two-way table? Add it to the table with the correct values.

b. Use the completed frequency table to make a new table showing the joint and marginal relative frequencies. Round to the nearest tenth of a percent.

c. The school board has decided that a salad bar should be added to the cafeteria if at least 30% of the students who currently do not eat in the cafeteria would start doing so. Should the salad bar be added?

© Houghton Mifflin Harcourt Publishing Company

Name _____ **Class** _____ **Date** _____

SELECTED RESPONSE

For Items 1–3, use the line plots below.

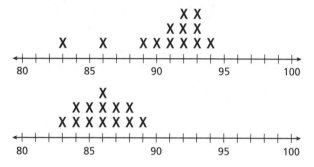

Class Scores on First Test (top)
and Second Test (bottom)

For Items 4–6, use the histograms below.

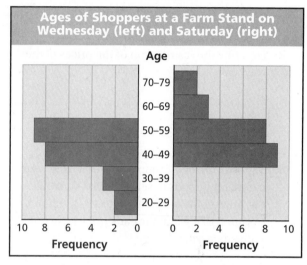

Ages of Shoppers at a Farm Stand on Wednesday (left) and Saturday (right)

1. How do the medians of the two sets of test scores compare?

   A. The median for the first test is greater than the median for the second test.

   B. The median for the first test is less than the median for the second test.

   C. The medians for the first and second tests are equal.

   D. The relationship cannot be determined.

2. For which test is the median greater than the mean?

   F. First test only

   G. Second test only

   H. Both tests

   J. Neither test

3. Which measure of center is appropriate for comparing the two sets of test scores?

   A. The median only

   B. The mean only

   C. Either the median or the mean

   D. Neither the median nor the mean

4. Which distribution is skewed toward older ages?

   F. Only the Wednesday distribution

   G. Only the Saturday distribution

   H. Both distributions

   J. Neither distribution

5. How do the spreads of the two distributions compare?

   A. The spread for the Wednesday data is much greater than the spread for the Saturday data.

   B. The spread for the Wednesday data is much less than the spread for the Saturday data.

   C. The spreads are roughly equal.

   D. The relationship cannot be determined.

6. Which measure of spread is appropriate for comparing the sets of ages?

   F. The interquartile range only

   G. The standard deviation only

   H. Either the interquartile range or the standard deviation

   J. Neither the interquartile range nor the standard deviation

© Houghton Mifflin Harcourt Publishing Company

CONSTRUCTED RESPONSE

For Items 7–10, use the box plot below.

**Prices (in Thousands of Dollars)
of Vehicles at a Used-Car Dealership**

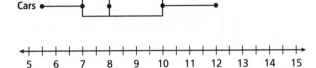

7. Describe the distribution of the prices of the used cars.

_____

_____

8. Suppose the dealership acquires a used luxury car that it intends to sell for $15,000. Would the price of the car be an outlier? Explain. (Assume that when the car's price is included in the data set, it has no effect on Q_3.)

_____

_____

9. The dealership also sells used SUVs. The prices (in thousands of dollars) of the SUVs are listed below. Add a box plot for the SUVs to the data display above.

6, 6, 7.5, 7.5, 8, 9, 11, 11, 11, 13, 14, 15

10. Compare the distribution of prices for the used SUVs with the distribution of prices for the used cars.

_____

_____

_____

_____

_____

_____

11. The table shows the temperature T displayed on an oven while it was heating as a function of the amount of time a since it was turned on.

a (sec)	T (°F)	a (sec)	T (°F)
31	175	250	300
61	200	285	325
104	225	327	350
158	250	380	375
202	275	428	400

a. Draw a line of fit on the scatter plot.

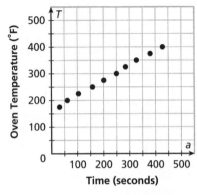

b. Find an equation of your line of fit.

_____

c. Perform linear regression to find the equation of the line of best fit and the correlation coefficient.

_____

d. Create a residual plot on a graphing calculator. Evaluate the suitability and goodness of fit of the regression equation.

_____

_____

_____

_____

e. Is the model a good predictor of the initial value? Why or why not?

_____

_____

© Houghton Mifflin Harcourt Publishing Company

Transformations in the Coordinate Plane

GPS
COMMON
CORE

© Houghton Mifflin Harcourt Publishing Company

Unpacking the Standards

Understanding the standards and the vocabulary terms in the standards will help you know exactly what you are expected to learn in this unit.

MCC9-12.G.CO.5

Given a geometric figure and a rotation, reflection, or translation, draw the transformed figure using, e.g., graph paper, tracing paper, or geometry software. Specify a sequence of transformations that will carry a given figure onto another.

Key Vocabulary

transformation *(transformación)* A change in the position, size, or shape of a figure or graph.

rotation *(rotación)* A transformation about a point P, also known as the center of rotation, such that each point and its image are the same distance from P. All of the angles with vertex P formed by a point and its image are congruent.

reflection *(reflexión)* A transformation across a line, called the line of reflection, such that the line of reflection is the perpendicular bisector of each segment joining each point and its image.

translation *(traslación)* A transformation that shifts or slides every point of a figure or graph the same distance in the same direction.

What It Means For You

You can change a shape's position and orientation in the plane without changing the actual shape or its size using translations, rotations, and reflections.

EXAMPLE

Reflecting the figures on the left half of the quilt across the vertical line will carry them onto the figures on the right half.

© Houghton Mifflin Harcourt Publishing Company

MCC9-12.G.CO.3

Given a rectangle, parallelogram, trapezoid, or regular polygon, describe the rotations and reflections that carry it onto itself.

Key Vocabulary

rectangle *(rectángulo)* A quadrilateral with four right angles.
parallelogram *(paralelogramo)* A quadrilateral with two pairs of parallel sides.
trapezoid *(trapecio)* A quadrilateral with exactly one pair of parallel sides.
regular polygon *(polígono regular)* A polygon that is both equilateral and equiangular.

What It Means For You

The rotations and reflections that carry a figure onto itself determine what kind of symmetry, if any, that the figure has. Reflections determine line symmetry, and rotations determine rotational symmetry.

EXAMPLE   Line symmetry and rotational symmetry

 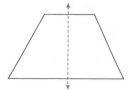

Parallelogram:	Isosceles Trapezoid:	Square:
no line symmetry	1 line of symmetry	4 lines of symmetry
no rotational symmetry	no rotational symmetry	90° rotational symmetry

MCC9-12.G.CO.5

Given a geometric figure and a rotation, reflection, or translation, draw the transformed figure using, e.g., graph paper, tracing paper, or geometry software. Specify a sequence of transformations that will carry a given figure onto another.

Key Vocabulary

rotation *(rotación)* A transformation that rotates or turns a figure about a point called the center of rotation.
reflection *(reflexión)* A transformation that reflects, or "flips," a graph or figure across a line, called the line of reflection, such that each reflected point is the same distance from the line of reflection but is on the opposite side of the line.
translation *(traslación)* A transformation that shifts or slides every point of a figure or graph the same distance in the same direction.

What It Means For You

Rotations, reflections, and translations do not change the shape or size of a figure. You can move a figure onto another of the same size by one or more of these transformations.

EXAMPLE

The diagram represents the whirling pockets of air that form behind a fast-moving truck.

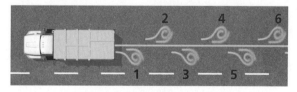

To carry whirl **1** onto whirl **2**: translate right and reflect up.

To carry whirl **2** onto whirl **3**: translate right and reflect down.

In the same way, you can carry each whirl onto the next.

UNIT 5

© Houghton Mifflin Harcourt Publishing Company

Key Vocabulary

angle of rotation *(ángulo de rotación)* An angle formed by a rotating ray, called the terminal side, and a stationary reference ray, called the initial side.

angle of rotational symmetry *(ángulo de simetría de rotación)* The smallest angle through which a figure with rotational symmetry can be rotated to coincide with itself.

center of rotation *(centro de rotación)* The point around which a figure is rotated.

line of symmetry *(eje de simetría)* A line that divides a plane figure into two congruent reflected halves.

line symmetry *(simetría axial)* A figure that can be reflected across a line so that the image coincides with the preimage.

reflection *(reflexión)* A transformation that reflects, or "flips," a graph or figure across a line, called the line of reflection, such that each reflected point is the same distance from the line of reflection but is on the opposite side of the line.

rigid motion *(movimiento rígido)* A transformation that does not change the size or shape of a figure.

rotation *(rotación)* A transformation that rotates or turns a figure about a point called the center of rotation.

rotational symmetry *(simetría de rotación)* A figure that can be rotated about a point by an angle less than 360° so that the image coincides with the preimage has rotational symmetry.

symmetry *(simetría)* In the transformation of a figure such that the image coincides with the preimage, the image and preimage have symmetry.

tessellation *(teselado)* A repeating pattern of plane figures that completely covers a plane with no gaps or overlaps.

transformation *(transformación)* A change in the position, size, or shape of a figure or graph.

translation *(traslación)* A transformation that shifts or slides every point of a figure or graph the same distance in the same direction.

© Houghton Mifflin Harcourt Publishing Company

16-1

Transformations in the Coordinate Plane

Extension: Properties of Rigid Motions

Essential question: *How do you identify transformations that are rigid motions?*

Video Tutor

MCC9–12.G.CO.2

1 ENGAGE **Introducing Transformations**

A **transformation** is a function that changes the position, shape, and/or size of a figure. The inputs for the function are points in the plane; the outputs are other points in the plane. A figure that is used as the input of a transformation is the **pre-image**. The output is the **image**.

For example, the transformation T moves point A to point A'. Point A is the pre-image, and A' is the image. You can use function notation to write $T(A) = A'$. Note that a transformation is sometimes called a *mapping*. Transformation T maps point A to point A'.

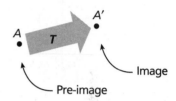

Coordinate notation is one way to write a rule for a transformation on a coordinate plane. The notation uses an arrow to show how the transformation changes the coordinates of a general point, (x, y).

For example, the notation $(x, y) \rightarrow (x + 2, y - 3)$ means that the transformation adds 2 to the x-coordinate of a point and subtracts 3 from its y-coordinate. Thus, this transformation maps the point $(6, 5)$ to the point $(8, 2)$.

REFLECT

1a. Explain how to identify the pre-image and image in $T(E) = F$.

_____

1b. Consider the transformation given by the rule $(x, y) \rightarrow (x + 1, y + 1)$. What is the domain of this function? What is the range? Describe the transformation.

_____

_____

_____

1c. Transformation T maps points in the coordinate plane by moving them vertically up or down onto the x-axis. (Points on the x-axis are unchanged by the transformation.) Explain how to use coordinate notation to write a rule for transformation T.

_____

_____

© Houghton Mifflin Harcourt Publishing Company

2 EXPLORE   **Classifying Transformations**

Investigate the effects of various transformations on the given right triangle.

- Use coordinate notation to help you find the image of each vertex of the triangle.

- Plot the images of the vertices.

- Connect the images of the vertices to draw the image of the triangle.

A $(x, y) \rightarrow (x - 4, y + 3)$ **B** $(x, y) \rightarrow (-x, y)$ **C** $(x, y) \rightarrow (-y, x)$

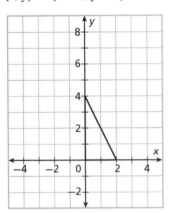 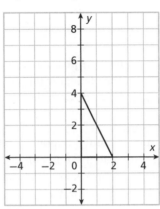 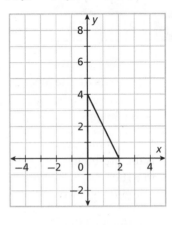

D $(x, y) \rightarrow (2x, 2y)$ **E** $(x, y) \rightarrow (2x, y)$ **F** $(x, y) \rightarrow (x, \frac{1}{2}y)$

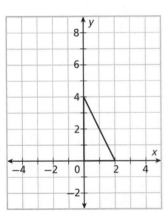 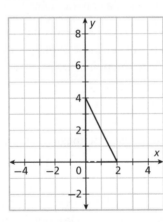 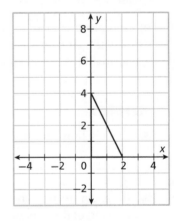

REFLECT

2a. A transformation *preserves distance* if the distance between any two points of the pre-image equals the distance between the corresponding points of the image. Which of the above transformations preserve distance?

_____

2b. A transformation *preserves angle measure* if the measure of any angle of the pre-image equals the measure of the corresponding angle of the image. Which of the above transformations preserve angle measure?

_____

© Houghton Mifflin Harcourt Publishing Company

A **rigid motion** (or *isometry*) is a transformation that changes the position of a figure without changing the size or shape of the figure.

PREP FOR **MCC9–12.G.CO.6**

3 EXAMPLE   Identifying Rigid Motions

The figures show the pre-image (△*ABC*) and image (△*A'B'C'*) under a transformation. Determine whether the transformation appears to be a rigid motion. Explain.

A

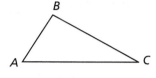 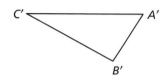

The transformation does not change the size or shape of the figure

Therefore, _____

B

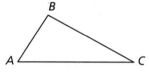 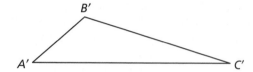

The transformation changes the shape of the figure.

Therefore, _____

C

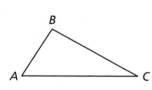 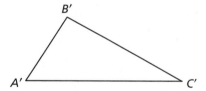

_____

_____

REFLECT

3a. How could you use tracing paper or a transparency to help you identify rigid motions?

_____

_____

_____

_____

3b. Which of the transformations on the previous page appear to be rigid motions?

_____

© Houghton Mifflin Harcourt Publishing Company

Rigid motions have some important properties. These are summarized below.

🔑 Properties of Rigid Motions (Isometries)

- Rigid motions preserve distance.
- Rigid motions preserve angle measure.
- Rigid motions preserve betweenness.
- Rigid motions preserve collinearity.

Reflections, rotations, and translations are all rigid motions. So, they all preserve distance, angle measure, betweenness, and collinearity.

The above properties ensure that if a figure is determined by certain points, then its image after a rigid motion is also determined by those points. For example, $\triangle ABC$ is determined by its vertices, points A, B, and C. The image of $\triangle ABC$ after a rigid motion is the triangle determined by A', B', and C'.

PRACTICE

Draw the image of the triangle under the given transformation. Then tell whether the transformation appears to be a rigid motion.

1. $(x, y) \rightarrow (x + 3, y)$

2. $(x, y) \rightarrow (3x, 3y)$

3. $(x, y) \rightarrow (x, -y)$

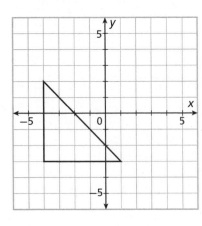

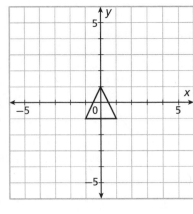

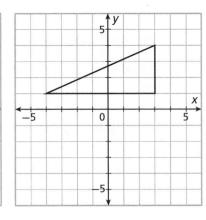

_____   _____   _____

4. $(x, y) \rightarrow (-x, -y)$

5. $(x, y) \rightarrow (x, 3y)$

6. $(x, y) \rightarrow (x - 4, y - 4)$

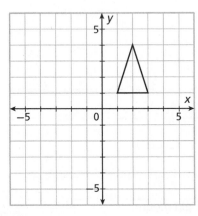

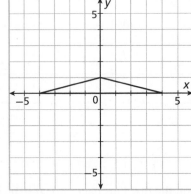

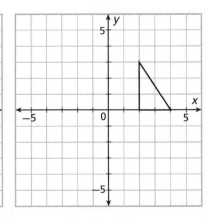

_____   _____   _____

© Houghton Mifflin Harcourt Publishing Company

The figures show the pre-image (*ABCD*) and image (*A'B'C'D'*) under a transformation. Determine whether the transformation appears to be a rigid motion. Explain.

7.

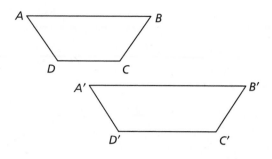

_____

_____

8.

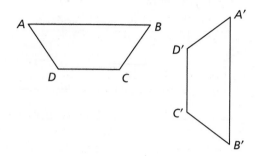

_____

_____

9.

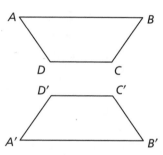

_____

_____

10.

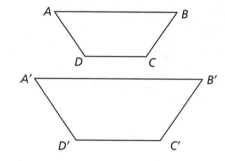

_____

_____

In Exercises 11–14, consider a transformation *T* that maps △*XYZ* to △*X'Y'Z'*.

11. What is the image of $\overline{XY}$? _____

12. What is $T(Z)$? _____

13. What is the pre-image of $\angle Y'$? _____

14. Can you conclude that $XY = X'Y'$? Why or why not?

_____

15. Point *M* is the midpoint of $\overline{AB}$. After a rigid motion, can you conclude that *M'* is the midpoint of $\overline{A'B'}$? Why or why not?

_____

_____

_____

© Houghton Mifflin Harcourt Publishing Company

16. Error Analysis A student claims that all of the transformations in Exercises 1–6 preserve angle measure. However, the student made an error. Which of the exercises shows a transformation that *does not* preserve angle measure? Use a protractor to estimate the measures of the angles in the pre-image triangle and image triangle to justify your answer.

_____

_____

_____

_____

© Houghton Mifflin Harcourt Publishing Company

Additional Practice

Use the figure for Exercises 1–3.

The figure in the plane at right shows the preimage in the transformation $ABCD \rightarrow A'B'C'D'$. Match the number of the image (below) with the name of the correct transformation.

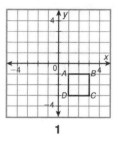

1

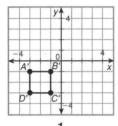

1

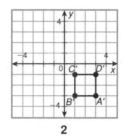

2

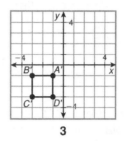

3

1. rotation _____

2. translation _____

3. reflection _____

4. A figure has vertices at $D(-2, 1)$, $E(-3, 3)$, and $F(0, 3)$. After a transformation, the image of the figure has vertices at $D'(-1, -2)$, $E'(-3, -3)$, and $F'(-3, 0)$. Draw the preimage and the image. Then identify the transformation.

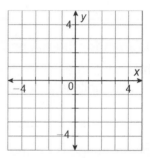

_____

5. A figure has vertices at $G(0, 0)$, $H(-1, -2)$, $I(-1.5, 0)$, and $J(-2.5, 2)$. Find the coordinates for the image of $GHIJ$ after the translation $(x, y) \rightarrow (x - 2.5, y + 4)$.

_____

Use the figure for Exercise 6.

6. A parking garage attendant will make the most money when the maximum number of cars fits in the parking garage. To fit one more car in, the attendant moves a car from position 1 to position 2. Write a rule for this translation.

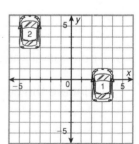

_____

7. A figure has vertices at $X(-1, 1)$, $Y(-2, 3)$, and $Z(0, 4)$. Draw the image of XYZ after the translation $(x, y) \rightarrow (x - 2, y)$ and a 180° rotation around X.

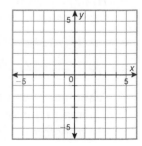

© Houghton Mifflin Harcourt Publishing Company

Problem Solving

Use the diagram of the starting positions of five basketball players for Exercises 1 and 2.

1. After the first step of a play, player 3 is at (−1.5, 0) and player 4 is at (1, 0.5). Write a rule to describe the translations of players 3 and 4 from their starting positions to their new positions.

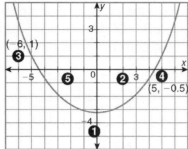

_____

_____

2. For the second step of the play, player 3 is to move to a position described by the rule $(x, y) \rightarrow (x - 4, y - 2)$ and player 4 is to move to a position described by the rule $(x, y) \rightarrow (x + 3, y - 2)$. What are the positions of these two players after this step of the play?

_____

Use the diagram for Exercises 3–5.

3. Find the coordinates of the image of *ABCD* after it is moved 6 units left and 2 units up.

_____

4. The original image is moved so that its new coordinates are $A'(-1, 7)$, $B'(-6\frac{1}{2}, 7)$, $C'(-5, 4)$, and $D'(-2\frac{1}{2}, 4)$. Identify the transformation.

_____

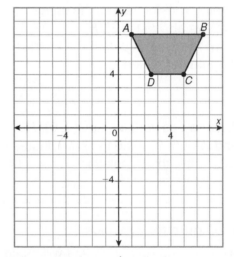

5. The original image is translated so that the coordinates of B' are $(11\frac{1}{2}, 17)$. What are the coordinates of the other three vertices of the image after this translation?

_____

6. Triangle *HJK* has vertices $H(0, -9)$, $J(-1, -5)$, and $K(7, 8)$. What are the coordinates of the vertices after the translation $(x, y) \rightarrow (x - 1, y - 3)$?

   A $H'(-1, 12)$, $J'(-2, 8)$, $K'(6, -5)$ C $H'(-1, -12)$, $J'(-2, -8)$, $K'(6, 5)$

   B $H'(1, -12)$, $J'(2, -8)$, $K'(-6, 5)$ D $H'(1, 12)$, $J'(2, 8)$, $K'(-6, -5)$

7. A segment has endpoints at $S(2, 3)$ and $T(-2, 8)$. After a transformation, the image has endpoints at $S'(2, 3)$ and $T'(6, 8)$. Which best describes the transformation?

   F reflection across the *y*-axis   H rotation about the origin

   G translation $(x, y) \rightarrow (x + 8, y)$ J rotation about the point (2, 3)

© Houghton Mifflin Harcourt Publishing Company

Reflections
Going Deeper

Essential question: *How do you draw the image of a figure under a reflection?*

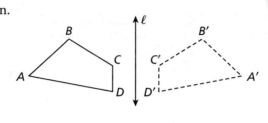

Video Tutor

One type of rigid motion is a reflection.
A *reflection* is a transformation that
moves points by flipping them over
a line called the *line of reflection*.
The figure shows the reflection of
quadrilateral *ABCD* across line ℓ.
Notice that the pre-image and image
are mirror images of each other.

MCC9–12.G.CO.4

1 EXPLORE   **Drawing a Reflection Image**

Follow the steps below to draw the reflection image of each figure.

A

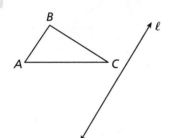

B

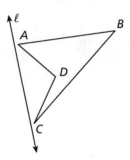

- Place a sheet of tracing paper over the figure. Use a straightedge to help you trace the figure and the line of reflection with its arrowheads.

- Flip the tracing paper over and move it so that line ℓ lies on top of itself.

- Trace the image of the figure on the tracing paper. Press firmly to make an impression on the page below.

- Lift the tracing paper and draw the image of the figure. Label the vertices.

REFLECT

1a. Make a conjecture about the relationship of the line of reflection to any segment drawn between a pre-image point and its image point.

_____

_____

1b. Make a conjecture about the reflection image of a point that lies on the line of reflection.

_____

_____

© Houghton Mifflin Harcourt Publishing Company

2 EXAMPLE Constructing a Reflection Image

Work directly on the figure below and follow the given steps to construct the image of △ABC after a reflection across line *m*.

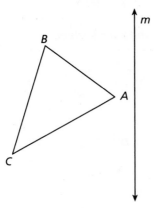

A Start with point *A*. Construct a perpendicular to line *m* that passes through point *A*.

B Label the intersection of the perpendicular and line *m* as point *X*.

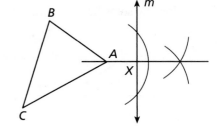

C Place the point of your compass on point *X* and open the compass to the distance *XA*. Make an arc to mark this distance on the perpendicular on the other side of line *m*.

D Label the point where the arc intersects the perpendicular as point *A'*.

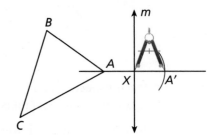

E Repeat the steps for the other vertices of △ABC. (*Hint:* It may be helpful to extend line *m* in order to construct perpendiculars from points *B* and *C*.)

REFLECT

2a. Reflections have all the properties of rigid motions. For example, reflections preserve distance and angle measure. Explain how you could use a ruler and protractor to check this in your construction.

_____

_____

2b. What steps should you take to construct the image of a point after a reflection across line *m* if the point lies on line *m*?

_____

_____

© Houghton Mifflin Harcourt Publishing Company

The table provides coordinate notation for reflections in a coordinate plane.

Rules for Reflections in a Coordinate Plane	
Reflection across the x-axis	$(x, y) \rightarrow (x, -y)$
Reflection across the y-axis	$(x, y) \rightarrow (-x, y)$
Reflection across the line $y = x$	$(x, y) \rightarrow (y, x)$

MCC9–12.G.CO.2

3 **EXAMPLE** **Drawing a Reflection in a Coordinate Plane**

You are designing a logo for a bank. The left half of the logo is shown. You will complete the logo by reflecting this figure across the y-axis.

A In the space below, sketch your prediction of what the completed logo will look like.

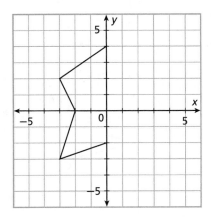

B In the table at right, list the vertices of the left half of the logo. Then use the rule for a reflection across the y-axis to write the vertices of the right half of the logo.

C Plot the vertices of the right half of the logo. Then connect the vertices to complete the logo. Compare the completed logo to your prediction.

Left Half (x, y)	Right Half (−x, y)
(0, 4)	(0, 4)
(−3, 2)	(3, 2)
(−2, 0)	

REFLECT

3a. Explain how your prediction compares to the completed logo.

_____

_____

3b. How can you use paper folding to check that you completed the logo correctly?

_____

_____

© Houghton Mifflin Harcourt Publishing Company

PRACTICE

Use tracing paper to help you draw the reflection image of each figure across line *m*. Label the vertices of the image using prime notation.

1.

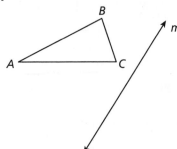

2.

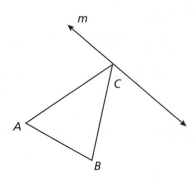

3.

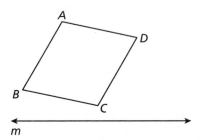

4.

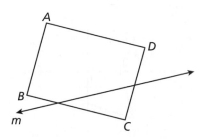

5.

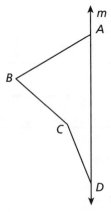

6.

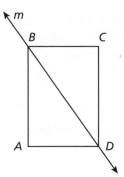

© Houghton Mifflin Harcourt Publishing Company

Use a compass and straightedge to construct the reflection image of each figure across line _m_. Label the vertices of the image using prime notation.

7.

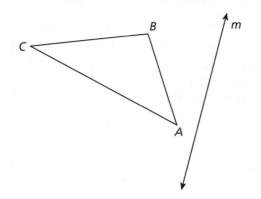

8.

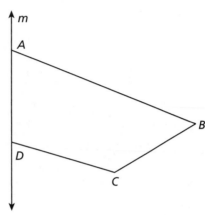

Give the image of each point after a reflection across the given line.

9. $(3, 1)$; _x_-axis

_____

10. $(-6, -3)$; _y_-axis

_____

11. $(0, -2)$; $y = x$

_____

12. $(-4, 3)$; _y_-axis

_____

13. $(5, 5)$; $y = x$

_____

14. $(-7, 0)$; _x_-axis

_____

15. $(-1, 5)$; $y = x$

_____

16. $(10, 6)$; _x_-axis

_____

17. $(8, 0)$; _y_-axis

_____

18. Plot several points on a coordinate plane. Then find their images after a reflection across the line $y = -x$. Use the results to develop a rule for reflection across the line $y = -x$.

_____

_____

_____

© Houghton Mifflin Harcourt Publishing Company

19. As the first step in designing a logo, you draw the figure shown in the first quadrant of the coordinate plane. Then you reflect the figure across the x-axis. You complete the design by reflecting the original figure and its image across the y-axis. Draw the completed design.

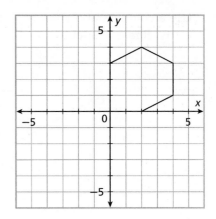

20. When point P is reflected across the y-axis, its image lies in Quadrant IV. When point P is reflected across the line $y = x$, its position does not change. What can you say about the coordinates of point P?

_____

_____

© Houghton Mifflin Harcourt Publishing Company

Additional Practice

Tell whether each transformation appears to be a reflection.

1.  _____

2. _____

3. _____

4. _____

Draw the reflection of each figure across the line.

5.

6.

7. Sam is about to dive into a still pool, but some sunlight is reflected off the surface of the water into his eyes. On the figure, plot the exact point on the water's surface where the sunlight is reflected at Sam.

Reflect the figure with the given vertices across the given line.

8. A(4, 4), B(3, −1), C(1, −2); y-axis

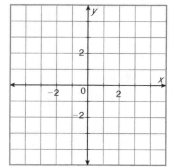

9. D(−4, −1), E(−2, 3), F(−1, 1); y = x

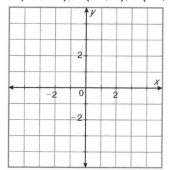

10. P(1, 3), Q(−2, 3), R(−2, 1), S(1, 0); x-axis

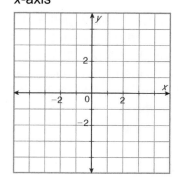

11. J(3, −4), K(1, −1), L(−1, −1), M(−2, −4); y = x

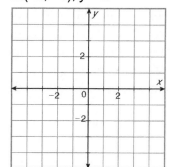

© Houghton Mifflin Harcourt Publishing Company

Problem Solving

1. Quadrilateral *JLKM* has vertices *J*(7, 9), *K*(0, –4), *L*(2, 2), and *M*(5, –3). If the figure is reflected across the line $y = x$, what are the coordinates of *M'*?

_____

2. In the drawing, the left side of a structure is shown with its line of reflection. Draw the right side of the structure.

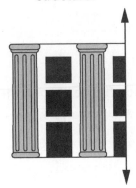

3. The function $y = -3^x$ passes through the point *P*(6, –729). If the graph is reflected across the *y*-axis, what are the coordinates of the image of *P*?

_____

Choose the best answer.

4. A park planner is designing two paths that connect picnic areas *E* and *F* to a point on the park road. Which point on the park road will make the total length of the paths as small as possible? (*Hint:* Use a reflection. What is the shortest distance between two points?)

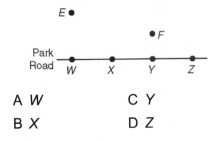

   A *W*   C *Y*
   B *X*   D *Z*

5. △*RST* is reflected across a line so that *T'* has coordinates (1, 3). What are the coordinates of *S'*?

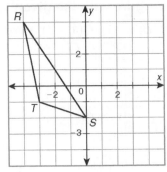

   F (0, 2)   H (2, 0)
   G (0, –2)   J (–2, 0)

6. △*MNP* with vertices *M*(1, 5), *N*(0, –3), and *P*(–2, 2) is reflected across a line. The coordinates of the reflection image are *M'*(7, 5), *N'*(8, –3), and *P'*(10, 2). Over which line was △*MNP* reflected?

   A $y = 2$
   B $x = 2$
   C $y = 4$
   D $x = 4$

7. Sarah is using a coordinate plane to design a rug. The rug is to have a triangle with vertices at (8, 13), (2, –13), and (14, –13). She wants the rug to have a second triangle that is the reflection of the first triangle across the *x*-axis. Which is a vertex of the second triangle?

   F (–13, 14)   H (–2, –13)
   G (–14, 13)   J (2, 13)

© Houghton Mifflin Harcourt Publishing Company

Translations
Going Deeper

Essential question: *How do you draw the image of a figure under a translation?*

You have seen that a reflection is one type of rigid motion. A *translation* is another type of rigid motion. A translation slides all points of a figure the same distance in the same direction. The figure shows a translation of a triangle.

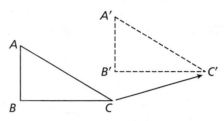

It is convenient to describe translations using the language of vectors. A **vector** is a quantity that has both direction and magnitude. The **initial point** of a vector is the starting point. The **terminal point** of a vector is the ending point. The vector at right may be named $\overrightarrow{EF}$ or $\vec{v}$.

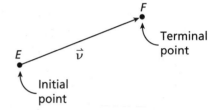

A vector can also be named using **component form**, $\langle a, b \rangle$, which specifies the horizontal change a and the vertical change b from the initial point to the terminal point. The component form for $\overrightarrow{PQ}$ is $\langle 5, 3 \rangle$.

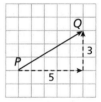

MCC9–12.G.CO.4

1 EXAMPLE Naming a Vector

Name the vector and write it in component form.

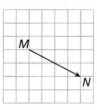

A To name the vector, identify the initial point and the terminal point.

The initial point is _____. The terminal point is _____.

The name of the vector is _____.

B To write the vector in component form, identify the horizontal change and vertical change from the initial point to the terminal point.

The horizontal change is _____. The vertical change is _____.

The component form for the vector is _____.

REFLECT

1a. Is $\overrightarrow{XY}$ the same as $\overrightarrow{YX}$? Why or why not?

_____

1b. How is $\overrightarrow{AB}$ different from $\overline{AB}$?

_____

© Houghton Mifflin Harcourt Publishing Company

You can use vectors to give a formal definition of *translation*.

A **translation** is a transformation along a vector such that the segment joining a point and its image has the same length as the vector and is parallel to the vector.

The notation $T_{\vec{v}}(P) = P'$ says that the image of point P after a translation along vector $\vec{v}$ is P'.

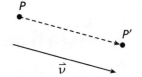

2 EXAMPLE   **Constructing a Translation Image**

Work directly on the figure below and follow the given steps to construct the image of $\triangle ABC$ after a translation along $\vec{v}$.

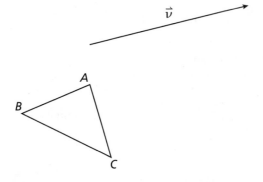

A Start with point A. Construct a line parallel to $\vec{v}$ that passes through point A.

B Place the point of your compass on the initial point of $\vec{v}$ and open the compass to the length of $\vec{v}$. Then move the point of the compass to point A and make an arc on the line parallel to $\vec{v}$. Label the intersection of the arc and the line A'.

C Repeat the process for points B and C to locate points B' and C'.

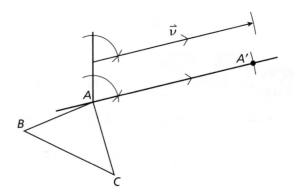

REFLECT

2a. Why do you begin by constructing a line parallel to $\vec{v}$?

_____

_____

A translation in a coordinate plane can be specified by the component form of a vector. For example, the translation along $\langle 3, -4 \rangle$ moves each point of the coordinate plane 3 units to the right and 4 units down.

More generally, a translation along vector $\langle a, b \rangle$ in the coordinate plane can be written in coordinate notation as $(x, y) \rightarrow (x + a, y + b)$.

© Houghton Mifflin Harcourt Publishing Company

3 EXAMPLE   Drawing a Translation in a Coordinate Plane

Draw the image of the triangle under a translation along $\langle -3, 2 \rangle$.

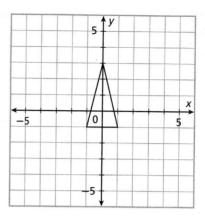

A   Before drawing the image, predict the quadrant in which the image will lie.

_____

B   In the table below, list the vertices of the triangle. Then use the rule for the translation to write the vertices of the image.

Pre-Image (x, y)	Image (x − 3, y + 2)
(0, 3)	
(1, −1)	
(−1, −1)	

C   Plot the vertices of the image. Then connect the vertices to complete the image. Compare the completed image to your prediction.

REFLECT

3a.   Give an example of a translation that would move the original triangle into Quadrant IV.

_____

3b.   Suppose you translate the original triangle along $\langle -10, -10 \rangle$ and then reflect the image across the y-axis. In which quadrant would the final image lie? Explain.

_____

_____

PRACTICE

Name the vector and write it in component form.

1.
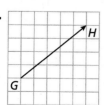

_____

2.
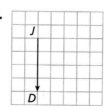

_____

3.
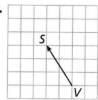

_____

© Houghton Mifflin Harcourt Publishing Company

Draw and label a vector with the given name and component form.

4. $\overrightarrow{MP}$; $\langle 3, -1 \rangle$

5. $\overrightarrow{CB}$; $\langle -3, 0 \rangle$

6. $\overrightarrow{HK}$; $\langle -5, 4 \rangle$

7. A vector has initial point $(-2, 2)$ and terminal point $(2, -1)$. Write the vector in component form. Then find the magnitude of the vector by using the distance formula.

_____

Use a compass and straightedge to construct the image of each triangle after a translation along $\vec{v}$. Label the vertices of the image.

8.

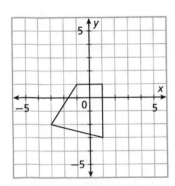

9.

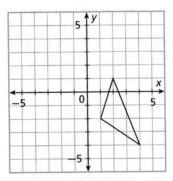

Draw the image of the figure under the given translation.

10. $\langle 3, -2 \rangle$

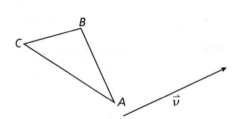

11. $\langle -4, 4 \rangle$

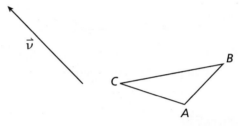

12. a. Use coordinate notation to name the translation that maps $\triangle ABC$ to $\triangle A'B'C'$.

_____

b. What distance does each point move under this translation?

_____

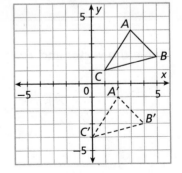

© Houghton Mifflin Harcourt Publishing Company

Additional Practice

Tell whether each transformation appears to be a translation.

1. _____

2. _____

3. _____

4. _____

Draw the translation of each figure along the given vector.

5.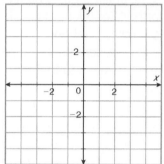

6.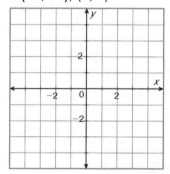

Translate the figure with the given vertices along the given vector.

7. $A(-1, 3)$, $B(1, 1)$, $C(4, 4)$; $\langle 0, -5 \rangle$

8. $P(-1, 2)$, $Q(0, 3)$, $R(1, 2)$, $S(0, 1)$; $\langle 1, 0 \rangle$

9. $L(3, 2)$, $M(1, -3)$, $N(-2, -2)$; $\langle -2, 3 \rangle$

10. $D(2, -2)$, $E(2, -4)$, $F(1, -4)$, $G(-2, -2)$; $\langle 2, 5 \rangle$

11. A builder is trying to level out some ground with a front-end loader. He picks up some excess dirt at (9, 16) and then maneuvers through the job site along the vectors $\langle -6, 0 \rangle$, $\langle 2, 5 \rangle$, and $\langle 8, 10 \rangle$ to get to the spot to unload the dirt. Find the coordinates of the unloading point. Find a single vector from the loading point to the unloading point.

_____

© Houghton Mifflin Harcourt Publishing Company

Problem Solving

1. A checker player's piece begins at *K* and, through a series of moves, lands on *L*. What translation vector represents the path from *K* to *L*?

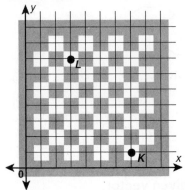

_____

2. The preimage of *M'* has coordinates (−6, 5). What is the vector that translates △*MNP* to △*M'N'P'*?

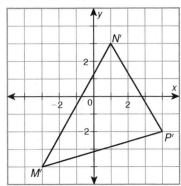

_____

3. In a quilt pattern, a polygon with vertices (3, −2), (7, −1), (9, −5), and (5, −6) is translated repeatedly along the vector ⟨4, 5⟩. What are the coordinates of the third polygon in the pattern?

_____

4. A group of hikers walks 2 miles east and then 1 mile north. After taking a break, they then hike 4 miles east and set up camp. What vector describes their hike from their starting position to their camp? Let 1 unit represent 1 mile.

_____

Choose the best answer.

5. In a video game, a character at (8, 3) moves three times, as described by the translations shown at right. What is the final position of the character after the three moves?

Move 1: ⟨2, 7⟩
Move 2: ⟨−10, −4⟩
Move 3: ⟨1, −5⟩

  A (−8, 3)   C (1, 1)

  B (−7, −2)   D (9, 2)

6. The logo is translated along the vector ⟨8, 15⟩. What are the coordinates of *R'*?

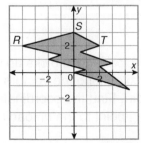

  F (4, 17)   H (15, 18)

  G (12, 17)   J (11, 19)

7. △*DEF* is translated so that the image of *E* has coordinates (0, 3). What is the image of *F* after this translation?

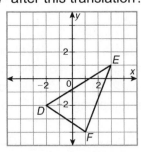

  A (1, −1)   C (−2, −2)

  B (4, −2)   D (−2, 6)

© Houghton Mifflin Harcourt Publishing Company

Rotations
Going Deeper

Essential question: *How do you draw the image of a figure under a rotation?*

You have seen that reflections and
translations are two types of rigid motions.
The final rigid motion you will consider is a
rotation. A rotation turns all points of the
plane around a point called the **center of
rotation**. The **angle of rotation** tells you the
number of degrees through which points
rotate around the center of rotation.

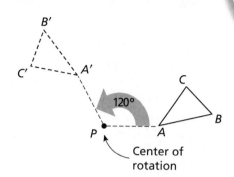

The figure shows a 120° counterclockwise
rotation around point *P*. When no direction
is specified, you can assume the rotation is
in the counterclockwise direction.

MCC9–12.G.CO.5

1 EXPLORE **Investigating Rotations**

Use geometry software to investigate properties of rotations.

A Plot a point and label it *P*.

B Plot three new points. Then use the segment
tool to connect the points to make a triangle.
Label the vertices *A*, *B*, and *C*.

C Select point *P*. Go to the Transform menu
and choose Mark Center. (This marks *P* as the
center of rotation.)

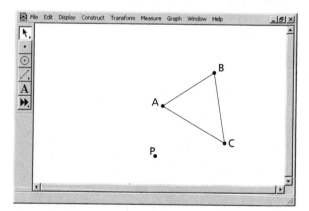

D Select the triangle. Go to the Transform
menu and choose Rotate. In the pop-up
window, use the default setting of a
90° rotation around point *P*.

E Label the vertices of the image *A'*, *B'*, and *C'*.

F Select points *P* and *A*. Go to the Measure
menu and choose Distance. Do the same for
points *P* and *A'*.

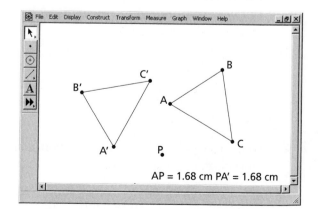

G Modify the shape or location of △*ABC* and
notice what changes and what remains
the same.

© Houghton Mifflin Harcourt Publishing Company

Video Tutor

1a. Make a conjecture about the distance of a point and its image from the center of rotation.

_____

1b. What are the advantages of using geometry software rather than tracing paper or a compass and straightedge to investigate rotations?

_____

_____

A **rotation** is a transformation about a point P such that (1) every point and its image are the same distance from P and (2) all angles with vertex P formed by a point and its image have the same measure.

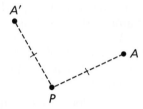

The notation $R_{P,\,m^\circ}(A) = A'$ says that the image of point A after a rotation of m° about point P is A'.

MCC9–12.G.CO.5

2 EXAMPLE **Drawing a Rotation Image**

Work directly on the figure below and follow the given steps to draw the image of $\triangle ABC$ after a 150° rotation about point P.

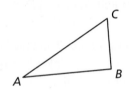

$\bullet$
P

A Draw $\overline{PA}$. Then use a protractor to draw a ray that forms a 150° angle with $\overline{PA}$.

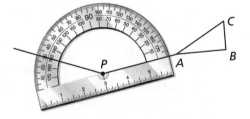

B Use a ruler or compass to mark point A' along the ray so that $PA' = PA$.

C Repeat the process for points B and C to locate points B' and C'.

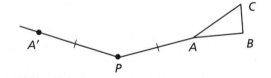

REFLECT

2a. Would it be possible to draw the rotation image of $\triangle ABC$ using only a compass and straightedge? Why or why not?

_____

_____

© Houghton Mifflin Harcourt Publishing Company

The table provides coordinate notation for rotations in a coordinate plane. You can assume that all rotations in a coordinate plane are rotations about the origin. Also, note that a 270° rotation is equivalent to turning $\frac{3}{4}$ of a complete circle.

Rules for Rotations in a Coordinate Plane	
Rotation of 90°	$(x, y) \rightarrow (-y, x)$
Rotation of 180°	$(x, y) \rightarrow (-x, -y)$
Rotation of 270°	$(x, y) \rightarrow (y, -x)$

MCC9–12.G.CO.2

3 EXAMPLE **Drawing a Rotation in a Coordinate Plane**

Draw the image of the quadrilateral under a 270° rotation.

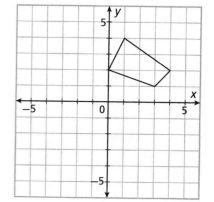

A Before drawing the image, predict the quadrant in which the image will lie.

_____

B In the table below, list the vertices of the quadrilateral. Then use the rule for the rotation to write the vertices of the image.

Pre-Image (x, y)	Image (y, −x)
(3, 1)	(1, −3)
(4, 2)	
(1, 4)	
(0, 2)	

C Plot the vertices of the image. Then connect the vertices to complete the image. Compare the completed image to your prediction.

REFLECT

3a. What would happen if you rotated the image of the quadrilateral an additional 90° about the origin? Why does this make sense?

_____

_____

3b. Suppose you rotate the original quadrilateral by 810°. In which quadrant will the image lie? Explain.

_____

_____

© Houghton Mifflin Harcourt Publishing Company

PRACTICE

Use a ruler and protractor to draw the image of each figure after a rotation about point *P* by the given number of degrees. Label the vertices of the image.

1. 50°

2. 80°

P •

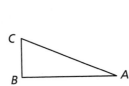

P •

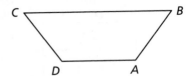

3. 160°

•
P

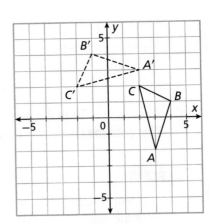

4. a. Use coordinate notation to write a rule for the rotation that maps △*ABC* to △*A′B′C′*.

_____

b. What is the angle of rotation?

_____

© Houghton Mifflin Harcourt Publishing Company

Draw the image of the figure after the given rotation.

5. 180°

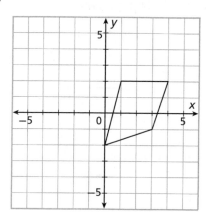

6. 90°

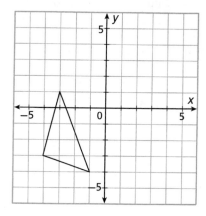

7. 270°

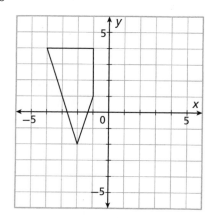

8. 180°

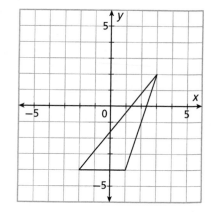

9. a. Reflect △*JKL* across the *x*-axis. Then reflect the image across the *y*-axis. Draw the final image of the triangle and label it △*J′K′L′*.

b. Describe a single rotation that maps △*JKL* to △*J′K′L′*.

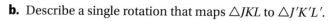

c. Use coordinate notation to show that your answer to part **b** is correct.

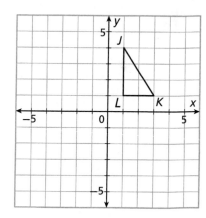

d. Describe a composition of reflections that maps △*J′K′L′* back to △*JKL*.

© Houghton Mifflin Harcourt Publishing Company

10. Error Analysis A student was asked to use coordinate notation to describe the result of a 180° rotation followed by a translation 3 units to the right and 5 units up. The student wrote this notation: $(x, y) \rightarrow (-[x + 3], -[y + 5])$. Describe and correct the student's error.

_____

_____

_____

_____

_____

© Houghton Mifflin Harcourt Publishing Company

Additional Practice

Tell whether each transformation appears to be a rotation.

1.  _____

2.  _____

3.   _____

4.  _____

Draw the rotation of each figure about point *P* by m∠*A*.

5.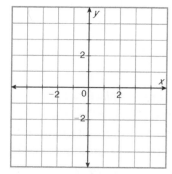

6.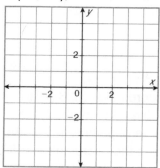

Rotate the figure with the given vertices about the origin using the given angle of rotation.

7. *A*(−2, 3), *B*(3, 4), *C*(0, 1); 90°

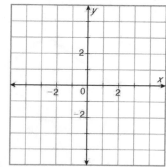

8. *D*(−3, 2), *E*(−4, 1), *F*(−2, −2), *G*(−1, −1); 90°

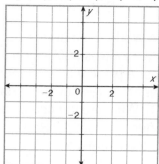

9. *J*(2, 3), *K*(3, 3), *L*(1, −2); 180°

10. *P*(0, 4), *Q*(0, 1), *R*(−2, 2), *S*(−2, 3); 180°

11. The steering wheel on Becky's car has a 15-inch diameter, and its center is at (0, 0). Point *X* at the top of the wheel has coordinates (0, 7.5). To turn left off her street, Becky must rotate the steering wheel by 300°. Find the coordinates of *X* when the steering wheel is rotated. Round to the nearest tenth. (*Hint:* How many degrees short of a full rotation is 300°?) _____

© Houghton Mifflin Harcourt Publishing Company

Problem Solving

1. △*ABC* is rotated about the origin so that *A'* has coordinates (−1, −5). What are the coordinates of *B'*?

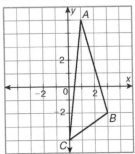

2. A spinning ride at an amusement park is a wheel that has a radius of 21.5 feet and rotates counterclockwise 12 times per minute. A car on the ride starts at position (21.5, 0). What are the coordinates of the car's location after 6 seconds? Round coordinates to the nearest tenth.

_____

3. To make a design, Trent rotates the figure 120° about point *P*, and then rotates that image 120° about point *P*. Draw the final design.

Choose the best answer.

4. Point *K* has coordinates (6, 8). After a counterclockwise rotation about the origin, the image of point *K* lies on the *y*-axis. What are the coordinates of *K'*?

   A (0, 5)   C (0, 8)

   B (0, 6)   D (0, 10)

5. △*NPQ* has vertices *N*(−6, −4), *P*(−3, 4), and *Q*(1, 1). If the triangle is rotated 90° counterclockwise about the origin, what are the coordinates of *P'*?

   F (−4, −3)   H (3, 4)

   G (−4, 3)   J (3, −4)

6. The Top of the World Restaurant in Las Vegas, Nevada, revolves 360° in 1 hour and 20 minutes. A piano that is 38 feet from the center of the restaurant starts at position (38, 0). What are the coordinates of the piano after 15 minutes? Round coordinates to the nearest tenth if necessary.

   A (0, 38)

   B (−38, 0)

   C (14.5, 35.1)

   D (35.1, 14.5)

7. The five blades of a ceiling fan form a regular pentagon. Which clockwise rotation about point *P* maps point *B* to point *D*?

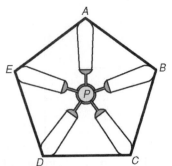

   F 60°   H 120°

   G 72°   J 144°

© Houghton Mifflin Harcourt Publishing Company

Compositions of Transformations
Going Deeper

Essential question: *How can you use more than one transformation to map one figure onto another?*

1 EXPLORE Investigating Reflections Across Parallel Lines

Use geometry software, or paper and pencil, to investigate properties of a double reflection across parallel lines.

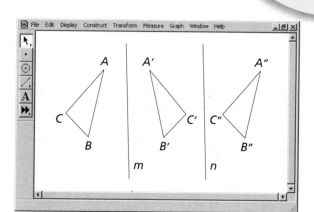

A Draw parallel lines *m* and *n*.

B Draw a triangle to the left of line *m*. Label the vertices *A*, *B*, and *C*. A sample triangle is shown.

C Reflect △*ABC* across line *m*. Label the vertices of the image *A'*, *B'*, and *C'*.

D Reflect △*A'B'C'* across line *n*. Label the vertices of the image *A"*, *B"*, and *C"*.

E Measure the distance between lines *m* and *n*, and lengths *AA"*, *BB"*, and *CC"*. What do you notice?

_____

_____

REFLECT

1a. What do you notice about $\overline{AA''}$, $\overline{BB''}$, and $\overline{CC''}$?

_____

1b. Describe a transformation that maps △*ABC* directly onto △*A"B"C"*.

_____

1c. How is the distance between lines *m* and *n* related to the transformation that maps △*ABC* directly onto △*A"B"C"*?

_____

1d. Is △*ABC* congruent to △*A"B"C"*? Explain.

_____

_____

© Houghton Mifflin Harcourt Publishing Company

2 EXPLORE | **Investigating Reflections Across Intersecting Lines**

Use geometry software, or paper and pencil, to investigate properties of a double reflection across intersecting lines.

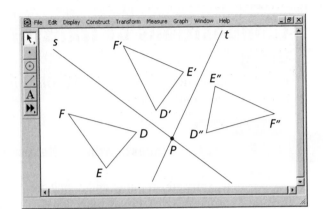

A Draw intersecting lines *s* and *t*. Plot a point where the lines intersect and label it *P*.

B Draw a triangle to the left of line *s*. Label the vertices *D*, *E*, and *F*.

C Reflect △*DEF* across line *s*. Label the vertices of the image *D'*, *E'*, and *F'*.

D Reflect △*D'E'F'* across line *t*. Label the vertices of the image *D''*, *E''*, and *F''*.

E Find the measure of ∠*DPD''* and the measure of the acute angle formed by lines *s* and *t*. What do you notice?

_____

REFLECT

2a. Describe a transformation that maps △*DEF* directly onto △*D''E''F''*.

_____

_____

PRACTICE

Show that △*ABC* is congruent to △*A''B''C''* by drawing two lines of reflection that can be used in a composition to map △*ABC* onto △*A''B''C''*.

1.

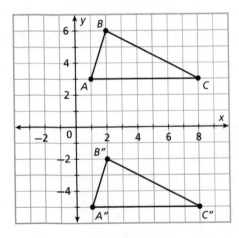

2.

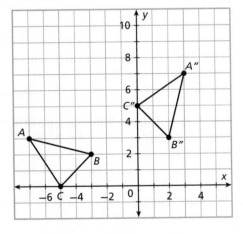

© Houghton Mifflin Harcourt Publishing Company

Additional Practice

Draw the result of each composition of isometries.

1. Rotate △XYZ 90° about point P
   and then translate it along $\bar{v}$.

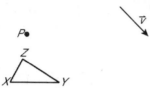

2. Reflect △LMN across line q and then
   translate it along $\bar{u}$.

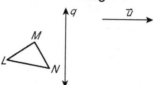

3. ABCD has vertices A(−3, 1), B(−1, 1),
   C(−1, −1), and D(−3, −1). Rotate
   ABCD 180° about the origin and then
   translate it along the vector ⟨1, −3⟩.

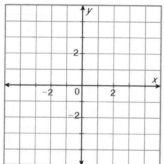

4. △PQR has vertices P(1, −1), Q(4, −1),
   and R(3, 1). Reflect △PQR across the
   x-axis and then reflect it across y = x.

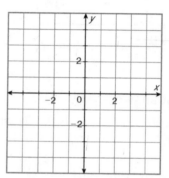

5. Ray draws equilateral △EFG. He draws two lines that make a 60° angle
   through the triangle's center. Ray wants to reflect △EFG across ℓ_1 and
   then across ℓ_2. Describe what will be the same and what will be different
   about the image of △E″F″G″ compared to △EFG.

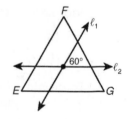

_____

_____

_____

Draw two lines of reflection that produce an equivalent transformation for each figure.

6. translation: STUV → S′T′U′V′

7. rotation with center P: STUV → S′T′U′V′

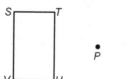

© Houghton Mifflin Harcourt Publishing Company

Problem Solving

1. A pattern for a new fabric is made by rotating the figure 90° counterclockwise about the origin and then translating along the vector ⟨−1, 2⟩. Draw the resulting figure in the pattern.

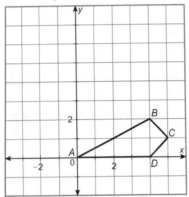

2. △LMN is reflected across the line y = x and then reflected across the y-axis. What are the coordinates of the final image of △LMN?

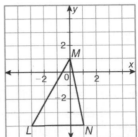

_____

Choose the best answer.

3. △EFG has vertices E(1, 5), F(0, −3), and G(−1, 2). △EFG is translated along the vector ⟨7, 1⟩, and the image is reflected across the x-axis. What are the coordinates of the final image of G?

   A (6, −3)   C (−6, 3)

   B (6, 3)   D (−6, −3)

4. △KLM with vertices K(8, −1), L(−1, −4), and M(2, 3) is rotated 180° about the origin. The image is then translated. The final image of K has coordinates (−2, −3). What is the translation vector?

   F ⟨6, 4⟩   H ⟨−1, −11⟩

   G ⟨6, −4⟩   J ⟨−10, −2⟩

5. To create a logo for new sweatshirts, a designer reflects the letter T across line h. That image is then reflected across line j. Describe a single transformation that moves the figure from its starting position to its final position.

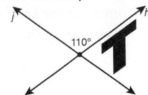

   A translation

   B rotation of 110°

   C rotation of 220°

   D reflection across vertical line

6. Which composition of transformations maps △QRS into Quadrant III?

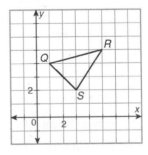

   F Translate along the vector ⟨−6, 4⟩ and then reflect across the y-axis.

   G Rotate by 90° about the origin and then reflect across the x-axis.

   H Reflect across the y-axis and then rotate by 180° about the origin.

   J Translate along the vector ⟨1, 2⟩ and then rotate 90° about the origin.

© Houghton Mifflin Harcourt Publishing Company

17-2

Video Tutor

Symmetry
Going Deeper

Essential question: *How do you determine whether a figure has line symmetry or rotational symmetry?*

A figure has **symmetry** if there is a rigid motion such that the image of the figure coincides with the pre-image.

A figure has **line symmetry** (or *reflection symmetry*) if the figure can be reflected across a line so that the image coincides with the pre-image. In this case, the line of reflection is called the **line of symmetry**.

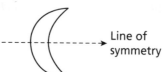

Line of symmetry

MCC9–12.G.CO.3

1 E X A M P L E Identifying Line Symmetry

Determine whether each figure has line symmetry. If so, draw all lines of symmetry. (Use the steps given for figure A to help you with the other figures.)

A Rectangle

- Trace the figure on a piece of tracing paper.

- Check to see if the figure can be folded along a straight line so that one half of the figure coincides with the other half. If so, the figure has line symmetry and the crease represents the line of symmetry.

- The rectangle has line symmetry. The two lines of symmetry are shown.

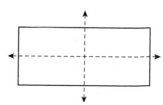

B Isosceles trapezoid   **C** Parallelogram   **D** Regular hexagon

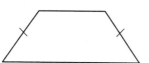   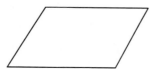

_____   _____   _____

REFLECT

1a. What can you say about a triangle that has exactly one line of symmetry? Why?

_____

_____

1b. Does every non-straight angle have a line of symmetry? Explain.

_____

© Houghton Mifflin Harcourt Publishing Company

A figure has **rotational symmetry** if the figure can be rotated about a point by an angle greater than 0° and less than or equal to 180° so that the image coincides with the pre-image. The smallest angle that maps the figure onto itself is the **angle of rotational symmetry**.

Angle of rotational symmetry: 90°

MCC9–12.G.CO.3

2 E X A M P L E   Identifying Rotational Symmetry

Determine whether each figure has rotational symmetry. If so, give the angle of rotational symmetry. (Use the steps given for figure A to help you with the other figures.)

A Rectangle

- Trace the figure on a piece of tracing paper.

- Without moving the tracing paper, firmly place the point of your pencil on the center point of the figure. Rotate the tracing paper. Check to see if the figure coincides with itself after a rotation by an angle less than or equal to 180°.

- The rectangle has rotational symmetry. The angle of rotational symmetry is 180°.

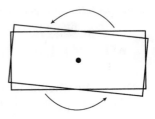

B Isosceles trapezoid

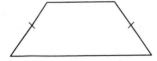

C Parallelogram

D Regular hexagon

_____   _____   _____

REFLECT

2a. Is it possible for a figure to have rotational symmetry but not have line symmetry? Explain.

_____

_____

2b. **Error Analysis** A student claims that a figure has rotational symmetry and that the angle of rotational symmetry is 360°. Critique the student's statement.

_____

_____

© Houghton Mifflin Harcourt Publishing Company

Additional Practice

Tell whether each figure has line symmetry. If so, draw all lines of symmetry.

1. _____

2. _____

3. _____

4. Anna, Bob, and Otto write their names in capital letters. Draw all lines of symmetry for each whole name if possible.

ANNA   BOB   OTTO

Tell whether each figure has rotational symmetry. If so, give the angle of rotational symmetry.

5.

6.

7.

_____   _____   _____

8. This figure shows the Roman symbol for Earth. Draw all lines of symmetry. Give the angle of any rotational symmetry.

_____

In the space provided, sketch a figure that has the given characteristics.

9. Exactly 1 line of symmetry

10. Angle of rotational symmetry: 180°
Exactly 2 lines of symmetry

© Houghton Mifflin Harcourt Publishing Company

1. Tell whether the window has line symmetry. If so, draw all the lines of symmetry.

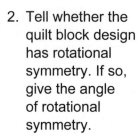

_____

2. Tell whether the quilt block design has rotational symmetry. If so, give the angle of rotational symmetry.

_____

3. Draw an example of a trapezoid that has no line symmetry and no rotational symmetry.

4. The figure is a net of an octahedron. Describe the symmetry of the net.

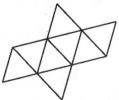

_____

Choose the best answer.

5. Which is a true statement about the figure with vertices $Q(-2, -4)$, $R(0, 1)$, $S(8, 1)$, and $T(5, -4)$?

   A $QRST$ has line symmetry only.

   B $QRST$ has rotational symmetry only.

   C $QRST$ has both line symmetry and rotational symmetry.

   D $QRST$ has neither line symmetry nor rotational symmetry.

6. Suppose you rotate this figure around its center point P by the given angle of rotation. Which angle measure would produce an image that coincides with the original figure?

   F 45°   H 90°

   G 60°   J 120°

7. Which of these figures has exactly three lines of symmetry?

   A

   B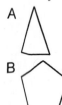

   C

   D

8. How many lines of symmetry does a regular pentagon have?

   F 0

   G 4

   H 5

   J 10

© Houghton Mifflin Harcourt Publishing Company

17-3

Tessellations
Connection: Using Transformations

Essential question: *How can you use transformations to describe tessellations?*

1 **E X A M P L E** **Describing Tessellations**

Describe the transformations that can map the tessellation onto itself. (The tessellation is made using congruent triangles, and it continues in all directions.)

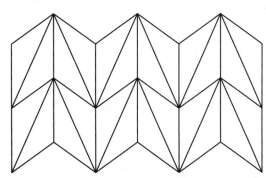

A Look for translations in the tessellation. If there are translations, then number two triangles in the tessellation and complete the statement below.

Triangle _____ maps onto triangle _____ by a translation.

B Look for rotations in the tessellation. If there are rotations, then number two triangles in the tessellation and complete the statement below.

Triangle _____ maps onto triangle _____ by a rotation of _____ about

_____.

C Look for reflections in the tessellation. If there are reflections, then number two triangles in the tessellation and complete the statement below.

Triangle _____ maps onto triangle _____ by a reflection.

REFLECT

1a. Describe a sequence of transformations that will map triangle 1 onto triangle 2 in part of the tessellation shown at the right.

_____

_____

_____

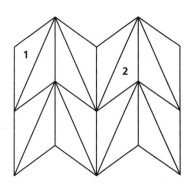

© Houghton Mifflin Harcourt Publishing Company

Describe the transformations that can map the tessellation onto itself. (The tessellation is made using congruent figures, and it continues in all directions.) You can number figures in the tessellation if you need to refer to them.

1.

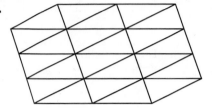

2.

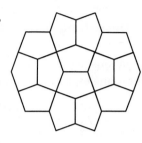

_____

_____

_____

_____

_____

        _____

        _____

        _____

        _____

3. Describe a sequence of transformations that will map figure 1 onto figure 2 in the tessellation.

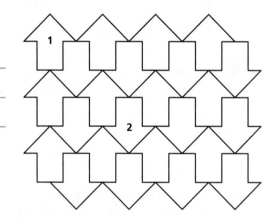

_____

_____

_____

4. Determine whether a concave quadrilateral can be used to create a tessellation. Explain your answer, using a drawing to support your answer.

_____

_____

_____

_____

© Houghton Mifflin Harcourt Publishing Company

Name _____ Class _____ Date _____

SELECTED RESPONSE

1. The function notation $R_{P,60°}(G) = G'$ describes the effect of a rotation. Which point is the image under this rotation?

   A. point R **C.** point G

   B. point P **D.** point G'

2. What is the image of the point $(4, -1)$ after a reflection across the line $y = x$?

   F. $(-4, 1)$ **H.** $(-1, 4)$

   G. $(4, 1)$ **J.** $(1, -4)$

3. Which of the following figures has an angle of rotational symmetry of 90°?

   A.

   B.

   C.

   D.

4. Which transformation is defined as a transformation along a vector such that the segment joining a point and its image has the same length as the vector and is parallel to the vector?

   F. reflection

   G. rigid motion

   H. rotation

   J. translation

5. Keisha wants to use a compass and straightedge to draw the image of $\triangle XYZ$ after a reflection across line m. What should she do first?

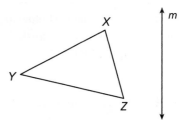

   A. Construct a perpendicular to line m that passes through point X.

   B. Construct a line parallel to line m that passes through point X.

   C. Copy $\angle X$ on the opposite side of line m.

   D. Copy $\overline{XZ}$ on the opposite side of line m.

6. You transform a figure on the coordinate plane using the rigid motion $(x, y) \rightarrow (-y, x)$. What effect does this transformation have on the figure?

   F. 90° rotation about the origin

   G. 180° rotation about the origin

   H. reflection across the x-axis

   J. reflection across the y-axis

7. Which is the best description of the symmetry of this regular pentagon?

   A. has neither line symmetry nor rotational symmetry

   B. has line symmetry but not rotational symmetry

   C. has rotational symmetry but not line symmetry

   D. has both line symmetry and rotational symmetry

© Houghton Mifflin Harcourt Publishing Company

8. Which transformation has a definition that is based on perpendicular bisectors?

    F. reflection

    G. rigid motion

    H. rotation

    J. translation

CONSTRUCTED RESPONSE

9. Work directly on the figure below to construct the image of $\triangle ABC$ after a translation along $\vec{v}$. Label the image $\triangle A'B'C'$.

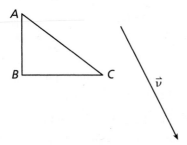

10. $\triangle RST$ has vertices $R(1, -3)$, $S(3, -1)$, and $T(4, -3)$. Give the coordinate notation for a transformation that rotates $\triangle RST$ 180° about the origin. Then give the coordinates of the vertices of the image of $\triangle RST$ under this transformation.

_____

_____

_____

11. In the space below, draw an example of a parallelogram that has exactly two lines of symmetry. Draw the lines of symmetry. Then give the most specific name for the parallelogram you drew.

12. In the space below, draw an example of a trapezoid that does *not* have line symmetry.

13. Perform the following transformations on the given right triangle and describe the effects.

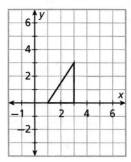

a. Plot the image of the triangle after the transformation $(x, y) \rightarrow (2x, 2y)$.

b. Plot the image of the triangle after the transformation $(x, y) \rightarrow (x, -y)$.

c. Explain why each transformation does or does not appear to be a rigid motion.

_____

_____

_____

_____

_____

_____

_____

_____

_____

© Houghton Mifflin Harcourt Publishing Company